German Intellectuals and the Nazi Past

This book analyzes how West German intellectuals debated the Nazi past and democratic future of their country. Rather than proceeding event by event, it highlights the underlying issues at stake: the question of a stigmatized nation and the polarized reactions to it that structured German discussion and memory of the Nazi past. Paying close attention to the generation of German intellectuals born during the Weimar Republic – the forty-fivers – this book traces the drama of sixty years of bitter public struggle about the meaning of the past. Did the Holocaust forever stain German identity so that Germans could never again enjoy their national emotions like other nationalities? Or were Germans unfairly singled out for the crimes of their ancestors? By explaining how the perceived pollution of family and national life affected German intellectuals, the book shows that public debates cannot be isolated from the political emotions of the intelligentsia.

A. Dirk Moses was educated in Australia, Scotland, the United States, and Germany. He has taught history at the University of Sydney since 2000. Moses' studies concern postwar Germany and comparative genocide, for which he has received numerous fellowships, including a Charles H. Revson Memorial Fellowship from the Center for Advanced Holocaust Studies at the United States Holocaust Memorial and Museum, a German Research Council Fellowship at the University of Freiburg, and an Australian Research Council Discovery Grant. He is the editor of *Empire, Colony, Genocide* (2008); *Colonialism and Genocide* (2007, with Dan Stone); and *Genocide and Settler Society: Frontier Violence and Stolen Aboriginal Children in Australian History* (2004). Moses is an associate editor of the *Journal of Genocide Research* and sits on the advisory boards of *H-German*, *Patterns of Prejudice*, and the *Online Encyclopedia of Mass Violence*.

German Intellectuals and the Nazi Past

A. DIRK MOSES

University of Sydney, Australia

CAMBRIDGE
UNIVERSITY PRESS

CAMBRIDGE UNIVERSITY PRESS
Cambridge, New York, Melbourne, Madrid, Cape Town, Singapore, São Paulo, Delhi

Cambridge University Press
32 Avenue of the Americas, New York, NY 10013-2473, USA

www.cambridge.org
Information on this title: www.cambridge.org/9780521145718

First published 2007
First paperback edition 2009

A catalog record for this publication is available from the British Library.

Library of Congress Cataloging in Publication Data

Moses, A. Dirk.
German intellectuals and the Nazi past / A. Dirk Moses.
　p.　cm.
Includes bibliographical references and index.
ISBN 978-0-521-86495-4 (hardback)
1. Germany – History – 1933–1945.　2. Collective memory – Germany (West)
3. Intellectuals – Germany (West) – Attitudes.　4. National socialism – Psychological aspects.
5. National characteristics, German.　I. Title.
DD256.5.M569　2007
943.087 – dc22　　2007005858

ISBN　978-0-521-86495-4 hardback
ISBN　978-0-521-14571-8 paperback

Contents

To my parents, John and Ingrid

Acknowledgments

This book has been a long time coming. A prototype was accepted by the Department of History at the University of California, Berkeley, as a Ph.D. dissertation in 2000, but its origins lie in the Midwest. Between 1992 and 1994, I was a graduate student at the University of Notre Dame, where I first began to ponder the Federal Republic and its vehement public debates about National Socialism and the Holocaust. A. James McAdams, an expert on contemporary Germany, encouraged this interest, and the Polish intellectual historian Andrzej Walicki taught me the existential significance of ideas for thinkers, an insight that has remained with me to this day. I have never had a chance to publicly acknowledge their support, or the friendship of Bill Miscamble, CSC, who suggested I follow his example of setting off for South Bend from Brisbane.

He could understand, then, that there was no ignoring the call of the Bay Area's eucalypts, and in 1994 I moved to Berkeley with its embarrassment of intellectual riches. Students of German history found a home in the Center for German and European Studies, ably led by Gerald Feldman, who, along with Norma Feldman–von Ragenfeld, became a mentor as well as a steadfast friend. Other members of the faculty were also inspirational teachers: Carla Hesse, Tom Laqueur, Peggy Anderson, Vicky Bonnell, and, not least, John Connolly, who gave his feedback over pints at the Bison. I was fortunate to encounter a cohort of gifted students, many of whom I later met on the road in Germany. Sharing the ups and downs of graduate school and beyond, they have become both friends and colleagues: Paige Arthur, Max Friedman, Jennifer Hosek, Marc Howard and Lise Howard, Christine Kulke, Ben Lazier, Sam Moyn, and Line Schjolden.

My supervisor, Martin Jay, warrants special recognition. He welcomed the itinerant student from abroad, stood by the project, wrote references, and opened doors. His own peerless intellectual histories were at once sources of guidance and inspiration. I thank him for his help and sage advice over the subsequent years as well. The Department of History was also incredibly supportive, awarding me successive research grants for travel in Germany, where I lived between September 1996 and January 2000.

In Freiburg, I was warmly received by Ulrich Herbert and his brilliant team, Bernhard Brunner, Sybille Buske, Isabel Heinemann, Jürgen Lillteicher, Christina von Hodenberg, Karin Hunn, Jörg Später, and Patrick Wagner, as well as by Jürgen Zimmerer, Nicolas Berg, Egbert Klautke, Gerd Leutenecker, Majid Sattar, and Sabine Russ from neighboring institutes. Uli integrated me into the German academic system, affording opportunities to present my theses at conferences and symposia, and even contriving financial support from the Deutsche Forschungsgemeinschaft. New friends Ingrid Horning, Reinhart Flessner, Annette Pehnt, and Christian Straub made Freiburg a congenial *Heimat*. From this base between the Black Forest and Kaiserstuhl, I could venture forth to the archives and meet the locals. Those who submitted to interview have my thanks: Hans Albert, Hans-Joachim Arndt, Ralf Dahrendorf, Andreas Flitner, Ludwig von Friedeburg, Imanuel Geiss, Antonia Grunenberg, Hartmut Jaeckel, Gerhard Kaiser, Jürgen Habermas, Karl-Ernst Jeismann, Reinhart Koselleck, Kurt Lenk, M. Rainier Lepsius, Hans-Joachim Lieber, Nikolaus Lobkowicz, Herman Lübbe, Hans Maier, Ernst Nolte, Dieter Oberndörfer, Otto Pöggeler, Günter Rohrmoser, Walter Rüegg, Gesine Schwan, Ernst Schulin, and Rudolf Vierhaus. Wilhelm Hennis, a virtual neighbor in Freiburg, always answered my many questions with unfailing courtesy and characteristic verve while I sat, sipping excellent tea, with his late wife in their elegant living room. I learned much from him. The staff of the Bundesarchiv in Koblenz, the Free University of Berlin's archive, and the Hauptstaatsarchiv of Nordrhein-Westfalen were also helpful.

Ned Curthoys and Andrew Beattie kindly proofread the doctoral manuscript after I moved to Sydney to take up a lectureship in 2000, while Martin Braach-Maksyvitis, Julia Kindt, and Neil Levi made suggestions about new material six years later. Our Sydney German history reading group gave two chapters a thorough going over, while other chapters were aired at seminars hosted by Volker Beghahn at Columbia and Peter Fritzsche and Matti Bunzl at Illinois. The belated transformation of the manuscript would never have been possible without Natasha Wheatley whose careful readings, intellectual partnership, and loving support were instrumental in redesigning its architecture. My colleagues in the Department of History at the University of Sydney understood that the revisions would take time, especially while I was working on new projects in comparative genocide; I am grateful for their forbearance.

I must also mention other friends and colleagues for their encouragement and assistance in this project: Avril Alba, Marion Berghahn, Alon Confino, Nick Doumanis and Helen Tirikidis, Beth Drenning, Geoff Eley and Gina Morantz-Sanchez, Norbert Finzsch and Michaela Hampf, Sean Forner, Konrad Jarausch, Konrad Kwiet, Geoff Levey, Harold Marcuse, Günter Minnerup, Jerry Z. Muller, Elliot Neaman, Jeff Olick, Jeff Peck, Randall Poole, Diethelm Prowe, Michael Rothberg, Katharina Vester, Lisa Yavnai, and Greg Zuschlag. Lew Bateman and Brian MacDonald at Cambridge were very patient editors with whom it was a pleasure to work. Most of all, I thank my parents, John and Ingrid, themselves fabulous scholars, whose humanism and ethical commitment are shining examples of the socially engaged life of the mind. This book is dedicated to them.

The end product of this global itinerary is not what some were anticipating. Having published and presented papers on the "forty-fivers" cohort of intellectuals (born in the 1920s and early 1930s), the expectation was that I would be their generational biographer. Although the forty-fivers feature in the book, I found that what required explanation was the underlying, transgenerational structure of political discourse and political emotions centered on questions of stigma, trauma, and basic trust in national traditions. This bundle of issues, highlighted for me by readings in psychology and anthropology as well as through an ethnographic immersion in German intellectual culture, accounted for the vehemence and polarization of public debates about the Nazi past in the Federal Republic. These debates were not seminars in the sky, ivory tower exercises, or common room spats. They were discursive battles in a cultural civil war to determine the meaning of German history and identity, a history that was now identified with evil and a national identity that was stigmatized. The intellectuals who threw themselves into verbal and written combat were not just reprising academic abstractions but fighting for national – and indeed personal – redemption. This is what I hope to have succeeded in showing in *German Intellectuals and the Nazi Past*.

Introduction

The proposition that the Federal Republic of Germany has developed a healthy democratic culture centered around memory of the Holocaust has almost become a platitude.[1] Symbolizing the relationship between the Federal Republic's liberal political culture and honest reckoning with the past, an enormous Memorial to the Murdered Jews of Europe adjacent to the Bundestag (Federal Parliament) and Brandenburg Gate in the national capital was unveiled in 2005. States usually erect monuments to their fallen soldiers, after all, not to the victims of these soldiers. In the eyes of many, the West German and, since 1990, the united German experience has become the model of how post-totalitarian and postgenocidal societies "come to terms with the past."[2] Germany now seemed no different from the rest of Europe – or, indeed, from the West generally. Jews from Eastern Europe are as happy to settle there as they are to emigrate to Israel, the United States, or Australia.[3]

---

[1] Bill Niven, *Facing the Nazi Past: United Germany and the Legacy of the Third Reich* (London and New York, 2002). For an excellent overview of postwar memory politics, see Andrew H. Beattie, "The Past in the Politics of Divided and Unified Germany," in Max Paul Friedman and Padraic Kenney, eds., *Partisan Histories: The Past in Contemporary Global Politics* (Houndmills, 2005), 17–38.

[2] For example, Daniel J. Goldhagen, "*Modell Bundesrepublik*: National History, Democracy and Internationalization in Germany," *Common Knowledge*, 3 (1997), 10–18. Making the same case for the Holocaust in an international context are Daniel Levy and Natan Sznaider, "Memory Unbound: The Holocaust and the Formation of Cosmopolitan Memory," *European Journal of Social Theory*, 5:1 (2002), 87–106. It is no coincidence that scholars of Germany have become central players in the global memory boom: Jeffrey K. Olick, ed., *States of Memory: Continuities, Conflicts, and Transformation in National Retrospection* (Durham, 2003); John Torpey, ed., *Politics and the Past: On Repairing Historical Injustices* (Lanham, Md., 2003); Jan-Werner Müller, ed., *Memory and Power in Post-War Europe: Studies in the Presence of the Past* (Cambridge, 2002).

[3] Jeffrey M. Peck, *Being Jewish in the New Germany* (New Brunswick, 2006); Leslie Morris and Jack Zipes, ed., *Unlikely History: The Changing German-Jewish Symbiosis, 1945–2000* (New York and Houndmills, 2000).

This rosy picture of the Berlin Republic is explicitly whiggish. Not for nothing was philosopher Jürgen Habermas hailed as the "Hegel of the Federal Republic," because his articulation of its supposedly "postconventional" identity presented the Berlin Republic as the end point of a successful moral learning process.[4] The Red-Green government of Gerhard Schröder (1998–2005) turned this philosophy into policy. Former minister for culture Michael Naumann justified the Berlin memorial by invoking the political theology of Habermas's friend, the theologian Johann Baptist Metz: the Republic's "anamnestic culture" of remembrance demanded such a commemorative gesture.[5] Twenty years after the "Historians' Dispute" (Historikerstreit) about the uniqueness of the Holocaust, "a culture of contrition" as the basis of German democracy seemed firmly embedded in German society.[6] Since (re)unification in 1990, historians and political scientists have begun attempting to explain this unexpectedly happy end to Germany's otherwise dismal twentieth century.[7]

Yet there are good reasons to regard the narrative in which Germany was redeemed by the memory of murdered Jews with some suspicion. No consensus ever obtained about remembering the Holocaust. Consider the tortured memory debates in Germany since the mid-1990s. Many Germans opposed the new memory politics, which they felt was imposed on them by distant leaders attuned to the expectations of Atlantic political and cultural elites. Research into the intergenerational transmission of German memory revealed a considerable gap between the pieties of official statements and the intimate sphere of the family, where stories of German suffering and survival endured half a century after the end of the Second World War.[8] Accordingly, the call for the

---

[4] Jann Ross, "Der Hegel der Bundesrepublik," *Die Zeit* (October 11, 2001), 45.

[5] Michael Naumann, "Remembrance and Political Reality: Historical Consciousness in Germany after the Genocide," *New German Critique*, 80 (Spring–Summer 2000), 22–23; Naumann, "Ohne Antwort, ohne Trost," *Die Zeit* (May 4, 2005). Cf. Peter Carrier, *Holocaust Monuments and National Memory Cultures in France and Germany since 1989: The Origins and Political Function of the Vél' 'dHiv' in Paris and the Holocaust Monument in Berlin* (New York, 2005).

[6] Karl Wilds, "Identity Creation and the Culture of Contrition: Recasting Normality in the Berlin Republic," *German Politics*, 9:1 (2000), 83–102.

[7] Ulrich Herbert, ed., *Wandlungsprozesse in Westdeutschland. Belastung, Integration, Liberalisierung 1945–1980* (Göttingen, 2002); Klaus Naumann, ed., *Nachkrieg in Deutschland* (Hamburg, 2001); Helmut Dubiel, *Niemand ist frei von der Geschichte* (Munich, 1999); Anne Sa'adah, *Germany's Second Chance: Trust, Justice, and Democratization* (Cambridge, Mass., 1998); Siobhan Kattago, *Ambiguous Memory: The Nazi Past and German National Identity* (Westport, Conn., 2001); Manfred Hettling, "Die Historisierung der Erinnerung – Westdeutsche Rezeptionen der nationalsozialistischen Vergangenheit," *Tel Aviver Jahrbuch für deutsche Geschichte*, 29 (2000), 357–78; Helmut König, *Die Zukunft der Vergangenheit: Der Nationalsozialismus im politischen Bewusstsein der Bundesrepublik* (Frankfurt, 2003); Michael Geyer, "The Politics of Memory in Contemporary Germany," in Joan Copjec, ed., *Radical Evil* (London, 1996), 169–200; Edgar Wolfrun, *Die geglückte Demokratie* (Stuttgart, 2006). Careful to avoid the temptation of teleology are Konrad Jarausch and Michael Geyer, *Shattered Pasts: Reconstructing German Histories* (Princeton, N.J., 2003).

[8] Olaf Jensen, *Geschichte Machen: Strukturmerkmale des intergenerationellen Sprechens über die NS-Vergangenheit in deutschen Familien* (Tübingen, 2004).

"normalization" of German history and national consciousness appeared regularly in public discourse.[9] Indeed, had not the writer Martin Walser complained infamously in 1998 that Holocaust memory was wielded like a "moral cudgel" to bully Germans into accepting a politically correct version of their past?[10]

Nor was the decision to construct the memorial in Berlin uncontroversial; in truth, it was highly divisive.[11] Then there were the many reminders of a half-forgotten past that appear regularly to rupture the moral smugness of official politics. In the so-called Flick affair in 2004, for instance, the son of a business tycoon who profited greatly under the Nazis by employing slave laborers, to whom his family has never paid compensation, moved his modern art exhibition to Berlin after protesters successfully hounded it from Switzerland. Herr Flick could not comprehend the motives of those who objected to the separation of his love for modern art and the moral issues surrounding his father's business dealings before 1945. Neither could Chancellor Schröder, who opened the exhibition by calling for the "normalization" of German memory.[12]

These were no isolated incidents. A year earlier, controversy had rocked the literary establishment when the celebrated rehabilitators of postwar German literature, the Gruppe 47, were accused of anti-Semitism. The seeming mania for uncovering apparent brown roots in public figures, particularly those with impeccable left-liberal credentials, continued with the claim that the prominent Germanists Walter Jens (b. 1923) and Peter Wapnewski (b. 1922) had been members of the Nazi Party. Historians were likewise shocked when it was revealed that Martin Broszat (1926–89), the longtime director of the celebrated Institut für Zeitgeschichte, which for decades had been at the forefront of innovative scholarship on Nazism, had joined the Nazi Party on April 20, 1944. In the same vein, the famous journalist and founder of *Der Spiegel* magazine, Rudolf Augstein (1923–2002), was revealed to have employed former Gestapo and SS officers in high positions in the 1950s. Then, in 2006, the Nobel

[9] Stuart Taberner, "'Normalization' and the New Consensus on the Nazi Past: Günter Grass's *Im Krebsgang* and the Problem of German Wartime Suffering," *Oxford German Studies*, 31 (2002), 161–86; Mitchell G. Ash, "Becoming Normal, Modern, and German (Again!)," in Michael Geyer, ed., *The Power of Intellectuals in Contemporary Germany* (Chicago, 2001), 295–313; Konrad H. Jarausch, "Normalisierung oder Re-Nationalisierung?" *Geschichte und Gesellschaft*, 21 (1995), 571–84; Jeffrey K. Olick, "What Does It Mean to Normalize the Past? Official Memory in German Politics since 1989," *Social Science History*, 22:4 (1998), 547–71; A. James McAdams, "Review Article: Germany after Unification – Normal at Last?" *World Politics*, 49:2 (1997), 282–308.

[10] Martin Walser, *Erfahrungen beim Verfassen einer Sonntagsrede: Friedenspreis der Deutschen Buchhandels 1998* (Frankfurt, 1998), 17–18.

[11] Michael S. Cullen, ed., *Das Holocaust-Mahnmal: Dokumentation einer Debatte* (Zürich and Munich, 1999); Ute Heimrod, Günter Schlusche, and Horst Seferens, eds., *Der Denkmalstreit – das Denkmal?* (Berlin, 1999); Claus Leggewie and Erik Meyer, *"Ein Ort, an den man gerne geht"* (Munich, 2005).

[12] Wolfgang Joop, "Soll die Flick-Sammlung nach Berlin? Darf in Deutschland Kunst ausgestellt werden, die angeblich mit Nazi-Vermögen finanziert wurde? Eine Debatte um Geld und Moral," *Die Welt* (November 22, 2004).

Prize–winning writer Günter Grass (b. 1927), a moralist associated with the left, admitted having been a member of the Waffen SS as a seventeen-year-old.[13] Even Habermas became the subject of speculation when the rumor that, in the 1980s, he had swallowed an order he had allegedly given as a Hitler Youth leader after it was presented to him by its addressee, was discussed in German newspapers.[14] The accumulation of these controversies in the first years of the new century led one journalist to remark on the seemingly never-ending "virulent identity crisis of the Germans."[15]

The virulence is also evident in the theme of "Germans as victims," which also made a reappearance after its high point in the 1950s. In 2002 the German public was treated to a heated debate about the morality of the Allied bombing campaign against German cities, a discussion saturated by graphic images of charred mounds of civilians that excited thoughts of Germans as victims of the British, the Americans, and perhaps even the Nazis.[16] Grass, too, signaled the preoccupation with German suffering in his novel, _Crabwalk (Im Krebsgang)_.[17] All the while, the organizations of German expellees agitate for a memorial site for their own suffering, much to the alarm of neighboring Poland and the Czech Republic, ever alert to any sign of irredentist politics in Germany.[18]

[13] Klaus Briegleb, _Mißachtung und Tabu: Eine Streitschrift zur Frage: "Wie antisemitisch war die Gruppe 47?"_ (Berlin, 2003); Hubert Spiegel, "Biographien Sprachlos: Germanisten als Hitlers Parteigenossen," _Frankfurter Allgemeine Zeitung_ (November 24, 2003); Peter Wapnewski, "Die Kartei hat immer Recht. Wie ich Mitglied der NSDAP wurde," _Die Zeit_ (November 27, 2003); Nicolas Berg, _Der Holocaust und die westdeutschen Historiker: Erforschung und Erinnerung_ (Göttingen, 2003); Otto Koehler and Monika Koehler, _Rudolf Augstein_ (Munich, 2002). The "68ers" now are found to be anti-Semites like their parents: Wolfgang Kraushaar, _Die Bombe im Jüdischen Gemeindehaus_ (Hamburg, 2005); "Warum ich nach sechzig Jahren mein Schweigen breche," Günter Grass in an interview with Frank Schirrmacher und Hubert Spiegel, _Frankfurter Allgemeine Zeitung_ (August 11, 2006). In July 2007 German newspapers claimed writers Martin Walser and Siegfried Lenz and cabarettist Dieter Hildebrandt had joined the Nazi Party as teenagers. "Walser, Lenz und Hildebrandt ware in der NSDAP," _Frankfurter Allgemeine Sonntagszeitung_ (July 1, 2007), 25.

[14] The public discussion began after Joachim Fest obliquely referred to the incident in his memoir, _Ich Nicht: Erinnerungen an eine Kindheit und Jugend_ (Reinbeck, 2006), 343. Christian Geyer, "Ein Fall Habermas? Der Verschluckte Zettel," _Frankfurter Allgemeine Zeitung_ (October 27, 2006).

[15] Thomas Lindemann, "Es kommt spät, aber zur rechten Zeit," _Die Welt_ (May 8, 2005).

[16] Robert G. Moeller, "Germans as Victims? Thoughts on a Post-Cold War History of World War II's Legacies," _History and Memory_, 17:1–2 (2005), 147–94.

[17] Jörg Friedrich. _Der Brand: Deutschland im Bombenkrieg 1940–1945_ (Munich, 2002); Lothar Kettenacker, ed., _Ein Volk von Opfern? Die neue Debatte um den Bombenkrieg 1940–45_ (Berlin, 2003); Robert Moeller, "Sinking Ships, Lost _Heimat_, and Broken Taboos: Günter Grass and the Politics of Memory in Contemporary Germany," _Contemporary European History_, 12:2 (2003), 147–81.

[18] Daniel Levy and Natan Sznaider, "Memories of Universal Victimhood: The Case of Ethnic German Expellees," _German Politics and Society_, 23:2 (2006), 1–27; Aleida Assmann, "On the (In)compatibility of Guilt and Suffering in Germany Memory," _German Life and Letters_, 59:2 (2006), 187–200; Norbert Frei, _1945 und wir: Das Dritte Reich im Bewusstsein der Deutschen_ (Munich, 2005); "Germans as Victims during the Second World War," special issue of _Central European History_, 38:1 (2005); Henning Sussner, "Still Yearning for the Lost Heimat? Ethnic

The viewpoint that the early twenty-first century marked the culmination of a collective moral learning process for Germany whose past has been successfully "mastered" seems increasingly untenable. That the "correct" answer to the Nazi past was found also ignores the proposition that such an answer is impossible to prove. Moreover, can a past such as Germany's be contained in a comfortable way? It is striking how long the debate has been framed by stark polarities: remembering or forgetting, too much memory or too little, its cynical instrumentalization or redeeming quality, capitulation in 1945 or liberation.[19] All evidence points to the fact that the meaning of memory is indeterminate, controversial, and never fully controlled by political elites.

This book suggests an alternative way of thinking about the past sixty years of German memory debates. Rather than posit linear progress or transformations in collective memory, it tries to explain the source of controversies about the national past between 1945 and 2005 as manifest enactments of an underlying structure of German political emotions. This structure was articulated in rival memory projects after the end of the Nazi regime, and it began to dissolve only at the beginning of the twenty-first century with the change of generations. As I show in Chapter 1, this structure was inscribed in the subjectivities of Germans as individuals because their past, and therefore their collective identity, had been polluted and stigmatized by the criminal deeds of the German regime between 1933 and 1945. This structure underlay discourse because it was intrinsic to postwar German identity. There was no escaping its stain: as a German, an individual necessarily partook in a national identity. As a structure, it framed the reaction to this stain in two ways, exemplified respectively by the "Non-German German" or the "German German": either Germans could try to convince themselves and others that they had invented a new collectivity, divorced from an unbearable past, or they could defend the viability of their collective identity by making the national past bearable through a variety of displacement strategies. (As subsequent chapters make clear, I also refer to Non-German Germans as "redemptive republicans" and leftists, and German Germans as "integrative republicans" and conservatives.) The structural gaze allows the reader to abjure the moralistic tone in some of the secondary literature. Like anthropologists, we are observing the workings of a foreign cultural system.

A Political Consensus

For all that, a consensus about German political institutions – as opposed to national identity – *did* develop over the past sixty years. Disputed as the meaning

German Expellees and the Politics of Belonging," *German Politics and Society*, 22:2 (2004), 1–26.

[19] Klaus Naumann made this aspect of German memory debates clear to me in a conversation in Hamburg in October 2003. See Jan-Holger Kirsch, "'Befreiung' und/oder 'Niederlage'? Zur Konfliktgeschichte des deutschen Gedenkens an Nationalsozialismus und Zweiten Weltkrieg," in Burkhard Asmuss et al., eds. *1945 – Der Krieg und seine Folgen: Kriegsende und Erinnerungspolitik in Deutschland* (Berlin, 2005), 60–71.

of the Nazi past was for the German collective self-representation, republican political institutions became secured by broad agreement in the political class and population. From the vantage point of the early twenty-first century, West Germany's epochal transformation – epochal in view of its moral and cultural ruin in 1945 – is easy to take for granted. With the guiding hand of the Allied occupation and the country's westernization and modernization, it was only a matter of time until liberalism took root and Germany became "like us," as one American commentator reassuringly put it.[20] The problem with this view is that it possesses the deterministic air of a script in which the happy ending is assured if the actors play their role. But that such a consensus would develop in the Federal Republic was not inevitable. Nor can the remarkable transformation in political culture that has taken place here be captured by the paradigms historians have employed, such as "westernization," "Americanization," and "modernization."

The modernization approach has gathered increasing adherents since the call of the Bonn contemporary historian Hans-Peter Schwarz to view the economic boom in the 1950s as a rapid modernization rather than as the restoration of an antidemocratic constellation of social forces. Was not the democratic system strengthened, rather than weakened, by this capitalist modernization, he asked?[21] The most significant product of this line of investigation has been the collection of Axel Schildt and Arnold Sywottek in which Schwarz's affirmative reading is both confirmed and differentiated.[22] Rapid modernization had indeed taken place, and the new system was consolidated, as Christoph Kleßmann put it, "under a conservative guardianship."[23] The westernization paradigm, advanced by historians at the University of Tübingen, examines the intellectual and cultural reorientation of the republic to the West, and especially to the United States, in the 1950s and 1960s.[24]

[20] Goldhagen, "Modell Bundesrepublik."

[21] Hans-Peter Schwarz, "Modernisierung oder Restauration? Einige Vorfragen zur künftigen Sozialgeschichtsforschung über die Ära Adenauer," in Kurt Düwell and Wolfgang Köllmann, eds., *Vom Ende der Weimarer Republic biz zum Land Nordrhein-Westfalen* (Wuppertal, 1984), 278–93; Schwarz, *Die Ära Adenauer. Gründerjahre der Republik, 1949–1957* (Stuttgart, 1981), 382. A similar argument is A. J. Nicholls, *Freedom with Responsibility: The Social Market Economy in Germany, 1918–1963* (Oxford, 1994).

[22] Axel Schildt and Arnold Sywottek, eds., *Modernisierung im Wiederaufbau. Die westdeutsche Gesellschaft der 50er Jahre* (Bonn, 1998); Axel Schildt, "Nachkriegszeit. Möglichkeiten und Probleme einer Periodisierung der westdeutschen Geschichte nach dem Zweiten Weltkrieg und ihrer Einordnung in die deutsche Geschichte des 20. Jahrhunderts," *Geschichte in Wissenschaft und Unterricht*, 44 (1993), 573–74; Thomas Schlemmer and Hans Woller, eds., *Die Erschließung des Landes 1949–1973* (Munich, 2001); Schildt, ed., *Gesellschaft im Wandel 1949–1973* (Munich, 2002).

[23] Christoph Kleßmann, "Ein stolzes Schiff und krächzende Möven: Die Geschichte der Bundesrepublik und ihre Kritiker," *Geschichte und Gesellschaft*, 11 (1985), 485.

[24] Anselm Doering-Manteuffel, *Wie westlich sind die Deutschen?* (Göttingen, 1999); Michael Hochgeschwender, *Freiheit in der Offensive? Der Kongreß für kulturelle Freiheit und die Deutschen* (Munich, 1998); Julia Angster, *Konsenskapitalismus und Sozialdemokratie: Die Westernisierung von SPD und DGB* (Munich, 2003).

There is much to be said for these approaches. They moved beyond the standard leftist view that regarded the 1950s as a decade of stagnation and dangerous authoritarianism when in fact rapid technical, industrial, and architectural changes transformed the face of the country.[25] Yet the processes and structural changes highlighted by these paradigms cannot account for the political consensus that has taken place among the West German intelligentsia over the past half-century.[26] After all, westernization also served as a synonym for the anticommunism that had rendered the German middle classes vulnerable to National Socialism. The self-understanding that opposed the "Christian West" to Soviet communism also disdained American popular culture and other apprehended manifestations of secular "materialism."[27] Here were mental continuities with the Nazi and pre-Nazi past that hindered consensus.

The same problem applies to modernization. Since the *Sonderweg* (special path of modernization) debate of the 1980s, it has become apparent that modernization and "bourgeois dominance" do not automatically issue in political liberalization. The reverse may even be the case. The *Sonderweg* was not an antimodern utopia, as some have misunderstood it, but an authoritarian, explicitly illiberal version of technical modernity.[28] The East Asian "tigers" – Singapore, Taiwan, South Korea – are contemporary examples of countries that have successfully industrialized without liberalizing their culture and political system, although the latter two are moving in that direction. If one considers the difficulties of combining a market economy and parliamentary politics in the rapidly transforming countries of Eastern Europe, the contingent relationship between economic system and political culture becomes equally apparent. Functioning liberal democracies appear to be the exception rather than the rule.[29]

What was different in the Federal Republic? The conventional view is that the Federal Republic was redeemed by the "1968 generation," not least by journalists and academics of that generation who have dominated the public sphere and universities. Born between 1938 and 1948, the so-called sixtyeighters are supposed to have corrected the political and moral deficiencies of

[25] Anselm Doering-Manteuffel, "Deutsche Zeitgeschichte nach 1945," *Vierteljahrshefte für Zeitgeschichte*, 41 (1993), 28–29.
[26] Paul Erker, "Zeitgeschichte als Sozialgeschichte. Forschungsstand und Forschungsdefizite," *Geschichte und Gesellschaft*, 19 (1993), 202–38; Werner Conze and M. Rainer Lepsius, eds., *Sozialgeschichte der Bundesrepublik: Beiträge zum Kontiniutätsproblem* (Stuttgart, 1983).
[27] Maria Mitchell, "Materialism and Secularism: CDU Politicians and National Socialism, 1945–1949," *Journal of Modern History*, 67 (1995), 278–308.
[28] For an example of the difficulty of linking liberalization to modernization, see Axel Schildt and Arnold Sywottek, "'Reconstruction' and 'Modernization': West German Social History during the 1950s," in Robert G. Moeller, ed., *West Germany under Construction: Politics, Society, and Culture in the Adenauer Era* (Ann Arbor, 1997), 439–40; and Arnold Sywottek, "Wege in die 50er Jahre," in Schildt and Sywottek, *Modernisierung im Wiederaufbau*, 13–42.
[29] For the origins of the *Sonderweg* thesis, see William Hagen, "Descent of the *Sonderweg*: Hans Rosenberg's History of Old-Regime Prussia," *Central European History*, 24 (1991), 24–50; cf. Hans-Ulrich Wehler, *Modernisierungstheorie und Geschichte* (Göttingen, 1975), and Barrington Moore, *Social Origins of Dictatorship and Democracy* (Boston, 1965).

German public and private life with their generational rebellion. In the words of one observer, "it was only in 1968 that the Federal Republic became a Western, liberal country. In Germany . . . the 1968 generation is seen not just as a cultural avant-garde but as Germany's saviour from its National Socialist past."[30] As this generation ages and the events of its youth pass into "history," we can make an elementary, analytical distinction – namely, between the consciously pursued project of the sixty-eighters and the cultural changes of which they were the bearer. The *intentions* and *outcomes* of 1968 are by no means the same. Let it be said: the aims of the sixty-eighter intellectuals were anything but liberal. They were divorced from reality by an illusory revolutionary self-understanding and were driven by a radicalizing voluntarism.[31] Wolfgang Kraushaar, himself a "sixty-eighter," drew attention to the fundamental anti- and illiberalism of the student leaders.[32] Older sympathizers of the student movement were appalled by this dimension of the protest.[33] It is difficult to make a case for the proposition that the liberal self-understanding of the Federal Republic was solely the result of 1968. The system and institutions that were established in 1949 were, among other things, its very target.

None of this is to deny that cultural modernity came with and through 1968, as it did in all Western countries. The political scientist Claus Leggewie argued plausibly that the movement was eminently successful if viewed as a "laboratory of the postindustrial society."[34] Conservatives are prepared to subscribe to this view.[35] What Jürgen Habermas called the "process of fundamental

---

[30] Heinz Bude, "The German *Kriegskinder*: Origins and Impact of the Generation of 1968," in Mark Roseman, ed., *Generations in Conflict: Youth Revolt and Generation Formation in Germany, 1770–1968* (Cambridge, 1995), 293. See also his *Das Altern einer Generation: Die Jahrgänge 1938 bis 1948* (Frankfurt, 1995).

[31] Detlev Claussen, "Chiffre 1968," in Jan Assmann et al., eds., *Revolution und Mythos* (Frankfurt, 1992), 219–29; Claus Leggewie, "Vergeßt '68! Denkt gefährlich!: Verrat am Ende des 20. Jahrhunderts," *Kursbuch*, 116 (1994), 148; Wolfgang Eßbach, "Protest Bewegung, Scheinrevolution, postmoderne Revolte? Nachdenken über '68," paper presented at the Albert-Ludwigs-University Freiburg, November 19, 1997; Dagmar Herzog, "'Pleasure, Sex, and Politics Belong Together': Post-Holocaust Memory and the Sexual Revolution in West Germany," *Critical Inquiry*, 24 (Winter 1998), 393–444; cf. Jürgen Habermas, "Die Scheinrevolution und ihre Kinder," in his *Protestbewegung und Hochschulreform* (Frankfurt, 1969), 188–201.

[32] Wolfgang Kraushaar, "Autoritärer Staat und anti-autoritäre Bewegung," 1999, 2 (July 1987), 103; cf. Fritz Walter, "Eine deprimierende Bilanz," *Die Woche* (May 22, 1998), 10: "The 68er revolt was no liberal revolution. The APO activists had contempt for no one more than the 'bloody liberals' [*liberalen Scheißer*], and they could not laugh more scornfully than about democracy, the constitution, and the division of powers." Cf. Hans Magnus Enzensberger, "Berliner Gemeinplätze," *Kursbuch*, 11 (1968), 151–69.

[33] Hellmut Becker, *Aufklärung als Beruf: Gespräche über Bildung und Politik* (Munich, 1992), 186.

[34] Claus Leggewie, "1968: Ein Laboratorium der nachindustriellen Gesellschaft?" *Aus Politik und Zeitgeschichte*, 20 (May 13, 1988), 13–20; cf. Christian Meier, "Nicht Zerstörung aber neue Herausforderung der Vernunft. Erwartungen an deutsche Intellektuelle nach 1989," in Martin Meyer, ed., *Intellektuellendämmerung? Beiträge zur neuesten Zeit des Geistes* (Munich, 1992), 81ff.

[35] See Wolfgang Jäger, "Vierzig Jahre Demokratie: Phasen der bundesdeutschen Nachkriegsgeschichte," *Die Politische Meinung*, 34 (March–April 1989), 10.

liberalization" – the transformation of authority relations in the family, work-place, and classroom and the readiness for democratic participation and protest – became an integral part of the West German landscape.[36]

At the same time, if we want to account for the continuity of those dimensions of the West German consensus that the sixty-eighters regarded as dubiously authoritarian – representative democracy, the social market economy, intellec-tual pluralism, and *Westbindung* (embedment in the West) – then an important factor is that 1968 *failed* in its explicit and avowed objectives.[37] This book argues that the answer to the question about the sources of German political reorientation can be found by looking at another generation: the comparatively neglected "generation of 1945," those young men and women (but mostly men – these were still patriarchal times) who were between fifteen and twenty-five years of age at the end of the war and who constituted the first postwar gen-eration of university students. The "forty-fivers" became the young academics and journalists in the 1960s who commenced the task of subjecting the national intellectual traditions to a searching critique in light of their experience of the rupture of 1945 when many of them had to begin reconsidering what they had been taught in the Hitler Youth or army.

Intellectuals and Memory

This book focuses on intellectuals and public debate among the forty-fivers, in particular those disputes over university reform, because they viewed univer-sities as the site of national defense and renewal. Simply cataloging debates is inadequate, however. Their terms need to be exposed and explained. I employ the concept of "political languages" from the history of political thought to capture the importance of background understandings of good and evil that stand behind the customary ideological differences. Because memories and ideas about Germany's past, present, and future are expressed linguistically, it is necessary to examine what Germans most adept at deploying these politi-cal languages have said and written about their collective past.

Postwar German intellectuals utilized two languages of republicanism in their debates, "redemptive" and "integrative," the former expressing the Non-German German wish for a republic divorced from corrupted national tradi-tions, and the latter articulating the German German imperative for positive,

---

[36] Jürgen Habermas, "Der Marsch durch die Institutionen hat auch die CDU erreicht," *Frank-furter Rundschau* (March 11, 1988), 11. Habermas was adapting the phrase of Karl Mannheim, who wrote about a "fundamental democratization." The Freiburg-based project on the Fed-eral Republic, led by Ulrich Herbert, similarly utilizes the liberalization concept: Herbert, *Wandlungsprozesse in Westdeutschland*; Christina von Hodenberg, *Konsens und Krise: Eine Geschichte der westdeutschen Medienöffentlichkeit 1945–1973* (Göttingen, 2006); Karin Hunn, *"Nächstes Jahr kehren wir zurück...." Die Geschichte der türkischen "Gastarbeiter" in der Bundesrepublik* (Göttingen, 2005).

[37] Jochen Vogt, "Have the Intellectuals Failed? On the Sociopolitical Claims and the Influ-ence of Literary Intellectuals in West Germany," *New German Critique*, 58 (Winter 1993), 7–8.

national continuities. If both languages were committed to a German republic, they entertained very different political visions of its future. Both laid claim to the German past to fashion narratives of legitimacy for their respective visions. The fact is that none of the languages of republicanism and the scholarly approaches they underwrote satisfactorily explains the development of a consensus about the political meaning of the Holocaust. As I argue in Chapter 2, the political consensus about the liberal political institutions of the new republic emerged out of a protracted and bitter public discussion about the *meaning* of the German past for the Federal Republic's present and future. West German democracy, then, is a *discursive* achievement, not an antifascist or conservative-integrationist one.

This book is not a conventional intellectual history. It relates the ideas of intellectuals to their political emotions. There is insufficient work linking individual subjectivity, social psychology, and intellectual life. Too often, ideas are isolated from the lives of their articulators, although it is readily apparent that the conceptual blockages and blindnesses that constitute the underlying structure of postwar German memory are bound up in the formative, adolescent experiences of the country's leading intellectuals. Close inspection of their writings undertaken in this book shows their intellectual production can be seen as stagings of their personal histories.[38] The embedding of ideas in individual and collective experiences is all the more important in Germany where the national past, guilt, shame, and democracy were of existential significance for its intellectuals. In this way, this book seeks to overcome the distinction between the history of ideas and the social history of intellectuals; the former runs the danger of denuding ideas of the existential meaning they possessed for intellectuals, and the latter tends to reduce ideas to a function of social status.[39]

A note on "intellectuals." It is customary in Germany to use the term in connection with dissident writers and/or leftist scholars about whom much has been written.[40] Less has been written about the historians, philosophers, sociologists, political scientists, and educationalists of this generation, many of whom made decisive interventions in the public sphere, served as ministers and political advisers, and liberalized German intellectual life.[41] I aim to redress

---

[38] Barbara Kosta, ed., *Recasting Autobiography: Women's Counterfictions in Contemporary German Literature and Film* (Ithaca, 1994).

[39] Daniel Wickberg, "Intellectual History vs. the Social History of Intellectuals," *Rethinking History*, 5:3 (2001), 383–95. German scholarship typically traces intellectual networks rather than analyzing texts. Michael Grunewald and Uwe Puschner, eds., *Das konservative Intellektuellenmilieu, seine Presse und seine Netzwerke* (Bern, 2003); Dirk van Laak, *Gespräche in der Sicherheit des Schweigens* (Berlin, 1993). American scholarship, by contrast, is more often interested in what intellectuals thought: Anson Rabinbach, *In the Shadow of Catastrophe: German Intellectuals between Apocalypse and Enlightenment* (Berkeley, 1997).

[40] Jochen Vogt, *"Erinnerung ist unsere Aufgabe." Über Literatur, Moral und Politik, 1945–1990* (Wiesbaden, 1991); Hauke Brunkhorst, *Die Intellektuellen im Land der Mandarine* (Frankfurt, 1987); Rob Burns and Wilfried van der Will, *Protest and Democracy in West Germany: Extra-Parliamentary Opposition and the Democratic Agenda* (London, 1988).

[41] Robert Holub, *Jürgen Habermas: Critic in the Public Sphere* (London and New York, 1991).

this imbalance. This book is a study of "professors and politics" rather than a treatment of literary figures like the important East German author Christa Wolf.[42]

Postwar German memory has been a popular field since the 1980s, and accordingly it has developed a conceptually reflective body of commentary.[43] A growing section of the literature addresses specific sites of modern German memory as case studies.[44] Other books treat the foundation years of postwar German memory and focus largely on political history.[45] Recently, the

---

[42] Studies in this genre are weighted on the pre-1945 period: John E. Toews, *Hegelianism: The Path of Dialectical Reason, 1805–1841* (Cambridge, 1980); Fritz Ringer, *The Decline of the German Mandarins: The German Academic Community, 1890–1933* (Cambridge, Mass., 1969); Hans Sluga, *Heidegger's Crisis: Philosophy and Politics in Nazi Germany* (Cambridge, Mass., 1995); Rudiger vom Bruch, *Wissenschaft, Politik und öffentliche Meinung: Gelehrtenpolitik im Wilhelminischen Deutschland, 1890–1914* (Husum, 1980); Gustav Schmidt and Jörn Rüsen, *Gelehrtenpolitik und politische Kultur in Deutschland, 1830–1930* (Bochum, 1986); Klaus Böhme, ed., *Aufrufe und Reden deutscher Professoren im Ersten Weltkrieg* (Stuttgart, 1975); Christian Jansen, *Professoren und Politik: Politisches Denken und Handeln der Heidelberger Hochschullehrer, 1914–35* (Göttingen, 1992); Hans-Peter Bleuel, *Deutschlands Bekenner. Professoren zwischen Kaiserreich und Diktatur* (Bern, 1968); Wolfgang J. Mommsen, ed., *Die Rolle der Intellektuellen, Künstler, und Schriftsteller im Ersten Weltkrieg* (Munich, 1995); Klaus Schwabe, *Wissenschaft und Kriegsmoral. Die deutschen Hochschullehrer und die politischen Grundfragen des Ersten Weltkrieges* (Göttingen, 1969); Marita Baumgarten, *Professoren und Universitäten im neunzehnten Jahrhundert. Zur Sozialgeschichte deutscher Geistes- und Naturswissenschaftler* (Göttingen, 1975). On the Federal Republic, there is Horst Schmitt, *Politikwissenschaft und freiheitliche Demokratie: Eine Studie zum "politischen Forschungs-programm" der "Freiburger Schule," 1954–1970* (Baden Baden, 1995).

[43] Jeffrey K. Olick, *In the House of the Hangman: The Agonies of German Defeat, 1943–1949* (Chicago, 2005); Olick, "Genre Memories and Memory Genres: A Dialogical Analysis of May 8th, 1945, Commemorations in the Federal Republic of Germany," *American Sociological Review*, 64 (June 1999), 381–402; Olick, "What Does It Mean to Normalize the Past?: Official Memory in German Politics since 1989," *Social Science History*, 22:4 (1998), 547–71. Wulf Kantsteiner, "Finding Meaning in Memory: A Methodological Critique of Collective Memory Studies," *History and Theory*, 41 (May 2002), 179–97; Alon Confino and Peter A. Fritzsche, eds., *The Work of Memory: New Directions in the Study of German Society and Culture* (Urbana, 2002); Robert Moeller, "What Has 'Coming to Terms with the Past' Meant in Post-World War II Germany? From History to Memory to the 'History of Memory,'" *Central European History*, 35:2 (2002), 223–56.

[44] S. Jonathan Wiesen, *West German Industry and the Challenge of the Nazi Past, 1945–1955* (Chapel Hill, 2001); Gavriel D. Rosenfeld, *Munich and Memory: Architecture, Monuments and the Legacy of the Third Reich* (Berkeley, 2000); Elliot Y. Neaman, *A Dubious Past: Ernst Jünger and the Politics of Literature after Nazism* (Berkeley, 1999); Sabine Moller, *Die Entkonkretisierung der NS-Herrschaft in der Ära Kohl: Die Neue Wache, das Denkmal für die ermordeten Juden Europas, das Haus der Geschichte der Bundesrepublik Deutschland* (Hannover, 1998); Brigitte Hausmann, *Duell mit der Verdrängung? Denkmäler für die Opfer des Nationalsozialismus in der Bundesrepublik 1980–1990* (Münster, 1998); Brian Ladd, *The Ghosts of Berlin: Confronting German History in the Urban Landscape* (Chicago, 1997); Kerstin Freudiger, *Die juristische Aufarbeitung von NS-Verbrechen* (Tübingen, 2002).

[45] Jeffrey Herf, *Divided Memory: The Nazi Past in the Two Germanys* (Cambridge, Mass., 1997); Robert Moeller, *War Stories: The Search for a Useable Past in the Federal Republic of Germany* (Berkeley, 2001); Norbert Frei, *Adenauer and the Nazi Past*, trans. Joseph Golb (New York, 2002).

evolution of German memory since unification has interested a number of scholars in German studies, history, and politics.[46] There are surprisingly few books that survey the entirety of German memory since the Second World War. One of them, Harold Marcuse's *Legacies of Dachau: The Uses and Abuses of a Concentration Camp, 1933–2001*, is a remarkable, indeed monumental work that analyzes German memory politics over nearly seventy years by investigating the evolution of and controversies surrounding the Dachau concentration camp.[47]

The purpose of this book is not to write a history of postwar German memory or memories (either of East or West Germany, or both) in this manner but to explain *why* and show *how* it is structured as it was, and to demonstrate how a political consensus developed. Because the texts and debates were played out in a public sphere, the book discusses the Federal Republic of Germany and not its East German counterpart. The first chapter explains the underlying structure of German intellectual stances to the recent past by showing how they were based on political emotions generated in family and adolescent socialization. The key issue is the difficulty of generating basic trust of intellectual elites in institutions and culture because of the continuities in personnel and attitudes from the previous regime. Chapter 2 outlines the rival languages of republicanism in the Federal Republic. The reactions of German intellectuals to the Nazi experience and Allied occupation after 1945 reveal that fundamental notions of good, evil, and a post-totalitarian redemptive community were the burning issues of the day. For much of the German intelligentsia, the liberal democratic outcome of West Germany was anything but inevitable because it was felt to be inadequate to the perceived problem of the moral "pollution" that the presence of former Nazis represented. The next chapter introduces what I contend to be the key generation of postwar German intellectual history. The forty-fivers comprised various intellectual groupings but were basically in thrall to the two languages of republicanism.

In the fourth and fifth chapters, I dramatize the underlying structure and languages of republicanism in the self-narration of two leading intellectuals. First, I discuss the "German German" Wilhelm Hennis, a prominent political theorist and public intellectual. The chapter is based on interview material as well as his published works. Then I move to unravel the "Redemptive Republicanism" of the "Non-German German" Jürgen Habermas. The chapter examines both his scholarly texts and public interventions, focusing on the 1940s and 1950s. The

---

[46] Niven, *Facing the Nazi Past; Anne Sa'adah, Germany's Second Chance: Trust, Justice, and Democratization* (Cambridge, Mass., 1998); Jan-Werner Müller, *Another Country: German Intellectuals, Unification and National Identity* (New Haven, 2000); Klaus Neumann, *Shifting Memories: The Nazi Past in the New Germany* (Ann Arbor, 2000); Mary Nolan, "The Politics of Memory in the Berlin Republic," *Radical History Review*, 81 (Fall 2001), 113–32.

[47] Harold Marcuse, *Legacies of Dachau: Uses and Abuses of a Concentration Camp, 1933–2001* (Cambridge, 2001); Peter Reichel, *Vergangenheitsbewältigung in Deutschland: Die Auseinandersetzung mit der NS-Diktatur von 1945 bis heute* (Munich, 2001); Mary Fulbrook, *German Memory after the Holocaust* (London, 1999).

point is not to praise a thinker about whom much adulatory work has been written already but to show how he at once articulated and was symptomatic of the political language and subjectivity of the left.

Having laid bare the underlying structure of German memory, in the next three chapters I show how the lack of basic trust in the Federal German institutions by much of the intelligentsia prefigured key debates in German intellectual and political culture in the 1960s and 1970s. In Chapter 6, I show how the role of science and technology was a prominent issue for intellectuals of all stripes, and how they wanted to reform the German university to make it a motor of the social reform that they hoped would rehabilitate Germany from its Nazi past. The competing projects of reform led inevitably to polarization and a sense of crisis. This anxiety is the subject of Chapter 7. For so-called nonconformist intellectuals on the left in particular, the reelection of conservative governments in the 1950s and early 1960s and the subsequent "grand coalition" with the Social Democrats were interpreted as incremental changes toward an authoritarian state. The panic was underwritten by particular memories of the Nazi past and the role of the university within it. The student rebellions of 1967–69 are usually understood as outbreaks of youthful exuberance in the name of freedom and countercultural experimentation. In fact, at least at the beginning, they were intended as defensive acts against a state perceived to be in thrall to German traditions that had led to 1933.

The common view that the forty-fiver generation of intellectuals was adamantly opposed to the radical nature of the 1968 movement is examined in Chapter 8. The evidence suggests that leftist and even liberal forty-fivers actually welcomed the protest initially, blaming the lack of reform for provoking the students. Only when revolutionary rhetoric and violence accompanied the movement did liberals and certainly conservatives commence a counter-campaign, mobilizing Nazi memories of their own by casting the students as "brown people from the left" who wanted to politicize the university like Nazi students had done. The battle lines drawn in the wake of 1968 continued to frame debate throughout the 1970s.

The subsequent three chapters cover the period between 1982 and 2006. Chapter 9 briefly introduces the polarized terms of debate in this period. It sets the stage for Chapter 10's analysis of the redemptive republican position by laying out the ambition of the conservative Kohl government to renationalize German identity in the 1980s. Non-German German intellectuals persisted in wanting Germans to abandon national identity altogether, while their conservative counterparts, as I show in Chapter 11, resisted the leftist stigmatization of German history and identity by entreating traditions as trustworthy sources of identification. The book concludes where it began: with the question of generational identification, the Nazi past, and the Federal Republican present. With the maturation of the fourth generation since 1945, the transmission of memory and concomitant feelings of pollution from the Germans who experienced Nazi years gradually came to an end. The underlying structure of German memory and its starkly polarized positions began to dissolve, and a new German patriotism based on Federal Republican traditions, now some sixty years old, was visible for the first time.

This book intervenes in a number of general debates. In particular, it contributes to scholarly and more general discussions on the nature of memory, trauma, transitional justice, and of course postwar Germany and the Nazi past. Many countries worldwide – in Latin America, in the postcommunist states of Eastern and Central Europe (including Yugoslavia at the moment), and South Africa – are in the process of working through their dictatorial pasts.[48] As the civil unrest in Chile about the trial of the former president Pinochet demonstrated, addressing the injustice that occurred only a few years earlier has grave political consequences. What I can show, based on the German experience, is that no party in the customary memory disputes in such societies possesses any epistemological advantage over the other. A future value consensus emerges incrementally out of contested struggles over collective memory.

---

[48] Martha Minow, *Between Vengeance and Forgiveness: Facing History after Genocide and Mass Violence* (Boston, 1998); A. Dirk Moses, "Coming to Terms with the Past in Comparative Perspective: Germany and Australia," *Aboriginal History*, 25 (2001), 91–115.

I

Stigma and Structure in German Memory

Many Germans and foreign observers regarded the (re)unification of Germany in 1990 as more or less a natural development, as if the breaching of the Berlin Wall late the year before had ended an artificial national division in the heart of Europe.[1] Finally, it seemed, the Germans had their nation-state back and could devote themselves to their national interests like any "normal" people. The celebrations were as heady in Berlin as they were further east when the iron curtain was pulled down after decades of Soviet domination. But concern accompanied euphoria from the outset. Some commentators worried that the breakup of the Soviet empire might herald ethnic chauvinism if the newly liberated nations reverted to nineteenth-century modes of identification to determine their boundaries and citizenship.[2] And sure enough, the spirit of peaceful revolution did not long outlast the posing of the democratic question about the constitution of "the people." The Czechs and Slovaks, for instance, soon decided on amicable divorce – though many of them united in hatred for Roma people – while corruption and economic stagnation belied the promise of capitalist prosperity that Thatcher and Bush had proclaimed in triumphant tones for postcommunist regimes at the end of history.[3]

For Germany, the defining of a national people over the past sixteen years has proved to be a Sisyphean project. The country's pretensions to cultural uniformity were challenged in three ways. West Germans were stunned by the alien mentality of their eastern compatriots, in particular regarding the divergent attitude to work, money, and state entitlements. Many "Wessies" wondered whether unification was such a good idea after all, especially in view of

---

[1] As Willy Brandt put it, "What belongs together, now grows together."

[2] Ralf Dahrendorf, *Reflections on the Revolution in Europe* (New York, 1990), and Michael Ignatieff, *Blood and Belonging: Journeys into the New Nationalism* (London, 1993).

[3] Vladimir Tismaneanu, *Fantasies of Salvation: Democracy, Nationalism, and Myth in Post-Communist Europe* (Princeton, N.J., 1998); Stefan Wolff, *Ethnic Conflict: A Global Perspective* (Oxford, 2006).

the new tax levied to pay for the massive transfers eastward.[4] They seemed to feel more at home amid the pastoral elegance of southern France, in an Italian piazza, or on a Greek island than in the shabby towns of Saxony, Thuringia, or Pomerania with their high unemployment, sullen inhabitants, and decidedly un-Mediterranean flair. Then there were the heated debates over refugees, naturalization laws, multiculturalism, and the stalled integration of "guest workers," as well as the periodic violence against them by neo-Nazis and disaffected youths. What was the status, for instance, of third-generation descendants of Turkish guest workers from the 1950s? Neither German nor Turkish, their hybridized identities did not fit the rigid categories of Central European national affiliation and citizenship.[5]

These are not new types of questions. They have been debated for more than two hundred years in the context of Jewish emancipation. Since 1990, they have been raised anew in relation to a third set of identity-related issues, namely, the numerous controversies about remembrance of the Nazi past. Which Germans are being addressed and in whose name are politicians speaking when they express contrition for what happened? Only the descendants of what is called "the perpetrator generation"? Germans and Jews are invariably juxtaposed as if they do not mix, like oil and water, although Germany is home for tens of thousands of Jews for whom German is their mother tongue.[6]

Of course, despite similarities, there is an important difference between the Turkish and Jewish cases. In the latter, the question of historical justice interposes itself at the site of national self-articulation. A "negative symbiosis" (Hannah Arendt) both unites and divides Germans and Jews.[7] Here the vocabulary of victims, perpetrators, and bystanders permeates the discussion, dividing the population into distinct lineages connected to the lives of parents and grandparents in the 1930s and 1940s. For this reason, public discussion about the common past is rooted in the intimate sphere of the family, through kitchen table conversations between the generations in which memories and experiences

[4] Marc Howard, "An East German Ethnicity? Understanding the New Division of Unified Germany," *German Politics and Society*, 13:4 (1995), 49–70.

[5] Jerome S. Legge Jr., *Jews, Turks and Other Strangers: The Roots of Prejudice in Modern Germany* (Madison, 2003); Simon Green, *The Politics of Exclusion: Institutions and Immigration Policy in Contemporary Germany* (Manchester, 2004); Adrian Del Caro and Janet Ward, eds., *German Studies in the Post-Holocaust Age: The Politics of Memory, Identity, and Ethnicity* (Boulder, Colo.: 2003); Andreas Huyssen, *Twilight Memories: Marking Time in a Culture of Amnesia* (New York, 1995), 67–84.

[6] For analyses of Jews in Germany, see Jeffrey M. Peck, *Being Jewish in the New Germany* (New Brunswick, 2006); Hans Erler, ed., *Erinnern und Verstehen: Der Völkermord an den Juden im politischen Gedächtnis der Deutschen* (Frankfurt and New York, 2003); Lynn Rapaport, *Jews in Germany after the Holocaust: Memory, Identity, and Jewish-German Relations* (Cambridge, 1997).

[7] Hannah Arendt first used this term in a letter to Karl Jaspers. See Katja Behrens, "The Rift and Not the Symbiosis," in Leslie Morris and Jack Zipes, eds., *Unlikely History: The Changing German-Jewish Symbiosis, 1945–2000* (New York and Houndmills, 2000), 32. Dan Diner adopts it in "Negative Symbiosis: Germans and Jews after Auschwitz," in Peter Baldwin, ed., *Reworking the Past: Hitler, the Holocaust, and the Historian's Debate* (Boston, 1990).

are transmitted, whether accurately or not, and collective identity formed with the necessary corollary: on whose side were "my people" all those years ago?[8]

For the most part, such conversations are conducted by those Germans whom National Socialism was supposed to benefit. But what about those whom it was supposed to exterminate? Many of their descendants live in Germany as well, and they occasionally remind the majority of the impossibility of presuming a seamless national identity and homogeneous collective "we/us." Indeed, that the rest of the world judges Germany not only by its treatment of Jews and other minorities but also by how it remembers the Second World War. In newspapers and learned journals, reporters and scholars from around the world keep careful watch on the German public sphere for signs of self-pity, lest its solemn duty to remember the Holocaust be downplayed and national feeling return. Yet, is there not a tension between demanding that Germany today is too diverse to admit of national modes of identification (i.e., Germany as a community of descent or fate) while simultaneously insisting that the supposedly ontologically stable entity called "the Germans" must confess guilt, express contrition, and atone for the Holocaust?[9] The tortuous construction of collective identity in Germany after Nazism and the Holocaust takes place within this tension. How do non-Jewish Germans recreate an identity in view of this aporia, especially if younger Germans can hardly be held even indirectly guilty for the Nazi murder of European Jewry? This book argues that we ought to employ the concepts of stigma and sacrifice rather than the guilt-shame couplet in order to understand the dynamics of German political emotions.

Dialogue across the Divide?

The "dialogue" between "Germans" and "Jews" demonstrates the dilemmas of post-Holocaust German identity creation. A hitherto ignored example occurred in late 1998, at the height of the debate about the proposed Berlin memorial to the Murdered Jews of Europe, and the dispute between the writer Martin Walser, who had attacked what he saw as a ritualized public commemoration of the Holocaust, and the leader of German-Jewry, Ignatz Bubis. In this overheated public sphere, the weekly magazine *Der Spiegel* asked three Jewish students in Berlin about their feelings regarding Holocaust memory in Germany. Mark Jaffé, Hilda Joffe, and Igor Gulko gave their answers in an interview-article entitled "Zum Hinschauen verdammt" (Condemned to Watch).[10] Hilda mourned the fact that her large extended family, once numbering more than

---

[8] On narratives of survival in German families, see Konrad Jarausch, "Living with Broken Memories: Some Narratological Comments," in Chrisoph Kleßmann, ed., *The Divided Past: Rewriting Post-War German History* (Oxford, 2001), 171–98.

[9] Symptomatic is Moishe Postone, "A Comment: The End of the Postwar Era and the Reemergence of the Past," in Y. Michael Bodemann, ed., *Jews, Germans, Memory: Reconstructions of Jewish Life in Germany* (Ann Arbor, 1996), 274.

[10] "'Zum Hinschauen verdammt': Die jüdischen Studenten Mark Jaffe, Hilda Joffe und Igor Gulko aus Berlin über den Streit um die Erinnerung an Auschwitz," *Der Spiegel* (December 7, 1998), 236–39.

ninety, had been decimated. "Today, we sit at a small table," she lamented. Mark said that it would be good if more people were personally conscious of what happened then, but – addressing Walser – he would prefer ritualized remembrance to none at all. Igor reported that he had non-Jewish friends who confessed that they find it difficult to be reminded daily of the Holocaust. One even felt molested by it. He could understand that they did not want to feel guilty for what their ancestors had done, but the alternative was unacceptable: forgetting and looking away. After all, he said, as a Jew he thought about it every day. Hilda said everyone was implicated. Members of the younger generation did not want to accept that perhaps their grandparents had participated in the exploitation and expulsion of Jews. Although they did not identify themselves as Non-German or as citizens of another nation-state, these three Jewish students equated "Germans" with the people who perpetrated the Holocaust against their relatives.[11]

How would Germans react to this notion? Stirring the pot of identity politics, *Der Spiegel* published a reply three weeks later by a non-Jewish student, Kathi-Gesa Klafke, under the revealing title "Also doch Erbsünde?" (So Inherited Sin after All?).[12] Kathi-Gesa, born in 1975, said she resented being made to feel guilty by the three Jewish students. Reality was too messy, she said, for human collectives, if they existed, to be absolutized or categorized neatly under terms like "victims" and "perpetrators": members of her own family had been persecuted, not all Jews had been angels and, what is more, many other nationalities participated in their murder. Pointing to her own Christianity, she said that only religion divided her from the Jewish students. To distinguish radically between Germans and Jews, as Hilda, Mark, and Igor had, was in fact racist. It was time, she declared, to confine "the Holocaust to history with the extermination of the Indians, the slave trade, serfdom, the gulag, colonization, the persecution of the Christians, the Inquisition, the Crusades . . . so that *everyone* can learn from them." What upset her was that "non-Germans are content to demonize the Germans, because something like that [the Holocaust] can only happen there." Germany was being victimized, she suggested. "No other country has so little national identity as the Germans and cares so much about what their neighbors think of them." The discrimination against Germans abroad was "absurd and is racism. And it is nothing else other than the instrumentalization of Auschwitz."

Anticipating the argument that as a German she is responsible for memory of Nazism and the Holocaust, Kathi-Gesa said that to link her closely to "what occurred then," as she put it, amounted to an accusation of "inherited sin" (*Erbsünde*), a concept she dismissed by asking why should Germans continue to endure being called perpetrators if people no longer accuse Jews collectively for crucifying Jesus. "I have a right to be held responsible only for my own actions,"

---

[11] According to Diana Treibers's study, Jewish families in Germany constitute their identity in opposition to surrounding German society: Treibers, *"Lech lecha": Jüdische Identiät der zweiten und dritten Generationen im heutigen Deutschland* (Pfaffenweiler, 1998).

[12] Kathi-Gesa Klafke, "'Also doch Erbsünde?'" *Der Spiegel* (December 28, 1998), 148–49.

she insisted. Her grandmother did not take Jewish furniture, she answered Hilda. "On the contrary, her own was burned, together with her house and family [referring to the bombing of German cities]. You and no one else have the right to judge in this way." In fact, to call "my generation" perpetrators, she concluded, would "achieve the opposite of contrition and awakening: rage and truculence."

This exchange is remarkable not only for the vehemence of Kathi-Gesa's reply, but also for its continuities with the reactions of Germans to their occupation in the immediate postwar period. Then Germans had been indignant about the accusation of "collective guilt" leveled at them by the American authorities in particular. "These Disgraces: Your Fault! You observed quietly and silently tolerated it. . . . That is your great guilt. You all are co-responsible for these gruesome crimes," the posters shouted in large print accompanied by pictures of piled remains of murdered camp victims. The subsequent denazification campaign, the prohibition for army personnel on fraternization with Germans, and rhetoric of a regressed national character that needed "reeducation," with its suggestion that the national culture was fatally flawed, emphasized further the impression of a collective-guilt accusation.[13]

The reaction to it was similar to that of Kathi-Gesa: recourse to Christian universalism, a lack of empathy for the victims of Germans, a reluctance to name the crimes (the vague references to "what occurred then"), an insistence on personal victim status and, above all, a rejection of collective guilt. There was even talk of Germany being treated like the Jews had been, as a pariah nation, indeed – with reference to Morgenthau's plans to deindustrialize the country and the dire food situation in 1946–47 – that Germany's national existence was imperiled.[14] The participants in the intense discussion about collective guilt immediately after the war – a debate in which all German commentators, irrespective of ideology or religion, flatly rejected the concept – insisted that the accusation was as invalid as blaming Jews collectively for putative crimes, as Kathi-Gesa Klakfe had repeated in 1998.[15]

The Exhaustion of Secular Vocabulary

The exchange between these students and recent research on the social psychology of members of groups that have committed transgressions shows that

[13] Donald Bloxham, "The Genocidal Past in Western Germany and the Experience of Occupation, 1945–6," *European History Quarterly*, 34:3 (2004), 305–35; Thomas Koebner, "Die Schuldfrage: Vergangenheitsverweigerung und Lebenslügen in der Diskussion, 1945–1949," in Thomas Koebner, Gert Sauermeister, and Sigrid Schneider, eds., *Deutschland nach Hitler* (Opladen, 1987), 301–29; Jeffrey K. Olick, *In the House of the Hangman: The Agonies of German Defeat, 1943–1949* (Chicago, 2005).

[14] Frank Stern, *The Whitewashing of the Yellow Badge: Antisemitism and Philosemitism in Postwar Germany*, trans. William Templar (Oxford, 1992), 305.

[15] Jan Friedmann and Jörg Später, "Britische und deutsche Kollektivschuld-Debatte," in Ulrich Herbert, ed., *Wandlungsprozesse in Westdeutschland. Belastung, Integration, Liberalisierung 1945–1980* (Göttingen, 2002), 53–90.

the guilt-shame couplet cannot account for the biblical notion of an "inherited sin" that affects entire groups.[16] Guilt is linked to individual responsibility, and whether individuals feel guilt for a violation committed by a member of their group depends on whether they regard the violation as ascribable to particular acts over which they had some control. But how can later generations be held guilty for events that occurred before they were born or when they were children? Indeed, how can collectives and groups be held guilty or innocent for mass crimes? The literature on "collective guilt" may be correct in pointing out that those ridden with guilt want to repair the damage, but its analysis is synchronic and therefore does not account for historical trauma.[17]

That the vocabulary of guilt and shame is insufficient, especially for transgenerational questions, is evident in Michael Schneider's observation that the relation "between the guilty and their offspring remains fixed as inexplicable, imprescriptable guilt, comparable to *Biblical guilt* within the framework of history."[18] Kathi's innovation was to introduce a temporal dimension to the anxiety about collective guilt: inherited sin (or guilt). This is indeed a biblical notion: I will visit "the iniquities of the fathers on the children, and on the third and the fourth generations of those who hate Me," God declares (Exodus 20:5, 34:6–7, and Deuteronomy 5:9). It circulates in a field of discourse with an ensemble of other biblical and religious terms about the German past: taboo, heresy, orthodoxy, sacrality, "thorn in the flesh" (*Stachel im Fleisch*). Not for nothing do journalists habitually resort to theological rhetoric to depict the relationship between Germans and their past. Only by remembering the Holocaust with contrition, wrote one, "can [Germans] again find their spiritual balance [*seelisches Gleichgewicht*]."[19]

Secular vocabulary exhausts itself when approaching what is routinely called "evil," perhaps the ultimate evil, itself a religiously connotated word from moral philosophy. For this reason, the German philosopher Karl Jaspers confessed

---

[16] Aleida Assmann and Ute Frevert, *Geschichtsvergessenheit: Vom Umgang mit deutschen Vergangenheiten nach 1945* (Stuttgart, 1999) is representative of the literature that limits itself to this dichotomy.

[17] This discussion draws on Brian Lickel, Tony Schmader, and Marchelle Barquissau, "The Evocation of Moral Emotions in Intergroup Contexts: The Distinction between Collective Guilt and Collective Shame," in Nyla R. Branscombe and Bertjan Doosje, eds., *Collective Guilt: International Perspectives* (Cambridge, 2004), 35–55. The extensive literature is cited in this chapter and others in this book. A useful start is also Bertjan Doosje and Nyla R. Branscombe, "Attributions for the Negative Historical Actions of a Group," *European Journal of Social Psychology*, 33 (2003), 235–48.

[18] Michael Schneider, "Fathers and Sons, Retrospectively: The Damaged Relationship between Two Generations," *New German Critique*, 31 (Winter 1984), 13 (emphasis added).

[19] Nicola Frowein, "Wenig Platz für Trauer," *ZDF Heue.de Magazin* (May 10, 2005), http://www.heute.de/ZDFheute/inhalt/7/0,3672,2290343,00.html. Cf. Hans-Ulrich Wehler, "Goldhagen Debatte: Wie ein Stachel im Fleisch," *Die Zeit* (May 24, 1996). See also Matthias Schmidt, "Von Schuld und Sühne, Versagen und Erneuerung: Zu Theorie und Praxis christlicher Annäherung an den Staat Israel," in Susanne Düwell and Matthias Schmidt, eds., *Narrative der Shoah: Repräsentationen der Vergangenheit in Historiographie, Kunst und Politik* (Paderborn and Munich, 2002), 263–77.

the limitations of his own finely grained moral distinctions in his famous 1947 book, *The Question of German Guilt*: "language fails" when a people's guilt brings it "face to face with nothingness."[20] Historians are dumb witnesses to a culture, a society, a people, wrangling with itself about the criminality of its past if they rest content with narrating the sequence of historical controversies such as those that have dotted the German public sphere since the war. They need to be alive to the subterranean biblical themes flowing beneath the surface froth of events, linking past and present through the continuity of German political emotions that are necessarily collective and therefore necessarily sensitive to anxieties about collective, inherited sin.

The notion of biblical guilt suggests a transgenerational curse or communal pollution, an insight of the sociologist Norbert Elias who thought that Germans "have to struggle again and again with the fact that the we-image of the Germans is *soiled* by the memory of the excesses perpetrated by the Nazis, and that others, and perhaps even their own consciences, blame them for what Hitler and his followers did."[21] Moreover, for the German ear, as Ralf Dahrendorf has pointed out, the term *Kollektivschuld* signifies more than collective guilt in English. "'Guilt' (*Schuld*) in German always has the undertone of the irredeemable, incapable of being canceled by metaphysical torment; *Kollektivschuld* binds every individual as such for all time."[22] In order to address the transgenerational aspects of guilt and shame, it is necessary to theorize more deeply what Elias means by "soiled": the "contamination," "pollution," "stain," and "taint" that is often said to mark postwar Germany.[23] According to the anthropologist Ghassan Hage, we need to understand such notions in the context of kinship and gift giving. Feelings connected to group life, such as pride, guilt, and shame, can be generated and then circulate only because of family life; it is in the family that parents pass on the gift of social viability to their children.[24] The gift of social life presupposes mutual obligations. The greater the gift's social viability, the more likely it is that the children will

---

[20] Karl Jaspers, *The Question of German Guilt*, trans. E. B. Ashton (New York, 1961 [1947]), 81.

[21] Norbert Elias, *The Germans: Power Struggles and the Development of Habitus in the Nineteenth and Twentieth Centuries*, trans. Eric Dunning and Stephen Mennell (New York, 1996), 16 (emphasis added). He mentions only once that the German collective has been stigmatized.

[22] Ralf Dahrendorf, *Society and Democracy in Germany* (New York and London, 1976 [1965]), 288–89.

[23] Eric L. Santner, *Stranded Objects: Mourning, Memory, and Film in Postwar Germany* (Ithaca, 1990), 45, asserts that Germany's "cultural reservoir has been poisoned" without explaining exactly how. More helpfully, Dan Diner explains that because the Holocaust was directed at the group existence of Jews, "it intuitively invites a presumption of collective guilt," that is, that the German group self is tainted because every member of the group is affected by a common memory of this past: Diner, *Beyond the Conceivable: Studies on Germany, Nazism, and the Holocaust* (Berkeley, 2000), 221. Cf. Konrad H. Jarausch, "Removing the Nazi Stain? The Quarrel of the German Historians," *German Studies Review*, 11 (May 1988), 285–301.

[24] Ghassan Hage, *Against Paranoid Nationalism: Searching for Hope in a Shrinking Society* (Sydney, 2003), 98.

be naturally inclined to participate constructively in the community. That is why recent research has found that memories of the war and interpretations of the Holocaust are mediated above all by family conversation rather than by the education system. The private sphere, more than the public sphere, is the site and first source of social memory.[25] Socially viable identities are impaired if children have difficulty identifying with their parents because they were implicated in crimes or refused to acknowledge the criminality of the Nazi regime.[26]

But the ambivalence that many younger postwar Germans felt toward their parents was not just due to the flawed social identity of the older generation; it is that parents were also sources of nurturing. The intense feelings of pollution stemmed from the fact that it was difficult to reject the gift out of hand. Referring to Adolf Eichmann's son, Hage explains: "Paradoxically, but more probably, it is because he inherited his father's evil through the love and protection that the latter gave him that he experienced such a form of oppressive pollution. It came with the gift of social life itself. The pollution defines one of the 'we' that constitute his social viability, and he was forced to relate to it."[27] There is no doubt that many German children felt polluted, and even saw themselves as victims of their parents. In various interview projects, a number of Germans described themselves as "the Jew of [the] family."[28] "Monika" made plain the consequences of having a Nazi father hanged as a war criminal – "that people would despise me, find me detestable, because of him." The relationship with her mother, who persisted in idealizing her disgraced husband, was fraught with ambiguity. She both pitied her and was frustrated by her obtuse unwillingness to recognize the criminality of her husband and the regime.[29] More drastic still, "Rudolf" believed that he "must not have any children. This line must come to an end with me. What should I tell the little ones about Grandpa?"[30] Helga Mueller was haunted by her Nazi father's past: "I feel his guilt on me – I've carried this burden ever since. . . . I have sensed (genocide victims) walking through

---

[25] Harald Welzer, Sabine Moller, and Karoline Tschuggnall, *"Opa war kein Nazi": Nationalsozial-ismus und Holocaust im Familiengedächtnis* (Frankfurt, 2002). For public memory, see Heinrich August Winkler, ed., *Griff nach der Deutungsmacht: Zur Geschichte der Geschichtspolitik in Deutschland* (Göttingnen, 2004); Edgar Wolfrun, *Geschichtspolitk in der Bundesrepublik Deutschland: Der Weg zur bundesrepublikanischen Erinnerung, 1948–1990* (Darmstadt, 1999); Wolfgang Duchkowitsch, Fritz Hausjell, and Bernd Semrad, eds., *Die Spirale des Schweigens: Zum Umgang mit der nationalsozialistischen Zeitungswissenschaft* (Münster, 2004).

[26] Dan Bar-On, "Children of Perpetrators of the Holocaust: Working through One's Own Moral Self," *Psychiatry*, 53:3 (1990), 229–45.

[27] Hage, *Against Paranoid Nationalism*, 99.

[28] Peter Sichrovksy, *Born Guilty: Children of Nazi Families*, trans. Jean Steinberg (London, 1988), 11; Gertrud Hardtmann, "The Shadows of the Past," in Martin S. Bergmann and Milton E. Jucovy, eds., *Generations of the Holocaust* (New York, 1982), 230: patients saw themselves as the "Jews" of their parent's generation.

[29] Dan Bar-On, *The Legacy of Silence: Encounters with Children of the Third Reich* (Cambridge, Mass., 1989), 280.

[30] Sichrovksy, *Born Guilty*, 56.

my bedroom."[31] Reinhard Heydrich's nephew, Thomas, found it necessary to "expiate this burden of guilt" for which he felt somehow responsible.[32]

Yet guilt does not explain more general anxieties about the collective self that are biblical in nature, namely, that Germany would be a cursed or pariah nation. German foreign policy elites have always been acutely conscious of the observation by U.S. occupation authority chief, John McCloy, that "The world will carefully watch the new Germany and one of the tests by which it will be judged will be its attitude toward the Jews and how it treats them."[33] Consequently, the first chancellor of the Federal Republic, Konrad Adenauer, insisted on a treaty of reparations with Israel in the face of bitter resistance in his own party because, "The name of our Fatherland must once again have a value which corresponds to the historical achievement of the German people in culture and economics." His colleague, Eugen Gerstenmaier, noted in the early 1950s that Germany lived in a ghetto surrounded by antipathy, but that "this treaty has the goal to bring Germany out of the ghetto completely and forever." "It seems to me," he added, that "it is time, it is high time, that we no longer let ourselves be ashamed. The honor of Germany requires it!"[34]

It is with this realization that Leah Rosh, the initiator of the Berlin Holocaust memorial, told the colloquium deliberating on its design in 1997 that their discussions were being registered "very closely" in Israel and the United States.[35] In fact, she had come up with the idea of the memorial after visiting Yad Vashem in Jerusalem and later learning about the plans for a memorial museum in Washington, D.C. Why was there no central memorial in Berlin, she had asked then? The resentment about expectations from abroad – interpreted as effectively violating German sovereignty – led the editor of the weekly magazine *Der Spiegel*, Rudolf Augstein, to remark about the wretched imperative to please U.S. "East Coast" elites with the memorial.[36] The right-wing Christian Democrat parliamentarian Martin Hohmann objected to the proposed Berlin memorial with similar language: "What do our voters say? Many speak about the issue only under their breath [*hinter vogehaltener Hand*]. That is not a good sign in a democracy. Overwhelmingly, the Holocaust Memorial is rejected, by many intellectuals as well as many Jewish fellow citizens. Not a few find the planned memorial to be a mark of Cain [*Kainsmal*], an expression of self-contempt."[37] Even Joschka Fischer, who welcomed the memorial, defended it

---

[31] Steve Pfarrar, "One by One: Descendants of the Third Reich and the Holocaust in Dialogue," *Daily Hampshire Gazette* (November 4, 1997), viewed at http://www.umass.edu/jewish/shofar1998/third.html.

[32] Bar-On, *The Legacy of Silence*, 144.

[33] Peck, *Being Jewish in the New Germany*, 135.

[34] Jay Howard Geller, *Jews in Post-Holocaust Germany, 1945–1953* (Cambridge, 2005), 251–52.

[35] Leah Rosh, "'Ansprache' at the Colloquium 11 April 1997," in Ute Heimrod, Günter Schlüsche, and Horst Seferens, eds., *Der Denkmalstreit – das Denkmal: Die Debatte um das "Denkmal für die ermordeten Juden Europas." Eine Dokumentation* (Berlin, 1999), 714.

[36] Rudolf Augstein, "'Wir sind alle verletzbar,'" *Der Spiegel* (November 30, 1998), 32–33.

[37] "Wer ist Martin Hohmann?" *Süddeutsche Zeitung* (October 31, 2003). Four years later, Hohmann was expelled from his party for an anti-Semitic speech accusing Jews of being (also)

in terms that shared the reference to external marks. "This barbaric crime will always be part of German history. For my country it signifies the absolute moral abomination, a denial of all things civilized without precedent or parallel. The new, democratic Germany has drawn its conclusions. The historic and moral responsibility for Auschwitz has left an *indelible mark on us*."[38]

The customary rhetoric of guilt that dominates the public discourse and scholarly literature on postwar German political emotions about collective identity and the Nazi past misses such voices mentioning inherited collective sin, national honor and disgrace, Cain and Abel, and indelible marks.[39] The inability of the guilt concept, including hybrids like "inherited guilt," to capture the nuances of collective political emotions indicated by the resort to religious and biblical language points to the need for alternatives.

Stigma

The conceptual work done by terms like pollution plainly add to our understanding of the moral-emotional dilemmas faced by postwar Germans. But even such language is unsatisfactory because it invests pollution with ontological status: it simply *exists*, with the implication that those who recognize it as a challenge to transformation are brave souls and those who disavow it to guard their nation's honor are craven and immoral. This is not a proposition that can withstand social scientific scrutiny because it overlooks the well-known fact, made famous by Mary Douglas's observation that pollution is "matter out of place," that a cultural system of meaning determines the polluting potential of any person or thing.[40] In accusing Germans of seeking to ignore the stain of the Nazi past – in effect, their crippled group self – commentators are blind to their own participation in the construction of the stain.[41] After all, "[o]nly he is defiled who is regarded as defiled."[42]

---

a perpetrator people. Most voters and supporters of the Christian Democrats, however, did not regard the speech as anti-Semitic. Fritz Schenk, *Der Fall Hohmann: Die Dokumentation* (Munich, 2004).

[38] Address by Joschka Fischer, Minister for Foreign Affairs, New York, commemorating the 60th Anniversary of the Liberation of the Nazi Concentration Camps, January 24, 2005, www.germany.info.org/relaunch/politics/new/pol_fischer_holocaust_UN_01_24_2005.html, viewed January 15, 2006 (emphasis added). Cf. Diner, *Beyond the Conceivable*, 218.

[39] Following Paul Ricoeur, Gesine Schwan relegates group emotions like defilement to the cultures of antiquity, thereby missing that they reappear with the Holocaust. See her *Politics and Guilt: The Destructive Power of Silence*, trans. Thomas Dunlap (Lincoln and London, 2001).

[40] Mary Douglas, *Purity and Danger: An Analysis of the Concepts of Pollution and Taboo* (London and New York, 1966), 40.

[41] Representative here is Michael Geyer, who is the only commentator beside Elias I have found who has attempted to conceptualize, even if briefly, the problem of stigma in postwar Germany: "The Stigma of Violence, Nationalism, and War in Twentieth-Century Germany," *German Studies Review*, 15 (Winter 1992), 75–110. Geyer suggests that the stigma exists apart from his positing of it: "The mark of Cain for the murder of a people is stamped on German history alone. This is the stigma of violence in Germany history," in Michael Geyer, "The Place of the Second World War in German Memory and History," *New German Critique*, 71 (Spring–Summer, 1997), 37.

[42] Paul Ricoeur, *The Symbolism of Evil*, trans. Emerson Buchanan (Boston, 1967), 36.

For this reason, we ought to think of postwar German memory in terms of stigma. In its Greek origins, it meant a bodily sign of inferior social status, a brand on a criminal or outcast. It is logically and causally prior to pollution because the stigmatized group self pollutes its members generations after the crime. As the sociologist Erving Goffman observed, "tribal stigma of race, nation and religion . . . can be transmitted through lineage and equally contaminate all members of a family."[43] Stigma also has the advantage of a greater array of meanings than pollution. For many within the cultural system, of course, it is a mark of not constructed but actual inferiority. But some of those subject to stigma regard themselves as victims of persecution rather than justifiable outcasts. And for the outside observer, the term highlights its socially bound meaning: stigma as a flawed *social* identity, an identity that is stigmatized only in a specific cultural system.[44] In other words, stigma is not a natural status but is contructed and maintained by the gaze of others.

For all that, evidence of stigma is not readily apparent in the confessions of Germans in autobiographical statements or interviews because stigma is not an emotion one experiences like guilt. Guilt can be felt without the gaze of others. But if people say "I feel stigmatized," they are referring to an externally imposed marker of social inferiority rather than an interior experience. This distinction means the clues to the existence of stigma must be sought in recourse, for instance, to the biblical vocabulary mentioned previously, as well as to philosophically incoherent concepts like collective guilt. Their prevalence indicates that anxiety about the stigma of the Nazi past is palpable in German memory discourse.

The right-wing parliamentarian quoted earlier, Martin Hohmann, signaled it when he expressed his concern that the Berlin memorial would be a *Kainsmal*, a mark of Cain. Writing in 1998, the editor of *Der Spiegel*, Rudolf Augstein, rejected the memorial project because its effect would be to stigmatize Germans likewise in terms of the story of Cain and Abel. "If we did not proceed with the Eisenman plan, which would be sensible, we get bashed in the world press only once. If we do, I fear that we will create anti-Semites out of those who would perhaps otherwise not be anti-Semites, and then we get bashed in the world press every year, for life, *until the seventh generation*."[45]

The writer, Martin Walser, also argued that the memorial was a provocation that would create anti-Semites and ensure that bad news about Germany would forever plague the country.[46] Augstein, who had become increasingly nationalistic throughout the 1990s – he was an early and vehement critic of Daniel J. Goldhagen's *Hitler's Willing Executioners* (1996), which he read as an indictment of Germans collectively as biological anti-Semites – continued by

---

[43] Erving Goffman, *Stigma: Notes on the Management of Spoiled Identity* (Englewood Cliffs, N.J., 1963), 14; Bruce G. Link and Jo C. Phelan, "Conceptualizing Stigma," *American Review of Sociology*, 27 (2001), 363–85.

[44] Goffman, *Stigma*, 17–19.

[45] Augstein, "'Wir sind alle verletzbar,'" 34 (emphasis added).

[46] Martin Walser, "Das Prinzip Genauigkeit: Über Victor Klemperer" (1995), *Werke*, vol. 12 (Frankfurt, 1997), 805.

asking whether "we can force our descendants to carry our personal shame."
Like Walser, he was also suspicious of Jews who advocated the institutionalization of this shame in the memorial, which he called a "monstrosity." Rejecting
the "somewhat superior" (*etwas überheblich*) suggestion of the German Jewish conservative politician and media personality, Michel Friedman, to educate
German youth to take co-responsibility for Auschwitz, he concluded that it was
impossible to do more than ensure it was taught academically at schools and
universities. The future was open – and ought not be stigmatized.[47]

The question of stigma arises in foreign policy, as well. Helmut Schmidt, the
West German chancellor in 1981, attempted to reject a stigmatized German
identity when he told the Israelis that his foreign policy would not be held
hostage to Auschwitz, after Menachem Begin had raised the collective-guilt
accusation when the Federal Republic agreed to sell Leopard tanks to Saudi
Arabia. Three years later, the next chancellor, Helmut Kohl, showed that guilt
and collective guilt were effectively synonyms for stigma when he told Israelis
on a visit to their country that he was blessed "by the grace of late birth"
(unlike Schmidt, who, born in 1918, had been a soldier in the war), with the
implication that he, and Germans generally, could not be stigmatized by the
Holocaust.[48] He also ventured to shield subsequent generations. "The young
German generation does not regard Germany's history as a burden but as a
challenge for the future. They are prepared to shoulder their responsibility. But
they refuse to acknowledge a collective guilt for the deeds of their fathers."[49]

These Germans felt the Holocaust was being instrumentalized to persecute
or victimize all Germans, even younger ones born long after the Second World
War. Stigma was also the underlying bone of contention in the celebrated Historians' Dispute of the mid-1980s. It was concern about the growing intensity
of Holocaust discourse in West Germany that led the historian Ernst Nolte (b.
1923) to give a controversial lecture on the "past that will not fade away."[50]
His target was the implicit stigma in the belief that the Holocaust was unique
and that accordingly the German people or nation and its history were abnormal, that is, permanently set off in horror from the traditions of other nations.
The writer Günter Grass (b. 1927) exemplified Nolte's concern when, in 1990
during the unification debates, he wrote that the civilizational rupture of the
Holocaust amounted to an ineffable evil, even a negative sublime that forever
marked his country: it "will never cease to be present; our disgrace will never
be repressed or mastered . . . Auschwitz will . . . never be understood.[51]

---

[47] Augstein, "'Wir sind alle verletzbar'"; cf. Michel Friedman, "'Der Streit über das Erinnern wird
gefährlich,'" *Die Welt* (November 23, 1998).
[48] See Michael Wolffsohn, *Eternal Guilt? Forty Years of German-Jewish-Israeli Relations*, trans.
Douglas Bokovoy (New York, 1993), 33, 35.
[49] Quoted in Klaus P. Fischer, *Nazi Germany: A New History* (London, 1997), 578.
[50] Ernst Nolte, "Vergangenheit, die nicht vergehen will," *Frankfurter Allgemeine Zeitung* (June 6,
1986).
[51] Günter Grass, *Schreiben nach Auschwitz* (Frankfurt, 1990), 9–10; Grass, "Schreiben nach
Auschwitz," *Die Zeit* (February 22, 1990).

The prominent leftist journalist Erich Kuby (1910–2005) wrote at the same time of Auschwitz as Germany's *Kainsmal* and followed Grass in disqualifying Germany from the right of unification because of its abnormal history. To "regard the German people as a people like any other leads, in the last instance, to see even the 'successes' of its criminal energy as totally normal."[52] A philosophically reflective version of this belief was provided by the philosopher Jürgen Habermas (b. 1929), who argued that national memory needed to be regarded in terms of a "dialectic of normalization." To continue to resemble a "normal" Western country, Germany needed to think of itself as abnormal, in other words, as stigmatized: "Following the break in civilization from which the Federal Republic emerged, the situation was so utterly abnormal that it was only the painful avoidance of a purely self-deceptive consciousness of 'normalcy' that allowed the rebirth of a halfway normal conditions in this country."[53] Germans ought to embrace the Holocaust, he thought, as an "element of a broken national identity" that is "branded [*eingebrannt*] as a persistent disturbance and warning."[54] These are some examples of stigma in public life, but its effects were also apparent in the intimate sphere of the family.

Stigma and the Origins of Structured Memory

The qualitative interview research on family life in postwar Germany reveals that the international construction of the Nazi past as stigma – as secular metaphor for evil, especially in the West – is incompatible with a positive German national subjectivity. Such an identity, like all national identities, is based on the affirmative continuity of ethnic traditions.[55] The *Schicksalsgemeinschaft* (community of destiny) that constitutes the nation, as Karl Deutsch observed long ago, is reproduced through intragroup communication, above all via family socialization.[56] Positively loaded childhood emotions connected with the intergenerational transmission of these traditions could not be reconciled with consciousness of these crimes unless they are displaced outside the ingroup. To have real empathy with victims of the Holocaust entailed a less affective relationship to the family, community, and nation, because acknowledging the implication – and thus the pollution – of these entities destroyed basic trust in them. To live with pollution as a constituent part of one's core identity was impossible, or at least tortuous, as some younger Germans' nightmares about

[52] Erich Kuby, *Der Preis der Einheit. Ein deutsches Europa formt sein Gesicht* (Hamburg, 1990), 84–103.
[53] Jürgen Habermas, *The Past as Future*, trans. Max Pensky (Lincoln and London, 1994), 28.
[54] Jürgen Habermas, "Der Zeigefinger: Die Deutschen und ihr Denkmal," *Die Zeit* (March 31, 1999).
[55] Anthony D. Smith, *The Ethnic Origins of Nations* (Oxford and New York, 1986).
[56] Karl Deutsch, *Nationalism and Social Communication: An Inquiry into the Foundation of Nationality*, 2nd ed. (Cambridge, 1966).

the Holocaust attest.[57] These crimes are, literally, unbearable for patriotic Germans. The chasm between victims and perpetrator, therefore, is impossible to bridge without doing violence to traditional patterns of national subjectivity.[58]

It was a zero-sum game. Surveys conducted in the Federal Republic over the decades confirm this conclusion. While by the 1990s, about 60 percent of Germans said they felt ashamed by the crimes committed by Germans against Jews; only a minority had "morally confronted and internalized both the perspective of the victim and the guilt of their fellow Germans." That is to say, only those who had "low identification with their national background" evinced "empathy for Holocaust victims."[59] These reactions show that the stigma of the Holocaust resulted in "psychological dissonance" among Germans, that is, discomfort caused by the violation of one's self-conception because of the conflict of two emotionally salient beliefs.[60] In this case, it was the incommensurability of regarding oneself as moral and socially respected but also as belonging to a group that was stigmatized as having committed the worst of all genocides, and within living memory.

There were two options for Germans. On the one hand, what one writer calls "the problem of their parents' moral degradation" was so great that children must disassociate their family from the Nazi contamination about which they know so much from public education.[61] This avoidance maneuver, probably the most common reaction in German families, continued to the third generation in the relationship of children to their grandparents, the war generation that is passing from the scene. In fact, as Harald Welzer and his colleagues found in their many interviews, the imperative to insulate the family unit from the Nazi contamination is so strong that a process of "cumulative heroization" takes place in which grandchildren imagine their grandparents as resisters or anti-Nazis despite evidence to the contrary. This phenomenon was by no means the

---

[57] Lutz Rosenkötter, "The Formation of Ideals in the Succession of Generations," in Martin S. Bergmann and Milton E. Jucovy, eds., *Generations of the Holocaust* (New York, 1982), 182: "The adolescent children of such parents can either share their right-wing ideals and, thus, openly oppose present-day society; or they may break with their parents, who, in their rigor, cannot bear to be questioned; or they may leave the matter open and go on living with conflicting ideals."

[58] For difficulties of reconciling descendants of victims and perpetrators, see Björn Krondorfer, *Remembrance and Reconciliation: Encounters between Young Jews and Germans* (New Haven and London, 1995). These tensions are manifested in literary representations of intergenerational relations. See Birte Giesler, "Krieg und Nationalsozialismus als Familientabu in Tanja Duckers Generationenroman *Himmelskörper*," in Lars Koch and Marianne Vogel, eds., *Imaginäre Welten im Widerstreit: Krieg und Geschichte in der deutschsprachigen Literatur des 20. Jahrhunderts* (Würzburg, 2006), 204–22.

[59] Lars Rensmann, "Collective Guilt, National Identity, and Political Processes in Contemporary Germany," in Branscombe and Doosje, *Collective Guilt*, 176.

[60] For this paragraph, I rely on the helpful analysis of Alexander L. Hinton, "Agents of Death: Explaining the Cambodian Genocide in Terms of Psychosocial Dissonance," *American Anthropologist*, n.s., 98:4 (1996), 818–31.

[61] Judith S. Kestenberg, introduction to Martin S. Bergmann and Milton E. Jucovy, eds., *Generations of the Holocaust* (New York, 1982), 165.

same as the much-discussed silence about the Holocaust said to have character-ized the 1950s.[62] On the contrary, the children studied the Holocaust intensively at school, and the more they knew about it, the greater the need to ensure that their family was not involved.[63] They were engaging in what Gabriele Rosen-thal calls "repair strategies" to exonerate the members of their family as people not involved in the undeniable Nazi criminality, perhaps even as victims of the regime and its consequences.[64] The need to absolve the family from Nazi crimes led to the need to absolve the nation of the crimes because the nation is thought of in familial terms – as a community of descent.[65] For the majority of Germans, talk of German guilt was experienced as a constant presentation of the national disgrace, that is, as a stigma. Their dissonance reduction strategy was to main-tain the conventional core self and its attachment to parents and Germany by denying that the group self ought to be stigmatized. Its rhetoric of normality, then, reflected a desire for national innocence – the end of stigma – so that the collective self ("we Germans") could become a nontraumatized component of the self. The writer Monika Maron (b. 1941) expressed this desire when she wrote that Germans abroad were victims of racism, and that younger Germans were not responsible for the Holocaust; there was no such thing as "inherited guilt" (*Erbschuld*).[66]

On the other hand, those children of Nazi parents who found that their gift of social life was unviable engaged in various strategies to invent new identities in order to escape the stigma of their collective identity. One option was to cut off all contact with the polluted generation and try to "make a fresh start," as did one young couple that did not invite their parents to their wedding.[67] More extreme still was the renunciation of one's national identity altogether by joining the people that one's family had persecuted, such as "Menachem," who became a rabbi and moved to Jerusalem. Or Liesel Appel, who, also a convert, recounted, "As soon as I could, I moved away . . . I felt compelled to

[62] Olick, *In the House of the Hangman*; Wolfgang Benz, "Postwar Society and National Socialism: Remembrance, Amnesia, Rejection," *Tel Aviver Jahrbuch für deutsche Geschichte*, 19 (2000), 1–12; Alon Confino, "Traveling as a Culture of Remembrance: Traces of National Socialism in West Germany, 1956–1960," *History and Memory*, 12:2 (2000), 92–121.

[63] Welzer, Moller, and Tschuggnall, "*Opa war kein Nazi*," 44–80; Karoline Tschuggnall and Harald Welzer, "Rewriting Memories: Family Recollections of the National Socialist Past in Germany," *Culture & Psychology*, 8:1 (2002), 1301–45. Cf. Santner, *Stranded Objects*, 34: children inherited not guilt but denial of guilt, "psychic structures that impeded mourning in the generations of their parents and grandparents."

[64] Gabriele Rosenthal, "National Socialism and Antisemitism in Intergenerational Dialogue," in Gabriele Rosenthal, ed., *The Holocaust in Three Generations: Families of Victims and Perpetra-tors of the Nazi Regime* (London, 1998), 240. Frederike Eigler, "Writing in the New Germany: Cultural Memory and Family Narratives," *German Politics and Society*, 23:3 (2005), 16–41.

[65] Nina Leonhard, *Politik- und Geschichtsbewusstsein im Wandel: Die politische Bedeutung der nationalsozialistischen Vergangenheit im Verlauf von drei Generationen in Ost- und West-deutschland* (Münster, 2002).

[66] Monika Maron, "Hat Martin Walser zwei Reden gehalten?" *Die Zeit* (November 19, 1998).

[67] Sichrovksy, *Born Guilty*, 27.

get as far away from my people as possible. I changed my identity, name, and religion."[68] Gottfried Wagner, a descendant of Richard Wagner, likewise left the country. Repelled by his family's perceived inability to deal critically with the past, he moved to Italy where, conscious of belonging to a "prominent family of Nazi perpetrators," he experienced his "identities as a multicultural and social involvement for which I have to exert myself daily with the intensive consciousness of a German who was born after the Holocaust."[69] Analogously, the most drastic reaction short of suicide for members of the perpetrator generation was literally to invent a new identity altogether, like Hans Schwerte and Hans-Robert Jauß, former SS officers who made prominent careers for themselves after the war as left-leaning literature professors.[70]

The problem of stigma and the psychological dissonance it caused for Germans who felt they could leave their German identity behind was solved by inventing a new German identity – a "Non-German German identity." The dominant emotion here besides guilt or shame was indignation. Indignation impelled them not simply to make amends in the manner of historical justice, which tries to alleviate some of the consequences of the crime and, as much as possible, restore relations that obtained as if the crime had not been committed.[71] Indignation also demanded the moral rehabilitation of the group. For example, Anna Rosmus, after whom the protagonist in the film *The Nasty Girl* is modeled, chose to rehabilitate her social environment morally by talking about the past and by campaigning to have survivors visit from abroad, to rename streets, and to erect memorials.[72] Similarly, the writer Carola Stern (1925–2000) who had been a Nazi youth leader, founded Amnesty International in West Germany after the war. Championing nonnational values like universal human rights allowed her to assume the role of the reformed sinner.[73] She had, in the words of Goffman, engaged in "a transformation of self

---

[68] Bar-On, *Legacy of Silence*, 169–70; Liesel Appel, "Honor Thy Mother: Reflections on Being the Daughter of Nazis," in Alan L. Berger and Naomi Berger, eds., *Second Generation Voices: Reflections by Children of Holocaust Survivors and Perpetrators* (Syracuse, 2001), 303–9.

[69] Gottfried H. Wagner, "To Be German after the Holocaust: The Misused Concept of Identity," in Berger and Berger, *Second Generation Voices*, 352.

[70] Jochen Hörisch, "'Verhaften Sie die üblichen Verdächtigen': Unheimliche Dimensionen in den Fällen Schneider/Schwerte, Paul de Man, Jauß," in Wilfried Loth and Bernd-A Rusinek, eds., *Verwandlungspolitik. NS-Eliten in der westdeutschen Nachkriegsgesellschaft* (Frankfurt and New York, 1998), 181–96; Helmut König, Wolfgang Kuhlmann, and Klaus Schwabe, *Vertuschte Vergangenheit. Der Fall Schwerte und die NS-Vergangenheit der deutschen Hochschulen* (Munich, 1997); Claus Leggewie: *Von Schneider zu Schwerte. Das ungewöhnliche Leben eines Mannes, der aus der Geschichte lernen wollte* (Munich, 1998).

[71] Jeremy Waldron, "Superseding Historical Injustice," *Ethics*, 103 (1992), 4–28; Paul Patton, "Historic Injustice and the Possibility of Supersession," *Journal of Intercultural Studies*, 26:3 (2005), 255–66.

[72] Anna E. Rosmus, "A Troublemaker in a Skirt," in Berger and Berger, *Second Generation Voices*, 283. See also Rosmus-Weniger, *Widerstand und Verfolgung am Beispiel Passaus, 1933–1939* (Passau, 1983).

[73] Carola Stern, *In den Netzen der Erinnerung: Lebensgeschichten zweier Menschen* (Reinbeck, 1986).

from someone with a particular blemish into someone with a record of having corrected a particular blemish."[74]

Such transformations were not limited to the individual. With that change comes a "concern with ingroup purification," an imperative to rehabilitate or regulate members of a community exhibiting the stereotypically stigmatized attribute, behavior that induces shame in the eyes of those who regard it stigmatized. "Stigma management" becomes the main imperative for those who feel they have developed a new German group self.[75] This phenomenon seems ubiquitous when cultural elites wish to gain acceptance for their group in the eyes of "civilized opinion." "Civilized opinion" encourages this dynamic. The United States occupation's denazification guidelines from August 1946 urged Germans to "cleanse" the country of "the stigma of moral joint responsibility for Nazi crimes and restore [Germany's] good name in the eyes of the world." The guidelines referred to "new Germans" as those willing to "clean their own house." This vocabulary was adopted by the new, liberal newspaper, the *Frankfurter Rundschau*, which criticized the "old Germanness" of the "Prussian tradition of catastrophe" and "militarism," and of course Nazism. The newspaper contrasted them unfavorably with the "new Germans" who embraced "free democracy," "social justice," and a "European spirit," and who welcomed the Nuremberg trials as a "purification... from Nazism."[76]

The observations of sociologist Zygmunt Bauman about the group emotions of emancipated German Jews regarding Eastern European Jews who had come to Germany at the end of the nineteenth century are particularly apposite because both groups were stigmatized and their elites were striving to overcome this social handicap. By incarnating the former, stigmatized Jewish identity, the presence of the Ostjuden induced feelings of shame and even provoked disavowal of "uncivilized kinsmen," leading to campaigns of stigma management.[77] Since the end of the war, much of the German intelligentsia has been scrutinizing the population in a similar manner, especially when intellectuals are embarrassed, in the eyes of the world, by "typically German" behavior.

These, then, were the two types of reactions to the stigmatization of the German collective self. How do we study it historically?

The Underlying Structure of Political Emotions

The language of German identity dramas invites a structural analysis because it was consistently framed in binary oppositions: forgetting versus remembering, denying the past versus working through the past, good Germans versus

---

[74] Goffman, *Stigma*, 20.

[75] Ibid., 131–32, 155.

[76] Quoted in Thomas Pegelow, "Killing with Words: Linguistic Violence, Nazi Power, and the Struggle of Germans of Jewish Ancestry" (Ph.D. dissertation, University of North Carolina, 2005), 515, 533–34.

[77] Zygmunt Bauman, *Modernity and Ambivalence* (Oxford, 1991), 132–35. Needless to say, I am not suggesting a symmetry in other aspects of this comparison.

bad Germans, truth versus error, sin versus redemption, sacred versus profane, and so on. We need not follow structural anthropology or linguistics in
positing deep mental structures, discerning laws of universal application, or
regarding discourse as a system of self-sufficient signs in order to find fruitful
an approach that thematizes the striking dualisms of the German memory discussion. By highlighting how the elements of binary oppositions are mutually
interdependent components in a specific cultural system, we can see that none
of the participants in a discursive field possess a vantage point over others.
The conceit of arrogating to oneself an epistemological (or moral) superiority
over others is inherent in the atomism of conventional analyses that regard the
terms of the memory discourse merely as elements in an aggregate without any
necessary relation to other terms.[78] To understand how the system works, then,
we need to observe its functioning rather than participate in it.

For all its merits, however, the structural gaze cannot explain why a particular vocabulary and emotions developed in any specific case. It is one thing to
point out that German memory discourse was – and at times remains – relent-
lessly polarized; it is quite another to account for this dualism.[79] This book
suggests the following answer. The criminal deeds of the Nazi regime between
1933 and 1945 bifurcated Germans' collective identity and group self; that is,
they were constituted by an underlying structure. The structure was underlying
because memories of this past were inescapable; no German could avoid their
inscription in his or her subjectivity. They constitute a structure because a strict
logic determined the individual's reaction to the shared, national past. Germans
could try to convince themselves and others that they had invented a new collectivity, divorced from an unbearable past, or they could defend the viability of
their collective identity by making the national past bearable through a variety
of displacement strategies – the dominant types here being, respectively, either
the "Non-German German" or the "German German."

These are, to be sure, metapsychological statements that posit a mutually
dependent relationship between individual and large-group identity with intergenerational implications – a relationship difficult to define.[80] Until recently,
psychologists have been satisfied to assert that certain events, for instance, can
be "internalized as powerful configurations that give the group structure and
unity" without showing how or why.[81] That membership of a large group was

---

[78] Jean Piaget, *Structuralism*, trans. Chaninah Maschler (New York, 1970), 7–8.

[79] See the articles of Eric Langenbacher, which usefully describe "German memory regimes" without explaining why its patterns occur and recur: "Changing Memory Regimes in Contemporary
Germany?" *German Politics and Society*, 21:2 (2003), 46–68; Langenbacher, "*Moralpolitik* versus *Moralpolitik*: Recent Struggles over the Construction of Cultural Memory in Germany,"
German Politics and Society, 23:3 (2005), 106–34.

[80] Skeptical of psychological approaches is Wulf Kansteiner, "Finding Meaning in Memory: A
Methodological Critique of Collective Memory Studies," *History and Theory*, 41:2 (2002),
179–97.

[81] Rita R. Rogers, "Intergenerational Exchange: Transference of Attitudes Down the Generations,"
in John G. Howells, ed., *Modern Perspectives in the Psychiatry of Infancy* (New York, 1979),
341; Rogers, "The Emotional Contamination between Parents and Children," *American Journal
of Psychoanalysis*, 36:3 (1976), 267–71. Similarly thin is Kai Erikson, "Notes on Trauma and

inherent in individual identity because the individual was also a social being, as a number of psychoanalysts and psychohistorians suggested, was as intuitively convincing as it was difficult to demonstrate.[82] The same went for the analogy between the structure of the individual self and group self. Heinz Kohut, for example, wanted to entertain the proposition that the structure of the self – "the central unconscious ambitions of the grandiose self and the central unconscious values of the internalized idealized parent imago" – could be applied to the group, but he did not undertake a systematic discussion of the relationship.[83]

If such statements were somewhat speculative, they at least began to supersede the methodological individualism of clinical psychology by positing a supra-individual, group self. Recent social psychologists have given firmer theoretical foundations to the relationship between the political emotions of individuals and the group self. The most elaborated attempt to answer these questions – to "investigate the psychology of we-ness" – has been undertaken by Vamik Volkan. Basing his approach on Erik Erikson's definition of core identity as comprising the subjective experience of inner sameness, he shows how solidarity with one's large group grows in children after the third year. The external world is gradually internalized because cultural objects act as "shared reservoirs for externalization." By adolescence, cultural membership is accepted – and in some cases, rejected – as part of one's core identity, and for this reason the group self (the "we-ness" of a collective) can act "as an invisible force in the unfolding drama" of the economy of individual emotion and intergroup interaction.[84] Elaborating on Freud's foundation text of social psychology, "Group Psychology and the Analysis of the Ego," he regards the group less as a mass libidinally fixated on a leader than as a tent that individuals cooperate in keeping up, its canvass serving as a second skin. Accordingly, attacks on the group are experienced as an attack on the self. In fact, "At times of collective stress . . . the tent's covering can take on greater importance than the various garments worn by the individual group members."[85]

This is not the place to explicate all aspects of Volkan's thought on trauma and cultural regression. For our purposes, his concept of the "chosen trauma" is

Community," in Cathy Caruth, ed., *Trauma: Explorations in Memory* (Baltimore, 1995), 183–99.

[82] W. R. Brion, "Group Dynamics; A Re-View," in Melanie Klein, Paula Heimann, and R. E. Money-Kyrle, eds., *New Directions in Psycho-Analysis* (Tavistock, 1955), 461; Peter Loewenberg, *Fantasy and Reality in History* (New York and Oxford, 1995); John Mack, "Nationalism and the Self," *Psychohistory Review*, 2 (1983), 52: "Who one *is* as a person, one's sense of self, contains a number of fantasies or self-representations among which are included one's conviction of belonging to a particular national or ethnic group"; George Klein, *Psychoanalytic Theory: An Exploration of Essentials* (New York, 1976), 179: the "we-ness" of group identity inheres in the "separateness and membership in a more encompassing entity."

[83] Heinz Kohut, *The Search for the Self: Selected Writings of Heinz Kohut, 1950–1978*, 2 vols., ed. and intro. Paul H. Ornstein (New York, 1978), 2:837n21.

[84] Vamik D. Volkan, *Bloodlines: From Ethnic Pride to Ethnic Terrorism* (Boulder, Colo., 1997), 25; Volkan, *Blind Trust: Large Groups and Their Leaders in Times of Crisis and Terror* (Charlottesville, Va., 2004), 38–41.

[85] Volkan, *Blind Trust*, 38.

the most relevant. He is interested in the indirect traumatization of the descendants of people who as a group have been subjected to some defeat or to shame and humiliation. The chosen trauma is an unconscious choice "to add a past generation's mental representation of a shared event to its own identity." It "reflects the traumatized past generations' incapacity for or difficulty with mourning losses connected to the shared traumatic event, as well as its failure to reverse the humiliation and injury to the group's self-esteem ('narcissistic injury') inflicted by another large group."[86]

Contrary to much of the literature on collective and historical memory, Volkan does not think that traumatic memories can be handed down intergenerationally.[87] What is transmitted – he calls it "deposited" – to the next generation are the damaged self-images of the parents who have been unable to mourn the damage done to their individual and group selves. Consequently, we are not dealing with the level of cognition, of historical interpretations by children, but with affect, with children's reactions to parents.[88] Children can either identify with the representations deposited (the "psychological gene") in their selves or can struggle against it.[89]

The cumulative affect of this self-image deposit based on the same event or narrative – at the level of a population of millions – means that large-group identity is effected. "Though each child in the second generation has an individualized personality organization, all share similar links to the trauma's mental representation and similar unconscious tasks for coping with that representation."[90] Because they share a reference to the same event, "a shared image of the tragedy develops," and "a new generation of the group is unconsciously knit together."[91] The unspoken experience of individual sameness over time that Erikson identifies as core identity is extended to the group. "Children develop *general* history-related unconscious fantasies because the traumatized self- and object-images passed on to children by their ancestors become amalgamated with their identity as a member of the traumatized large group, which is part of their core identity."[92] These fantasies manifest themselves in specific tasks like, say, diminishing a humiliation so the parent will have less to mourn. The

---

[86] Vamik D. Volkan, Gabriele Ast, and William F. Greer, *The Third Reich in the Unconscious: Transgenerational Transmission and Its Consequences* (New York and London, 2002), 42; Volkan, *Bloodlines*, chap. 3.

[87] "People do not transmit to their progeny their memories of historical experience, for memory can belong only to the survivor of trauma and cannot be transmitted": Volkan, Ast, and Greer, *The Third Reich in the Unconscious*, 43.

[88] Volkan, *Blind Trust*, 49.

[89] Vamik D. Volkan "Intergenerational Transmission and 'Chosen' Traumas: A Link between the Psychology of the Individual and That of the Ethnic Group," in Leo Rangell and Rena Moses-Hrushovski, eds., *Psychoanalysis at the Border* (Madison, 1996), 258.

[90] Vamik Volkan, "Traumatized Societies," in Sverre Varvin and Vamik D. Volkan, eds., *Violence or Dialogue? Psychoanalytic Insights on Terror and Terrorism* (London, 2003), 231.

[91] Volkan, *Blind Trust*, 49.

[92] Volkan, Ast, and Greer, *The Third Reich in the Unconscious*, 41.

specific mission varies from generation to generation but the task is not to forget the chosen trauma as an identity-conferring mission.[93]

Although he has cowritten a book on postwar Germany, Volkan does not indicate what the tasks for young Germans have been other than to follow the standard refrain that they suffer from an "inability to mourn," a reference to the well-known book by Alexander Mitscherlich and Margarethe Mitscherlich he clearly admires.[94] Nor does he reflect on how the chosen trauma functions in a society or nation that, although defeated, is regarded as the perpetrator rather than a victim. For all its insights, Volkan's social psychology needs to be supplemented to satisfactorily explain how otherwise well-adjusted individuals and smoothly functioning societies feel that "something has gone wrong with their sense of collective self," as Tanya M. Luhrmann puts it. Drawing on Volkan's work, Luhrmann has developed the concept of the "traumatized social self," by which she means the self-representation a person possesses that defines what it means to be a good member of a community, and that is "now associated with failure, moral inadequacy, embarrassment and guilt."[95] For many, the national collective self is a self-representation that matters intensely. The feelings associated with group pride or shame affect the emotional economy of the individual. A chosen trauma may inhere in a perpetrator group as well, then. Even if a group has started a conflict and inflicted the most damage, its members will feel victimized by the enemy, with attendant feelings of humiliation and helplessness, after it was defeated. The deflation of the collective self-representation and self-idealization will be all the greater if the defeat is compounded with the shame of having committed genocide.

But are people emotionally attached to the "traumatized social self" in a uniform way? If we examine cases like Germany, we see that the loss of "we-ness" is internalized in two different ways. It can lead to efforts either to defend the culture or to renovate it. This structure of political emotions – the dualism of subjectivities related to the collective self – can be traced to the question of "basic trust" in a national culture, that is, the confidence in the predictability and moral reliability of the familial and social environment. And the issue of such basic trust arises in adolescence.

These concepts are taken from Eric Erikson who posits the mid-teenage years as a specific developmental stage in which the ego begins to understand the contingency of history, and thus realizes that the adolescent needs to forge a personality that is both authentically its own and socially recognized.[96] This

---

[93] Ibid., 37; Volkan, "Traumatized Societies," 230–31.

[94] Alexander Mitscherlich and Margarete Mitscherlich, *The Inability to Mourn: Principles of Collective Behavior*, trans. Beveley R. Placzek (New York, 1975).

[95] Tanya M. Luhrmann, "The Traumatized Social Self: The Parsi Predicament in Modern Bombay," in Marcelo M. Suarez-Orozco and Antonius C. G. M. Robben, eds., *Cultures under Siege: Collective Violence and Trauma* (Cambridge, 2000), 185.

[96] For Erikson, identity is always psychosocial: Erikson, *Identity and the Life Cycle* (New York and London, 1959), 57–67, 108–9, 122, 132; Erikson, *Childhood and Society*, 2nd ed. (New York, 1963), 247–51.

task was complicated if "something is rotten in the state of Denmark" – Erikson referred to Hamlet – and the youthful sense of basic trust in the nation is ruptured. An identity crisis arises, and the relation between the generations is reversed. The young "tell the old whether the life as represented by the old and as presented to the young has meaning; and it is the young who carry in them the power to confirm those who confirm them and, joining the issues, to renew and to regenerate, or to reform and to rebel." The identity crisis is resolved when the adolescent joins a tradition that can be ethically affirmed and that provides a personal link to the fate of the community, which Erikson assumes to deserve trust.[97]

If Erikson's resolution of the adolescent crisis overemphasizes social integration – he is inclined to speak of youth rebellion in terms of delinquency[98] – it nonetheless opens the way for a consideration of disruptive identity dramas when basic social trust was violated. What if the corruption is experienced as so deep that Hamlet feels he has to make invidious choices? To be or not to be? Here is the origin of the dualism we seek to uncover, and it is no coincidence that Lévi-Strauss himself regarded Hamlet's question as underlying the binary structure of reality.[99]

But how is this dualism inscribed in subjectivities, and what is the nature of the political emotions released? In the German case, it was rage expressed against parents and grandparents for the pollution and stigmatization of the collective self that they had bequeathed the younger generation. The rage of the Non-German Germans – Erikson would call theirs a "negative identity"[100] – against the polluted collective self-image was split off and projected onto German Germans, who represented the polluting agent and who acted as emotional reservoirs against whom scorn could be constantly directed to stabilize a Non-German German identity. This projective identification allowed Non-German Germans simultaneously to disavow their own national selves while excoriating the national selves of their compatriots.[101] Most Non-German Germans were not as reflective as Joschka Fischer, who in 1984, told fellow Greens that "even in rebellion, one could not wipe the filth of the Fatherland from ones boots. One would always be caught in a web called Germany, and so the basic political feeling of my generation, the 68ers, could be summed up as: vomiting with indignation [*zum Kotzen*]."[102]

---

[97] Erik H. Erikson, "Youth: Fidelity and Diversity," in Erik H. Erikson, ed., *Youth: Change and Challenge* (New York and London, 1963), 5–20.

[98] Erik H. Erikson, *Identity: Youth and Crisis* (New York and London, 1968).

[99] Claude Lévi-Strauss, *The Naked Man: Introduction to a Science of Mythology*, vol. 4 (London, 1981), 694.

[100] Erikson, *Identity and the Life Cycle*, 139–43.

[101] For the Kleinian background for this conclusion, see Marcelo M. Suarez-Orozco and Antonius C. G. M. Robben, "Interdisciplinary Perspectives on Violence and Trauma," in Suarez-Orozco and Robben, *Cultures under Siege*, 28–31; and Robert M. Young, "Psychoanalysis, Terrorism, and Fundamentalism," *Psychodynamic Practice*, 9:3 (2003), 307–24.

[102] Joschka Fischer, "Identität in Gefahr!" in Thomas Kluge, ed., *Grüne Politik: Eine Standortbestimmung* (Frankfurt, 1984), 28–29.

For German Germans, by contrast, constructing the Nazi past as stigma and secular metaphor for evil in the West is incompatible with national subjectivity. Consequently, the stigma needs to be warded off by denationalizing the causes of the Nazi catastrophe and ascribing them to non-German causes. What is more, German Germans similarly engage in projective identification, disavowing their own resentments and genealogical relationship to the Nazi *Volksgemeinschaft* by displacing them onto Non-German Germans, regarding themselves, the vast majority of Germans, as victims of persecution.[103]

For all the polarization, however, German political culture changed over the years. The process of constructing and rejecting stigma was culturally productive, as the next chapter explains.

---

[103] Cf. Charlotte Kahn, "The Different Ways of Being a German," *Journal of Psychohistory*, 20:4 (1993), 391.

2

The Languages of Republicanism and West German Political Generations

Studying a structure demands what Jean Piaget called "a special effort of reflective abstraction."[1] We need, the anthropologist Claude Lévi-Strauss explained, to look "beyond the empirical facts to the relations between them," which "reveals and confirms that these relations are simpler and more intelligible than the things they interconnect."[2] By studying intellectuals whose political emotions dramatize the structure of German subjectivities, we can reveal these relations in the case of postwar German memory and identity. Intellectuals and writers are no different from other Germans in having to wrestle with political emotions. In fact, because their identity projects are so elaborately articulated in public language, they embody the affects and unconscious fantasies about their large-group identity as Germans in oblique but sometimes disarmingly candid ways. Because of the high level of reflection in their thinking for and against the nation, intellectuals are more likely to develop internally consistent and coherent positions, and, consequently, we can "read off" the logic and structure of their political emotions from their writings. Dissecting their writings is thereby at once an exercise in biographical study and detection of those deeper, often quasi-religious currents that subtend public discourse. Nonetheless, while agreeing with Nietzsche that "every great philosophy" is "the personal confession of its author and a kind of involuntary and unconscious memoir," this book does not contend that the link between individual intellectual life and social psychology affords access to the political emotions of every German.[3] Consistent with the focus on the relation between individual and group, this particular exercise in abstraction uncovers the subjectivities of those for whom the fate of their nation was a burning personal question, who regarded it as an

[1] Jean Piaget, *Structuralism*, trans. Chaninah Maschler (New York, 1970), 137.
[2] Claude Lévi-Strauss, *The Naked Man: Introduction to a Science of Mythology*, vol. 4 (London, 1981), 687.
[3] Friedrich Nietzsche, *Beyond Good and Evil*, "On the Prejudices of the Philosophers," part I, sec. 6, *Basic Writings of Nietzsche*, ed. and trans. Walter Kaufman (New York, 1992), 203.

object about which they were entitled to worry and about whose fate they were socially qualified to propound.[4]

The nexus between political emotions and political languages was evident in the heated debates about the nature of postwar German democracy. In January 1958 a young journalist at Southwest German radio, Horst Krüger, published an open letter in a leading daily newspaper under the provocative title of "No Is Not a Program."[5] Its addressee was an anonymous "Herr S," whom Krüger described as one of the "nonconformist" intellectuals who rejected the new Federal Republic because it did not measure up to their high moral standards. They came from a variety of backgrounds. "Pacifists and passionate anticlerics, real democrats and some literary utopians, left-socialists who fear nothing more than communism because, as ex-communists, they had experienced it first hand, some passionate Christians, militant antifascists, and then that circle of bourgeois individualists who from an unconscious anarchism and homelessness always like to join such groups." These "nonconformists," Krüger argued, had excessive expectations of the new state. It was not perfect, he conceded, but it was an improvement on the state that preceded it; moreover, the danger of communism was at hand. The intellectuals failed to recognize that utopian politics could not be reconciled with a liberal order. Moreover, where was their indignation about the political situation in the eastern bloc countries? In these circumstances, Krüger concluded, they should accept the current state and work for reform within its parameters.

This was a standard argument of liberals and conservatives in the Cold War in all Western countries, but what sets this article apart is the generational and existential significance Krüger attached to the issues. Born in 1919, he had met a similarly aged Herr S in a prisoner-of-war camp in 1945, the site of a formative experience that determined their respective postures toward the nascent West German state. Krüger could well understand the source of his anonymous friend's disdain for this state. It issued from the tremendous disappointment with the failure of West Germans to use the opportunity of their defeat to set out on a radically new political path, divorced from old, discredited traditions:

Your "no" was in its depth a moral protest born of the pure and passionate will for a better state than the one we saw collapse in 1945. You justifiably refer to the period between 1945 and 1948 in which the German people, shaken by the enormity of the catastrophe, really appeared to break in one wave with all the bad traditions of its history. This time, it really was an exciting and fascinating epoch in which material poverty, in a peculiar way, appeared to open Germans to a spiritual-intellectual and a moral basis of history. After all, of the many journals that appeared at the time to think

[4] Ghassan Hage, *White Nation: Fantasies of White Supremacy in a Multicultural Society* (Sydney, 1998).

[5] Horst Krüger, "Das Nein ist kein Programm. 'Offener Brief' an einen Nonkonformisten," *Frankfurter Allgemeine Zeitung* (January 23, 1958), 6. His memoir from 1966 is *A Crack in the Wall: Growing Up under Hitler*, trans Ruth Hein (New York, 1986).

through the crisis, one was called *Die Wandlung* [The Transformation], which was more than a slogan, namely a program.

Krüger had to agree that this hoped-for rebirth or regeneration had not taken place:

Today even such a title [*Die Wandlung*] would be impossible. Who in Germany wants to transform him- or herself? You refer to this hopeful time back then that was prepared to change; you speak of a missed opportunity, and I think that you see a serious problem. Indeed, the great hoped-for transformation has not occurred. The material upswing after the currency union [in 1948] covers over all deep cleavages, and since then one tries to escape them in a rapid and superficial manner. It is virtually impossible to measure how much repressed bad conscience became a drive in the today's so-called German economic miracle.

Yet, however understandable this reaction, and however true their warning about reactionary developments in West German politics (unidentified in his article), Krüger continued, the intellectuals' Cold War anti-Americanism and distance to politics missed the point. "I will never forget," he wrote, "that America took the nightmare from me and my generation and that today and tomorrow it still takes from my nights the nightmare of a Soviet termite-state. What would we be without this continent?" A flawed liberal order was the best of possible worlds at the time.

This long-forgotten article is worth recalling because it expresses the enduring problem of the intellectual history of the Federal Republic: the dilemma of republican democracy in a post-totalitarian, postgenocidal society. On the one hand, such societies must distance themselves in all respects from the evil regime that they replaced in order to establish their moral credibility. On the other, they must usually integrate a substantial number of persons who were implicated in the crimes of that regime if the new republic is to be a stable entity. West Germany institutionalized this ambivalence. It was the successor regime of the Nazis, liable for its political crimes, while regarding itself as the legitimate representative of the German cultural nation (*Kulturnation*).

This tension was expressed by the two opposing languages of republican democracy. In one political language, a republican foundation entails a cathartic break with a deemed evil past. It is, as Hannah Arendt argued, not just liberation from tyranny, but an adventure in freedom with the "pathos of novelty." On this reading, republican foundations generally follow upon revolutions, they mark the beginning of a radically new order, and they are motivated by indignation at suffering and evil.[6] I call this the "redemptive" language of republicanism. Such was the case with the French and American revolutions, whose fighting citizenry serve as the symbol of popular sovereignty. In these cases, the republican value consensus is thrashed out at the time of the foundation, often by a violent moment of inner "cleansing" of the recalcitrant representatives and supporters of the succeeded order.

[6] Hannah Arendt, *On Revolution* (New York, 1963), 21–28, 31, 66.

In the rival political language, the promulgation of a republican constitution and the establishment of democratic institutions suffice. A moment of revolutionary self-emancipation is unnecessary, and the citizens of a new republic learn the ways of self-government gradually, much in the manner of the French Third Republic, which was founded after defeat in war and civil unrest, and which survived for seventy years. The value consensus, so this language has it, develops of its own accord over time, and the personal continuities from the previous regime are integrated slowly into the new dispensation.[7] Accordingly, this model of republicanism is "integrationist." It prizes toleration over virtue.

These rival versions of republicanism reflected the underlying structure of German political emotions by highlighting the question of basic trust in the new order. This problem manifested itself in the two modes of legitimacy and temporality. Integrative republicanism conceives of politics in terms of institutional continuities, whereas the other ascribes to society as a whole a sacred or epic origin. The former is concerned with moments of transition, the latter with moments of creation.[8] Neither of these languages possesses an unblemished record of historical success. Inner cleansing has had totalitarian consequences and has not necessarily guaranteed a subsequent consensus because it provokes counterrevolution and is difficult to institutionalize, as in the case of France in the 1790s.[9] But the failure to establish some kind of consensus at the moment of foundation also means that powerful groups, which never reconcile themselves to the new state, remain strategically placed to overthrow it for authoritarian, even totalitarian alternatives in times of crisis, as the respective fates of the French Third Republic and the Weimar Republic show.[10] A tension exists between continuity and rupture that made the determination of a republican value consensus virtually impossible.

Republican Sensibilities

The redemptive reaction in Germany was expressed by the leftist Roman Catholic publicists Eugen Kogon (1903–87) and Walter Dirks (1901–91), who placed their hopes on a "constructive social revolution." They called for a "productive utopia" of a non-Marxist, "humanized," democratic socialist Germany in a united Europe, free from the war-mongering clique of "capitalists, Nazis,

---

[7] Philip Nord, *The Republican Moment: Struggles for Democracy in Nineteenth Century France* (Cambridge, Mass., 1995).

[8] J. G. A. Pocock, *Politics, Language and Time: Essays on Political Thought and History* (Chicago, 1971), 244.

[9] François Furet, *Revolutionary France, 1770–1880*, trans. Antonia Nevill (Oxford, 1992).

[10] My categories differ from those of Anne Sa'adah, *Germany's Second Chance: Trust, Justice, and Democratization* (Cambridge, Mass., 1998), 3–5, 55–56. While her ideal type of the "institutional" strategy of democratic legitimation corresponds broadly to what I refer to as integrationist republicanism, her second "cultural" strategy does not contain the sense of radical rupture based on moral indignation.

bureaucrats, and party leaders," whom they held responsible for fascism.[11] One day, Dirks wrote with prescience, Germans would be able to enjoy the moral status born "of the special wisdom and mercy that was heavily guilty and implicated in immense disaster, and which has purified itself in self-determination and active contrition."[12] National integrity would be restored by penance. The moral energy released by the suffering that such leftist and religious commentators had witnessed issued in the hope for a new beginning and radically better future.

Who was to carry out the revolution? Inspired by the antifascist committees that had shot up spontaneously from the ground in 1945, Hans Werner Richter (1908–93), with Alfred Andersch (1914–18), an editor of *Der Ruf* and founder of the literary circle Gruppe 47, looked to the "youth returning from the war" in whose perceived condition of radical alienation from the German past he saw a chance for cultural rebirth.[13] "From the shifting of life-feeling, from the power of the experiences to which the young generation was exposed and that shook them, lies today the only opportunity for a *spiritual rebirth* and *an absolute and radical new beginning.*"[14] Andersch agreed: "The European movement toward unity in socialist praxis and humanistic freedom is being tirelessly carried forward by the young forces in both of the largest parties."[15]

But the hoped-for revolution did not eventuate. Yesterday's men, as the politicians of the Weimar period were derisively called, took over the reigns of power and prevented the desired collectivist and democratic socialist refoundation. With the help of the Allies, they marginalized the antifascists, cemented the capitalist economic system, and set up the frontiers of the Cold War.[16] Rather than beginning something radically new, these critics complained, Germany's elites resumed as if nothing had happened since 1933. German history had come to an end, yet they sought to perpetuate it nonetheless. Did they not realize, Dirks wrote in exasperation, that they were continuing a project that had failed once already and that "bore the seeds of its own demise"?[17] The French

[11] W(alter) D(irks), "Bundesrepublik Deutschland," *Frankfurter Hefte*, 4 (1949), 457–59.

[12] Walter Dirks, "Die Zweite Republik. Zum Ziel und zum Weg der deutschen Demokratie," *Frankfurter Hefte*, 1 (1946), 12–24.

[13] On the literary journals established at this time, see Clare Flanagan, *A Study of German Political-Cultural Periodicals from the Years of Allied Occupation, 1945–1949* (Lewiston, N.Y., 2000). See also Wolfgang Schivelbusch, *In a Cold Crater: Cultural and Intellectual Life in Berlin, 1945–1948* (Berkeley, 1998), and Michel Grunewald and Hans Manfred Bock, *Der Europadiskurs in den deutschen Zeitschriften (1945–1955)* (Bern and Frankfurt, 2001).

[14] Hans Werner Richter, "Warum schweigt die junge Generation?" in Hans Schwab-Felisch, ed., *Der Ruf: Eine deutsche Nachkriegszeitschrift* (Munich, 1962), 32 (emphasis added).

[15] Alfred Andersch, "Das junge Europa formt sein Gesicht," in ibid., 21–26.

[16] Günter Plum, "Versuche gesellschaftlicher Neuordnung. Ihr Scheitern im Kräftefeld deutscher und alliierter Politik," in Institut für Zeitgeschichte, ed., *Westdeutschlands Weg zur Bundesrepublik, 1945–1949* (Munich, 1976), 90–117.

[17] Walter Dirks, "Die restaurative Charakter der Epoche," *Frankfurter Hefte*, 5 (1950), 942–54, 946. See also Eugen Kogon, "Die Aussichten der Restauration," *Frankfurter Hefte*, 7 (1952), 165–77.

resistance poured scorn on the postwar settlement across the Rhine in the same terms.[18]

Dirks and Kogon did not trust the new dispensation because they did not think it was actually new. In a famous article in 1950, Dirks described the postwar reconstruction as a "restoration" that gripped Europe and Germany. Restoration was not a reaction, it should be noted, a policy that was consciously carried out by specific agents to revert to the past. Restoration was "a proceeding, a process, a situation, an atmosphere" in which many subjects continued unconsciously to go about their business according to familiar formulas. Unlike the active sins of commission of reactionaries, those of the unwitting agents of restoration were sins of omission: failing to grasp the opportunity for regeneration. "The really guilty ones are those who are called to renewal, but are too comfortable to accept the ardor of the feeling, the exertion of the idea, the effort and risk of the deed and service, and the cross of sacrifice."[19]

It is no accident that such prose was suffused with the religious pathos of redemption. We are dealing here, after all, with a reaction to events that were experienced as metaphysical evil, and with the dismay that they were not taken as an occasion for conversion. "After the lessons we were given, after the blows that we had to accept from a retributive God, after the crimes in which we were involved, no one can deny that we had our hour. We have missed it."[20] All those who hoped for radical change were crestfallen by the path of West German democracy. Writing in the 1960s, the psychoanalysts Alexander and Margarethe Mitscherlich admitted that "We are indeed all oppressed by a profound disappointment that not only did the immeasurable suffering of World War II, the indescribable slaughter that accompanied it, have no cathartic effect but that, on the contrary, there have been multiple metastases of the evil of war."[21] Richter voiced the same sentiment, which he projected onto the younger Germans:

Thus in those first years, I rejected almost everything that developed under the influence of the occupying forces: the foundation of both German states, which I held to be disastrous, the restoration of the capitalist economic order on the one hand, and the command economy on the other. . . . The youth returning from the war did not impose themselves, which we had optimistically expected, but the older generations did . . . men, who after the unprecedented collapse, attempted to take up where the social and party-political development in the Weimar Republic had left off. We were marginalized. . . . The

---

[18] Sa'adah, *Germany's Second Chance*, 14–23.

[19] Dirks, "Der restaurative Charakter der Epoche," 944. An explicitly Marxist-inspired study in this tradition is Erich-Ulrich Huster et al., *Determinanten der westdeutschen Restauration, 1945–1949* (Frankfurt, 1972).

[20] Dirks, "Der restaurative Charakter der Epoche," 950.

[21] Alexander Mitscherlich and Margarete Mitscherlich, *The Inability to Mourn: Principles of Collective Behavior*, trans. Beverley R. Placzek (New York, 1975), 303.

object of our rejection and critique in the subsequent years would be what we called the "restoration" ... the restoration of the old.[22]

The standard set by the German cultural left was high. Anything less than a vaguely conceived revolution was deemed a restoration. "The restoration is the fear of the revolution."[23] Here lies the origin of the two enduring features of redemptive republican consciousness in West Germany: the tainted birth of the Federal Republic and the "missed opportunity" for a radically new beginning, both the responsibility of the old elites, which, if not themselves Nazis, had failed miserably to withstand them in 1933. These were no men to lead Germany into the future. For much of the intelligentsia, the new German democracy had been corrupted by moral pollution and politically endangered by ex-Nazis and fellow travelers. The Federal Republic was not trustworthy.

These myths prefigured the emotional posture of many Germans toward the Federal Republic for the next sixty years. But it was not just that the evil of National Socialism was not redeemed by a rebirth in 1949. It was also perceived to have continued into and infected the new state itself. Already by 1954, Kogon felt moved to write that in view of the massive presence of former Nazis in all walks of life, and especially in positions of power, the left stood "virtually with [our] backs to the wall."[24] Arendt herself remarked that Germans "did not particularly mind the presence of murderers at large in the country."[25] The Basic Law may have been replete with the rhetoric of human dignity and individual rights, but the social and political reality of the new republic hardly lived up to these lofty ideals.

Consequently, the "nonconformist" intellectuals regarded the Federal Republic with considerable suspicion. Dirks spoke for many when he wrote in June 1949 that the promulgation of the Basic Law was not "an occasion for celebration," being "no more than the rules of the game for a period of transition."[26] The affirmation of the new order was impossible for many Germans on the left because the necessary opportunism of integrating millions of ex-Nazis provoked moral outrage and disgust, especially in view of the fate of their countless victims, not to mention the plight of the survivors. Indignation and suspicion have driven many Germans until the early years of the twenty-first century. They shared the outrage of the young Marx: "But war upon the state of affairs in Germany!"[27]

[22] Hans Werner Richter, *Briefe an einen jungen Sozialisten* (Munich, 1974), 114–15, cited in Helmut L. Müller, *Die literarische Republik. Westdeutsche Schriftsteller und die Politik* (Weinheim and Basel, 1983), 52.

[23] Dirks, "Der restaurative Charakter der Epoche," 953.

[24] E(ugen) K(ogon), "Beinahe mit dem Rücken zu der Wand," *Frankfurter Hefte*, 9 (1954), 641–45.

[25] Hannah Arendt, *Eichmann in Jerusalem: A Report on the Banality of Evil*, rev. ed. (New York, 1977), 16.

[26] D(irks), "Bundesrepublik Deutschland," 458.

[27] Karl Marx, "Contribution to the Critique of Hegel's Philosophy of Right: Introduction," in Robert C. Tucker, ed., *The Marx-Engels Reader*, 2nd ed. (New York, 1978), 55–56.

This outrage did not produce the "Non-German German" emotional reaction among the founding generation of the republic. Its rejection of the German "restoration" was perfectly consistent with its sense of German nationality. Nationally based arguments had a long tradition in the political left. For many, the integrity of organized labor during the Nazi period was evidence that the group self was not irredeemably polluted. As one young man admitted, his communist grandfather was "a symbol for me, proof that the 'other' Germany had always existed as well."[28] In the immediate postwar years, leftists were as averse to the nascent rhetoric of collective guilt as other Germans.[29] The old elites and not the workers or people were responsible for fascism. Kogon spoke for many when he worried that Germany would become a pariah nation like the Jews had been, and he insisted that guilt could only be personal, never collective.[30]

The tone for Social Democrats was set by their leader Kurt Schumacher, who possessed impeccable anti-Nazi credentials. Like most Europeans at the time, he was also an ardent patriot. It was natural for nations to pursue their own interests, he insisted, and so a free Europe should comprise nation-states of equal status – without American or Soviet domination. Nor ought Germany be subservient to its neighbors. Indeed, a democratic socialist Germany should act as a third force between the warring fronts of the Cold War. Schumacher appealed to Germans by claiming that only the Social Democrats (SPD) were real patriots, because the Christian Democrats (CDU) had sold out to the occupation forces of the West by accepting the country's division; they had become "patriots of other states." Moreover, as the party of property and the Roman Catholic Church, the CDU represented the antidemocratic forces that relied on foreign support to exploit German workers. In the tradition of socialist internationalism, he argued that Germany required democratic (and therefore national) self-determination, and it was the SPD's role to create "a new spirit of national self-confidence" in the defeated Germans so that they could play their new, important role.[31]

If the "old left" was as wedded to national identity as other Germans, the "sixty-eighter" generation (born between 1938 and 1948) of the German "new left" found such an identity an intolerable burden because intergenerational relations had been poisoned by pollution and stigma. As Norbert Elias observed at the time, "they were aware, perhaps with a certain astonishment, that the world at large blamed the German people for the creation of a violent regime which went far beyond the normally bearable forms of inhumanity. In other

[28] Peter Sichrovsky, *Born Guilty: Children of Nazi Families*, trans. Jean Steinberg (London, 1987), 158.

[29] Frank M. Buscher, "Kurt Schumacher, German Social Democracy and the Punishment of Nazi Crimes," *Holocaust and Genocide Studies*, 5:3 (1990), 261–73.

[30] Jeffrey K. Olick, *In the House of the Hangman: The Agonies of German Defeat, 1943–1949* (Chicago, 2005), 185.

[31] Lewis J. Edinger, *Kurt Schumacher: A Study in Personality and Political Behavior* (Stanford, 1965), 150–51.

words, they found that the stigma attached not only to individual people who had been personally involved in the acts of violence of the Hitler period, but to the entire nation."[32] For this reason, the sixty-eighters' commitment to socialism represented a "type of distancing and purification ritual in relation to the sins of the fathers."[33] These rituals were designed to produce a new German: the Non-German German.

The integrationist vision prevailed for the first decades of the Republic.[34] Many factors conspired to prevent a redemptive republican foundation along the lines of the French or American model. To begin with, the Parliamentary Council of German politicians charged by the occupation authorities with drafting a constitution regarded the document it produced as a temporary measure that was to obtain only until Germans in the Soviet-occupied zone could join their compatriots in the west. The Basic Law, as it called the constitution, was provisional, and consequently the Parliamentary Council was not displeased that its deliberations were unaccompanied by the public interest and emotion that usually attends the foundation of a state and the promulgation of a constitution. The patrician liberal politician and inaugural president of the new republic, Theodor Heuss, ensured that the Basic Law was not even put to a popular vote.[35] Ordinary Germans, for their part, barely took notice of the Parliamentary Council, concerned as they were with providing for their subsistence at the time of the Russian blockade of Berlin (June 23, 1948–May 12, 1949) and the currency reform after June 1948. The Allied military governors, they thought, would retain ultimate political control anyway. In 1949 only 25 percent of them preferred the black, red, and gold flag of the Weimar Republic and liberal tradition, an equal number opting for the black, red, and white flag of Imperial Germany, while 35 percent expressed no opinion at all.[36]

Arendt insisted on "the enormous difference in power and authority between a constitution imposed by a government upon a people and the constitution by which a people constitutes its own government."[37] But a constitution generated by the German population was no option at the time, and the politicians' elitist suspicion of the people they represented was well founded. In 1948 an Allensbach poll recorded that 57 percent of Germans affirmed the proposition that National Socialism was a good idea badly carried out.[38] There was still a

---

[32] Norbert Elias, *The Germans: Power Struggles and the Development of Habitus in the Nineteenth and Twentieth Centuries*, trans. Eric Dunning and Stephen Mennell (New York, 1996), 252–53.

[33] Ibid., 261.

[34] Diethelm Prowe, "Demokratisierung in Deutschland nach 1945," in Dietrich Papenfuß and Wolfgang Schneider, eds., *Deutsche Umbrüche im 20. Jahrhundert* (Cologne, 2000), 447–57.

[35] Manfred Overesch, *Deutschland, 1945–1949: Vorgeschichte und Gründung der Bundesrepublik* (Königstein, 1979), 156.

[36] Dennis L. Bark and David R. Gress, *A History of West Germany*, vol. 1 (Oxford, 1989), 235.

[37] Arendt, *On Revolution*, 144.

[38] Erhard H. M. Lange, "Entstehung des Grundgesetzes und die Öffentlichkeit: Zustimmung erst nach Jahren," *Zeitschrift für Parlamentsfragen*, 10 (1979), 378–402.

widespread feeling among most Germans that liberal capitalism of the Anglo-American model had failed them and that some kind of statist, semiliberal alternative was preferable. This was not a people to effect a republican revolution against the Nazi incubus and its legacy. In view of this observation and its interpretation of the weaknesses of the Weimar constitution, the Parliamentary Council elected not to include its plebiscitary elements in the Basic Law. Germans had already conducted a revolution, namely, the "national revolution" against the "ideas of 1789" in 1933.

The Weimar Syndrome and the Discursive Refoundation of the Republic

This dichotomy of political emotions and political languages meant that the Federal Republic faced an acute legitimacy dilemma. In order to secure its legitimacy, West German elites had to turn a blind eye to the tangible legacy of the Nazi past highlighted by the theories of fascism of the left, because to accept the continuity from the past would disqualify the liberal-democratic foundation of the state in 1949. Conversely, the new state continued to suffer a legitimacy deficit for redemptive republicans because they feared it was endangered by ex-Nazis or authoritarian political traditions. The hope of liberals like Krüger that West German politics could be run along the lines of the Western democracies ignored the fact that a Western political culture did not yet exist and that the distrust of the republic's institutions and population by the German intelligentsia was based on very real continuities in personnel from the Nazi regime.[39] This dilemma, and the ensuing political polarization would persist until the early twenty-first century when basic trust in German society had developed among intellectuals. At the same time, to dismiss the redemptive republicanism of the left as naive and destructive moralism, as some commentators have been wont, is to fail to see that the dream of renewal and the project of transformation were inevitable responses to a perceived special evil: the odium of the National Socialist regime and the absence of a moral catharsis after 1945.[40]

This recognition does not mean we must accept the claim that the republic was "refounded" in the 1960s when leftist and liberal intellectuals and the generational rebellion of students began challenging the conservative hegemony. Or that the current open attitude of many Germans to their past should be

---

[39] Norbert Frei, *Vergangenheitspolitik. Die Anfänge der Bundesrepublik und die NS-Vergangenheit* (Munich, 1996); Frei, *Karrieren im Zwielicht: Hitlers Eliten nach 1945* (Frankfurt, 2001); Wilfried Loth and Bernd-A. Rusinek, eds., *Verwandlungspolitik: NS-Eliten in der westdeutschen Nachkriegsgesellschaft* (Frankfurt and New York, 1998); Michael R. Hayse, *Recasting West German Elites: Higher Civil Servant, Business Leaders, and Physicians in Hesse between Nazism and Democracy* (Oxford and New York, 2003).

[40] Hans-Peter Schwarz, *Die Ära Adenauer: Gründerjahre der Republik, 1949–1957* (Stuttgart, 1981); Fritz Walter, "Eine deprimierende Bilanz," *Die Woche* (May 22, 1998), 10.

traced to the sixty-eighters.[41] To argue that "1968" constituted the "intellectual foundation" of the Federal Republic ignores a vital aspect of the story – namely, that for many Germans like Horst Krüger the establishment of the state in 1949 was in fact a legitimate foundation that would be threatened by an attempt to "start again." It may have required reform but hardly a "new beginning." Whereas redemptive republicans thought that Germany had yet to develop an adequate answer to the Nazi experience, liberals and moderate conservatives thought that the Federal Republic constituted the fundamentals of precisely such an answer. The "nonconformists" were so appalled by the Nazi past and its undeniable continuities into the new state that they rejected those elements of it that liberals and moderate conservatives cherished: political parties, representative democracy, and membership in the Western alliance. Liberals, for their part, thought the differences between the Federal Republic and its predecessor more important than any similarities.

This dilemma was compounded by the practice common to all players of building their vision of a democratic Germany on the foundation of a theory about the demise of the Weimar Republic. This practice, which at times bordered on an obsession – most of the politicians in the 1950s had experienced the period as adults – can be called the "Weimar syndrome."[42] The syndrome meant that the fate of the Bonn Republic itself was cast in terms of Weimar's fate. "Bonn is not Weimar," the Swiss journalist F. R. Alleman assured Germans in 1956, confirming what was uppermost in people's minds. Twelve years later, in the wake of the right-wing electoral success and student mobilization, the political scientist Karl Dietrich Bracher was also moved to ask whether Bonn was in fact Weimar after all.[43] In a discourse of crisis structured like this, different factions of the intelligentsia defined one another as the dangerous tradition responsible for the destruction of German democracy in the past. The syndrome thus tended to escalate conflict because opponents always fulfilled the threatening clichés of the other.[44]

Moreover "republicanism" is what political theorists call an "essentially contested concept." Such concepts like "art," "social justice," or "the Christian life" are necessarily open, persistently vague, and definable in various ways. No criteria exist by which to adjudge one definition as true, and no amount of

[41] Clemens Albrecht, Günter C. Behrmann, Michael Bock, Harald Homann, and Friedrich H. Tenbruck, *Die intellektuelle Gründung der Bundesrepublik. Eine Wirkungsgeschichte der Frankfurter Schule* (Frankfurt and New York, 1999); Helmut Dubiel, *Niemand ist frei von der Geschichte. Die nationalsozialistische Herrschaft in den Debatten des Deutschen Bundestages* (Munich, 1999); Sa'adah, *Germany's Second Chance*.

[42] A. Dirk Moses, "The Weimar Syndrome in the Federal Republic of Germany: Carl Schmitt and the Forty-Five Generation of Intellectuals," in Holger Zaborowski and Stephan Loos, eds., *Leben, Tod und Entscheidung: Studien zur Geistesgeschichte der Weimarer Republik* (Berlin, 2003), 187–207.

[43] Karl Dietrich Bracher, "Wird Bonn doch Weimar?" *Der Spiegel* (March 13, 1967), 60–68.

[44] J. G. A. Pocock, "Verbalizing a Political Act: Toward a Politics of Speech," in Michael Shapiro, ed., *Language and Politics* (Oxford, 1984), 38–39.

discussion can settle the issue.[45] This is equally the case with the national past to which everyone appealed in order to buttress his or her respective cases. By framing contemporary public dramas in terms of Weimar politics, the "Weimar syndrome" contributed to the hysteria and paranoia of postwar West German politics. Ironically, then, the passionate effort of Bonn intellectuals to ensure that the turmoil of the 1920s would not ruin the Federal Republic meant that some of the spirit of those years would live on decades later nonetheless.

During the 1950s, the differences between liberals and leftists were obscured by their common front against the older generation of illiberal intellectuals who rejected the language of democracy. But this loose coalition disintegrated during the 1960s, and especially after the radicalization of the student movement in 1967, when many liberal forty-fivers (and older German Jewish émigrés, like Ernst Fraenkel) saw in the students and the New Left the attempt to radically refound a republic that they had fought to liberalize in the 1950s and early 1960s. Forty-fivers on the left, by contrast, like Habermas, saw the generational protest as the chance to effect the democratic socialist foundation that the state had missed in 1949. The subsequent bitter and protracted cultural and intellectual conflict polarized the forty-fivers, as each identified in the other the enemy of democracy.

The temporary victory of the left wing of the forty-fivers was not 1968, but the *Machtwechsel* (change of power) of 1969. At the federal and state levels of government, they gained power and influence and attempted to "refound" the country. "We are only now just beginning," proclaimed Chancellor Brandt. The book traces the reform debates and ensuring polarization, based as it was on mutual hostility and fear. There is evidence to suggest that liberals, like Hans Maier, who was not associated with the Carl Schmitt school, feared a socialist *Machtergreifung* in the early 1970s. In this context liberals joined conservatives in organizations like the Bund Freiheit der Wissenschaft to resist the leftist reform attempts, above all in education. The ambitions of the left for a cultural refoundation of the republic set off fears among liberals and conservatives. The left and conservative political languages and groups became caricatures of one another. For example, Habermas constantly accused his opponents of seeking out an "inner enemy" (in a reference to Carl Schmitt [1888–1985]) against whom the majority could conduct a "pogrom," while Hermann Lübbe warned of the dangers of moralized politics that inexorably culminated in terrorism.[46]

For all that, the syndrome was also responsible for the gradual generation of a political consensus. Paradoxically, the paranoia generated by the fear that the other side would seize power in a reenactment of 1933 worked to spur the

[45] W. B. Gallie, "Essentially Contested Concepts," in Max Black, ed., *The Importance of Language* (Edgewood Cliffs, N.J., 1962), 121–46; William E. Connolly, *The Terms of Political Discourse*, 3rd ed. (Princeton, N.J., 1993), 10–41.

[46] A. Dirk Moses, "The State and the Student Movement, 1967–1977," in Gerard J. De Groot, ed., *Student Protest: The Sixties and After* (London and New York, 1998), 129–39.

contending wings of the intelligentsia to defend "the republic" when they felt their opponents were on the ascendancy. During the 1980s and 1990s, the commitment developed to the republican institutions and culture as they existed, rather than as they should be. The ensuing consensus emerged unintended from the dust of the political and intellectual battlefield rather than out of conscious design. The apparent "refoundation" of the republic in the 1960s and 1970s by the left was not the victory of the redemptive republicans, but the beginning of the resolution of the legitimacy dilemma by the left's incremental acceptance of the liberal order and the concession of liberals and conservatives that nefarious continuities from the Nazi period needed to be addressed.

Neither language of republican democracy accounts satisfactorily for the actual development of the West German republican consensus. Neither side succeeded in imposing its vision: there were no cathartic moments or purges, nor was there a seamless integration of Nazi elites and toleration of illiberal mentalities and practices. The republican consensus in West Germany emerged out of a protracted and bitter public discussion about the meaning of the German past for the Federal Republic's present and future. This symbolic conflict was the post facto, functional equivalent of the foundational debates that many other republics have *at the time* of their foundation.[47] West German democracy was a *discursive* achievement, not an integrationist or redemptive one. A political consensus was reached, then, neither by force nor by stealth, but by open discussion in which rival claims about the meaning of the past were made, modified, or rejected. The experience of the Federal Republic shows that the development of common values is an open process, a hermeneutical circle, a permanent debate. Of course, the incremental development of basic trust in political institutions and political culture did not mean that the customary cut and thrust of politics disappeared. It meant that agreement was reached about its institutions so that the election of the opposition political forces did not entail a completely different or "other" republic, as it was still put in West Germany in the 1970s.

Intellectual Generations

Which Germans were responsible for the discursive democratization of the Federal Republic? To date, most attention has been focused on the West German "founder" generation, which was socialized before the First World War (like the first chancellor, Konrad Adenauer [1876–1967]), or on the sixty-eighters.[48] In fact, it was the generation in between, whose members include world-famous

---

[47] Cf. Wolfgang Jäger, "Verfassung und Identität in westlichen Demokratien," *Politische Studien*, special issue, "Vor 40 Jahren: Grundgesetz Bundesrepublik Deutschland" (1989), 147–54.

[48] Frank R. Pfetsch, "Die Gründergeneration der Bundesrepublik. Sozialprofil und politische Orientierung," *Politische Vierteljahresschrift*, 27 (1986), 237–51; Marie-Luise Recker, "'Bonn ist nicht Weimar.' Zur Struktur und Charakter des politischen Systems der Bundesrepublik Deutschland in der Ära Adenauer," *Geschichte in Wissenschaft und Unterricht*, 44 (1993), 287–303.

intellectuals like Jürgen Habermas and Ralf Dahrendorf (both born in 1929), which was uniquely committed to the new state as an emphatically republican project of reform. These were the young Germans of the 1940s on whom Andersch and Richter set so much store and in whom they were so disappointed. The generation goes by a variety of names – "Hitler Youth," "skeptical," "reconstruction," "searching," "betrayed," "*Flakhelfer*," "Auschwitz" – indicating its indeterminate and contested identity. I call them "the forty-fivers" because the collapse of the Nazi regime and beginning of liberal freedoms was the turning point of their lives and the beginning of their own (and Germany's) intellectual and emotional (*geistige*) reorientation.[49] "What really determined my political views was 1945," wrote Habermas. "At that point the rhythm of my personal development intersected with the great historical events of the time."[50]

This is the key generation in West Germany's legitimacy dilemma, not only because its members came of age in the late 1950s and early 1960s and ran the Federal Republic until the 1990s. Their experiences meant they were uniquely placed to commence the process of discursive republican value development. In the first place, the new state became part of their emotional and intellectual economy. Whether it was legitimate was a question of immediate existential significance because they had to adopt one side of this dilemma to answer their own personal quest for meaning and orientation in the years of perplexity after the end of the war. "For the first time in my life," Horst Krüger related, "a state exists that in its fundaments I could affirm."[51] Because they were socialized during the Nazi period and immediately thereafter, they possessed no direct experience of pre-Nazi Germany. Their relationship to "restorative traditions" was therefore different from that of older Germans. The democratic system was not something to which preexisting German traditions needed to be adapted: it was their second home. As the jurist Ernst Wolfgang Böckenförde (b. 1931) observed of his generation of young Roman Catholics, "It sought...to understand this order [i.e., West Germany] on its own terms, its structure and mode of functioning, and to situate itself within it." Fulfilling the promise of a civil and Christian society was this generation's aim, and despite the different answers that it developed, he feels licensed to speak of it as "sharing a group journey."[52]

The central question of experience raises the issue of intellectual and political generations because they are experiential collectives based on temporal and

[49] Joachim Kaiser, "Phasenverschiebungen und Einschnitte in der Kulturellen Entwicklung," in Martin Broszat, ed., *Zäsuren nach 1945: Essays zur Periodisierung der deutschen Nachkriegsgeschichte* (Munich, 1990), 69–74. Claus Leggewie follows him in "The 'Generation of 1989': A New Political Generation?" in Peter Monteath and Reinhard Alter, eds., *Rewriting the German Past: History and Identity in the New Germany* (Atlantic Highlands, N.J., 1997), 103–14. Harold Marcuse prefers the term "48ers." See his *Dachau: The Uses and Abuses of a Concentration Camp, 1933–2003* (Cambridge, 2001).

[50] Peter Dews, ed., *Habermas: Autonomy and Solidarity* (London, 1986), 73.

[51] Krüger, "Das Nein ist kein Programm."

[52] Ernst Wolfgang-Böckenförde, *Der deutsche Katholizismus im Jahre 1933: Kirche und demokratisches Ethos* (Freiburg, 1988), 10.

spatial proximity. Experience is a notoriously vague category.[53] For that reason, social scientists have preferred to address its *consequences* rather than its *origins* by using cohort and statistical analysis of, say, voting patterns, when attempting to explain political behavior in generational terms.[54] The theoretical literature on the subject is essentially an extended footnote on Karl Mannheim's analysis of 1928, because he offers an explanation of how and why generational experiences arise in the first place.[55] Mediating between French positivists, who understood generations primarily as a biological phenomenon, and German romantics, who saw in their cycles the mystery of the historical process itself, Mannheim combined the objective and subjective dimensions of generation formation. The historical context into which one is born was an objective fact, and to this extent years of birth shared with class membership a definite and ascertainable temporal and spatial "location" that limits individuals "to a specific range of potential experience, predisposing them for a certain characteristic mode of thought and experience, and a characteristic type of historically relevant action."[56] This is the basic insight of the sociology of knowledge: social being determines thought. What Fredric Jameson writes of historical periods can be applied to generations: it "is not understood as some omnipresent and uniform shared style or way of thinking and acting, but rather the sharing of an objective situation, to which a whole range of varied responses and creative innovations is then possible, but always within that situation's structural limits."[57]

For an "actual" generation to arise, the potentially new experiences inherent in a particular generational location need to be released by the participation of the relevant persons in the social and intellectual currents at moments of "dynamic destabilization." Such participation during the adolescent years of identity crisis and formation identified by Erikson (approximately between seventeen and twenty-five years of age) brings a generation into "fresh contact"

[53] Martin Jay, *Songs of Experience: Modern American and European Variations on a Universal Theme* (Berkeley, 2005).

[54] Ulrich Hermann, "Das Konzept der 'Generation,'" *Die Neue Sammlung*, 27 (1987), 364–77; M. Rainer Lepsius, "Generation," in Martin Greiffenhagen, Sylvia Greiffenhagen, and Rainer Prätorius, eds., *Handwörterbuch zur Politischen Kultur der Bundesrepublik Deutschland* (Opladen, 1981), 172–75; Alan Spitzer, "The Historical Problem of Generations," *American Historical Review*, 78 (December 1973), 1353–85; Jürgen Reulecke and Elisabet Müller-Luckner, *Generationalität und Lebensgeschichte im 20. Jahrhundert* (Munich, 2003).

[55] Karl Mannheim, "The Problem of Generations," in his *Essays on the Sociology of Knowledge*, ed. Paul Kecskemeti (London, 1952), 276–320; Robert Wohl, *The Generation of 1914* (Cambridge, Mass., 1979), 73–84; Mary Gluck, *Georg Lukacs and His Generation, 1900–1918* (Cambridge, Mass., 1985); Peter Loewenberg, "The Psychohistorical Origins of the Nazi Youth Cohort," in his *Decoding the Past: The Psychohistorical Approach* (Berkeley and Los Angeles, 1985), 209–39; Nancy Winter, "Political Generations, Micro-Cohorts, and the Transformation of Social Movements," *American Sociological Review*, 62 (1997), 760–78.

[56] Mannheim, "The Problem of Generations," 291.

[57] Fredric Jameson, "Periodizing the 60s," in his *The Ideologies of Theory: Essays, 1971–1986*, vol. 2 (London, 1998), 178–218, 179.

with the "historical process." It is not necessary to share Mannheim's quasi-Hegelian belief in a unified and coherent historical process to find useful his insight that generational experience is incarnated in a "natural view of the world" that operates as a lifelong interpretive grid. One can speak of "spectacular events" that lead to the shattering of received categories of interpretation ("shock effect," "cognitive dissonance") and the necessity of redrawing cognitive maps. A learning process is set in motion in which the subject seeks the information and categories with which to make sense of the new circumstances, a journey in which charismatic teachers often play an influential role.[58]

Intellectuals play an important part in this regard because the experience of generations is not solely the result of the synchronic interaction of cohorts and their historical context. Generational consciousness also contains a diachronic dimension: generations rely upon the preexisting political languages – Mannheim calls them "fundamental integrative attitudes and formative principles" – with which to come to terms with their circumstances. Others use the term "memory trace," which is not simply a copy of an experience but its simultaneous distortion, because a process of "telescoping" and selection occurs through specific "schemata" and "scripts" provided by culturally determined "semantic memory."[59] Here is the link to political languages, defined by John Pocock as "a number of already formed and institutionalized structures" that have been created by unknown others and that are publicly available. They make political communication possible at all.[60] Intellectual generations are formed by and in turn continue and develop the political languages at their disposal. The gestation of generational experience is simultaneously the development of existing political languages, and reconstructing the formation of intellectual generations is an exercise in intellectual history.

Any complex society comprises various, indeed competing political languages, a fact that raises the question of generational unity, because of the pluralism of interpretive possibilities for immediate experience (*Erlebnis*) due to the variety of integrated narratives that constitute the mediated experience of *Erfahrung*. Mannheim argued that generations are never homogeneous entities for precisely this reason. They are, rather, question-posing collectives that compete internally to answer their common immediate experience.[61] If, as R. G. Collingwood contended, historians should write about the answers to particular questions that change with each particular context, rather than about the answers to putative eternal questions, then it is important to bear in mind the particular question of each intellectual generation.[62]

---

[58] Helmut Fogt, *Politische Generationen. Empirische Bedeutung und theoretisches Modell* (Opladen, 1982), 83–85.
[59] Jay Winter and Emmanuel Sivan, "Setting the Framework," in Jay Winter and Emmanuel Sivan, eds., *War and Remembrance in the Twentieth Century* (Cambridge, 1999), 6–39.
[60] Pocock, "Verbalizing a Political Act," 30–31.
[61] Hans Jaeger, "Generationen in der Geschichte. Überlegungen zu einem umstrittenen Konzept," *Geschichte und Gesellschaft*, 3 (1977), 444.
[62] R. G. Collingwood, *An Autobiography* (Oxford, 1939), 62.

The generational question of the forty-fivers was how and why National Socialism could come to power; its mission was to ensure that the Federal Republic would succeed. The normative political language in West Germany was the language of republicanism, but its vocabulary was just as bifurcated as the national past was interpretable, and the generation was split. It was an illusion of Richter and Andersch to expect "the youth returning from war" to take matters into their hands and effect the rebirth of the country. As we will see in the next chapter, ever since the forty-fivers have been condemned as a politically passive generation of craven conformists. In fact, they were split from the outset. The forty-fivers adopted different interpretations to meet various personal crises related to national feeling. In the years of cognitive and emotional reorientation after the war, members of this generation adopted competing conceptions of republican democracy as "cultural ideologies" that resolved their adolescent identity crises.

The generational units of the forty-fivers drew competing genealogies of the catastrophe that they had experienced, and they sought to secure the vision of republicanism and those traditions that they valued and had incorporated into their own vulnerable identities. These languages were framing scripts that, in the words of John E. Toews, served as a "healing exorcism" because they connected "historical knowledge as articulated in the narrative scripts (or metanarratives) into which individuals must insert their personal stories and cultural, public 'memory.'"[63] In order to understand these competing languages of republicanism, it is necessary to reconstruct their arguments on particular issues because these arguments laid bare how they constituted the world. Political languages compete with one another to provide the best argument about the meaning of power-defining concepts. And the criteria of what counts as a successful argument for each language express the investments of those whose polarized political emotions constitute the underlying structure of public discourse.

[63] John E. Toews, "Historiography as Exorcism: Conjuring up 'Foreign' Worlds and Historicizing Subjects in the Context of the Multiculturalism Debate," *Theory and Society*, 27 (1998), 535.

3

The Forty-fivers

A Generation between Fascism and Democracy

Who were the forty-fivers? The precise boundaries of the generation are porous. The educationalist Rolf Schörken (b. 1928) identifies those born between 1921 and 1929, while the political scientist Hans-Joachim Arndt (1923–2004) casts his net a little more widely to include those born between 1920 and 1933.[1] The Social Democratic intellectual Günter Gaus (1929–2004) and many others, however, insist that those born in the late 1920s and early 1930s constitute a generation distinct from those born in the early years of the Weimar Republic. A man born in the early 1920s was most likely a soldier in World War II, spending at least six years in uniform and then several years in a prisoner-of-war camp.[2] *Flakhelfer* (the operators of antiaircraft canons, born between 1927 and 1929) or *Pimpfe* (the ten- to fourteen-year-olds), by contrast, had a far less militarized experience and would have spent little if any time in a POW camp. Gaus concluded that consequently slightly older men were more resigned and less optimistic after the war than the younger ones. The younger ones, he thinks, transferred their Nazi idealism to the hope for cultural and political renewal in

---

[1] Rolf Schörken, *Jugend 1945. Politisches Denken und Lebensgeschichte* (Frankfurt, 1990), 16; Hans-Joachim Arndt, *Die Besiegten von 1945. Versuch einer Politologie für Deutsche samt Würdigung der Politikwissenschaft in der Bundesrepublik* (Berlin, 1978), 252. For this generation in East Germany, see Dorothee Wierling, "The Hitler Youth Generation in the GDR," in Konrad H. Jarausch, ed., *Dictatorship as Experience: Towards a Socio-Cultural History of the GDR*, trans. Eve Duffy (New York and Oxford, 1999), 307–24.

[2] Günter Gaus, *Die Welt der Westdeutschen: Kritische Betrachtungen* (Cologne, 1986), 72; Jürgen Habermas, "Carl Schmitt in der politischen Geistesgeschichte der Bundesrepublik," in his *Die Normalität einer Berliner Republik* (Frankfurt, 1995), 119; Wilhelm Hennis, "Politikwissenschaft als Beruf," *Freiburger Universitätsblätter*, 2 (June 1998), 25–48, 37; Ernst Schulin, "Ratlos und Unsicher. Ernst Nolte stellt das Geschichtsdenken des zwanzigsten Jahrhunderts dar," *Frankfurter Allgemeine Zeitung* (October 8, 1991), L23; Martin Greiffenhagen, *Jahrgang 1928. Aus einem unruhigen Leben* (Munich, 1988); Claus Leggewie, *Die 89er. Portrait einer Generation* (Hamburg, 1995), 84; Dirk van Laak, *Gespräche in der Sicherheit des Schweigens. Carl Schmitt in der politischen Geistesgeschichte der frühen Bundesrepublik* (Berlin, 1993), 13; Paul Nolte, "Die Historiker der Bundesrepublik," *Merkur*, 53 (May 1999), 413–32.

the late 1940s, and became as disappointed with the West German "restoration" in the 1950s and Cold War (including the German military alliance with the West) as they were in National Socialism.[3] Similarly, Alexander and Margarethe Mitscherlich thought that the values of those with the experience of group solidarity from the front did not collapse in 1945, as they did for the Hitler Youth. The former distinguished between Germany and National Socialism and fell back on an identification with the nation (the "good Germany") in which they retained basic trust. Not so for the former Hitler Youth, who were plagued by an inability to bond to collectives.[4]

The war undeniably touched the members of these years of birth in profoundly different ways, whether in terms of gender or front experience.[5] Obviously, we are speaking of non-Jewish Germans. By the time the war broke out in 1939, Jewish Germans had been forced into emigration, like the future American historians Peter Gay (b. 1923), Wilma Iggers (b. 1921), Georg G. Iggers (b. 1926), Peter Loewenberg (b. 1930), and Fritz Stern (b. 1927). Those who resisted, like Sophie Scholl (1921–43), were murdered.

Nonetheless, there are good reasons to maintain that those born roughly between 1922 and 1932 belong to a single *intellectual generation*. The argument about the varying experiences during the war is based on an unsatisfactory theory of experience. It confuses *Erlebnis* with *Erfahrung*. Searching for some alleged seminal event that can explain all subsequent developments in reconstructing an intellectual generation is therefore a fruitless quest. It is necessary to investigate how a common condition, which produced a "generational question," was "worked up" in different ways. Experience is interpreted memory.[6]

It is difficult to make direct correlations about the relationship between precise years of birth and political emotions as Gaus and others have supposed. Certainly, ex-soldiers like the political scientist Iring Fetscher (b. 1922), politician Erhard Eppler (b. 1926), historian Martin Broszat (1926–89), and educationalists Andreas Flitner (b. 1922) and Hartmut von Hentig (b. 1925) did not seem as alienated from their German identity as Habermas, but their criticisms of the Federal Republic were located left of center nonetheless. Nor was there a shortage of the slightly younger former antiaircraft assistants (*Flakhelfer*) and Hitler Youth with conservative or national orientations, such as the political

---

[3] Cf. Heinz Bude, *Bilanz der Nachfolge. Die Bundesrepublik und der Nationalsozialismus* (Frankfurt, 1992), 84–85; Helmut Schmidt, "Politischer Rückblick auf eine unpolitische Jugend," in Helmut Schmidt et al., *Kindheit und Jugend unter Hitler* (Berlin, 1992), 188–254.

[4] Alexander Mitscherlich and Margarethe Mitscherlich, *The Inability to Mourn: Principles of Collective Behavior*, trans. Beverley R. Placzek (New York, 1975), 217.

[5] Tilman Fichter, *Die SPD und die Nation: Vier sozialdemokratische Generationen zwischen nationaler Selbstbestimmung und Zweistaatlichkeit* (Frankfurt, 1993), 63; Jürgen Herbst, *Requiem for a German Past: A Boyhood among the Nazis* (Madison, 1999); Gerhard Rempel, *Hitler's Children; The HJ and the SS* (Chapel Hill, 1989).

[6] See Kathleen Canning, "Feminist History after the Linguistic Turn: Historicizing Discourse and Experience," *Signs*, 29 (1994), 368–97.

scientists Dieter Oberndörfer (b. 1929), Hans Maier (b. 1931), and Bernard Willms (1931–91), political commentator Johannes Gross (1932–99), historians Hellmut Diwald (1929–93) and Thomas Nipperdey (1927–92), legal scholar Martin Kriele (b. 1927), and philosophers Günter Rohrmoser (b. 1927) and Robert Spaemann (b. 1927).

Despite their different private experiences during the war, these young Germans faced the same existential predicament in 1945: the need to reflect on their cognitive map in view of the bankruptcy of the ideals they had been taught and the criminality of the regime in which they had been socialized. The first postwar student generation came into contact with German intellectual traditions in light of the experience of rupture and the radical suspicion of inherited tradition. What they would make of that experience, and which lessons they would draw from the past, would be a product of the concepts and categories they learned.

But what was the generational *Erlebnis* and concomitant question? The political scientist and publicist Christian Graf von Krockow (b. 1927) says of his generation that "It was old enough to consciously experience the war, and the power and fall of the Third Reich; it was young enough to start again." The medieval historian, Karl Ferdinand Werner (b. 1924), wrote that "It is no retrospective interpretation of my personal experience of '1945,' the shock of which struck me in the last weeks of the war in 1944, that I date my determination to gather information about how crimes of such proportion could occur in Germany. This resulted from a conviction, which I possessed already then, that the German historians were co-responsible for the German fate through their contribution to the perversion of our political-historical thinking."[7]

The historian Imanuel Geiss (b. 1931) spoke for many when he wrote that "Many German history students of my age were driven by the search for the underlying cause of what Meinecke called the 'German Catastrophe.'"[8] Their generational mission was: "It should, as far as we were able to do anything about it, never happen to others again."[9] And this aim meant, concretely, ensuring that the Federal Republic – Germany's and their own second chance – would be safe for democracy. In the case of the forty-fivers, the shared "experiential matrix" of war, ideological fanaticism, and political and social breakdown released a charge of moral energy to answer the question of how German history came to "1933," and the mission of how to prevent it from recurring.[10]

---

[7] Karl Ferdinand Werner, "Ein Historiker der 'Generation 1945' zwischen 'deutsche Historie,' 'Fach' und Geschichte," in Hartmut Lehmann and Otto Gerhard Oexle, eds., *Erinnerungsstücke. Wege in die Vergangenheit* (Vienna, Cologne, and Weimar, 1997), 241.

[8] Imanuel Geiss, "A German Historian Looks at His Century," *The Poppy and the Owl*, 19 (1996), 3–7, 6–7.

[9] Christian Graf von Krockow, "Das Mißverhältnis der Erfahrungen – Versuch zu einem Dialog," in Claus Richter, ed., *Die überflüssige Generation: Jugend zwischen Apathie und Aggression* (Munich, 1979), 205–7.

[10] For the concept of "experiential matrix," see John E. Toews, *Hegelianism: The Path of Dialectical Reason, 1805–1841* (Cambridge, 1980), 99–100.

A Conformist Generation?

The dominant view is that the forty-fivers did *not* produce an answer to National Socialism and were apolitical conformists. In this regard, two early books have been of lasting influence: Helmut Schelsky's *Die skeptische Generation* (The Skeptical Generation), and the Mitscherliches' *Die Unfähigkeit zu Trauern* (The Inability to Mourn), probably among the most cited and little read works in the history of the Federal Republic.[11] They are classics and can be still read with profit, but their enormous impact may lie in their sloganlike titles into which contemporaries could read their own meanings.[12]

Schelsky wrote *Die skeptische Generation* as a synthetic overview of the empirical literature on German youth in the 1950s. Although he professed sociological distance from the subject, his own ideological baggage and biography clearly played a decisive role in his interpretation. Schelsky (1912–84) had been an enthusiastic Nazi in his youth, appearing in a storm trooper uniform to disrupt the lectures of disliked professors in the early 1930s. Like many intellectuals who were attracted initially by National Socialism's antibourgeois and anticapitalist pretensions to a "third way," Schelsky eventually became disenchanted with the regime and "ideologies" in general. After the war, he devoted his long and influential academic career to the new Federal Republic, which he hoped to disabuse of all utopian alternatives to the "reality" of industrial society.[13] For that reason, he championed (and, to a large extent, created) the reputation of the forty-fivers, whom he called "skeptical" by defending it against the criticisms of older educationalists like Eduard Spranger, who felt that postwar youth lacked idealism, missionary zeal, and a pioneering spirit.[14] He construed this vice as a virtue by highlighting the epochal significance of the forty-fivers' apprehended "skepticism." Unlike preceding German generations – the "youth movement" at the turn of the century (to which Spranger had belonged) and the "political youth" of the interwar years (of which Schelsky had been a member) – postwar youth had responded to the disappointment of the Nazi defeat, the sobering

---

[11] Franz-Werner Kersting, "Helmut Schelsky's *Die skeptische Generation* von 1957," *Vierteljahrshefte für Zeitgeschichte*, 50 (2002), 465–95.

[12] Two prominent political scientists, Martin Greiffenhagen (b. 1928) and Christian Graf von Krockow (b. 1927) agree that theirs was a skeptical generation, but they come to differing conclusions about what that means. Greiffenhagen thinks the term should be read as the Greeks would have used it, that is, as searching and intellectually curious. See his *Jahrgang 1928: Aus einem unruhigen Leben* (Munich, 1988), 55. Krockow regards it as a synonym for "anti-idealism," which is probably closer to Schelsky's intention. See his "Das Mißverhältnis der Erfahrungen," 207.

[13] Helmut Schelsky, *Auf der Suche nach Wirklichkeit: Gesammelte Aufsätze* (Düsseldorf and Cologne, 1965); Horst Baier, ed., *Helmut Schelsky – ein Soziologe in der Bundesrepublik* (Stuttgart, 1986); Axel Schildt, "Ende der Ideologien? Politisch-ideologishe Strömungen in den 50er Jahren," in Axel Schildt and Arnold Sywottek, eds., *Modernisierung im Wiederaufbau. Die Westdeutsche Gesellschaft der 50er Jahre* (Bonn, 1998), 627–35.

[14] Helmut Schelsky, *Die skeptische Generation: Eine Soziologie der deutschen Jugend* (Düsseldorf and Cologne, 1957), 115–20. His other target was educationalists who insisted that youth culture was an autonomous and not transitional stage of human development.

realization of its ideological manipulation, and the considerable material hardship of the postwar years, by abjuring a "special social role." Its rejection of those utopian ideals ("community," "wholeness") that prevented a reconciliation with modern civilization ended the dangerous *Sonderweg* of bourgeois youth rebellion and, so Schelsky contended, had normalized German society.[15] The "skeptical" and apolitical concentration on the private world of work and family was precisely what was needed to reconstruct a shattered country.

To be sure, what he wrote about German adolescents of the late 1940s and 1950s could be applied to most Germans at the time. As Friedrich Tenbruck has shown, most Germans withdrew into the private spheres of family and work. Schelsky, it appears, was projecting onto the forty-fivers his positive assessment of the 1950s and the "end of ideology" *Zeitgeist* in West Germany.[16]

If Schelsky praised the absence of idealism and a generational mission to change the world, the psychoanalysts Alexander and Margarethe Mitscherlich viewed this absence as a symptom of individual and collective mental illness. West Germans, they thought, were gripped by a "psychic immobilism and inability to tackle the problems of the present-day society in a socially progressive fashion."[17] This situation was understandable, at least in the immediate postwar years. The enormity of the German crime was such, so the argument went, that its "working through" would call forth feelings of guilt and shame that were incommensurable with "the self-esteem needed for continued living." In order to avoid melancholia (that is, depression), Germans "de-realized" their memories of the war and their narcissistic attachment to Hitler and his ideology by viewing themselves as victims and by investing their psychic energies in the rebuilding of the economy.[18]

The problem was the persistence of this denial and defensiveness into the 1950s and 1960s. The cost was high: the retention of the personality structure that had been vulnerable to Hitler's overtures in the first place. The psychological rivalry with the father remained unresolved and could be projected again onto imaginary enemies. West Germany, the Mitscherliches feared, threatened to act out its collective pathology in fits of compulsive behavior, particularly in the realm of foreign policy, where it possessed "brutally aggressive proclivities" and was susceptible to "unbridled aggressive adventures."[19] By the mid-1960s, they held that the time had come for Germans to admit their guilt and mourn their lost ideals in a process the couple referred to as *Trauerarbeit* (the work of

---

[15] Ibid., 84–88, 493.

[16] Friedrich Tenbruck, "Alltagsnormen und Lebensgefühle in der Bundesrepublik Deutschland," in Richard Löwenthal and Hans-Peter Schwarz, eds., *25 Jahre Bundesrepublik Deutschland – eine Bilanz* (Stuttgart, 1974), 289–310; Hans Braun, "Das Streben nach 'Sicherheit' in den 50er Jahren. Soziale und politische Ursachen und Erscheinungen," *Archiv für Sozialgeschichte*, 18 (1978), 279–306.

[17] Mitcherlich and Mitscherlich, *The Inability to Mourn*, 63.

[18] Ibid., 26–27.

[19] The Mitscherliches believed that East Germany's fears of a West German invasion were "not entirely ungrounded." Ibid., 50.

mourning). Facing the Nazi past was at once a cure for the crippled German ego, which remained stunted by a childish reliance on authoritarian individuals and collectives, and the path to social renewal, because autonomous citizens were by definition oriented to reform and the humanization of their environment.

No discussion of *The Inability to Mourn* can overlook its treatment by Tilman Moser. In a widely read critique, the former student of the Mitscherliches assailed their conflation of psychological and moral categories.[20] Moser argued that the Mitscherliches, on the one hand, explained convincingly why Germans could not detach themselves from an authoritarian collective and feel for their victims but, on the other hand, condemned Germans for just this inability. Moser contended that a consistent approach to what he calls this "poisonous mental underground" entailed empathizing with the subjects. In this way, one could recognize that their self-pitying posture possessed an existential basis: archaic feelings of guilt for causing the war and the Holocaust, and archaic feelings of punishment in the form of civilian bombing, millions of German refugees, casualties, and destroyed life narratives. With this historicizing insight, it would have been possible to "create space" for the exhausted German psyche to recognize gradually the reality of the suffering that Germans had inflicted on others.

The Mitscherliches were prevented from taking this approach, Moser suggested, by the unrealistically high hopes they entertained for postwar political renewal. The massive damage could be redeemed, it almost appeared, were it taken as the occasion for the admission of guilt, expression of contrition, and resolution to take the high road to socialist democracy. Hoping that a sense of guilt would lead to a psychological catharsis and political creativity, they were dismayed, even enraged, when their patients dissembled with the usual strategies of self-justification. Moreover, the sixty-eighters (Moser's own generation) seized the book as a means of avoiding an empathetic engagement with their parents, which would have entailed assuming the burden of the tainted familial and national legacy. Moser went so far as to claim that the escapist and moralistic accusations of the younger generation, far from breaking the silence about the Nazi past in German families, in fact prolonged the self-exculpating mechanisms of the parents by a decade or two.[21]

Like the sixty-eighters, the Mitscherliches demanded of forty-fivers that they feel guilt even if they had not participated directly in Nazi crimes. They wanted them to feel subjectively guilty for an imputed objective guilt, and for this reason they posed a false alternative. Either the subjects admit their guilt and resolved

[20] Tilman Moser, "Die Unfähigkeit zu trauern: Hält die These einer Überprüfung stand?" *Psyche*, 46 (May 1992), also in his *Vorsicht Berührung. Über Sexualisierung, Spaltung, NS-Erbe und Stasi-Angst* (Frankfurt, 1992), 203–20. Cf. Alon Confino, "Traveling as Culture of Remembrance," *History and Memory*, 12:2 (2000), 93–96; Anthony D. Kauders, "History as Censure: 'Repression' and 'Philosemitism' and Postwar Germany," *History and Memory*, 15:1 (2003), 97–122.

[21] Cf. Michael Schneider, "Fathers and Sons, Retrospectively: The Damaged Relationship between Two Generations," *New German Critique*, 31 (Winter 1984), 3–52.

to start anew by adopting the Mitscherliches' interpretation of the past, or they were denying their guilt, repressing the past, and continuing in their bad old ways. By conflating the clinical and political, these critics participated in a destructive ad hominem discourse of accusation and denial, because those who disagreed with the political dimension of the argument were seen necessarily to be repressing the past. And, indeed, Moser was subject to precisely such a criticism from the Mitscherlich camp.[22]

Significantly, Schelsky and the Mitscherliches agreed implicitly about the meaning of youth movements and their relation to politics. Betraying a characteristically German romantic bias, all three authors framed youth movements as rebellions against bourgeois society and as redemptive sources of cultural renewal.[23] Although they evaluated the situation from opposite standpoints, they considered politics as a radical, totalistic, and transformative project of collective will formation. A very continental conception of politics is implicit in the hope for, and fear of, the catalytic role of youth movements.

The forty-fivers have been judged on the basis of these culturally specific background assumptions. The failure of the antifascist project of redemptive republicanism in Trizonia in the early postwar years delighted Schelsky as much as it dismayed the Mitscherliches, and from it they all concluded that the forty-fivers were an apolitical and conformist generation. A vulgar version of this viewpoint was voiced by the sixty-eighters:

The generation of the first phase, which was born in the Weimar Republic, experienced the crisis of the Depression, was socialized in the Hitler Youth during the "Third Reich," and later in the trenches and antiaircraft batteries. After the collapse, the first priority was eating [*Fressen*, in a reference to Bertold Brecht] and only then morality. But they were acutely conscious that the Nazis had lost the war. This did not by any means turn them into antifascists.... The first postwar generation was generally opportunistic and did not produce a political answer to National Socialism.[24]

Heinz Bude's widely read *Deutsche Karrieren* (German Careers) stands in this tradition. Following Schelsky and Mitscherlich, he readily admits that the forty-fivers were the successful bearers of *Modell Deutschland*. But they remain for him a generation of shallow *Macher* (operators), bereft of the psychological resources to develop their own projects of reform and renewal.[25] The

---

[22] The responses to Moser are Margarethe Mitscherlich-Nielsen, "Was können wir aus der Vergangenheit lernen?" *Psyche*, 47 (August 1993), 743–53; Christian Schneider, "Jenseits der Schuld? Die Unfähigkeit zu trauern in der zweiten Generation," *Psyche*, 47 (August 1993), 754–74; Dieter Rudolf Knoell, "Die doppelte als einseitige Vergangenheit," *Psyche*, 47 (August 1993), 775–94. Moser replied to his critics in "Nachwort zur Kritik an der *Unfähigkeit zu trauern*," in his *Politik und seelischer Untergrund* (Frankfurt, 1993), 198–203.

[23] Frank Trommler, "Mission ohne Ziel. Über den Kult der Jugend im modernen Deutschland," in Thomas Koebner et al., *"Mit uns zieht die neue Zeit." Der Mythos Jugend* (Frankfurt, 1985).

[24] Tilman Fichter and Siegward Lönnendonker, "Von der APO nach TUNIX," in Richter, *Die überflüssige Generation*, 139–41.

[25] Heinz Bude, *Deutsche Karrieren* (Frankfurt, 1984). Claus Leggewie replicates this analysis in his portrayal of West German generations: Leggewie, *Die 89er*, 87–88.

forty-fivers had been forced to conform and internalize the social-Darwinistic worldview of the Nazi socialization.[26] Arno Klönne (b. 1931), leading historian of the Hitler Youth, drew the political conclusions. "The effect of the Hitler Youth education was less the production of a larger group of fanatical-activist young National Socialists than much more in the training of the youths in system conformity, in the renunciation of political and social will-formation and spontaneity, and in the prevention of political experience, including the formation of social utopias: put briefly, in the political-social incapacitation [*Entmündigung*] of youth."[27]

The conclusion of the literature is that this generation was politically docile or passive, that it could not be relied upon to defend democracy, and that it did not develop a political answer to National Socialism. "The lesson the HJ generation drew from the past... was *Pflichtbewußtsein*, a willingness to do one's duty, or better *Leistungsbereitschaft*, a willingness to give it everything one had, largely irrespective of whatever state form or political system happened to be in operation at the time."[28]

Our view of this generation, then, has been a product of redemptive republicanism. Because the generation was not revolutionary, it was restorative, with all the concomitant negative connotations. Such polemically loaded terms do not make for useful analytical concepts.

So did the Nazi regime succeed in producing the fascist personality for which it strove? How deeply was Nazism embedded in German youth in and after 1945? The historian Rolf Schörken tried to answer the first question in a semiautobiographical work on the sixteen- and seventeen-year-olds who staffed the antiaircraft batteries after 1943 (*Flakhelfer*).[29] Like Klönne, Schörken saw a wide spectrum of reactions in his cohort, only a minority of whom were convinced Nazis. The special experience of the *Flakhelfer* – who lived fairly militarized lives, separated from school, family, and Hitler Youth groups – actually increased the prestige of the army, which embodied the "good Germany," at the expense of the Nazi Party. The specific group dynamics that developed in these units resulted in an inner distancing from Nazi ideology and its hyperbolic propaganda. Schörken even spoke of "blockages" that thwarted the Nazi project, although he conceded that slightly older boys, for whom the point of reference was the foreign policy successes of Hitler until 1941, rather than the saturation

[26] Christian Schneider, Cordelia Stillke, and Bernd Leineweber, *Das Erbe der NAPOLA: Versuch einer Generationsgeschichte des Nationalsozialismus* (Hamburg, 1996); cf. Johannes Leeb, *"Wir waren Hitlers Eliteschüler": Ehemalige Zöglinge der NS-Ausleseschulen brechen ihr Schweigen* (Hamburg, 1998).

[27] Matthias von Hellfeld and Arno Klönne, eds., *Die betrogene Generation: Jugend in Deutschland unter dem Faschismus. Quellen und Dokumente* (Cologne, 1985), 345.

[28] Alexander von Plato, "The Hitler Youth Generation and Its Roles in the Two Post-War German States," in Mark Roseman, ed., *Generations in Conflict* (Oxford, 1995), 218.

[29] Rolf Schörken, *Luftwaffenhelfter und Drittes Reich. Die Entstehung eines politischen Bewußtseins* (Stuttgart, 1984); Schörken, *Die Niederlage als Generationserfahrung. Jugendliche nach dem Zusammenbruch der NS-Herrschaft* (Weinheim and Munich, 2004).

bombings of German civilians, were more vulnerable to Nazi overtures. In a later investigation, Schörken argued that the remnants of explicit Nazi ideology disappeared almost overnight in the summer of 1945, except for those unlucky enough to languish in prisoner-of-war camps dominated by fanatical officers.[30]

Many forty-fivers were emotionally bound to Hitler, and the defeat of Germany was a personal collapse of sorts. Günter Grass (b. 1927) is a good example of a "true believer" in the "final victory" (*Endsieg*).[31] Of the 550,000 youths recruited into the military from the cohort born in 1928, some 95,000 went to the Waffen SS.[32] One and a half million of his generation died in the war, 60,000 of those born between 1927 and 1929 dying in its last year.[33] No doubt "true believers" were among them, but to claim that they were all clamoring to die a hero's death is a caricature.[34] Even the subjects about whom the Mitscherliches wrote had not been fanatical Nazis.[35] Consider the leftist educationalist Wolfgang Klafki (b. 1927). In an autobiographical essay, he traced the course of his emotional loyalty to Hitler, to whom he remained faithful until the end. Like many of his contemporaries, he actually disliked the Nazi Party and did his best to avoid the clutches of the Waffen SS, which actively canvassed among sixteen- and seventeen-year-old boys after 1943. He attributed any misrule or maladministration to corrupt party officials, distinguishing them from the benevolent Führer and the respected Wehrmacht. For all that, the deconversion process was rapid and nontraumatic.

When, soon after May 9, 1945, information and trustworthy evidence about the actual goals of National Socialism and Hitler as its leading representative became accessible, and as I learned about the gruesome proportions of the perpetrated crimes, the "superstructure" of the idealized Hitler-image collapsed and with that the central element of the identification pattern.... I experienced this process not as a crisis, but as a liberation from a false orientation and as the opening of newer, more positive horizons.[36]

Contemporaries report feelings of relief felt by many Hitler Youths that the war was finally over, and that it was possible to "come to oneself." Helmut

---

[30] Rolf Schörken, "Singen und Marschieren. Erinnerung an vier Jahre Jungvolk, 1939–1943," *Geschichte in Wissenschaft und Unterricht*, 7 (July–August 1998), 447–61; cf. Eva Gehrken, "Singen und Maschieren – das war doch nicht alles!" *Geschichte in Wissenschaft und Unterricht*, 2 (1999), 118–19.

[31] Heinrich Vormweg, *Günter Grass* (Hamburg, 1986).

[32] Bernd Wegner, *The Waffen-SS: Organization, Ideology, and Function*, trans. Ronald Webster (Oxford and Cambridge, Mass, 1990), 350.

[33] Karl-Heinz Jahnke, *Hitlers letztes Aufgebot. Deutsche Jugend im sechsten Kriegsjahr, 1944/45* (Essen, 1993), 35.

[34] Waldtraut Rath recounts that the boys in her class feared military service because it meant a near certain death: "Kindheit und Mädchenjahre im Dritten Reich," in Wolfgang Klafki, ed., *Verführung, Distanzierung, Ernüchterung. Kindheit und Jugend im Nationalsozialismus* (Weinheim and Basel, 1988), 193.

[35] Mitscherlich and Mitscherlich, *The Inability to Mourn*, 212–14.

[36] Wolfgang Klafki, "Politische Identitätsbildung und frühe pädagogische Berufsorientierung in Kindheit und Jugend unter dem Nationalsozialismus – Autobiographische Rekonstruktion," in Klafki, *Verführung, Distanzierung, Ernüchterung*, 168.

Schmidt said the same in his farewell speech to the West German parliament in 1986.[37]

A historicizing approach might recognize that the experience of compulsion and politicization in the Hitler Youth until 1945, and of civil society and the rule of law thereafter, afforded the forty-fivers a unique perspective on the virtues of the Federal Republic. The writer Peter Rühmkorf (b. 1929) wrote about the effects of the rupture in the following terms:

> I am talking about the feeling of life in that age group for whom fascism, war, and dictatorship had just still become consciousness-forming. It was a group for whom the new beginning related to their age coincided with radical change, and who experienced that ascent out of nothingness into nothing more than an increase in goods with dissipating idealism and awakening criticalness.[38]

The new order was patently superior, humane, and liberal because it safeguarded the private sphere from state violation. This is the primal experience of liberalism. The forty-fivers did produce an answer to the Nazi past: the Federal Republic as a project of consolidation and reform.[39]

Ultimately even the generation's redemptive republicans – that is, Non-German German left-liberal intellectuals – like politician and academic Peter von Oertzen (b. 1924), sociologist Ludwig von Friedeburg (b. 1923), and political scientists Werner Hoffmann (1922–69), Kurt Lenk (b. 1929), and Jürgen Seifert (1928–2005) were radical reformers rather than revolutionaries. It was illusory of idealists like Hans-Werner Richter to look for a revolution from this generation. Ultimately, even Habermas and figures like Günter Grass set limits to the radicalism of sixty-eighters with whose intuitions they otherwise sympathized. Such generational tensions became evident in the forty-fivers' rejection of the youth rebellion of the late 1960s, with the provocative reproach that they knew the dangers of utopianism and youthful romanticism because they had experienced them personally in the Hitler Youth. Günter Gaus, regarded by all as a left-liberal intellectual, expressed this notion well when he told the student leader Rudi Dutschke in 1967: "The difference between your generation and those who are today between forty and fifty appears to me to lie in the fact that you, the younger ones, do not possess the understanding of the redundancy of ideologies that we have gained over the past decades."[40] This is the first German generation in the twentieth century that oriented itself, without reservation, to the West and the Enlightenment. It is the first German generation

[37] Schörken, "Singen und Maschieren."

[38] Peter Rühmkorf, "Das lyrische Weltbild der Nachkriegsdeutschen," in Hans-Werner Richter, ed., *Bestandaufnahme: Eine deutsche Bilanz* (Munich, 1962), 442, cited in Sigrid Wiegel, "'Generation' as Symbolic Form: On the Genealogical Discourse of Memory since 1945," *Germanic Review*, 77:4 (2002), 274.

[39] This observation may be made of reforming police officers of this generation. See Klaus Weinhauer, *Schutzpolizei in der Bundesrepublik* (Paderborn, 2003).

[40] Rudi Dutschke, *Mein langer Marsch: Reden, Schriften und Tagebücher aus zwanzig Jahren*, ed. Gretchen Dutschke-Klotz (Reinbek, 1980), 49.

whose intellectuals were, exceptions notwithstanding, committed to a democratic and republican system of government, even if they disagreed about its precise meaning.[41]

An Intellectual Revolution

The generational "revolution" of the forty-fivers did not entail a personal denunciation of the older generation or subversion in the manner of the sixty-eighters. Indeed, forty-fivers have been criticized for their complicity in the silence after the war: unlike the sixty-eighters, they did not challenge their teachers and professors – the parents' generation – about their previous commitments.[42] The controversy among German historians about the wartime activities of the discipline's founding fathers was an aspect of the problem. The students of Werner Conze (1908–86) and Theodor Schieder (1908–84) – Hans-Ulrich Wehler and Wolfgang J. Mommsen, for example – were criticized for not calling them to account for their past lives.[43]

There were a number of reasons for this state of intergenerational relations in the 1950s. The extent of the complicity of the university teachers in the Nazi regime was often unknown and, in any case, it was more or less impossible to challenge, openly or even privately, a German university professor in the 1950s, such was their power and prestige. Moreover, the oedipal conflict between forty-fivers and their fathers was felt to have been rendered superfluous by the manifest discrediting of "the father" in the wake of the catastrophe that his generation had visited upon Germany and the world. Writing in 1965, the forty-fiver Karl Markus Michel (1929–2000) averred that "After 1945, the young men in Germany found only ruins. What the fathers had created was so odious that it made a mockery of any criticism. And the fathers themselves hardly appeared as great criminals, rather as pitiful objects of seduction, cowardly partakers, and willing victims of a crazy and barbarous

[41] Hans-Ulrich Wehler, "Zur Lage der Geschichtswissenschaft in der Bundesrepublik, 1949–1979," in his *Historische Sozialwissenschaft und Geschichtsschreibung* (Göttingen, 1980), 21–22; Klaus Schönhoven, "Aufbruch in die sozialliberale Ära: Zur Bedeutung der 6oer Jahre in der Geschichte der Bundesrepublik," *Geschichte und Gesellschaft*, 25 (1999), 123–45.

[42] Sibylle Hübner-Funk, *Loyalität und Verblendung. Hitlers Garanten der Zukunft als Träger der zweiten deutschen Demokratie* (Potsdam, 1998); Ralph Giordano, *Die zweite Schuld oder Von der Last Deutsche zu sein* (Hamburg, 1987); Gesine Schwan, *Politik und Schuld. Die zerstörerische Kraft des Schweigens* (Hamburg, 1997); Helm Stierlin, "Der Dialog zwischen den Generationen über die Nazizeit," in Barbara Heimannsberg and Christoph J. Schmidt, eds., *Das Kollektive Schweigen* (Cologne, 1992), 247–66.

[43] Franziska Augstein, "Schlangen in der Grube," *Frankfurter Allgemeine Zeitung* (September 14, 1998), 49; Volker Ullrich, "Späte Reue der Zunft," *Die Zeit* (September 17, 1998), 53; Hans-Ulrich Wehler, "In den Fußstapfen der kämpfenden Wissenschaft," *Frankfurter Allgemeine Zeitung* (January 4, 1999), 48; Götz Aly, "Stakkato der Vertreibung, Pizzikato der Entlastung," *Frankfurter Allgemeine Zeitung* (February 3, 1999), 46; Willi Oberkrome, "Historiker im 'Dritten Reich': Zum Stellenwert volkshistorischer Ansätze zwischen klassischer Politik- und neuer Sozialgeschichte," *Geschichte in Wissenschaft und Unterricht*, 2 (1999), 74–99.

system."[44] As the Mitscherliches noted, "there thus was no one to fight, no one to protest against."[45] Then there was the essential integrative function of discretion about the past in the 1950s. "Not a single university, local government, private factory, or business could have been reconstructed," noted the philosopher Hermann Lübbe (b. 1926), "if the dominant tone between colleagues, who had to cooperate with one another, had been an accusational 'how could you have...'"[46]

For these reasons, the struggle of the forty-fivers with the older generation was displaced to another sphere: German intellectual traditions. Never before did Germany undergo such soul-searching and *Traditionskritik* (critique of tradition).[47] The task was to identify and root out those intellectual traditions, discourses, ideologies, and political languages that had led to the "German Catastrophe." In their doctoral and habilitation dissertations in the 1950s and early 1960s, the forty-fivers tried to cleanse the country's intellectual traditions, either by their explicit criticism, as in Lübbe's critique of the "ideas of 1914," or by directly addressing recent events in the manner of Karl Dietrich Bracher's (b. 1922) study on the collapse of the Weimar Republic, Waldemar Besson's (1929–1971) survey of Württemberg in the Weimar Republic, and Ernst-Wolfgang Böckenförde's (b. 1931) review of the Roman Catholic Church on the eve of the Nazi seizure of power; or like the sociologists, who swapped the discredited domestic tools for methods and questions learned in England and the United States, where many of them spent time during the 1950s.[48] The sociologist M. Rainer Lepsius (b. 1927) spoke for many when he wrote that "It was important for me to deflate the traditional German modes of thought, which, moreover, were tainted by National Socialism."[49] In their different ways, the forty-fivers conducted what Wolfgang J. Mommsen (1930–2004) has described

[44] Karl Markus Michel, *Die Sprachlose Intelligenz* (Frankfurt, 1968), 71. This book is a collection of essays that appeared originally in *Kursbuch* between 1965 and 1967.

[45] Mitscherlich and Mitscherlich, *The Inability to Mourn*, 218.

[46] Hermann Lübbe, "Deutschland nach dem Nationalsozialismus 1945–1990. Zum politischen und akademischen Kontext des Falles Schneider alias Schwerte," in Helmut König, Wolfgang Kuhlmann, and Klaus Schwabe, eds., *Vertuschte Vergangenheit: Der Fall Schwerte und die NS-Vergangenheit der deutschen Hochschulen* (Munich, 1997), 202.

[47] Joachim Radkau, *Die deutsche Emigration in die USA. Ihr Einfluß auf die amerikanische Europapolitik, 1933–1945* (Düsseldorf, 1971), 57.

[48] Hermann Lübbe, *Politische Philosophie in Deutschland* (Basel, 1963); Wilhelm Hennis, "Zum Problem der deutschen Staatsanschauung," *Vierteljahreshefte für Zeitgeschichte*, 7 (1959), 1–13; Karl Dietrich Bracher, *Die Auflösung der Weimarer Republik* (Stuttgart, 1955); cf. Werner Conze's review of Karl Dietrich Bracher's book in *Historische Zeitschrift*, 183 (1957), 378–82; Waldemar Besson, *Württemberg und die deutsche Staatskrise, 1918–1933* (Stuttgart, 1959); Ernst-Wolfgang Böckenförde, *Der deutsche Katholizismus im Jahre 1933* (Basel, 1981); Ralf Dahrendorf, *Gesellschaft und Freiheit* (Munich, 1961).

[49] M. Rainer Lepsius, "Soziologie als angewandte Aufklärung," in Christian Fleck, ed., *Wege zur Soziologie nach 1945. Biographische Notizen* (Opladen, 1996), 188.

as their "revolution" against the intellectual roots of fascism, seeking to rupture the continuities that led to 1933.[50]

These studies are the origin of the discursive, post facto, debates about the nature of West German republicanism. In particular, their target was the conservative revolutionary thinking of the 1920s and 1930s with which their own teachers had sometimes been associated. As we will see, their criticisms of this tradition predisposed them to view the younger generation, the sixty-eighters, in the same light. For this reason, right-wing commentators, like Armin Mohler (the first historian and postwar defender of the conservative revolution)[51] and Günter Maschke, identified in this generation an unusually active group of intellectuals who have (unfortunately in their view) moved West Germany to the West. "This generation is the generation of critique for the sake of critique. Nothing of what has been painstakingly rebuilt is safe from its obsession with negation." Writing in 1965, Mohler attacked the "men under forty" as members of a "sour generation" who were disappointed by their Nazi elders. "This led to a false conclusion. Until then, they had believed in the Reich with all the limitlessness of their youth. From then on [1945], everything around them was sh____." "If it is not the best of all nations, then it must be the worst.... Nothing compares with the German crimes, not even closely – from a wounded national feeling arises a peculiar nationalism with a negative valence. German history is a tale of singular folly."[52]

Maschke, who in an earlier life gloried in the reputation as the "Dutschke of Vienna," became a national-conservative disciple of Carl Schmitt, and held the forty-fivers responsible for weakening German substance.[53] "This generation, too young to understand the punishment it received, became the victim of the world of community studies, the care packet, American scholarships for 'the science of democracy' (political science), and the legends of British parliament."[54] Maschke included those figures who in leftist circles were considered dangerous neoconservatives – Wilhelm Hennis (b. 1923), Hermann Lübbe, and Friedrich Tenbruck (1919–94).[55]

If the 1960s was the decade of "orientation crisis" when the tired social and political formulas of Wilhelmine Germany began to lose their tenability,

---

[50] Wolfgang J. Mommsen, "Gegenwärtige Tendenzen in der Geschichtsschreibung der Bundesrepublik," *Geschichte und Gesellschaft*, 8 (1981), 162.

[51] Armin Mohler, *Die Konservative Revolution in Deutschland, 1918–1932*, 2nd ed. (Darmstadt, 1972).

[52] Armin Mohler, *Was die Deutschen Fürchten* (Stuttgart, 1965), 133–36.

[53] For his youthful commitment to the New Left, see Günter Maschke, "Cubanische Taschenkalender," *Kursbuch*, 30 (December 1972), 129–47.

[54] Günter Maschke, "Die Verschwörung der Flakhelfer," in Hans-Joachim Arndt, ed., *Inferiorität als Staatsräson: Sechs Aufsätze zur Legitimität der BRD* (Krefeld, 1985), 93–118.

[55] Frank Niess, "Neue Rechte," in Sylvia Greiffenhagen and Martin Greiffenhagen, eds., *Handwörterbuch zur politischen Kultur der Bundesrepublik Deutschland* (Wiesbaden, 1981), 263–67.

and the culture was open for redefinition, answering the crisis was conducted largely by the forty-fivers.[56] One commentator called this generation the "first political generation" of the Federal Republic, because it was the bearer of the original federal republic consciousness and westernization, which occurred well before "1968."[57] He mentioned Bracher, Hermann Lübbe, M. Rainer Lepsius, and Wilhelm Hennis. He could have added other intellectuals who participated in forming the public culture of the republic, like the philosophers Hans Albert (b. 1921), Karl-Otto Apel (b. 1922), and Odo Marquard (b. 1928); historians Hans Buchheim (b. 1922), Arnulf Baring (b. 1932), Andreas Hillgruber (1925–89), Reinhart Koselleck (1923–2006), Hans-Ulrich Wehler (b. 1931), Hans Mommsen (b. 1930) and Wolfgang Mommsen (1930–2004), Eberhard Jäckel (b. 1929), Hermann Glaser (b. 1928), Helga Grebing (b. 1930), Ernst Nolte (b. 1923), and Gerhard A. Ritter (b. 1929); political scientists Peter Brückner (1922–83), Hans-Joachim Lieber (b. 1923), Thomas Ellwein (b. 1927), Helge Pross (1927–86), Harry Pross (b. 1923), Erwin Scheuch (1928–2003), Dieter Oberndörfer (b. 1929), Martin Greiffenhagen (b. 1928), Manfred Hättich (1925–2003), and Alexander Schwan (1931–1989); theologian Dorothee Sölle (1929–2003); Germanist Walter Jens (b. 1923); publishers and writers Rudolf Augstein (1923–2002) and Joachim Fest (1927–2006); writers Carl Amery (1922–2005), Rolf Hochhut (b. 1931), Heiner Müller (1929–85), Hans Magnus Enzensberger (b. 1929), Martin Walser (b. 1927), Christian Geissler (b. 1928), Siegfried Lenz (b. 1926), Gudrun Tempel (b. 1926), and Christa Wolf (b. 1929). This generation of journalists was also instrumental in liberalizing the public sphere in the later 1950s.[58]

Successful as the intellectual style of the forty-fivers' generational rebellion was in stabilizing and gradually reforming the republic, it also meant that the mental "base" on which the Nazi "superstructure" rested survived the rupture of 1945 largely intact. Schörken called it the *Kultur von rechts* (right-wing culture): patriarchal and hierarchical thinking, as well as the widespread "we identification" that made the 1950s the "authoritarian society" that it has been depicted as, notwithstanding the dynamism of its economy and incipient consumer culture. This last gasp of the culture of imperial Germany overlapped sufficiently with National Socialism to permit many Germans to support the Nazis without changing any of their convictions.

---

[56] Lutz Niethammer, "Stufen der historischen Selbsterforschung der Bundesrepublik Deutschland. Ein Forschungsessay," in Deutsches Institut für Fernstudien, Universität Tübingen, ed., *Nachkriegsjahre und Bundesrepublik Deutschland: Deutsche Geschichte Nach 1945*, part 1 (Tübingen, 1985), 23–34; Werner Klose, *Generation im Gleichschritt, die Hitlerjugend: Ein Dokumentarbericht*, rev. ed. (Oldenburg, 1982), 268–69.

[57] Klaus Naumann, "'Neuanfang ohne Tabus.' Deutscher Sonderweg und politische Semantik," *Blätter für deutsche und internationale Politik*, 4 (1994), 442–43.

[58] Christina von Hodenberg, "Mass Media and the Generation of Conflict: West Germany's Long Sixties and the Formation of a Critical Public Sphere," *Contemporary European History*, 15:3 (2006), 367–95.

Sixty-eighters and Forty-fivers

Lübbe agreed that "without doubt there was much mute narrow-mindedness and unchanged identification with the ideological orientations that enabled one to participate" in the Nazi regime. But he thought that the restoration of public morality in public institutions was decisive, because it initiated a long-term learning process: the point is not that there were scandals about ex-Nazis – post-totalitarian societies *always* have continuities from the past – but that scandals were possible in the first place.[59] Successful as the accommodation between the forty-fivers and older Germans proved to be, however, it was limited to the public world of politics and work, and not surprisingly Lübbe restricted his examples to these realms. Habermas, by contrast, recalled that in the sub-political niches of the family and *Stammtisch* (the regulars' table at the pub), the silent majority "remembered the sufferings of its own rather than those of its victims."[60] Morality, it appeared, was anything but restored in the private sphere. It is not difficult to see how the sixty-eighter generation, which was raised by this silent majority, and that was not a party to the unwritten contract of discretion between the forty-fivers and the older generations, deduced that West Germany was an immoral place.

The price to be paid for the missing "cleansing" in the second half of the 1940s, then, was the generational rebellion of "1968." The radicalism exhibited then was the result of real psychological damage caused by the intergenerational transfer of the psychological legacy of Nazism. The cost of the functionally necessary silence in the 1950s was the intergenerational transfer of the psychological consequences of pollution and stigma. To dismiss the sixty-eighters as confused middle-class revolutionaries fails to consider the reasons for their distrust of the Federal Republic.[61] They manifested one aspect of the country's legitimacy dilemma, that is, the blind spot in the culture of integrative republicanism in the 1950s.

The Structure of Political Emotions

To understand the real continuities that persisted in the Federal Republic and to which "1968" was a reaction requires careful differentiation. Gabriele Rosenthal shows that by late 1944 most of the forty-fivers she interviewed had given up the belief in "final victory" and that, paradoxically, it was the true believers, like Günter Grass, who had joined the Waffen SS, who made the cleanest break with the regime after 1945 because the collapse of their world demanded a systematic, critical reflection on their prior commitments. Here is an origin of

---

[59] Hermann Lübbe, "Verdrängung? Über eine Kategorie zur Kritik des deutschen Vergangenheitsverhältnisses," in Bad Homburg Forum für Philosophie, ed., *Zerstörung des moralischen Selbstbewußtseins: Chance oder Gefährdung?* (Frankfurt, 1988), 220–21.

[60] Jürgen Habermas, "On How Postwar Germany Has Faced Its Recent Past," *Common Knowledge*, 5 (Fall 1996), 7–8.

[61] Michael Burleigh, "Habitus Corpus," *Times Literary Supplement* (March 29, 1996), 5–6.

the redemptive republican reaction.[62] Redemptive republicanism appealed to those young Germans who felt guilty about their own former commitment to, or association with, the Nazi regime and who wanted to comport themselves in good conscience toward the new situation, confident that they had found the moral and historical answer to fascism. It also appealed to those who had not been committed to the regime, like Jürgen Habermas, who were shocked at the enormity of the Holocaust and by the absent contrition of Germans afterward. Although these mostly leftist young Germans linked Nazism and the Holocaust to perceived pathologies in modernity, they viewed their own country and the German educated middle class (*Bildungsbürgerturm*) as incarnating these pathologies in a particularly virulent way. They became most suspicious of "the German" element in their own selves and their immediate environment and committed themselves to universal values that stood above national traditions. Redemptive republicanism tended to postnationalism among the forty-fivers.

For the damaged subject, like Christoph Oehler (b. 1929), whose father had been the curator of the Nietzsche Archive in Frankfurt and an active Nazi, the attraction of a new beginning was the chance of regenerating the self that had been polluted by the Nazi regime.[63] The conversion moment in redemptive republicanism paralleled the need for a personal conversion of the subject and a new beginning. The leftist jurist Jürgen Seifert went so far as to write of the "Hitler in ourselves" and of his struggle to recognize that Hitler in his own person.[64] With reference to men like Peter von Oertzen, who had been a committed Nazi officer during the war and had turned to Marxism thereafter, the leftist sociologist Oskar Negt (b. 1934) thought that 1945 "was the end of all security, and whoever searched for answers that pointed to the future had to win distance from the destroyed world of his dreams and ideals that lively critique and reflection releases."[65]

The longtime member of the Institute for Social Research in Frankfurt, Ludwig von Friedeburg wrote in similar terms. His father had been a Nazi admiral in the Second World War who committed suicide in its final days, and he was himself a submarine officer and responsible for the commission of the last submarine from the Kiel shipyards. Reflecting on his youth, he wrote that "I

---

[62] "Warum ich nach sechzig Jahren mein Schweigen breche," Günter Grass in an interview with Frank Schirrmacher und Hubert Spiegel, *Frankfurter Allgemeine Zeitung* (August 11, 2006); Günter Grass, "Schreiben nach Auschwitz," in his *Nachdenken über Deutschland*, vol. 1, ed. Dietmar Keller (Berlin, 1990); Gabriele Rosenthal, *Die Hitler-Jugend Generation: Biographische Thematisierung als Vergangenheitsbewältigung* (Essen, 1986), 54, 97–99, 317, 370. These findings corroborate those of the Mitscherliches, *Die Unfähigkeit zu Trauern*, 252.

[63] Christoph Oehler, "Erinnerungen an Theodor W. Adorno und Max Horkheimer," in Klaus F. Geiger, ed., *Einblicke Ausblicke. Eine Festschrift für Ingrid Haller* (Cassell, 1996), 58–66.

[64] Jürgen Seifert, "Der lange Weg, Hitler in mir zu überwinden. Ein Gespräch," *Vorgänge*, 1 (1984), 34–42.

[65] Oskar Negt, "Radikalität und Augenmass. Zur Denkweise eines sozialistischen Grenzgängers zwischen Politik und Wissenschaft," in Jürgen Seifert, Heinz Thörner, and Klaus Wettig, eds., *Soziale oder Sozialistische Demokratie? Beiträge zur Geschichte der Linken in der Bundesrepublik* (Marburg, 1989), 42.

learned very early on to look away." Although he was not directly implicated in war crimes, and although he recognized that only a minority of the millions of *Wehrmacht* shot civilians, he found all guilty for making such crimes objectively possible by their service to the regime. It was difficult to face up to this objective guilt, and "it has taken me decades [to face this past], and I am tempted constantly to find apologetic explanations. Without the help of others, it is very difficult to face the truth."[66] He had no doubt that he had, in fact, found "the truth." Redemptive republicans were not nominalists. They did not argue that Germans should talk about the Nazi past in order to explore its implications. They already knew the answer, and it was not the Federal Republic as founded in 1949. It is easy to see the affinity of this psychology with the Protestant tradition of inner examination and concomitant emphasis on conversion and the maintenance of faith in a particular vision.

They experienced "the restoration" as Dirks and Kogon did, and they gritted their teeth in the dark years (as they remember it) of the Adenauer chancellorship. And they poured scorn on the other members of their generation who they did not think had moved beyond their youthful loyalties. "I grew up with the special [Nazi] announcements ringing in my ear," recalled Günter Grass. "I always succumbed to the rapture of the [military] successes. Toughness that was measured exclusively by military achievements became the favorite idea of my generation."[67] Habermas was bitterly disappointed in the largely negative reaction of many of his cohort to the student movement, noting that the students had reacted more politically to the Vietnam War than "we older ones reacted to that national incubus [*Ungeist*] during the first two decades after the end of the war."[68]

Whereas redemptive republicanism sought rupture and regeneration, integrative republicanism based the new state on positive cultural and intellectual continuities, whether that of the German cultural nation or liberalism. These forty-fivers, while recognizing the criminality of the regime, did not feel personally guilty, and therefore rejected von Friedeburg's "truth." They did not think that German history had come to an end and needed fundamental reconstruction. While they engaged in thoroughgoing critiques of German intellectual history to isolate the perceived bacillus that had led to Nazism, they sought to rehabilitate German traditions.

In order to explain the bitterness of intellectual conflict and the hysterical fears of the left or right, it is important to highlight the existential importance of these political languages for these thinkers. The interpretative lenses they borrowed from their university teachers were their sources of moral and political

---

[66] Ludwig von Friedeburg, "Zur Eröffnung der Ausstellung 'Vernichtungskrieg, Verbrechen der Wehrmacht, 1941–1944," speech in Kiel, January 1, 1999.

[67] Günter Grass, "Vom Ritterkreuz und von der Wut über den zu verlierenden Milchpfennig," in Freimut Duve, ed., *Die Restauration entlässt ihre Kinder oder der Erfolg der Rechten in der Bundesrepublik* (Reinbeck, 1968), 71–74.

[68] Jürgen Habermas, *Philosopish-politische Profile* (Frankfurt, 1971), 10.

orientation during the years of perplexity after the war. They functioned as "cultural ideologies" to which the forty-fivers "converted," because they solved their personal and political crises by offering all-encompassing explanations for the past, analyses of the present, and perspectives for the future. For this generation, visions of the past and of republicanism were of existential significance. As John E. Toews described for the young Hegelians, the particular system of meaning offered a form of personal salvation. The forty-fivers solved their own problems attempting to institutionalize "true" republicanism in West Germany.[69]

The forty-fivers' relationship with their teachers was therefore of paramount importance. These teachers were the men (it was mostly men), often returned emigrants, like Theodor W. Adorno (1903–69), Max Horkheimer (1885–1973), Helmut Plessner (1892–1985), Ernst Fraenkel (1898–1975), Siegfried Landshut (1897–1968), Hans Rothfels (1891–1976), Wolfgang Abendroth (1906–85), and René König (1906–92), and, in London, Karl Popper (1902–94) but also Germans who had remained, like Joachim Ritter (1903–74) and Gerhard Ritter (1888–1967), Theodor Schieder, Werner Conze, and Rudolf Smend (1882–1975), who offered the forty-fivers the intellectual tools with which to free themselves from their Hitler Youth formation and make their own way.

The political languages of the forty-fivers were learned at the feet of such men, but they cut their own path, and one should not draw mechanical lines of continuity: Hans Mommsen was no national conservative like his teacher, Rothfels, nor did Iring Fetscher and Andreas Flitner share the politics of their mentor, Eduard Spranger. Finally, there is the importance of the "America" or "England" experience for this generation, which made it consistently "Western" in outlook. Important as they were as examples of functioning democracies, one should not assume that the forty-fivers took on board automatically the Anglophone way of politics and methodology. Wilhelm Hennis, for instance, always rejected "American Social Science," as he put it.

A Republican Consensus

These political languages articulated the underlying structure about memory of the German past because they were inscribed into the national subjectivity of Germans. Nowhere had the collective ego ideal been compromised more starkly than in postwar Germany. The extent of the Nazi crimes committed by Germans in the name of Germany made such an implication inescapable. Germany's "chosen trauma" produced two diametrically opposed reactions. One reaction, which underwrote redemptive republicanism, regarded German national subjectivity as irredeemably polluted, and sought to construct a political community cleansed of national ideals and values. The radicalism of this project should not be underestimated. It was to recast Germans as essentially

---

[69] Toews, *Hegelianism*, 89–90; Carl Schorske portrays Theodore Herzl's "conversion" to Zionism in similar terms. See his *Fin-de-Siècle Vienna: Culture and Politics* (New York, 1980), 159.

non-German, that is, as European citizens of a republic, cut off from their pre-Nazi history. The social theorists who have devised metanarratives to clothe their moral impulse call such an identity "postconventional," that is, "postnational." Where it identified traces of negative continuity, it engaged in rituals of purification.

The alternative reaction of integrative republicanism was defensive. It was to protect the integrity of the national ideal by ascribing the causes of the disaster to another source. It devised metanarratives of its own to ensure that German nationality was not stigmatized. German history before 1945 will be shown not to have been a one-way street to 1933 or 1941. Such stories were designed to permit Germans to retain basic trust in one another and their history, and therefore to feel good about being German despite the Nazism and the Holocaust.[70]

The two subjectivities formed a symbiosis as rival identity projects that presupposed the existence of the other. The nationalist one advanced its case against the antinationalist one, and vice versa. Without the redemptive republican suspicion of national traditions, they would not need explicit defending. But without the moral shock of the Holocaust, such radical suspicion would not have arisen. Postwar German collective identities were inherently structured along these fissures of national subjectivity. For that reason, controversies about the past did not recede into oblivion, irrespective of consensus about the country's political institutions.

The political dimension of the consensus that developed over decades was, as the liberals always had it, the Federal Republic as a liberal and democratic state. Its moral dimension was the new beginning demanded by redemptive republicans. It was able to develop because neither language of republicanism was able to impose itself, leading to a gradual discursive moral refoundation of the polity within the institutional structures of 1949. The Federal Republic needed both dispositions, because it was functionally necessary to integrate the largely Nazified population into the new order, which would have been impossible had the majority of the forty-fivers attempted an antifascist revolution after the war. The new state could not be made on the basis of redemptive republicanism. But neither, in the long run, could it be made without it.

---

[70] For example, see Alfons Heck, *The Burden of the Hitler Legacy* (Frederick, Colo., 1988).

4

The German German

The Integrative Republicanism of Wilhelm Hennis

Wilhelm Hennis is one of the Federal Republic's most prominent political thinkers, best known in the English-speaking world for his books and articles on Max Weber.[1] He has been a pugnacious commentator on political events and theory since the 1950s and is regarded as one of the "grand old men" of the country as a whole. An integrative republican from the outset of the new state, he was also a "German German" who developed an account of the nation's past that rescued its traditions from moral pollution.

Born into a Protestant horticultural family in Hildesheim in 1923, Wilhelm Hennis did not have a typical German childhood. He spent five years in Venezuela (1933–38), where his father, disaffected with the new political situation in Germany, accepted the offer of the Venezuelan president to establish a silkworm industry. Instead of mixing with his *Volksgenossen* (German comrades) in the *Jungvolk* (the Hitler Youth for ten- to fourteen-year-olds), he attended primary school with the locals and emigrant Jewish children from Germany. Still, as there were no secondary schools there and because his family set enough store on a proper German education, they returned to Germany in 1938. Hennis senior may not have liked the regime but not enough to prevent him and his family from living in Nazi Germany

The younger Hennis likewise had an ambivalent relationship to Nazi Germany. On the return journey from South America, he visited the biennale in Venice, where he was put off by the "degenerate" art of Europe, to which he saw German art as a healthy antidote. And he shared with his compatriots the national enthusiasm about the "liberation" and "repatriation" of ethnic Germans who were brought into the Reich by Hitler's foreign policy successes in 1938.[2] Yet, at his Protestant boarding school in Dresden, he sought to preserve himself from the danger of "inner damage," as he later expressed it, by

---

[1] Wilhelm Hennis, *Max Weber: Essays in Reconstruction* (London 1988).
[2] He candidly admits these adolescent reactions in "Begegnung mit moderner Kunst," *Göttinger Universitäts-Zeitung*, 12 (June 21, 1946), 9–10.

immersing himself in literature and art. Oswald Spengler was popular at the
time, and Hennis read *Jahre der Entscheidung* (Years of Decision) as a sixteen-
year-old. "I lived at such a level of abstraction that the little things like 'service,'
the 'parade,' and the *Jungvolk* group did not count for me."[3] Like many other
scions of the educated middle class (*Bildungsbürgertum*), he turned to the elitist cultural criticism of Jakob Burckhardt, Spengler, and Nietzsche to maintain
distance from the "masses" and the plebeian vulgarity of the Nazis.[4] Hennis
was typical of many educated members of his generation: retaining an elitist
skepticism of the Nazis, but sharing a basic national orientation.

He gladly served in the navy to which he was called up in 1942. But he
listened when he could to foreign radio, and he rejected an offer to serve as a
Nazi political attaché while he was the assistant to an admiral. This decision
resulted in disciplinary action and ultimate transfer to front duty, where he was
later indicted on spurious charges of dereliction of duty, proceedings that were
ended only by the capitulation of Germany in April 1945. He had no reason to
love the regime, and he experienced the end of the war as a liberation. Half of
his classmates did not return from the front, and none from the parallel class at
the government grammar school. Males born in 1923 were among the hardest
hit by the war.[5] "We had survived... it was good to be alive." A few months
later, after early release from Allied captivity, he enrolled in law and history at
Göttingen University at the tender age of twenty-two.[6]

What lessons did Hennis learn from his three years of military experience
and the catastrophic consequences of the regime? Because he felt he had maintained an inner distance to the regime, his political world did not collapse,
and he felt morally intact as an individual and as a patriotic German. Indeed,
the basic assumptions of his reading and milieu had been confirmed. In the last
months of the war, as military proceedings hung over his head, he was comforted
by Karl Jaspers's *Max Weber: Deutsches Wesen im politischen Denken, im
Forschen und Philosophieren* (Max Weber: German Essence in Political Thinking, Research, and Philosophizing), a book that Jaspers wrote to wean German
youth from "their confused and wrongheaded jabbering" and win them for

---

[3] Oswald Spengler, *Jahre der Entscheidung. Deutschland und die Weltgeschichtliche Entwicklung* (Munich, 1933); Wilhelm Hennis, "Politikwissenschaft als Beruf: 'Erzählte Erfahurng' eines
Fünfundziebzigjährigen," *Freiburger Universitätsblätter*, 140 (July 1998), 28, 31. Reprinted in
his *Regieren im modernen Staat. Politikwissenschaftliche Abhandlungen* (Tübingen, 1999), 381–
445.

[4] Cf. Iring Fetscher (b. 1922), "Reflexionen über meine geistige Entwicklung," in his *Arbeit und
Spiel. Essays zur Kulturkritik und Sozialphilosophie* (Stuttgart, 1983), 5. Hans Albert (b. 1921)
was also taken by Spengler as a young man.

[5] Of men born in 1923, 37 percent (243,810) died during the war. The most decimated in per-
centage terms were those born in 1921 (38.95 percent). See Bernhard B. Kroener, "Die per-
sonelle Resourcen des Dritten Reiches im Spannungsfeld zwischen Wehrmacht, Bürokratie und
Kriegswirtschaft, 1939–1942," in Militärgeschichtliches Forschungsamt, ed., *Das Deutsche Reich
und der Zweite Weltkrieg* (Stuttgart, 1988), 986.

[6] Wilhelm Hennis, "Man lebte noch...," in Werner Filmer and Heribert Schwan, eds., *Mensch,
der Krieg ist aus. Zeitzeugen erinnern sich* (Düsseldorf, 1985), 174–79.

Weber's sobriety.[7] Hennis was nothing if not sober, a posture he combined with an aesthetic irony in the face of a bourgeois world that had seemingly come to an end. He felt able to distinguish between a perceived "good Germany," which he thought he represented, and its perversion in National Socialism. Though well aware of the criminality of the regime, he thought "reeducation" was unnecessary.[8] In this regard, he differed from those who had been devoted to the regime. They were psychologically obliged to direct their libidinal energies elsewhere, and the United States often offered a suitable object of uncritical attraction.[9] The experience of being delivered up to forces around and above him had convinced Hennis that he must lead a politically responsible life. The importance of leadership and judgment had also been impressed upon him, as had a nascent distrust of the irrationality of the large crowds he had experienced in seaports during the war.

How did he deal with personal continuities from the past? Nearly all students at German universities in the immediate postwar years had been in the army, and in those desperate years many wore old uniforms with the markings removed. It was an unwritten rule among them not to talk about their recent experiences.[10] Hennis felt especially indebted to his university teachers who represented the Germany with which he identified. This sympathy was naturally directed to his "revered teacher" Rudolf Smend, but it extended also to the likes of constitutional theorists Ernst Forsthoff (1902–74) and Ernst-Rudolf Huber (1903–90), who, at least for a while, had been active supporters of the Nazi regime and had gained academic positions as students of the regime theorist Carl Schmitt.[11] Such men incarnated for the young Hennis the tortured soul of Germany itself, shining beacons of Central European intellectual culture, erring in their search for their nation's rightful place in Europe. There had to be room for such men in the new Germany.[12] There was no need for patricide. As we will see, this was a posture that someone like Jürgen Habermas was unable to share. But there were limits. Like Habermas, Hennis did not extend his sympathy to Carl Schmitt himself, who was seen as an enemy of the new republic.[13]

---

[7] Wilhelm Hennis, "Politikwissenschaft als Disziplin. Zum Weg der politischen Wissenschaft nach 1945," *Neue Politische Literatur*, 3 (1999), 3; Karl Jaspers, *Max Weber. Deutsches Wesen im politischen Denken, im Forschen und Philosophieren* (Olbenburg, 1932); Jaspers to Hannah Arendt, January 3, 1933, in *Hannah Arendt/Karl Jaspers Correspondence, 1926–1969*, ed. Lotte Kohler and Hans Saner, trans. Robert Kimber and Rita Kimber (New York, 1985), 17.

[8] Hennis, "Man lebte noch," 178.

[9] Hans-Ulrich Wehler, "Historiography in Germany Today," in Jürgen Habermas, ed., *Observations on the "Spiritual Situation of the Age*," trans. Andrew Buchwalter (Cambridge, Mass., 1985), 255n25.

[10] Hennis, "Politikwissenschaft als Beruf."

[11] Huber replaced Professor Schücking in Kiel, and Forsthoff ousted Hermann Heller in Frankfurt. See Joseph W. Bendersky, *Carl Schmitt: Theorist for the Reich* (Princeton, N.J., 1983), 203. On Huber, see Ralf Walkenhaus, *Konservatives Staatsdenken. Eine wissenssoziologische Studie zu Ernst Rudolf Huber* (Berlin, 1997).

[12] See Martin Greiffenhagen, *Jahrgang 1928. Aus einem unruhigem Leben* (Munich, 1988) for Huber's candor about his past with the forty-fiver Greiffenhagen.

[13] Hennis, "Politikwissenschaft als Disziplin."

University Studies and Intellectual Influences

Hennis had two aims in his studies. To learn the law – an interest sparked by his brush with military caprice – and to read everything he could by Max Weber. His leading question was that of the forty-fivers generally, namely: "How could the collapse of 1933 have occurred... and how could one prevent it occurring again?... What did one have to do to place the new democratic order on a stable footing?"[14] Hennis studied with the constitutional theorist Smend and supplemented his reading with Anglo-American literature at vacation courses in Oxford in 1948 (which he attended with the historian Annelise Timm, who later immigrated to Canada)[15] and 1950, and twice at Salzburg courses on American studies. After completing his dissertation and law exams in 1951, Hennis became the first academic assistant in the German Bundestag with Adolf Arndt, the legal expert of the Social Democratic Party.[16] In the summer of 1952, he was invited to the Harvard International Seminar for four months by Henry Kissinger, and he toured the country visiting the leading departments of political science, where he met many luminaries of the German academic emigration: Leo Strauss, Eric Voegelin, Carl Joachim Friedrich, Franz Neumann, and Otto Kirchheimer. As he had during his England sojourn, he saw in the host country a functioning democracy, but unlike some of his generational cohort, he did not think that Germans should copy American social science.[17] In March 1953 he became the academic assistant of the Social Democratic politician and political scientist Carlo Schmid at the University of Frankfurt, where he was a neighbor of the Institute for Social Research ("the Frankfurt School"). After completing his habilitation thesis, he took up a professorship in Hamburg from 1962 to 1967, before being called to Freiburg in 1968, where he has remained ever since.

What intellectual and political project did Hennis develop during these years? How did he analyze the mistakes of the past? Which traditions were to blame? How did he propose to make a republic out of a population of monarchists and ex-Nazis? What was the key to making democracy succeed this time? What, indeed, did Hennis mean by democracy, and what were its elements? How much would Germany have to change? What would provide the glue that held this new experiment together? These questions can be answered by examining the intellectual traditions that formed Hennis's worldview and by tracing how he used these traditions to answer the generational question of the forty-fivers.

---

[14] Ibid., 13; cf. Hennis, "Politikwissenschaft als Beruf," 44: "My basic experience remained the failure of Weimar; that could not be permitted to recur."

[15] Annelise Thimme, "Geprägt von der Geschichte. Eine Außenseiterin," in Hartmut Lehmann and Otto Gerhard Oexle, eds., *Erinnerungsstücke. Wege in die Vergangenheit* (Vienna, Cologne, and Weimar, 1998), 153–224.

[16] Dieter Gosewinkel, *Adolf Arndt* (Frankfurt, 1990).

[17] Hennis, "Politikwissenschaft als Beruf," 42. The forty-fivers spent a lot of time in the United States, but they brought back different lessons. Compare, for example, Dieter Oberndörfer, Hartmut von Hentig, and Horst Ehmke.

Hennis's ideas were compounded of materials from many sources. In addition to Weber and Burckhardt, it is possible to identify three formative influences: Smend, Joseph Schumpeter, and Siegfried Landshut. They provided him with not only the concepts and categories but also the personal models of intellectual engagement.

In Hennis's first year at university, the German translation of Joseph Schumpeter's (1883–1950) *Capitalism, Socialism and Democracy* appeared, and it was read with "great fascination" in Smend's seminar. Hennis understood it, especially its final section, as an extension of Weber's theory of democracy, which he regarded as the most plausible.[18] On this exegesis, the classical theories of democracy, which posited that a unified people's will was supposed to be expressed by democratic government, were anachronistic because no such will could be identified under modern conditions. The increasing complexity of these conditions had rendered economic and social processes inexplicable for the majority of citizens who had no direct control over or responsibility for them. Largely ignorant of national and international affairs, they yielded easily to irrationalism and the grand simplifiers who sought to manipulate them.

Schumpeter proposed a theory of democracy that replaced the notion of direct representation with its mediation by political parties that competed with one another for governmental power. He drew on the antiliberal theories of elites such as Gustave Le Bon, Georges Sorel, Vilfredo Pareto, and Robert Michels in order to develop a conception of democracy that he thought could survive in an age when liberal democracies had fallen throughout Europe.[19] Political parties were the creatures of informed and engaged political elites, and Schumpeter held such parties to be the key factor in stable democratic regimes because they provided the continuity of the tradition that restrained both the state and labile population. They *were* the political nation and leaders of civil society who stood against the state and guaranteed the constitution of liberty. The difference between England and Germany, Schumpeter thought, following Weber, was the lack in the latter of an elite that was prepared to put its stamp on the polity. Germany possessed "no class or group whose members looked upon politics as their predestined career."[20] And such a class was needed in a democracy, because the experience of the majority of the population was profoundly unpolitical, limited as it was to local rather than national experience.

The problem of political experience was likewise a concern of Rudolf Smend (1882–1975). During the Weimar period, he developed an organic theory of the constitution to move beyond both the "pure law" theory of Hans Kelsen and the radical emphasis on state sovereignty of Carl Schmitt. Like Schmitt, he was

---

[18] Wilhelm Hennis, "Integration durch Verfassung? Rudolf Smend und die Zugänge zum Verfassungsproblem nach 50 Jahren unter dem Grundgesetz," *Juristische Zeitschrift*, 10 (1999), 1–20, 19n29. Reprinted in his *Regieren im modernen Staat*, 367–68.

[19] See the discussion in Jerry Z. Muller, ed., *Conservatism: An Anthology of Social and Political Thought from David Hume to the Present* (Princeton, N.J., 1997), 223, 275.

[20] Joseph Schumpeter, *Capitalism, Socialism and Democracy*, 3rd ed. (London, 1950), 291.

a conservative who was deeply disturbed by the fragmentation of national life wrought by modernity. The ever-increasing differentiation of capitalist society had ruptured the unified experience that subjects or citizens once possessed of their common life, distancing them from the vital sources of social renewal. How were states that the people experienced as foreign and even alienating to command popular loyalty? Such concerns were not limited to conservatives. Writing in the late 1930s from the safety and stability of England, Karl Mannheim confessed that once he had not entertained "much hope of learning anything from a study of the liberal and democratic countries, for he involuntarily shared the feeling prevalent in Central Europe that the democratic system had run its course."[21]

Unlike Schmitt, Smend argued that the state should integrate civil society, rather than remain sovereignly neutral above it. The state was not an autonomous coercive force, but a unified "value totality," and the individual was integrated into it to the extent that he or she experienced it as an "essential moment." But because it was impossible for the modern individual to possess an overview of this value totality, integration took place at the level of symbols, like flags, national festivals, and state leaders, which afforded the opportunity for "intensive experience."[22] Thus in 1928 Smend had no hesitation in claiming that fascism was "the great gold mine" (*Fundgrube*) of insights into the phenomena of integration, "independent of its value and future."[23] In an article published in 1943, Smend dropped the reference to fascism but declared that the urgent task remained the winning back of the lost original social unity because it remedied the "sickness unto death" and "yearning for experience" of isolated, romantic subjectivity, which was dissipated in the private sphere of sport clubs, conversation, and radio listening, instead of being directed toward the "value totality" of the state. "I need not emphasize how much this is the conscious intention of the German present," he added diplomatically.[24]

Vulnerable as Smend's theory was to a collapse into fascism, it was considered modern and innovative because his state, like that of Hobbes, was based only on the will of its members, and not on an ontologically privileged source, like God, a race, a language, or geography. In this sense, Smend was a radically immanent, even norm-free thinker. Unlike many contemporary constitutional theorists, he was concerned with the effective, as opposed to the written, formal constitution. The real constitution was the ensemble of factors that contributed to the political integration of society, and these factors should be the object of political and constitutional inquiry. Influenced by Ernst Renan's dictum that a nation is a "daily performed plebiscite," Smend argued that the viability of a

---

[21] Karl Mannheim, *Man and Society in an Age of Reconstruction* (New York, 1940), 5.

[22] Rudolf Smend, "Verfassung und Verfassungsrecht," in his *Staatsrechtliche Abhandlungen und andere Aufsätze*, 2nd ed. (Berlin, 1968), 163.

[23] Ibid., 141, 157.

[24] Rudolf Smend, "Politisches Erlebnis und Staatsdenken seit dem 18. Jahrhundert," in *Staatsrechtliche Abhandlungen*, 360.

state rested not on its appeal to transcendent values or on its independence from civil society, but in its successful attraction of "social forces" to the common life of the state.[25] The state existed only to the extent that it could reproduce itself. The theory of integration, then, was oriented to practical politics rather than model building or abstract theorizing.[26]

The problem with Smend's integration theory was, as he later admitted, that if the form of the state was in principle open and not informed by norms or purposes beyond itself, it contained no barriers to fascist techniques of integration.[27] Moreover, despite its dialectical pretensions, the theory entailed an undialectical effacing of individual subjectivity by its passive incorporation into the totality of the state, which was always privileged as the authentic site of meaning and orientation. Integration was, in fact, a synonym for the legitimation of rule (*Herrschaft*).[28] Unlike Schmitt, however, Smend was not encumbered by a *völkisch* preoccupation that could hinder integration. For this reason, Smend admired France, which he considered the most modern of nation-states, because it assimilated the Alsatians, while Germany marginalized perceived "imperial enemies."[29] Consequently, he left the right-wing Deutsche Nationale Volkspartei in 1930 after Alfred Hugenberg sought to move it in an outright authoritarian direction, and he defended the Weimar constitution, including its controversial social rights, against Carl Schmitt, as the only means available for integrating the nation and making it a "living unity."

Only days before the Nazi seizure of power, Smend delivered an address to the students and faculty of Berlin University on the occasion of the sixty-second anniversary of the foundation of the German Reich in 1871. There he echoed the widespread feeling at the time that crass egoism and interest politics were sundering the nation. But he also told the students, many of whom were ardent Nazis, that they did not take account of the emancipatory dimension of the "bourgeois epoch." In a barb aimed at Schmitt, he recalled that the "bourgeois world" had also transformed them from subjects (*Untertanen*) into citizens. The anarchism of bourgeois life found its correction in the national idea and its realization in 1871, which gave the bourgeoisie the focus of unity and ethical (*sittliche*) commitment beyond its own narrow interests. The national mission of securing an appropriate place for Germany in Europe had been badly damaged by the Versailles Peace Treaty, he regretted, but it was up to the students to commit themselves to its repair rather than lose themselves "in the absorptive, religious-like pretensions of the great political movements."[30] It was no surprise

[25] Ernest Renan, "What Is a Nation?" in H. K. Bhabba, ed., *Nation and Narration* (London, 1990), 8–23.

[26] Smend, "Verfassung und Verfassungsrecht," 122.

[27] Rudolf Smend, "Integrationslehre," in *Staatsrechtliche Abhandlungen*, 474–81.

[28] Smend, "Verfassung und Verfassungsrecht," 150.

[29] Hennis, "Integration durch Verfassung?" 380.

[30] Rudolf Smend, "Bürger und Bourgeois im deutschen Staatsrecht," in *Staatsrechtliche Abhandlungen*, 309–26.

that Schmitt later replaced Smend in his professorial chair in Berlin, forcing him to Göttingen.[31]

Smend enjoyed enormous prestige after the war, partly because he was perceived to be a victim of the Nazi regime, although a transfer to a chair at Göttingen hardly counted as persecution. But his postwar writings did betray a marked liberalization and moral sensitivity that was more appealing to many forty-fivers than the sermonizing of a Karl Jaspers in Heidelberg.[32] In his open lecture to the students of Göttingen University as its rector in the winter semester of 1945–46, Smend sought to remedy the normative deficit of his integration theory by identifying the vulnerability of Germany to fascism in his "fathers' and grandfathers' generation" of political thinkers. They had forgotten that the state was not simply a power apparatus for the implementation of capricious policies, but a just order under law. Jakob Burckhardt's portrait of the Renaissance state marked this decline, but it was Max Weber, so Smend argued, who brought the tradition of amoral politics into twentieth-century German thought. To be sure, Weber also had accurately analyzed the problematic, apolitical character of German political culture, dominated as it was by the bureaucratic rather than by the political-democratic type of elite.[33] But in seeking to develop a democratic-political ethic of his own in the well-known "ethics of responsibility," Smend continued, Weber had gone too far. For by completely separating power from ethics and making the former the realm of demons to which one had to sell one's soul, he made it possible for power to be worshiped in its own right and for it to be wielded without limit.[34]

A year later, Smend made the same criticism of Lutheranism because it denied Christianity the right to develop an ethic of public life, thereby abetting the amorality of politics and the passivity of the population.[35] The problem for Germany today was that "the collapse of the German Reich in so much filth and guilt" increased the feeling of skepticism, indeed the "nearly nihilistic rejection" of participation in the new state. How, then, were the Germans to "find the correct path back" to the combination of ethics (*Sittlichkeit*) and politics? The English balance of ethics and necessity offered an example. The task today, he

---

[31] Peter Caldwell, *Popular Sovereignty and the Crisis of German Constitutional Law: The Theory and Practice of Weimar Constitutionalism* (Durham and London, 1997), 142–44.

[32] On Jaspers as a moral figure, see Anson Rabinbach, "The German as Pariah: Karl Jaspers's *The Question of German Guilt*," in his *In the Shadow of Catastrophe: German Intellectuals between Apocalypse and Enlightenment* (Berkeley, 1997), 127–65.

[33] Smend referred to Weber's article on the passivity of German people after 1900 in "Parliament and Government in the New Germany," which appears as an appendix in Günther Roth and Claus Wittich, eds., *Economy and Society* (New York, 1968); Joseph Schumpeter, "Das soziale Antlitz des Deutschen Reiches," in his *Aufsätze zur Soziologie* (Tübingen, 1953), 214–25.

[34] Raymond Aron made the same criticism of Weber in his "Max Weber and Power-Politics," in Otto Stammer, ed., *Max Weber and Sociology Today* (New York, 1971), 83–132. In this regard, Weber and Schumpeter shared common ground.

[35] Rudolf Smend, "Unsere Einordnung in die Ökumene," *Göttinger Universitäts-Zeitung*, 2 (December 20, 1946), 2–4.

concluded briefly, "certainly concerns democracy, but above all it concerns a new, political basic posture that can carry it."[36]

Hennis listened carefully to Smend's speech, and although he did not initially share the criticism of Weber, he was impressed enough to want to become his student. As might be expected, Smend's seminars were essentially a criticism of the positivist turn in German constitutional thinking since the middle of the nineteenth century.[37] It was the formalism of legal positivism that had turned attention away from the political realities of the constitution toward a conception of the state as a sovereign legal personality beyond ethical standards. Positivism and the concomitant "inner alienation of the humanity of the German nineteenth century from the political world," Smend taught, were particularly German.[38]

Hennis held his first presentation in Smend's seminar on Karl Löwith's celebrated article "Weber and Marx" and on Siegfried Landshut's (1897–1968) *Kritik der Soziologie*. The latter author was to be of great importance to Hennis. The German Jewish political theorist was a veteran of the First World War and afterward had studied with the stars of German philosophy and sociology. But his Jewish ancestry and uncompromising attacks on positivist sociology had led to the rejection of his habilitation thesis in 1928 and his expulsion from Hamburg University in 1933. After living a threadbare existence in Egypt and Palestine for eighteen years, he was invited back to Hamburg in 1951 to a chair in political science, a position that he occupied until his retirement in 1967.[39]

Landshut was such an important although regrettably neglected figure that he is worth treating in some detail. He represented an important tradition in German thought that Hennis continued in the postwar period. What appears to be the influence of, say, Hannah Arendt on Hennis's thought was, in fact, that of Landshut. In an early seminar with Smend, Hennis read Landshut's 1925 essay, "Über einige Grundbegriffe der Politik" (On Some Basic Concepts of Politics), which moved him to study politics rather than the law. The article represented, he adjudged later, "essentially the new beginning of political science [*wissenschaftliche Politik*] in Germany."[40] It also reinforced Hennis's understanding of modernity as an epoch of alienation from the wellsprings of political life. This kind of analysis allowed him to identify the origins of Germany's historical problems in general European problems.

---

[36] Rudolf Smend, "Staat und Politik," in *Staatsrechtliche Abhandlungen*, 363–79. See also his "Zwischen den Jahren," *Göttinger Universitäts-Zeitung*, 3 (January 10, 1946), 1.

[37] Hennis, "Integration durch Verfassung?" 379.

[38] Ibid., 377.

[39] Rainer Nicolaysen, *Siegfried Landshut. Die Wiederentdeckung der Politik: Eine Biographie* (Frankfurt, 1997).

[40] Siegfried Landshut, "Über einige Grundbegriffe der Politik," *Archiv für Sozialwissenschaften und Sozialpolitik*, 54 (1925), collected in his *Kritik der Soziologie und andere Schriften der Politik* (Neuwied and Berlin, 1969), 261–306; Wilhelm Hennis, "Zu Siegfried Landshuts Wissenschaflichten Werk," *Zeitschrift für Politik*, 17 (1970), 4, reprinted in his *Politik und praktische Philosophie. Schriften zur politischen Theorie* (Stuttgart, 1977), 275–93.

Landshut's general argument was an attack on the modern nation-state and accompanying nationalist pathos. They were perverted derivatives of a "basic structure" of human "togetherness" (*miteinanderleben*) that Thomas Aquinas had identified as the common human nature welding individual households into a political unity. Although he did not explicate the historical location of this "basic structure" in any detail, it is clear that Landshut regarded as its key feature the organic unity in the medieval world of what would be called subsequently the "state" and "society," because elites were able, at least in some degree, to control their political environment, and because their rule was oriented toward the common good. Landshut was surveying the chaotic world of international relations in the mid-1920s, riven as they were by nationalist chauvinism and resentment, and he sought to find the way back to the origins of human political "togetherness": "Only the orientation on the *finis societatis* [social ends]," he averred, "can give the appropriate horizon from which political action, which has lost its orientation, can find guidance."[41]

Why did the synthesis of medieval universalism and dynastic political unity disintegrate? Landshut saw the seeds of decline in Christianity itself because its radical belief in human equality, articulated in a secularized form by Jean-Jacques Rousseau, could no longer tolerate the inequality and corruption of the early modern state. Rousseau tried to resolve the conundrum of freedom, equality, and political authority by making sovereign the self-governing people themselves. In order to weld the competing interests into the unity of the "general will," the state had to be depersonalized and stand above social conflict. But in doing so, Landshut argued, the modern state became the product of human division and compromise (*Gegeneinandersein*). More significantly, state and society were sundered, and henceforth a self-conscious and autonomous state cultivated the authentic energies of human political unity for its own nationalist purposes. Contemporary mass movements, he contended, were the compensatory phenomena of the irreconcilable divisions of modernity.

Revealing his reception of Karl Marx's theory of alienation, Landshut thought of modernity as the release from human control of humanly created institutions that subsequently hindered the restoration of political sociability. "The decisionless togetherness is sucked into the autodynamism that institutions assume when they have been detached from their orientation to human existence [*menschliche Dasein*]."[42] Just as the state was a human creation over which humans had lost control, so public opinion (*Öffentlichkeit*), which was a "fundamental phenomenon" of common political life that had become sovereign in modernity, had likewise become alienated from humans. Evidently influenced by Martin Heidegger, with whom he had studied in Freiburg and Marburg, Landshut deplored the anonymity and irresponsibility of public

---

[41] Landshut, "Grundbegriffe," 261.
[42] Ibid., 262. It was no coincidence that Landshut was greatly impressed by the young Marx and edited an early collection of his writings: Landshut and Jacob Peter Meyer, eds., *Der historische Materialismus. Die Frühschriften* (Leipzig, 1932).

opinion, creature as it had become of the financial imperatives of mass-media circulation. Far from disclosing the openness of the political situation and the variety of policy options as it was supposed to, it closed them down.[43]

In the context of German politics in the 1920s, Landshut was saying that the nationalist press and categories that prestructured the political horizon were blinding decision makers to other choices open to the country. True sovereignty lay in the ability to understand the openness of the situation and make decisions freely, rather than in rattling the sword of national self-assertion. The automatic effect of public opinion to rule out the particularity, and to efface the openness, of a situation undermined political responsibility because politicians slavishly followed it: where public opinion ruled, no one did.[44]

But that is not all. Nationalist public opinion also generated the "tendency to [imperialist] expansion," because the state was concerned solely with its power, which was "limitless" when not tied to "the appropriate 'finis' of human togetherness." What Hegel called a philosophy of history was really the "self-description of its [humanity's] own decisionlessness." Nation, *Volk*, state – the political idols of Weimar Germany – were a far cry from a true human political community. Like Hannah Arendt, Landshut thought that situations were fundamentally open and able to be changed by human agency where this fact was recognized. The present only appeared inexorably determined by social and economic laws because political life had become alienated from human control. It was necessary, therefore, to replace the "rotting traditions with which we nourish ourselves" with a critique founded on the "basic structure" of political community itself.

Providing practical orientation for politics at the time was the purpose of his major work, the rejected habilitation thesis of 1928, which appeared a year later under the title of *Kritik der Soziologie*.[45] Its purpose, as the title suggested, was to point out the inadequacy of the sociological question (*Fragestellung*) and method for the crisis of modern society. Landshut's target was sociology, because its determinism and attribution of agency to blind forces undermined human agency and further obfuscated the reality of the political. *Kritik der Soziologie* also developed further the earlier argument about the origins of modernity and the source of the social crisis.

The problem with sociology, Landshut argued, was its stated aim of providing abstractions and decision-making rules of social phenomena, because such laws and abstractions could not reveal anything about particular situations, which necessarily comprised "concrete historical relations and connections [*Zusammenhänge*]." In this regard, he shared Smend's criticism of legal positivism for blinding political theory to the realities of constitutional life.

---

[43] Landshut, "Grundbegriffe," 292–93.
[44] Ibid., 297. Cf. his critique of neocolonial aspirations of German imperialists in "Eine Frage europäischer Politik," *Die Gesellschaft*, 3 (1926), 124–33. See the discussion in Nicolaysen, *Siegfried Landshut*, 81–84.
[45] Now in his *Kritik der Soziologie und andere Schriften der Politik*, 11–18.

Landshut took Max Weber as an example of where the sociological method went down the wrong path. While Weber asked the correct questions – elucidating the cultural meaning of contemporary social phenomena – he appealed to "ideal types" and other abstractions that were based on an erroneous epistemology. Researchers' questions were not determined by their value commitments, as Weber had maintained, but originated in the "historical material" itself. Rejecting Weber's neo-Kantiansim, Landshut averred that reality was not a chaotic manifold upon which researchers imposed their capricious categories; it was "in" them already. What led to a research question was the perceived "questionability" (*Fraglichkeit*) of the reality in which one lived. And it yielded an answer because it could articulate a human structure of motivation and meaning. The purpose of inquiry was not to search for timeless laws and empty concepts that supposedly stood "behind" reality, but to gain insight into the historical connections that led to the current situation.[46] Everything, after all, was historical, including such apprehended laws and concepts. Sociology did not explain human alienation; it expressed it.

How did this misunderstanding arise? To answer the question, Landshut applied his own method and sought the origins of sociology in the antinomies of capitalist modernity. Sociology was itself an answer to a particular "questionableness" – namely, the inability to combine the strivings for freedom and equality in conditions where much of the population possessed no property and was hopelessly dependent on the owners of capital. That this situation was considered a problem, however, rested on a culturally specific "Western-Christian" emphasis on human "personality" (*Persönlichkeit*). The sociological perspective identified these hindrances as the result of inexorable social laws. In fact, Landshut countered, the problem could be explained historically by examining the secularization of Christian conceptions of freedom and the rise of the modern state, as he had in his 1925 article. Unlike the ancient, Aristotelian teaching that freedom and happiness lay in participation in communal life, Christian freedom and equality were essentially unpolitical and otherworldly virtues. After the wars of religion in the sixteenth and seventeenth centuries, a powerful state was required to guarantee peace, but at the cost of political sociability. In this way, the political world became alienated from the population of European states. Society, rather than the common good and political sociability, became the focus of human happiness, and consequently society became the focus of a discipline about human freedom and "self-determination," thereby replacing philosophy as the queen of sciences, which itself had taken the place of theology.[47]

The sociological question was in fact parasitical on the original question of Aristotelian political philosophy: the question of the good life. Weber and Marx, he continued, were motivated by this search, but in their answers they had been seduced by the mechanistic talk of the "causal-automatism" and "effective

[46] Ibid., 17–24.
[47] Ibid., 112–13.

factors" of the sociological imagination. Although he did not use the term "practical philosophy," Landshut made clear that the problem of inequality and alienation could be understood correctly only by examining the "real relations of meaning and motivation" that led to them. For once they had been uncovered and the determinism of sociology abandoned, men and women were presented with a fundamentally open situation in which they could act to recover the possibility of political action.[48]

What Schumpeter, Smend, and Landshut shared was a commitment to the academic study of politics concerned with political life as it actually occurred, rather than with developing models, concepts, or abstractions. Their political science was antipositivist, empirical rather than theoretical, inductive rather than deductive. The problem with positivism, however, was more than methodological. It was symptomatic of human alienation from the political world as a whole, an alienation that culminated in the German fascism that they all experienced in some form. From them, as from Burckhardt and Weber, Hennis learned to see the crisis of the twentieth century as a problem of European modernity rather than a German "special path" away from modernity. The challenge for Germans, then, was to become emancipated citizens who exercised freedom rather than be cowed subjects of an alienated state. "Working through the Nazi Past" was unnecessary.

The Early Writings

As a cofounder of the important *Göttinger Universitäts-Zeitung* and the local branch of the Junge Sozialisten (Jusos or Sozialistische Deutsche Studentenbund: the youth wing of the Social Democratic Party, SDS), Hennis used his position to impress upon his peers what he saw as the important issues confronting them. Along the lines of Richard Löwenthal's (alias Paul Sering) *Beyond Capitalism*, which the Jusos in Göttingen devoured at the time, his socialism was moral and non-Marxist, unlike that of his friend and comrade Peter von Oertzen (b. 1924), who had been an enthusiastic Nazi officer and turned to Marxism as an answer. Hennis's position needs to be appreciated in its historical context. To be a Social Democrat in the conservative law faculty in Göttingen was the exception rather than rule, as was his readiness, already in 1946, to admonish those who truculently sang Nazi songs and doubted whether they had been really liberated.[49]

This admonition was made in the context of a report on a local art exhibition. Art was no esoteric pastime for Hennis and the forty-fivers: it offered the

---

[48] Hannah Arendt makes the same arguments in *Crises of the Republic* (New York, 1969), 5–12.

[49] Many ex-soldiers took several years to get over the loss of the war and destruction of their ideals. For example, the Waffen SS soldier Jürgen Girgensohn (born 1924), the future Social Democratic minister of culture in North-Rhine-Westphalia, recalled such an attitude and the singing of forbidden Nazi songs in his POW camp in the immediate postwar years. Heiner Wember, *Umerziehung im Lager. Internierung und Bestrafung von Nationalsozialisten in der britischen Besatzungszone Deutschlands* (Essen, 1991), 171.

interpretive resources to answer the burning question he posed sympathetically for his fellow students: "And now we are 'free.' But whether we really are, and if so, 'what for': 'what do we do with this freedom?' This is the question." In Jean Anouilh's *Antigone* he saw the choice they all confronted because "This Antigone is the person of a fully disoriented time, perhaps just the person of our time." Antigone no longer believed in anything, nor possessed the strength to create meaning herself. "She is a person who has to wait forever for a prophet who will proclaim a new 'objective' meaning." Hennis contrasted Antigone's passivity with Creon, who did not believe in a "meaning to history" or in reason as the essence of humanity. On the contrary, like a "statesman" and "with both feet on the ground," he insisted on the duty to develop the will to create meaning oneself. In the spirit of Max Weber's, "Science as Vocation," a speech delivered to German students immediately after the First World War that warned of the dangers of utopianism and cultural pessimism, Hennis implored his fellow students to abandon their "longing for harmony" and attraction for "prophets" like Oswald Spengler, which he called a "sickness."[50] His message was clear: there was no point in waiting for someone to deliver the answer to the existential crisis of his generation; it had to develop one itself. Twenty years later, Hennis would give the same warnings about cultural pessimism and the dangers of "finding" meaning in "prophets" to the student movement.

Here, then, already in 1946, were the key elements of Hennis's orientation: a distrust of political enthusiasts, sectarians, and ideologues, but also a sense that the seemingly limitless personal freedom offered by Western liberal democracies was insufficient if not undergirded by ideals or sources of meaning. But what should they be? Three years later, he articulated his analysis in political terms during the West German rearmament debate when he aimed his pen at the anticommunist ideologues of the pro-rearmament lobby.[51] West Germany should not rearm, he insisted, because it would alarm the Soviets and provide ammunition for antidemocratic forces in West Germany: anticommunism was insufficient nourishment for the new German democracy and could benefit only fascism and nationalism: "No west European people . . . is more vulnerable to an anticommunist fanaticism than we Germans."[52] Communism and fascism, he argued, were symptoms of the "worldwide crisis" of liberal democracy whose "sovereignty of bourgeois freedom" could no longer provide orientation.

Like many Europeans at the time, he was convinced that the "bourgeois epoch" of the nineteenth century had come to an end. Reflecting the moderate socialism of the SDS, he upbraided German elites for wanting again to play grand politics instead of "in a peaceful spirit constructing what the Soviets think

---

[50] Wilhelm Hennis, "Begegnung mit moderner Kunst. Barlach, Hindemuth, Anouilh und wir," *Göttinger Universitäts-Zeitung* (June 21, 1946), 9–10. Hartmut von Hentig (b. 1925) was a student at Göttingen at the same time and was similarly impressed by Anouilh's *Antigone*. See his *Aufgeräumte Erfahrung. Texte zur eigenen Person* (Munich, 1983), 41.

[51] Wilhelm Hennis, "Krieg aus Angst. Wiederaufrüstung im Schatten der Vergangenheit," *Deutsche Universitäts-Zeitung*, 1 (1949), 7–8.

[52] Hennis, "Politikwissenschaft als Beruf," 39.

they can do only with brutal violence: a just community of human dignity." In late 1940s, he thought the bottle of Western democracy needed to be filled with the wine of democratic socialism.

Although the coming Federal Republic was not to be a democratic socialist state, Hennis thought that the Basic Law incarnated those values which made it qualitatively different from its predecessors. In the first defense of the new order by a forty-fiver, Hennis attacked those who cast doubt on the opportunity that the first election for the first West German parliament in 1949 presented for the country. There had been grumbling in the *Göttinger Universitäts-Zeitung* that the new Basic Law was only "provisional" and not "inwardly" supported by the majority; it did not represent a plausible "idea of state" (*Staatsidee*), and it would be best for it to end soon so that the German people could determine their constitution in freedom.[53] Werner Weber, a disciple of Carl Schmitt and a new professor at Göttingen, added his voice to the skeptical chorus by using his inaugural lecture to compare critically the Weimar constitution with the Bonn Basic Law. He lamented the weakening of the emergency law and the executive in the new system, and especially its institutionalization of political parties as the bearers or mediators of "the people's will," which he assumed to be a unified entity. By limiting the participation of "the people" to the periodic election of the parliament, he complained, the Basic Law prevented the plebiscitary and democratic "self-representation" of the people.[54] At this moment, both the right and left in German politics were dissatisfied with the foundation of the new republic, because it had not issued from "the people" itself.

Hennis modeled his answer on Smend's address at Berlin University in 1933. He was equally worried that, once again, German students would not commit themselves to a German democracy. And just as Smend rejected Schmitt's caricature of modernity, so Hennis attacked the categories with which Werner Weber analyzed the situation in 1949. But where Smend had looked to the past for inspiration, Hennis looked to the present. The issue at stake was not whether to have some constitution formulated by Germans alone in the future, but to have the "inner readiness" to decide to see the situation realistically today. And this stance meant seizing the opportunity provided by the new organs of state to make what was possible of the new system. In the first place, the "provisionality ideology" overlooked the fact that a future constitution would be essentially no different from the Basic Law. "It would be a republican, democratic, parliamentary, and federal constitution." Second, West Germans had to become accustomed to the division of Germany because it was probably a condition for the growing together of Western Europe and the price for the lost war.

Hennis reserved his biggest criticism for Werner Weber's complaint that the German people were prevented from political self-realization by the domination

---

[53] Werner Kalisch, "Das Provisorium," *Göttinger Universitäts-Zeitung*, 10 (1949), 1–3.
[54] Werner Weber, "Weimarer Verfassung und Bonner Grundgesetz," *Göttinger Universitäts-Zeitung*, 14 (1949), 6–8. It was expanded into a book of the same name later in the year (Göttingen, 1949).

of political parties. Such rhetoric was dangerous, because it implied the existence of a unified people and, therefore, a concomitant one-party state as its most appropriate political expression. Citing the Social Democratic politician of the Weimar period, Hermann Heller, he argued that there was no such will, because of the great social tensions that obtained in the modern state. "Antagonism," not the harmony of interests, characterized modernity. Consequently, the mediation of political parties was necessary to enable citizens to articulate themselves politically. "Whoever does not want such mediation, propagates – whether he wants to or not – an identification of the part with the whole that characterizes the total state. If National Socialism discredited political parties together with democracy, today – it appears to me – conceptual confusion reigns when the parties are discredited in the name of democracy." Without using the word "pluralism," he praised political parties as guarantors of freedom because their reflection of social differences prevented totalistic or one-party solutions to political problems.

Although he did not copy Smend's nationalistic rhetoric, Hennis shared his teacher's view that the task at hand was fulfilling the promise of nineteenth-century liberalism: reintegrating the state into national life and transcending personal interest by foregrounding the common good. He therefore urged his fellow students to support the new state despite its problems. Indeed, such a posture contained a deep, individual, almost redemptive meaning. "For it concerns not simply the state and a just political life, but also our most personal moral being in relation to that readiness for the state, that inner decision to which the election calls us." By incorporating the idea of the whole and common good into one's self, one was saved from isolation and idiosyncrasy.[55]

The important point to note is that the call for a German "new beginning" came from the right, using plebiscitary, indeed, *völkisch* rhetoric. In order to recommend the new order, Hennis had to reject the idea of a radical new beginning. On his view, Germany had experienced enough of radical, new beginnings and, as we will see, he thought that the problem of German history was not the continuity of premodern traditions but their continual rupture. In defending parliamentary democracy against Weber, and implicitly against Dirks, Kogon, Richter, and Andersch, he represented and articulated the integrative republican program.

The Dissertation

This mission was set out in detail in Hennis's doctoral dissertation from 1951: "The Problem of Sovereignty." This important document contains virtually all the themes that Hennis would pursue in his later work. It also reveals in acute form the issue of continuity and rupture in German intellectual traditions. The dissertation contains two parts: a reconstruction of the gradual repression of the sovereignty question in the nineteenth and twentieth centuries

---

[55] Wilhelm Hennis, "Vierzehnter August," *Göttinger Universitäts-Zeitung*, 15 (1949), 1–3.

in German political and constitutional thought, followed by his own legitimation of sovereignty. Whereas German theorists had removed political and social categories from their *Staatslehre* (theory of the state), Hennis resolved to restore them. The theoretical point of his argument was to demonstrate the inadequacy of a purely legal and formal, as opposed to the political, view of sovereignty. Its practical purpose was, like the arguments of Smend and Landshut, to recast a culturally and politically (but not *völkisch*) conceived nation-state as a source of political orientation in the "disintegrating" conditions of modernity.[56] Its polemical target was the cultural left that wanted to dissolve German sovereignty into a united Europe.

Hennis's method was a "material," sociologically oriented analysis in which the aporias of reflective political thought indicated problems with class relations. German constitutional thinking since the industrial revolution, he averred, reflected a particular German constellation of social and political forces. Germany had taken a separate path from general Western European development in the nineteenth century, and consequently, unlike in France, where the "democratic nation" had defeated the feudal world and grand bourgeoisie. In Germany, however, the *Bürgertum* (middle class) failed in 1848 and 1871 to successfully assert a liberal democratic order against the monarchical principle. Having lost its belief in a self-conscious political mission, the *Bürgertum* retreated to an "unpolitical culture-aestheticism" and power worship and conceived of the state merely as an instrument of order. Hennis followed his teachers in maintaining that this bourgeois misdevelopment resulted in the negation of political life, the decline of civic freedom, and the denial of social responsibility by a substantial part of Germany's elite. For this reason, Hennis found German liberalism and the ideology of the *Rechtsstaat* (state governed by law) an inadequate answer to contemporary challenges. "Hundreds of years of absolutist rule in Russia, Spain, Italy, and east European countries had produced the same effect," he wrote, because the broad mass of the population had never, or only very recently, "carried responsibility for the political whole."[57]

If Hennis upbraided German liberal positivism for its other worldly apoliticism, he reserved his harshest judgments for Schmitt, whom he called "the *Wegbereiter* [pathbeater] of the Third Reich."[58] Echoing Smend's earlier criticism, he chastised Schmitt for never understanding that the purpose of constitutions was to regulate social and political conflict.[59] Schmitt offered no real alternative, because he effectively defined the "state of exception" as the very pluralism that marked the Weimar constitution itself. Hennis conceded that there were

---

[56] Wilhelm Hennis, "Das Problem der Souveränität. Ein Beitrag zur neueren Literaturgeschichte und gegenwärtigen Problematik der politischen Wissenschaften" (Dr. Phil. dissertation, Göttingen University, 1951).

[57] Ibid., 12–16, 106, 128–29.

[58] Ibid., 36–40.

[59] Cf. Rudolf Smend, "Bürger und Bourgeois im deutschem Staatsrecht," in *Staatsrechtliche Abhandlungen*, 320.

emergency situations in which it was conceivable that positive law might need to be overridden. But he held Schmitt's position to be untenable, indeed dangerous, because no legal order could arise from his decisionistic and capricious voluntarism. The French and British, after all, were able to account for such contingencies in their constitutions. Schmitt's anthropology was so extreme in its Hobbesian pessimism, Hennis pointed out, that it implied the permanent necessity of a dictator to prevent civil war or revolution.

Hennis held Schmitt's theory of sovereignty to be "unusually representative" of a certain strain of German political thought that he saw as a fatal legacy of the romantic movement's alienation from politics, although, ironically, Schmitt himself had attacked "political romanticism."[60] German political thought possessed a tension between "sublime spirituality" and "legal" apoliticism, on the one hand, and cynical realism, power worship, and the state as a "real personality," on the other. Schmitt, of course, belonged to the latter tendency that, according to Hennis, also included the young Marx, Hegel, Treitschke, and Karl Mannheim.[61] All these thinkers understood themselves as particularly realistic and illusion-free, especially in relation to the West and its ideals, but ended up calling either for the "total revolution" against reality or for resigned acceptance. "In both cases, one does not correctly regard the reality in which one stands. One views it in cramped and in exaggerated terms, as naively enthusiastic [*schwärmerisch*] or with nihilistic skepticism." This is the same criticism that he made of his fellow students in his newspaper article in 1946, and his own mediation of ideal and reality repeated the position he articulated then: "For a rational and credible humane approach, human reality is . . . constituted precisely by the fact that in this world people have tasks to perform and goals for which to strive and for which they should strive, which they know they very often will not reach, but that are not in principle unrealizable. This approach is as foreign to the naive enthusiast as it is to the small-minded disillusioned skeptic."[62]

Hennis saw a positive point of departure in Schmitt's rival, Hermann Heller, who offered the "most important presentation of the problem [of sovereignty] in the recent past." Most attractive was his reincorporation into *Staatslehre* of the practical political issues: what were the state's "purposes and functions"? Nonetheless, Hennis found Heller's theory inadequate because it reflected too strongly the political chaos of the Weimar Republic and the resentment against the Versailles treaty of 1919. In his critique of Kelsen, Heller overemphasized the moment of autonomous state decision, thereby ignoring how laws were actually made. His preference for orders of "rule" (*Herrschaft*) over orders of "contract" indicated that he did not permit public opinion and civil society an

---

[60] Carl Schmitt, *Political Romanticism*, trans. Guy Oakes (Cambridge, Mass., 1986).
[61] Hennis, "Das Problem der Souveränität," 53.
[62] Ibid., 43–56. Hennis uses this formulation again in "Das Modell des Bürgers," *Gesellschaft – Staat – Erziehung*, 2 (1957), 330–339. Collected in his *Politik als praktische Wissenschaft. Aufsätze zur politischen Theorie und Regierungslehre* (Munich, 1968), 213–23.

input into sovereign state decisions. Accordingly, he did not pose the question of freedom "that is so essential for Anglo-Saxon thinking on the state" because he thought all liberalism and individualism led inexorably to anarchy. The question of freedom was rooted in the "experience of the truly 'total' state" that Heller was denied by his premature death in 1933.[63]

In fact, Hennis pointed out, the state had far less room to maneuver than Heller thought. It never possessed a choice between stark alternatives. It was, rather, a matter of "guiding" (*Lenkung*) social and political "forces" in light of common, historically bequeathed collective goals. He referred to "natural law" in the sense that law was "found" by a process of consensus construction with political partners. This was Hennis's interpretation of Smend's integration theory. The caprice of the state could be limited only by the need for cooperation with the forces of civil society, as Landshut had also insisted. Implicit in Hennis's criticism was the need to activate civil society or what he called public opinion (*öffentliche Meinung*) to prevent state authoritarianism. This point remained undeveloped in the dissertation and received detailed treatment later in the 1950s.

For now, the question remained why and how the sovereign state should take notice of public opinion at all. Hennis turned to the Christian-liberal Zurich school of political theory, which argued that the state could be limited only by its own ideal, that is, by justice. "A state power only appears legitimate to us that does not include certain aspects of life in its sphere of positive and transpositive competencies: a state that makes clear that the aim of a total 'grasp' of human life is prevented by law."[64] Several years later, Hennis made the same point in these terms:

When politics has no content and the state no specific task, then everything can become political and subject to the state, and why not – I draw the conclusions from the Schmittian line of thinking – the "racial" blood component of a person, the paintings that he loves, the music to which he likes to listen, or the books that he likes to read?... The total evacuation of the state and politics made possible the total politicization of all realms of social and intellectual life. Only when a state has a purpose or a task, can one limit it, namely to this purpose or task, irrespective of how all encompassing it may be.[65]

The target here was the German tradition of regarding the state as a "personality" that needed to develop itself and could not be tied to ethical standards.[66]

---

[63] Hennis, "Das Problem der Souveränität," 80. Hennis repeated the criticism in his habilitation thesis, *Politik als praktische Philosophie. Eine Studie zur Rekonstruktion der politischen Wissenschaft* (Neuwied and Berlin, 1963), 77.

[64] Hennis, "Das Problem der Souveränität," 72.

[65] Wilhelm Hennis, "Zum Problem der deutschen Staatsanschauung," *Vierteljahreshefte für Zeitgeschichte*, 7 (1959), 1–12. Reprinted in his, *Politik als praktische Wissenschaft*, 11–36. Here Hennis appears to rely on Franz Neumann, "The Concept of Political Freedom," in his *The Democratic and the Authoritarian State* (Glencoe, Ill., 1957), 194.

[66] There is an excellent survey and analysis of this tradition in historical thought in Georg G. Iggers, *The German Conception of History: The National Tradition of Historical Thought from Herder to the Present*, rev. ed. (Middletown, Conn., 1983).

As we will see later, Hennis's criticism of the "democratization" campaign of the late 1960s was made in these terms.

Far from detracting from the state's "dignity," as conservatives like Ernst Forsthoff and Werner Weber thought, the ideal of justice added to it. For above the state were "higher values" that, in turn, Hennis contended, were rooted "in the human person." A state was democratic when its constitution incarnated these human values: justice, fraternity, equality, and decency. Democracy was not to be tied to a social "bearer," like the middle class, or even "the people." Why, after all, should one place its fate in hands of a fickle people in the age of "totalitarian majorities"?[67] Like his teachers, Hennis believed that the political realm – decision making about the common good – possessed ontological status whose neglect threatened to enslave citizens to an alien state apparatus. "The essence of humans is their self formation as political beings; they themselves are never the measure of all things."[68] Concretely, this meant that active civic consciousness was required by democracies to uphold and redeem the values for which the state stood.

Hennis doubted West Germans of the 1950s possessed such a spirit. They did not think in political categories and were less likely to do so now than ever before. The essential problem was that of appropriate political experience, as Smend and Schumpeter had diagnosed. In analyzing the situation, Hennis also drew on the recent Anglo-American social psychology he read at the Salzburg seminars in 1948 and his time in Oxford in 1950.[69] This literature repeated the view of modernity as a process of alienation and rationalization that radically impoverished the political experience of certain social groups, particularly the petit bourgeois, intellectuals, and the unemployed, which, almost inevitably, became vulnerable to the totalitarian temptation. The "net of insecurities" that rendered the world "unpredictable" had led the German middle class, which comprised "conservative- and tradition-oriented people," to see an answer in fascism. They had not adjusted as well to the modern world as the peoples of Western Europe.

It is noteworthy that in this regard Hennis agreed with left-liberals, like Ralf Dahrendorf, who also attacked the "unmodern" aspects of German society. Unlike Dahrendorf, however, Hennis did not see an answer in modernizing the society as a whole. His question was to find a source of adjustment for the "anomie" that modern life inexorably caused, and he found the answer in a certain tradition of political thought. Unlike the right-wing "crisis literature," it sought the means by which humans could affect these tendencies without simultaneously positing an idealized distant future that could be realized only at the

---

[67] Hennis, "Das Problem der Souveränität," 70, 84–85, 87.

[68] Ibid., 112.

[69] Talcott Parsons, "Some Sociological Aspects of the Fascist Movements," *Social Forces*, 21:2 (December 1942), 38ff.; Parsons, *Essays in Sociological Theory Pure and Applied* (1949); Edward Shils, *The Present State of American Sociology* (1948), 40–52; Elton Mayo, *The Social Problems of an Industrial Civilization* (Boston, 1945); Robert Merton, "Social Structure and Anomie," in *Social Theory and Social Structure* (Glencoe, Ill., 1949).

expense of freedom, as Soviet communism did. A political scientific approach was not just diagnostic, Hennis insisted, but prescriptive, remedial, practical, and normative. It had to seek to identify the origins of the crisis and develop means of "containing or overcoming" it.[70] Where to find the answer?

The place to look, Hennis thought, was premodern political theory because it conceived of sovereignty – and this meant the normative problem of its legitimacy – in political rather than narrowly legal terms. Hennis isolated three aspects of the tradition for consideration: autarchy, "inner unity," and civic consciousness. Autarchy was no longer feasible or desirable in an age of global economic interdependence. The drive for autarchy, as Landshut had argued, lay behind imperialism and now represented an "unbearable danger for the peaceful coexistence of peoples." The purpose of integration was to maintain some unity in the face of social disintegration. Arguing against the antinationalism of leftist intellectuals of the time, Hennis maintained that historical consciousness and cultural individuality performed the important function of compensating for the unraveling social unity. For a state founded on more than power, cultural individuality was an essential precondition because it lent government rule historical legitimacy. Attempts to substitute transnational for national loyalties would only hasten the alienating rationalization caused by the modernization process. Finally, civic or political consciousness was more necessary for a democratic polity than any other type because it required the active responsibility of citizens for the common good. Fascism and communism succeeded most where the "mass of citizens lead a politically isolated and uninvolved existence." Because they had won their appeal by making the state the center of citizens' lives, democracy needed to do likewise.[71]

What did Hennis mean by freedom? He did not mean simple negative liberty, which he described as the "anticommunity individualism of nineteenth-century liberalism." Obviously, the limitation of the state was an important but insufficient condition for freedom. Freedom also meant responsibility for the whole, the common good. State-oriented as this may appear, Hennis regarded such responsibility as the antidote to the authoritarian traditions of German *Obrigkeit* (authoritarianism) because it prevented the state from alienating itself from and subsequently dominating civil society. But in modern conditions, he observed, the population was far removed from such a sense of responsibility. If the problem of modernity was anomie, and anomie meant an irresponsible isolation from political life, then the "permanent task of state formation" was "to lead [the citizen] back to such a sense of responsibility." The purpose of sovereign individual nation-states was not to effect the self-rule of "a people," but to serve as sites of self-administration, where individuals could fulfill communally given duties and thereby their human nature.

---

[70] Hennis, "Das Problem der Souveränität," 125. For the engaged role of political science, Hennis cited Edward Shils, "Social Science and Social Policy," *Philosophy of Science*, 6:3 (July 1949), 219ff.

[71] Hennis, "Das Problem der Souveränität," 116–17.

Politics as Practical Philosophy

As a student and young academic, Hennis was still unclear precisely where modern political thought had gone awry. His trip to the United States in 1952, when he met Leo Strauss and Eric Voegelin, provided the stimulus. Although Hennis does not count himself as their student, there is little doubt that he was influenced greatly by their criticism of positivism and modernity, and by their advocacy of an ethical role for political science. Equally important was the catalog of the Göttingen University library, which maintained the Aristotelian system of ordering disciplines in large leather binders from the 1820s. After reading Otto Brunner's *Adliges Landleben and europäischer Geist* (Aristocratic Rural Life and European Spirit), in which the Aristotelian division of the "practical disciplines" (ethics, politics, and economics as responsible for the "whole household") was set out, Hennis felt he had finally found the reason for the decline of the political in Europe: the gradual erosion of both the Aristotelian conception of politics as governance for the common good and its handmaiden, political science as a "practical science" whose object was praxis rather than theory or pure knowledge.[72]

Remedying this situation was the purpose of his famous habilitation thesis, *Politik als praktische Philosophie* (Politics as Practical Philosophy), an intellectual and disciplinary history of this decline.[73] Where did politics take the fatal turn from a practical to a theoretical orientation? By showing the contingent nature of these developments, Hennis aimed to release the present situation from the perceived arrogance of "modern thinking" and to make it available for conscious human intervention, in the same way as Landshut had done more than forty years earlier.[74] It was Descartes, Hennis began, who reduced knowledge to one pole of the Aristotelian distinction: henceforth, only theoretical knowledge – knowledge of phenomena that obeyed immanent rules and that was independent of human action – counted as scientific, for example, mathematics and geometry. This decline continued especially with Thomas Hobbes, who, in his effort to imbue political philosophy with the certainty of natural science, omitted human agency and the classical political virtues of *phronesis* and *prudentia* because they could not be measured and accounted for precisely in terms of cause and effect.[75] This mechanistic anthropology robbed political science of its humanistic task because, if everything were determined by cause and effect, there could be no place for human striving for the telos of the common good and the good life.

Politics was an uncertain business, Hennis maintained, and it necessarily entailed the making of value judgments. True, their veracity could not be

---

[72] Hennis, "Politikwissenschaft als Beruf," 38, 43–44; Hennis, "Politikwissenschaft als Disziplin," 10. See Hennis's first publication in a scholarly journal: review of G.-E. Lavau, *Parties Politique et Réalités Sociales*, in *Politische Literatur*, 2 (1953), 422–24.

[73] Hennis, *Politik als praktische Philosophie*. The habilitation thesis was completed in 1959.

[74] Ibid., 38.

[75] Ibid., 41–51.

demonstrated with mathematical certainty, but insofar as political activity was a struggle for competing purposes and goods, it was also teleological because it assumed that particular purposes and goods should be followed for certain reasons.[76] Moreover, value judgments had real consequences. The inability of modern political thinking to distinguish between good government and tyranny was evident in the belief of the civil servants of the Nazi state that they had to serve "the state" as such rather than a state devoted to the common good. Hennis, following Leo Strauss, whose book *On Tyranny* he had read during his visit to the United States in 1952, and whose translation into German he was later to publish, believed that this ancient distinction offered the teleological orientation of which positivism had robbed political thinking. Modern theories may be able to account for the rise of totalitarianism, but they did not go to its essence. A value-laden distinction between freedom and tyranny was required for such an insight. "The chapter on tyranny in book eight of Plato's *Republic* or Xenophon's *Hiero* reveal more about the National Socialist regime than most of the sociological or social-psychological explanatory attempts." Instead of searching for an illusory theoretical knowledge of politics and distancing itself from its own environment in a vain effort to gain an "objective" viewpoint, political science "should sharpen consciousness about the given problems for us today" that have, "to use Max Weber's terminology, 'cultural significance.'" And, in doing so, it should not shy from making value judgments.[77]

Hennis was vague about the values that should inform the answers to such problems, because he was not advocating a normative, static utopia animated by Christianity or antiquity.[78] He was urging that political discourse be conducted against the horizon of certain basic values – justice, decency, and freedom – in the interests of the common good that awaited definition in each particular case. It was an open discourse but one that set obvious limits to available options: tyranny was obviously ruled out by such a basic consensus. Still, Hennis also implied that the "problems of cultural significance" were objectively pregiven and awaited revelation by proper political thinking. What set him apart from Strauss was his belief that these problems were historically bequeathed national-ethical (*sittlich*) tasks, which he juxtaposed to the empty abstraction of "the

[76] Ibid., 60–61; Alfred Cobban's influential article argued that political philosophy was doomed when it renounced making value judgments in order to obtain a desired objective viewpoint. See his "The Decline of Political Theory," *Political Science Quarterly*, 68:3 (1953), 321–37. It appeared in German as "Der Verfall der politischen Theorie," *Der Monat*, 6 (1954).

[77] Hennis, *Politik als praktische Philosophie*, 70–71. Leo Strauss, *On Tyranny: An Interpretation of Xenophon's Hiero* (New York 1948); *Über Tyrannis*, afterword by Alendre Kojève (Neuwied and Berlin, 1963). There is a good discussion of Strauss's thought in this connection in Alfons Söllner, "Leo Strauss: German Origin and American Impact," in Peter Kielmansegg, Horst Mewes, and Elisabeth Glaser-Schmidt, eds., *Hannah Arendt and Leo Strauss: German Émigrés and American Political Thought after World War II* (Cambridge, 1995), 121–37, esp. 127.

[78] Hennis has been misleadingly categorized as an "ontological-normative" thinker. See Wolf-Dieter Narr, *Theoriebegriffe und Systemtheorie*, vol. 1, *Einführung in die moderne politische Theorie*, ed. Wolf-Dieter Narr and Frieder Naschold (Stuttgart, Berlin, Cologne, and Mainz, 1969), 42n6; Kurt Lenk, "Methodenfragen der politischen Theorie," in Hans-Joachim Lieber, ed., *Politische Theorien von der Antike bis zur Gegenwart* (Bonn, 1991), 1000.

state" as a transhistorical category and to the nihilism of existentialism and decisionism.[79] Unlike the Frankfurt School, then, and at about the same time as Hans-Georg Gadamer's *Truth and Method* and Hannah Arendt's *Viva Acta*, Hennis advocated the perspective from within one's environment and the productivity of prejudgments as the antidote to totalitarianism rather than their critical dissolution.[80] The norms of practical philosophy were immanent, not transcendent, a posture that Habermas, for example, could not follow because he regarded immanent German norms as polluted.

Consequently, Hennis advocated the rehabilitation of the (pre-Hegelian) dialectical or topical method for political thinking. Topical thinking took the object of inquiry in reference to a specific problem and weighed up the different viewpoints on it. The answer would never be more certain than the balance of probabilities, but it would give the best, that is, the most convincing reasons. This mode of scholarly inquiry was necessarily dialogical and underlined the centrality of speech for human sociability and the political. He who restricted speech was a tyrant. Equally dangerous, however, was skepticism about the efficacy of discussion altogether. Descartes' inability to honor topical-dialectical thinking had led to the "dark irrationalism" of decisionism for which no good reasons can ever be adduced.[81] Although Hennis did not adumbrate a catalog of schemata under which particulars were to be subsumed, he assumed that inherited notions of the common good would suffice. Accordingly, he did not say how agreement could be reached where no consensus obtained about the criteria for adjudging the plausibility of a given argument. To the extent that he presumed such a consensus, topical thinking was circular, because its purpose was to secure such a consensus by the force of argument alone. Nonetheless, Habermas would find stimulation for his theory of the "ideal speech situation" in Hennis's utilization of the topics in political thinking, although he would take these ideas in a different direction.[82]

The Theory of Representative Democracy

Politics as Practical Philosophy took over the Aristotelian postulate, set out in the *Nicomachean Ethics*, that an immature character was not qualified to

---

[79] Hennis, *Politik und praktische Philosophie*, 59–60, 64, 79–80.
[80] Manfred Riedel has called attention to the origins of the revival of practical philosophy in Germany in Heidegger's Freiburg lectures on Aristotle. Hennis was no Heideggerian, but his criticism of positivism was influenced by Landshut, who, like Gadamer, Helmut Kuhn, and Ludwig Landgrebe, had studied with Heidegger and who welcomed Hennis's book. See Riedel, "Seinsverständnis und Sinn für das Tunliche," in Hans Maier et al., eds., *Politik, Philosophie, Praxis. Wilhelm Hennis zum 65. Geburtstag* (Stuttgart, 1988), 280–302.
[81] Hennis, *Politik und praktische Philosophie*, 96–97, 107. The relevant chapter of Hennis's book has been translated as "Political Science and the Topics," *Graduate Faculty Philosophy Journal*, 7 (Spring 1978), 35–77. For an analysis of the debate in which Hennis intervened, see Otto Pöggeler, "Dialektik und Topik," in Manfred Riedel, ed., *Rehabilitierung der praktischen Philosophie*, vol. 1, *Rezeption, Argumentation, Diskussion* (Frieburg, 1974), 291–331.
[82] Jürgen Habermas, "The Classical Doctrine of Politics in Relation to Social Philosophy," in his *Theory and Practice*, trans. John Viertel (Boston, 1973), 79–81.

participate in the conversation of political science. "Whoever is not in the position to understand the advantages of the free versus the slavelike life will not
be able to appreciate a theory of freedom."[83] Judgment, not just pure intellect, was a prerequisite for knowledge. It was in this vein that Hennis made
the "office" (*Amt*) and public sphere (*Öffentlichkeit*) the pillars of his theory
of representative democracy, which he saw best incarnated in Great Britain
and the United States. Significantly, those states had endured not because of
their modernity but, on the contrary, because they had forgotten less of the
past wisdom than continental Europe and, above all, Germany. Consolidating
representative democracy, then, did not mean modernizing the country, as Ralf
Dahrendorf advocated. Rather,

We must return to those forms of thought and [academic] disciplines from which the
modern concept of the state emancipated itself; and in Germany more radically than in
England or the United States, where elements of the older theories have been preserved
into the present to a much greater extent than on the continent, and especially Germany. We Germans are not a particularly conservative, tradition-bound people; rather
Germany – at least intellectual Germany – stands, since the beginning of the nineteenth
century, for the most radical modernity. Marxism, Historicism, and Existentialism were
formed here. After lagging behind for a long time, Germany has become...the most
ardent *Vortrupp* of that *Neuzeit* whose end one can now diagnose.[84]

The political traditions and tone-setting elites in the Anglophone countries had
resisted the plebiscitarian model of democracy. The purposes of the English
state were not decided by the capricious will of the people. Hennis's target
was the continental metaphysics of will, whether incarnated in the absolutist
state or, subsequently, in the people. As he argued in his dissertation, democracy was explicitly *not* the self-rule of the people. Decisive was the goal of
realizing certain timeless virtues: justice, decency, freedom. The virtue of representative democracy was its origins in the feudal "office," which guaranteed an
"order of freedom" because an office was a trust that comprised independently
given duties for the common good that were not at the disposal of popular
will.[85] The problem with German history was the gradual replacement of the

---

[83] Hennis, *Politik und praktische Philosophie*, 40.
[84] Hennis, "Zum Problem der deutschen Staatsanschauung," 15. Hennis, "Meinungsforschung
und repräsentative Demokratie. Zur Kritik politischer Umfragen," in his *Politik als praktische
Wissenschaft*, 144. Originally *Meinungsforschung und repräsentative Demokratie. Zur Kritik
politischer Umfragen* (Tübingen, 1957). Karl Mannheim made a similar analysis: "In contrast
with Germany, England is among those countries in which the recent tendencies in mass society
have been stayed by the persistence of the older organic ties and their accompanying effects."
Mannheim, *Man and Society in an Age of Reconstruction*, 61, 88.
[85] Wilhelm Hennis, "Amtsgedanke und Demokratiebegriff," in *Staatsverfassung und Kirchenord-
nung. Festgabe für Rudolf Smend* (Tübingen, 1962), 51–70. Reprinted in his *Politik als praktische
Wissenschaft*, 50. J. G. A. Pocock and Keith Michael Baker have come to similar conclusions
about the difference between English and continental political culture.

representative and "office" dimension in its institutions and political thought by the plebiscitary model, "whose originator [*Stammvater*] is Rousseau."[86]

The task today, Hennis argued, was to restore the lost tradition. The Federal Republic's Basic Law adumbrated all the essential ethical postulates that the new German democracy required, but public opinion was the key because it was the means by which the political nation – the country's elites – could hold the state to these values. Public opinion, however, was not simply the general views in the population. Such a view, popularized by polls and surveys, in fact undermined the representative nature of the constitution by privileging a seemingly "authentic" public will against the elected representatives and leaders of civil society. Public opinion, in Hennis's sense, was qualitative. True to his Aristotelian assumptions, and following Schumpeter, he argued that it was the viewpoint of those with responsible positions who were thus able to make informed judgments. Consequently, Hennis placed particular emphasis on the role that universities and professors played in constituting public opinion in the tradition of the German mandarins.[87] While it would be going too far to suggest that Hennis equated the modern "masses" and their preoccupation with the private sphere with Aristotle's slaves, and the contemporary makers of public opinion with the free men and citizens of the ancient city-state, there is no doubting that he saw a parallel between the two cases. Only those who took responsibility for the common good by engaging in the political issues of the day were really qualified by their public mode of life (*Lebensführung*) to be able to give advice to governments.[88]

For this reason, Hennis was lukewarm about the direction that political education was taking in the Federal Republic.[89] Political education was a child of the "reeducation" program of the American occupation authorities, and the discipline of political science was established at least in part to train the coming German elites in ways of democracy.[90] For Hennis, *politische Bildung*, as it was called, reeked of Rousseauean activism because it encouraged citizens to participate in politics as an end in itself. This intention, he observed provocatively, had been realized all too well in the recent German past. Yet the preparedness for political participation and protest was precisely the task that Habermas

---

[86] Wilhelm Hennis, "Der Begriff der Öffentlichen Meinung bei Rousseau," *Archiv für Rechts- und Sozialphilosophie*, 43 (1957), 111–15; Hennis review of J. J. Rousseau, *Über Kunst und Wissenschaft* in *Deutsche Universitäts-Zeitung*, 23–24 (1946), 30.

[87] Hennis, "Meinungsforschung und repräsentative Demokratie," 136, 146, 158.

[88] Wilhelm Hennis, "Rat und Beratung im modernen Staat," in *Politik als praktische Wissenschaft*, 65–80.

[89] Hennis to Fraenkel, June 1, 1962, BA Koblenz, N 1274–44 (Bundesarchiv, Koblenz, Germany); Wilhelm Hennis, "Der Begriff der öffentlichen Meinung bei Rousseau," *Archiv für Rechts- und Sozialphilosophie*, 43 (1957), 111–15.

[90] Hans Karl Rupp, "Democratizing a Country and a Discipline: The (Re-) Establishment of Political Science as Political Education in West Germany after 1945," in Rainer Eisfeld, Michael Th. Greven, and Hans Karl Rupp, *Political Science and Regime Change in 20th Century Germany* (New York, 1996), 55–109.

and his colleagues had set out as the vanguard of democracy in *Student und Politik*.[91]

This notion was an anathema for Hennis. In the conditions of large nation-states, the Rousseauean ideal of participation was a dangerous illusion because it raised the expectation among citizens that they were able to control its complex affairs. Of course, one did what one could at the local level, but beyond that sphere another virtue was required, namely judgment. This was the virtue that Hennis, following Smend, saw based on "correct experience." Were citizens to recognize the complexity of national affairs and vote for the most competent political party? Would they, as Hennis lamented of his leftist colleagues, "moralize limitlessly, complain, judge, and passionately 'take a stance' without troubling themselves to reflect on the factual foundations of their engagement"? Or would they give themselves over to simplistic, utopian solutions that would blame social woes on, say, the Jews, the slogans of which were "still ringing in our ears." Cultivating a "realistic experience" of national life should be the task of political education. His model citizen, then, was someone who participated in local affairs and took an interest in national ones. Such a citizen was immune to the seduction of "utopian poison" and was true to his or her political self. "A person, who neglects the political, and allows it to be lost to his essence, betrays his nature."[92]

Elitist as Hennis's position was, he felt it was "progressive" nonetheless. For in the early Federal Republic, as he pointed out, a populist conception of public opinion would entail giving credence to the irredentist voices in the population that strove for German unification and nonrecognition of West Germany's eastern borders. In such matters, statesmanlike leadership was called for. Echoing Landshut's complaint about the surrogate rule of (a debased) public opinion, Hennis complained that the plebiscitary model led to government by the slavish following of opinion polls, rather than by the informed and considered decisions of elected representatives.[93]

As might be expected, Hennis was attacked bitterly by intellectuals on the left. Opinion polls and surveys were not just employed by political parties but constituted one of the research methods of his neighbors at Frankfurt University, the Institute for Social Research. Two years earlier, in 1955, the Institute had published a large interview project, the *Group Experiments* on political consciousness in the Federal Republic, which Hennis mocked for its accusation that the distinction he made between general and truly public opinion was a "naive elite theory."[94] Although he did not follow the right-wing criticism that played down the finding of widespread authoritarianism in West German

[91] Jürgen Habermas et al., *Student und Politik. Eine soziologische Untersuchung zum politischen Bewußtsein Frankfurter Studenten* (Neuwied, 1961).

[92] Wilhelm Hennis, "Das Modell des Bürgers," *Gesellschaft, Staat, Erziehung*, 2 (1957), 330–39. Reprinted in his *Politik als praktische Wissenschaft*, 210.

[93] Hennis, "Meinungsforschung und repräsentative Demokratie," 147.

[94] Hennis referred to *Gruppenexperiment*, vol. 2, *Frankfurter Beiträge zur Soziologie* (Frankfurt, 1955). 21. See his "Meinungsforschung und repräsenatitive Demokratie," 135n46.

society, he objected to such research methods as manifestations of a social scientific denial of human freedom because, on his understanding of its premises, everything was thought to be the product of "social forces." He said the same of the Marxism of Critical Theory. "There can be no qualitative differences in public opinion where everything is a reflex of social relations."[95] This was the same complaint that an increasingly conservative Max Horkheimer made against Habermas's work at the time.[96]

Hennis explicitly idealized the early nineteenth-century model of the public sphere because it was representative in character: opinion holders were qualified and responsible leaders of civil society. In an interesting connection, Jürgen Habermas also idealized the "bourgeois public sphere," and he shared Hennis's historical narrative of its decline in the gradual democratization and commercialization over the nineteenth and twentieth centuries. This was perhaps no coincidence: Hennis had given his younger colleague his card catalog file on the subject in the late 1950s.

The institute responded in kind to Hennis's attack. Werner Thönnessen wrote a bitter attack in *Diskus*, the Frankfurt University magazine, to which Hennis responded with equal vehemence.[97] Wolfgang Abendroth, in the *Neue Gesellschaft*, objected to Hennis's "old liberalism" that omitted the participation of the population, and he went so far as to accuse him of proximity to (unnamed) constitutional theorists who had welcomed the Nazi dictatorship.[98] Hennis remarked privately to Ernst Fraenkel that "If Abendroth has an affinity to Carl Schmitt, then it is via Rousseau and the democratic chain of identification. They always agreed in their rejection of the liberal state of law, even if their motives were totally different."[99] Otto von der Gablentz, professor at the Otto Suhr Institute at the Free University in Berlin, wrote to his colleague Fraenkel that, while he agreed with Hennis's vision of an engaged political science, he worried that his foregrounding of premodern political thought would lead him, "probably involuntarily, to become the voice of the spiritual and political reaction."[100] Speaking for the Ritter school of neo-Hegelianism based in Münster, Bernhard Willms complained similarly that the missing "dialectical moment" in *Politik und Praktische Philosophie* meant that Hennis could not incorporate individual freedom in his schema, and that

---

95 Hennis, "Meinungsforschung und repräsenatitive Demokratie," 152–60. On the debate surrounding the *Gruppenexperimente*, see Rolf Wiggershaus, *The Frankfurt School: Its History, Theories, and Political Significance*, trans. Michael Robertson (Cambridge, Mass., 1994), 477–78.
96 See Wiggershaus, *The Frankfurt School*, 554.
97 Werner Thönnessen, "Demokratie und öffentliche Meinung," *Diskus*, 6:7 (1957), 193–96. Hennis replied in "Aufklärung der Dialektik," *Diskus*, 7:7 (1957), 201–4.
98 Wolfgang Abendroth review of Wilhelm Hennis, *Meinungsforschung und repräsentative Demokratie* (Tübingen, 1957), in *Die Neue Geselleschaft*, 4:6 (November–December 1957), 472–74.
99 Hennis to Fraenkel, December 8, 1957, BA Koblenz, NL 1274-24.
100 Von der Gablentz to Fraenkel, February 18, 1961, BA Koblenz, NL 1274-40.

therefore he was an advocate of "totalitarianism."[101] Fraenkel himself shared Abendroth's reservation about Hennis's reliance on the thinkers of the eighteenth century but, unlike the Marburg political scientist, he welcomed his "passionate" defense of the representative principle and warning about the danger of "Caesarism."[102] The political scientist Thomas Ellwein may have been closer to the mark with his observation that Hennis's was a "nostalgic glance" into the past.[103]

Abendroth's and Willms's polemics were well wide of the mark and revealed more about their own commitments than about Hennis's project. While it was true that Hennis did not utilize Hegelian categories, and that at times he wrote in a pointed way about the decline of public virtue at the expense of individual, negative freedom, it is clear that he valued such freedom as a constitutive, if insufficient, moment in modernity. The transition from the status of royal subject to republican citizen was epochal because the freedom that had been reserved for a privileged elite was now conferred upon all.[104] But the task of realizing it had been rendered difficult by the instability and anomie caused by rapid modernization. Capitalism and Manchester liberalism thwarted consciousness of citizenship by limiting the horizon of the population to the private sphere. In Hennis's conception, political science should remind the people of the role to which they were called: to be citizens of the state for which they should take responsibility, and to serve the common good.

The Nazi Past and the Dilemma of Integrative Republicanism

How did the issue of the foundation of the Federal Republic relate to the Nazi past in Hennis's thought? The answer is that he had to oppose a political education that laid the blame for Nazism at the door of German history or a supposed German national character. The fascist potential, he contended, was prevalent

---

[101] Bernard Willms, "'Ein Phoenix zu viel.' Bemerkungen zu zwei Versuchen über Zerstörung und Erneuerung einer Wissenschaft," *Der Staat*, 3 (1964), 488–98. On the Münster school, see Jan-Werner Müller, *A Dangerous Mind: Carl Schmitt in Post-War European Thought* (New Haven, 2003).

[102] Ernst Fraenkel review of Wilhelm Hennis, *Meinungsforschung und repräsentative Demokratie* (Tübingen, 1957), in *Archiv des öffentlichen Rechts*, 44 (1958), 360–62. Their correspondence on this matter is in BA Koblenz, NL 1274–24, letters July 3, 7, and 8, 1958. Fraenkel was an enthusiast of Jacob L. Talmon and was instrumental in securing a German translation of his book *The Origins of Totalitarian Democracy* (London, 1952); See Fraenkel to Talmon, June 22, 1958, and Westdeutscher Verlag to Fraenkel, May, 10, 1958, BA Koblenz, N 1274–28. Cf. Ernst Fraenkel, "Die repäsentative und die plebizitäre Komponente im demokratischen Verfassungsstaat" (1958), in his *Deutschland und die westlichen Demokratien* (Stuttgart, 1964), 113–51.

[103] Thomas Ellwein, "Überlegungen zum Thema," in Thomas Ellwein, Manfred Liebel, and Inge Negt, eds., *Die Spiegel Affäre*, vol. 2, *Die Reaktion der Öffentlichkeit* (Freiburg, 1966), 17. See also Manfred Friedrich, "Restitution einer Wissenschaft," *Neue Politische Literatur*, 9 (1964), 541–56.

[104] Wilhelm Hennis, "Motive des Bürgersinns," *Festgabe für Carlo Schmid* (Tübingen, 1962), 97–107. Reprinted in his *Politik als praktische Wissenschaft*, 213–34.

in all modernizing societies. One should not look for some cancerous cell in, say, Luther and trace its pernicious growth until it overwhelmed the country in 1933. The German problem was the lack of resistance, which was caused by its greater distance than the Anglophone countries from the emollient political traditions of premodern Europe.[105]

By virtue of this interpretation, Hennis was able to protect his national German subjectivity from the accusations of Non-German Germans and the victorious Allies that questioned any form of German collective identification. He did not doubt that many German ideals had been destroyed by the Nazi experience – the state, duty, nationalism – and he proclaimed the "never-to-be-compensated guilt of our people" for having abandoned German Jews in their hour of need.[106] Germans had failed to practice the virtue of fraternity, the basic political friendship between free and equal citizens that had to animate any republic. Representative democracy was based on trust because voters needed to have confidence in officeholders and in one another. Public opinion and political speech were possible only in conditions of mutuality and dialogue. Citizens needed to be able to look one another freely in the eye.[107]

There is an obvious problem with this argument. Germans did not simply abandon Jews. Germans actively persecuted them, and Hennis seemed unable or unwilling to consider the proposition that specifically German traditions had led to this persecution.[108] He chose explicitly *not* to follow the left and other liberals like Karl Dietrich Bracher in thematizing the recent Nazi past, which would discredit Germany's elites and endanger their leadership function.[109] Although he did not deny a role to the discipline of contemporary history (*Zeit-geschichte*) in the curriculum of political education, Hennis thought too much attention to the totalitarian experience would issue in an irrational "limitless excitement" (*Aufregung*) that could tip into "petit bourgeois resignation."[110] Excessive reflection on the Nazi past, he thought, reproduced the customary German lopsided relationship to politics and should therefore be avoided. What Hennis had in mind were judgments that relativized the difference between the Federal Republic and eastern bloc countries because the former was viewed as essentially as undemocratic and illiberal as the latter. But his real target was the redemptive republicanism of Non-German Germans that stigmatized West

---

[105] Hennis, "Zum Problem der deutschen Staatsanschauung." As an exemplar of this approach, Hennis cited Dietrich Gerhard, "Regionalismus und ständisches Wesen als Grundthema europäischer Geschichte," *Historische Zeitschrift*, 174 (1952), 307–37.

[106] Wilhelm Hennis, "Vom Sinn des. 20. Juli," in Hennis and Karl D. Schmidt, *Deutscher Widerstand, 1933–1945* (Hamburg, 1965), 225–37. Reprinted in his *Politik als praktische Wissenschaft*, 225–30.

[107] Hennis, "Zum Begriff der öffentlichen Meinung," in his *Politik als praktische Wissenschaft*, 42, 46.

[108] Wilhelm Hennis, "Zum Begriff und Problem des politischen Stils," *Gesellschaft, Staat, Erziehung*, 9 (1964), 225–37. Reprinted in his *Politik als praktische Wissenschaft*, 230–44.

[109] Hennis, "Meinungsforschung und repräsentative Demokratie," 156–57.

[110] Hennis, "Motive des Bürgersinns," 223.

Germany as a false start, a "restoration" of discredited German traditions. Here we see the new state's legitimacy dilemma most starkly.

The limits of the integrative solution to the dilemma are evident in Hennis's prescription for political consciousness. Important was the spirit (*Gesinnung*) of identification with the customs of community of which the citizen was a part. Politics should not be based on universal values and the nonconformist ideal of the Frankfurt School's model of participation and protest. It was precisely the particularity of the community that provided the motivation for political activity. The virtuous citizen integrated himself or herself into "a tradition that he or she interpreted as a model, as in Anglo-Saxon countries." Rather than distance from the social environment, escape from one's private world and identification with its common goods and aims was required.[111]

This recommendation was all very well in societies whose traditions were not open to such suspicion. Clearly, Hennis did not distrust this community and its customs as his left-liberal colleagues did. He did not see what they saw, namely, that German customs were the source of moral and political pollution. To some extent, their differences were semantic: what the left called typically German – anti-Semitism, authoritarianism, and so on – Hennis identified as characteristic of modernity in general. He, too, recognized the continuity of unhealthy attitudes and mentalities, but he chose to attribute them to another source, thereby saving German identity from complete ruin. For those for whom it was polluted, there was no alternative but to "start again."

In order to legitimate the Federal Republic, Hennis needed to play down attention to the recent past. His liberal-conservative illusion was that Anglo-Saxon-style politics could be institutionalized with a population uninterested in reflecting critically on its implication in the Nazi regime and an intelligentsia alienated from this population and the state. In his anxiety to have Germans identify with the new republic, Hennis did not realize that it was impossible for many of his compatriots to ignore the impact of the past on the present. Hennis wanted to base the new republic on German continuities that others regarded as polluted and stigmatized. What is more, he advocated a republican consciousness based on fraternity at a time when the transparency of true political friendship and mutuality was rendered impossible by the presence in the population of mass murderers and unrepentant Nazis. As long as such people occupied positions of authority in West Germany, it was impossible for many of its citizens to place basic trust in its institutions. This suspicion lay behind the opposition to the emergency laws in the 1960s.

As an integrative republican and German German, Hennis had to oppose those who saw in the pollution of the Nazi past a reason to question the legitimacy of the new Federal Republic. That his message was not heard by the younger generation, let alone by many left-liberal forty-fivers, testifies to the consequences of this pollution and the enormity of the evil that lay behind it.

---

[111] Fraenkel was not pleased with this argument. See Fraenkel to Hennis, May 29, 1962, BA Koblenz, NL 1274.

5

The Non-German German

The Redemptive Republicanism of Jürgen Habermas

Those Germans who felt indignant about the crimes committed by Germans and for their subsequent lack of contrition sought to construct a political community cleansed of nationalist ideals and values. The radicalism of this project should not be underestimated. It was to recast Germans essentially as European citizens of a republic cut off from the national traditions that led to Auschwitz. These are the Non-German Germans. They were not like the few who converted to Judaism in order to escape their Germanness. Nor did they resemble the German refugees, for whom the professor of German literature Hugo Kuhn coined a new term after he encountered them on his study tour of Australian universities in 1960. "In the concert halls of Melbourne and Sydney, we felt as we used to in Breslau. What a forced-export of cultivated and culture-conscious Germans has gone across the entire globe! Hitler has indeed brought together German and German-conscious Europeans in all the world – but as German Anti-Germans [*deutsche Gegen-Deutsche*]."[1] This orientation may have even preceded the Nazis: we know from Thomas Mann that a "German self-antipathy" (*deutscher Selbst-Antipathie*) has existed for more than a thousand years![2]

Non-German Germans are not to be confused with the so-called "anti-Germans" (*Antideutsche*) for whom "Germany must die so we can live," and who insist that "After Auschwitz, we have no right to be German."[3] For this sect of the German left, the average German was "Otto Normalvergaser" (Otto Normal-gasser), a petit bourgeois with barely concealed genocidal and

---

[1] Hugo Kuhn, "Europäische Reflexionen in Australien," *Die Zeit* (March, 17, 1961), 13. I thank my father John A. Moses for furnishing me with this long-forgotten article that he clipped while studying in Germany in the early 1960s.

[2] Thomas Mann, *Doktor Faustus*, vol. 6, *Gesammelte Werke* (Frankfurt, 1960), 51.

[3] Cited by Richard Schroeder, "Verführtes Denken? Zur Rolle der Ideologie in der DDR," in Wolfgang Hardtwig and Heinrich August Winkler, eds., *Deutsche Entfremdung: Zum Befinden in Ost und West* (Munich, 1994), 158.

anti-Semitic urges.[4] Incarnating the "self-hating German,"[5] like those young Germans who concealed their nationality while traveling abroad, the anti-Germans regard the German problem in terms of the country's fascist reaction to the crises of capitalism. They supported anything that negates German nationalism and, for that reason, were fiercely critical of German and European anti-Zionism, particularly on the left. Solidarity with Israel was paramount.[6]

As this example shows, identity dilemmas could not be reduced to questions of left-right politics. It was the Greens and peace movement, after all, that in the early 1980s raised the issue of German national sovereignty against NATO and the USSR. And an anti-Israel reflex, replete with Nazi analogies, in relation to the contemporaneous invasion of Lebanon, was equally evident in sections of the left at the same time.[7] The Non-German Germans, by contrast, were not constituted purely by negation. They wanted to transform their social environment by making it nonnational. But why use this specific term? The Non-German German is, of course, an adaptation of the famous term, "Non-Jewish Jew," coined by the Polish Jewish historian, Isaac Deutscher. The link between the two identities is more than semantic. A universalist, postnational orientation constitutes their inner affinity. The non-Jewish Jew is the Jewish heretic, the rebel, perhaps especially for the Marxist Deutscher, the revolutionary. His heroes were Baruch Spinoza, Heinrich Heine, Karl Marx, Rosa Luxemburg, Leon Trotsky, and Sigmund Freud. It is true that many of them left not only Judaism but any Jewish identity behind, yet Deutscher insisted that they belonged to a venerable Jewish tradition nonetheless.[8]

---

[4] Eike Geisel, *Die Banalität des Guten: Deutsche Seelenwanderungen* (Berlin, 1992), 17. This term is a play on *Otto Normaverbraucher*, the average citizen, as in "the man on the Clapham omnibus."

[5] This term is used by Klaus Rainer Röhl (b. 1928) in his angry settling of accounts with former, fellow leftist: Röhl, "Morgenthau und Antifa: Über den Selbsthaß der Deutschen," in Heimo Schwilk und Ulrich Schacht, eds., *Die selbstbewußte Nation: "Anschwellende Bockgesänge" und weitere Beiträge zu einer deutschen Debatte* (Berlin, 1994), 85–100.

[6] Vigilant in combating contemporary manifestations of the problem, they now identify Islamism as a form of National Socialism, and condemn "Old Europe's" stance of diplomatic solutions to Iran's nuclear aspirations as a form of "collaboration." See the new journal, *Promodo: Zeitschrift in eigener Sache*, 1 (October 2005), 46, www.promodo-online.org, which carried an announcement for an "antideutsche Konferenz": "Kritik und Parteilichkeit Aufruf zur antideutschen Konferenz am 18. und 19. November 2005 in Berlin." See also www.redaktion-bahamas.org and www.jungleworld.org. I am grateful to Norbert Finzsch for drawing my attention to these references. A critique by a former anti-German is Robert Kurz, *Die Antideutsche Ideologie: Vom Antifaschismus zum Krisenimperialismus* (Münster, 2003).

[7] Susann Heenan, "Deutsche Linke, Linke Juden und der Zionismus," in Dietrich Wetzel, ed., *Die Verlängerung der Geschichte: Deutsche, Juden und der Palästinakonflikt* (Frankfurt, 1983), 109, cited in Anson Rabinbach, "Introduction: Reflections on Germans and Jews since Auschwitz," in Anson Rabinbach and Jack Zipes, eds., *Germans and Jews since the Holocaust: The Changing Situation in West Germany* (New York, 1986), 10.

[8] Isaac Deutscher, *The Non-Jewish Jew and Other Essays*, ed. and intro. Tamara Deutscher (London, 1968), 27.

Precisely because Jews did not have their own nation-state and always had to contend with the Other, even in Galician Shetls where Deutscher grew up, they were not permitted "to reconcile themselves to ideas which were nationally or religiously limited, [which] induced them to strive for a universal *Weltanschauung*."[9] By leaving tradition behind, these Non-Jewish Jews resolved a tension in Jewish identity in the cosmopolitan, universalistic, and international direction that Deutscher preferred. That tension, he argued, inhered in the Jewish God who was unitary yet universal, but revealed himself to a single chosen people. The tension was resolved by figures like Spinoza whose ethics, Deutscher wrote, remained Jewish "except that his was Jewish monotheism carried to its logical conclusion and the Jewish universal God thought out to the end; and once thought out to the end, that God ceased to be Jewish."[10]

Why was the Non-Jewish Jew important for world history in Deutscher's view? In his Marxist voice, he argued that the "moral and political heritage, that the genius of the Jews who have gone beyond Jewry has left us the message of universal human emancipation." Later, he wrote less of a flattening-out of national or cultural differences than of "supra-national forms of social existence" that retained some cultural particularity. Writing in the 1960s, he was convinced that the age of the nation-state was coming to an end.[11]

There are obvious connections to Germany. It is not that Deutscher's Polish Jewish family was originally from Nuremberg and that his father remained in thrall to German culture. His son Isaac, after all, was fascinated by Yiddish and Polish culture. The connection was that the articulator of the Non-German German idea, Habermas, was thinking in similar terms at the same time as Deutscher was writing in the late 1950s. Like Deutscher, he moved from particularism to universalism. And, like Deutscher, he favored a world released from national egoism, and he also argued that world history was moving beyond the nation-state.

Jürgen Habermas's Non-German Germanism

Jürgen Habermas, born in 1929, is an ideal figure with whom to trace the evolution of the redemptive republican orientation in the Federal Republic. As the country's most important social philosopher, he was able to articulate this political language in the most sophisticated terms. Little is known of his youth, but one can surmise that it was not perfectly happy. For the boy had a severe cleft palate and could talk only with great difficulty, nor was he able to participate in the sporting activities that were so important for children in the

---

[9] Ibid., 30.

[10] Ibid.

[11] Above all, he rejected the imperative that his "dominant emotion" must be "belonging to Jewry," by which he meant feeling compelled to support Israel, to which he referred as "this new [nationalist] Hebrew mutation of the Jewish consciousness." Ibid., 92, 56.

area. Moreover, in the "racial state" of Nazi Germany, and indeed beforehand, such disabilities were marked as "inheritable diseases" that further isolated and marginalized the sufferer. Habermas's father, Ernst, head of the local chamber of commerce and a staunch nationalist, joined the Nazi Party, but his mother was a sensitive, intellectual personality who kept an apolitical distance to the world of great ideologies.[12] Confessionally, Habermas's hometown of Gummersbach is dominated by pietism, and its culture of inwardness, spiritual rebirth, and "new reformation" no doubt suffused the Habermas household: his grandfather had been a Protestant minister and head of the local seminary.[13]

Habermas joined the Hitler Youth despite his disability, serving as a field nurse toward the war's end, but avoiding the call-up for the final, futile defense of the area by absconding into the local countryside. He wrote that he experienced the war's end as a liberation. A few weeks after Germany's surrender, he saw the Allied films of the concentration camps and realized that he had been living in a system run by criminals. It was a great moral shock.

At the age of 15 or 16, we sat before the radio and experienced what was being discussed before the Nuremberg tribunal; when others, instead of being struck silent by the ghastliness, began to dispute the justice of the trial, procedural questions, and questions of jurisdiction, there was that first rupture, which still gapes. Certainly, it is only because I was still sensitive and easily offended that I did not close myself to the fact of collectively realized inhumanity in the same measure as my elders.[14]

Ever since, he has been unable to possess a basic trust in his social environment. It had become polluted. "There is nothing at all to which I have an unambivalent attitude, at least apart from very rare moments.... This has to do with very personal experiences, which I would rather not speak about, but also with critical moments – for example with the coincidence of great events and my own puberty in 1945."[15]

The experience of alienation from national tradition was shared by ex-soldiers. Habermas's student friend in Bonn, Karl-Otto Apel (b. 1922), felt that "everything was false" for which he had fought as a soldier and, therefore, that it was impossible to return to some "normality."[16] The left-wing educationalist Hans-Jochen Gamm (b. 1925) was handed over to the Russians by the Americans after 1945 and spent four years as a prisoner of war in Eastern Europe. Before setting him free, the Soviets made him and other POWs visit Auschwitz, and it was this experience that set him against the perceived fruits of German

---

[12] There is a portrait of Ernst Habermas in Benno von Wiese, *Ich erzähle mein Leben. Erinnerungen* (Frankfurt, 1982).

[13] Peter Dews, ed., *Habermas: Autonomy and Solidarity* (London, 1986).

[14] Jürgen Habermas, "The German Idealism of the Jewish Philosophers" (1961), in his *Philosophical-Political Profiles*, trans. Frederick G. Lawrence (Cambridge, Mass., 1983), 41.

[15] Dews, *Habermas: Autonomy and Solidarity*, 126.

[16] Karl-Otto Apel, "Zurück zur Normalität? Oder können wir aus der nationalen Katastrophe etwas Besonderes gelernt haben?" in Forum für Philosophie, Bad Homburg, ed., *Zerstörung des moralischen Selbstbewußtseins: Chance oder Gefährdung?* (Frankfurt, 1988), 94.

hypernationalism.[17] This was also the reaction of Günter Grass, who had been a Waffen-SS soldier on the eastern front near Gdansk.[18]

Contrast this reaction with the German German historian Reinhart Kosel-leck, who was similarly forced to visit Auschwitz as a POW. He did not attribute the Holocaust to overreaching German ambition, nor did he iden-tify or empathize with the victims to the exclusion of his own suffering and that of his comrades. He certainly recognized the enormities that Germans had inflicted, but they did not disturb his national loyalty, and he was able to repress the news of the massacres of Babi Yar in order to carry out his duties in good conscience, as he admitted in retrospect.[19]

The question was whom to blame. Of course, Germans had instigated and committed the crimes, but had they been expediting a barbarous mission of a specific German national destiny that needed to be abandoned outright after 1945? Or had they been in thrall to a totalitarian ideology that, now consigned to history, made "Germany" essentially harmless? The reaction to the Nazi past and its crimes provoked widely divergent reactions, but they possessed an iron logic. To the extent that one attributed its causes to particularly German characteristics, one was forced to reconfigure one's identity in Non-German German terms by effecting a radical break with inherited traditions. By contrast, to the extent that one felt, like Hennis, Koselleck, and others, that the causes were generally modern and European as well as German, it was possible to distinguish Germans from Nazis and therefore feel more comfortable with the continuity of personnel into the new regime.

A Moral Renewal?

The late 1940s was a time of intellectual opening for the forty-fivers, and Habermas fell upon the cheap series of "RoRoRo" books and the Marxist books available at a local communist bookstore, as well as the literature of Sartre, Wolfgang Borchert, Alfred Andersch, Richter, and, later, Heinrich Böll. Because of his acute moral sensitivity, he shared with some of these authors the hope that the Nazi past would be the occasion for a break with the past. "We believed that a spiritual and moral renewal was indispensable and inevitable."[20] "I thought then . . . if only there had been some spontaneous sweeping away, some explosive act, which then could have served to begin the formation of political authority. After such an eruption we would have at least known what we couldn't go back to."[21] Later he would write, as Jaspers did, that his hopes

---

[17] Hans-Jochen Gamm, "Pädagogischer Ausgangspunkt: Ein mecklenburgischer Tagelöhner-karten," in Wolfgang Klafki, ed., *Verführung, Distanzierung, Ernüchterung. Kindheit und Jugend im National-sozialismus* (Weinheim and Basel, 1988), 81–107.

[18] Günter Grass, "Der lernende Lehrer," *Die Zeit* (May 29, 1999), 41–43.

[19] Reinhart Koselleck, "Glühende Lava, zur Erinnerung geronnen," *Frankfurt Allgemeine Zeitung* (May 6, 1995).

[20] Dews, *Habermas: Autonomy and Solidarity*, 35.

[21] Ibid., 75.

"at that time were so unrealistic that I cannot begin to relate them to the present day."[22]

If such hopes seemed unrealistic, they were nonetheless widely shared. As the writer Wolfdietrich Schnürre (1920–89), a founding member of the Gruppe 47, recalled in 1961:

Let us recall the first postwar years: think of the hopes that we had. Think of the fear that would not leave us.... We were scared that one would not draw the right political conclusions from the merciless debacle of those twelve bestial years. We were scared that one would not draw the line sharply enough against the National Socialists. And we were, above all, scared that German militarism might rise again.[23]

At the same time, the novelist Siegfried Lenz (b. 1926) recalled:

I was nineteen at the end of the war, and the first newspaper that was free from lies I read in the POW camp. At that time, there was the hope of a purification, the wish to do at least the minimum of justice for all victims in that one brought to justice those responsible and excluded them [from power]. Whoever was prepared to continue our history would have to work assiduously, without other considerations, for the justice of the defenseless and victims – not to answer the hatred of the executioner with that of the judge, but to make credible our morality.[24]

But, as we know, such a moral cleansing and a radical new political beginning did not occur, and these writers observed with dismay how the old elites reestablished themselves. "What our reality is can be seen in the tenured judge who broke the law, doctors who once worked in the euthanasia programs and now practice privately, pampered functionaries of a brutal state who now again have a state function."[25] Schnürre echoed these comments: "Soon the Nazis, who were never really removed from power and who were declared harmless by the law, inherited the democracy and, with the camouflage of bonhomie and joviality, trickled into the public offices, the economy, politics, justice, journalism, medicine, the arts, and academia."[26]

Indeed, by the mid-1950s, left-wing commentators were speaking of a creeping "renazification" by which the restoration was being affected. Such was the resurgence of ex-Nazis in public life, the professions, and the economy after the very popular amnesty laws of 1949 for war criminals, including murderous *Einsatzgruppen* commanders, and especially after the so-called 131 law of 1951 that permitted "burdened" civil servants to reclaim their jobs, that Kogon was moved to write that democrats were "virtually with their backs to the wall" of the resistance bunkers.[27] The ex-Nazis, who by no means had abandoned the

---

[22] Ibid., 35.
[23] Wolfdieter Schnurre, "Das falsche Gleis," in Martin Walser, ed., *Die Alternative oder brauchen wir eine neue Regierung?* (Reinbeck, 1961), 68–69.
[24] Siegfried Lenz, "Die Politik der Entmündigung," in Walser, *Die Alternative*, 133–34.
[25] Ibid., 134.
[26] Schnürre, "Das falsche Gleiss," 69.
[27] E(ugen) K(ogon), "Beinahe mit dem Rücken an der Wand," *Frankfurter Hefte*, 9:9 (September 1954), 641–45. See Norbert Frei, "Das Problem der NS-Vergangenheit in der Ära Adenauer,"

predispositions that had led them to support the former regime, now conspired against those critics who had opposed Hitler, he exclaimed. As contemporary historian Karl Dietrich Bracher pointed out, the integration of these people had dire consequences for public culture.[28] The *Deutsche Universitäts-Zeitung* worried in 1952 about intellectual conformity of "planned opinion formation" due to nationalist resentments and prejudices.[29] The journalist Harry Pross (b. 1923) went so far as to write that "in its political significance and effect, this law [article 131] is no better than Hitler's law on the protection of German career civil service," a law that expelled Jews from the civil service.[30] A young Imanuel Geiss (b. 1931), who thirty years later was to break with the leftist camp during the Historians' Dispute, complained in 1955 that the *Abendland* groups of conservative intellectuals hankered for an authoritarian regime "similar to that founded by Dollfuss in Austria twenty years ago, and that still exists in Franco-Spain."[31] The Social Democrat Hans Tietgens (b. 1922) commented dryly that "When concentration camps are supposed to be made up for by autobahns, something must be wrong with the spiritual-intellectual [*seelisch-geistig*] economy."[32]

Habermas was outraged that Germans did not take seriously enough the crimes that had been committed by many of their number and in their collective name.[33] The postwar behavior of Heidegger, Carl Schmitt, and Ernst Jünger had appalled Habermas and ruptured his relations with them after his youthful enthusiasm. "You cannot imagine what this legacy did to bourgeois students after the war," he said in an interview, "who encountered an essential continuity in the universities."

There was no break in terms of persons or courses. The two pre-eminent thinkers – who determined the direction of my philosophical interests – were Heidegger and Gehlen. The expressionist poet with whom everybody identified was Benn. Nobody told us about their past. We had to find out step by step for ourselves. It took me four years of studies, mostly just by accident looking into books in libraries, to discover what they had been thinking only a decade or decade and a half ago. Think what that meant.[34]

Of their postwar lack of remorse and contrition, Habermas wrote that "The moral and psychological implication was devastating," and this reaction applied to no one more than his revered teacher, the Bonn philosopher

in Bernd Weisbrod, ed., *Rechtsradikalismus in der politischen Kultur der Nachkriegszeit. Die verzögerte Normalisierung in Niedersachsen* (Hannover, 1995), 19–31.

[28] Karl Dietrich Bracher, "Rechtsradikalismus in der Bundesrepublik," *Colloquium*, 10:2 (1956), 9–11.

[29] Editorial, "Konformismus," *Deutsche Universitäts-Zeitung*, 7:2 (1952), 5.

[30] Harry Pross, "Nazismus – Vor und Nach Hitler (1961)," in his *Vor und Nach Hitler. Zur deutschen Pathologie* (Freiburg, 1962), 143–62.

[31] Imanuel Geiss, "Auf dem Wege zum 'Neuen Abendland,'" *Neue Gesellschaft*, 2:6 (November–December 1955), 41–46.

[32] Hans Tietgens, "Unbewältigte Vergangenheit," *Kulturarbeit*, 10:4 (1958), 73–76.

[33] Jürgen Habermas, *Die Normalität einer Berliner Republik* (Frankfurt, 1995), 33.

[34] Dews, *Habermas: Solidarity and Autonomy*, 196.

Erich Rothacker.[35] Habermas was particularly disturbed, for example, by the appointment of Hans-Christoph Seebohm (1903–67) as the transport minister in Konrad Adenauer's first cabinet, a man who once belonged to the right-wing German People's Party in the Weimar Republic. Habermas witnessed him at a preelection rally in Göttingen in 1949, where imperial regalia and nationalist pomp were on show, including the first verse of the German anthem, "Deutschland über Alles." The twenty-year-old student was incensed and stormed out of the meeting "in an emotional furor."[36] That such an unrepentant man as Seebohm who embodied a continuity from a discredited past could form an integral part of the new order did not incline Habermas to trust it as the definitive answer to the Nazi experience.

The foundation of the Federal Republic was hardly the new, moral beginning for which he had hoped: "The first great political disappointment came with the formation of the government in 1949," he wrote, in stark contrast to the sentiments of Wilhelm Hennis.[37] Arno Klönne, who would later join Habermas as a student of the socialist political scientist Wolfgang Abendroth in Marburg, had hoped similarly for "something other than bourgeois arrangements" in the founding of the Federal Republic.[38] The foundation was, as Dirks and Kogon decried, a restoration rather than a new beginning. Although this was not his later position, the young Habermas's experience of Germany and, as we will see, modernity as a whole was that of a fallen, sinful world. Not surprisingly, he employed medical metaphors to refer to such corruption: "hygiene," "cleansing," "disease," and "infection."

The United States, the Cold War, Anticommunism, and Rearmament

Redemptive republicans were dismayed with the United States because its plans for West Germany dashed their hopes. Gerhard Schoenberner (b. 1931) pointed out that the outbreak of the Korean War changed U.S. occupation policy and stabilized West German material circumstances, "simultaneously destroying the chance for a political-moral new beginning. Overnight one dropped the plans for a democratic reeducation and tried to win over the Germans as allies in an anticommunist bloc. Hitherto one had done everything to destroy

---

[35] Ibid., 197. On Rothacker, see Thomas Weber, "Arbeit am Imaginären des Deutschen. Erich Rothackers Ideen für eine NS-Kulturpolitik," in Wolfgang Fritz Haug, ed., *Deutsche Philosophie 1933* (Hamburg, 1989), 125–58.

[36] Dews, *Habermas: Solidarity and Autonomy*, 35, 73. Seebohm, from a German Bohemian family that lost considerable property with its expulsion from the territory after the war, represented the right-wing in Adenauer's first government. His scandalous weekend speeches constantly embarrassed the chancellor, who was forced to discipline him on several occasions. In 1960 he became head of the Sudeten German organization. See Walter Henkels, *99 Bonner Köpfe* (Frankfurt, 1965), 232–34.

[37] Dews, *Habermas: Autonomy and Solidarity*, 74.

[38] Arno Klönne und Jürgen Reulecke, "'Restgeschichte' und 'neue Romantik': Ein Gespräch über Bündisch-Jugend in der Nachkriegszeit," in Franz-Werner Kersting, ed., *Jugend vor einer Welt in Trümmern* (Weinheim and Munich, 1998), 87–106.

Hitler-Germany, and so one hurried to restore the remaining torso."[39] Making the same point, Hans-Jochen Gamm complained of the "bitter consequences" of German remilitarization: "The West Germans were permitted by the Allies to collectively repress the past for the benefit of their integration into the Western alliance. The Western integration represented a surrogate achievement for a true inner and outer cleansing from fascism."[40] Anticommunism and ex-Nazis entered into an unholy alliance, not only preventing a new, moral beginning but, worse still, facilitating the rehabilitation of ex-Nazis. "If all the signs are not misleading," wrote Kurt Nemitz in 1955, "then the anticommunist fighting experience is a legitimation that increasingly paves the way for even heavily burdened functionaries of the Nazi regime to return to public life."[41]

By accepting ex-Nazis into the new state, the "antitotalitarian" consensus of integrative republicanism functioned to discredit those critics who objected to their integration.[42] This Cold War consensus was, in fact, not freely reached but propagated as official policy with the perverse consequence that anti-Nazi critics of the policy found themselves marginalized in the political culture of the 1950s. For this reason, the Berlin-based political thinker Otto von der Gablentz, himself on the left-wing of the CDU, wrote disparagingly of a "totalitarian anticommunism" that compelled political and intellectual conformism.[43] Writing somewhat later, Wolfgang Abendroth's former colleague, Werner Hofmann (1922–69), asked provocatively whether West German conservatives would use the term "totalitarianism" to refer to the authoritarian regimes in Spain, Portugal, or Greece that they supported? Obviously not, but what was more, the language of totalitarianism meant that even the memory of Nazism was used to attack anti-Nazis today.

> Whoever finds something to complain about with our Nazi past is supposed now, above all, to oppose the *current* dictatorship on German soil; he should line up in that social unity-front of defense that today stretches from the business councils to the unions ... the organizations of the old SS-soldiers, to the churches. Long ago, under the sign of the new antitotalitarianism, the former totalitarians have been able to find their place.[44]

This was the cost of integrative republicanism.

Habermas's doubts about the new order were strengthened by the rearmament debate in the early 1950s, and he found himself attracted, like Geiss and Erhard Eppler, to the new party of Gustav Heinemann, who left the CDU

[39] Gerhard Schoenberner, "Zerstörung der Demokratie," in Walser, *Die Alternative*, 137–45.
[40] Hans-Jochen Gamm, *Führung und Verführung: Pädagogik des Nationalsozialismus*, 2nd ed. (Frankfurt, 1984), 24.
[41] Kurt Nemitz, "Das Regime der Mitläufer. Soziologische Notizen zur Renazifizierung," *Neue Gesellschaft*, 11:3 (May–June, 1955), 39–45.
[42] Gesine Schwan, "Antikommunismus und Antiamerikanismus. Deutsches politisches Bewusstsein nach 1945," *Blätter für deutsche und internationale Politik*, 1 (1999), 77–87.
[43] Otto von der Gablentz, *Die versäumte Reform: Zur Kritik der westdeutschen Politik* (Cologne and Opladen, 1960).
[44] Werner Hofmann, *Stalinismus und Antikommunismus: Zur Soziologie des Ost-West Konflikts*, rev. ed. (Frankfurt, 1969), 132–33.

on pacifist grounds. On behalf of the Gesamtdeutsche Volkspartei (The All-German People's Party), Eppler polemicized against Germany's involvement in the Cold War and poured scorn on the idea that America offered Germans a viable social system. The American and Soviet arms race posed a grave threat to Germany, and so he advocated a "third force" of European and nonaligned countries to oppose the two power blocs and deescalate the conflict. Consequently, he opposed the Federal Republic's "West integration," because only a united Germany in a united Europe could move beyond the Cold War fronts.[45] Habermas argued similarly for the "historical chance" for disarmament outside the Soviet and North American hegemony. The consequent social and economic progress in those nonaligned countries would force the belligerents of the Cold War to relinquish their stockpiling. "It is the chance to banish war from the world by virtue of the punishment of [economic] decline."[46]

Eppler, Habermas, and many other redemptive republicans also entertained hopes of a "third way" not only as a power bloc between the Soviet Union and Western military alliance but also between communism and capitalism. They were devastated, for example, by Adenauer's determination not to respond to Soviet overtures in 1952 about negotiating toward a neutral, demilitarized Germany.

Whatever view is taken today of the political significance of Stalin's Note of March 1952, this was a date that played a major role in my own life because in rejecting this offer the Federal Republic ensured the military integration of the Federal Republic into the Western hemisphere. This meant that we had to abandon all hope of a neutralist solution which might have prevented the two social systems of German soil from becoming sealed off from each other.[47]

Habermas and Klönne identified a particular generational posture in this regard. "We are the better Europeans," Habermas wrote in 1955 with reference to his student generation, because "we don't have the national resentments" of the government leaders "who think in terms of [power] blocs" and for whom there is no "European integration against the policy of the fortified front between east and west." Accordingly, he defended the *ohne mich* (without me) spirit of skeptical distance that many younger Germans had for the policies of the new regime and NATO against conservative politicians who sought support of the government's foreign policy goals just as Hennis had criticized it.[48] This attitude, the fruit of "especially painful experiences of the collapse" (of Germany in 1945), had a positive dimension for those "who once

[45] Erhard Eppler, *Haller Tagblatt* (September 6, 1953), in his *Einsprüche* (Freiburg, 1986), 55–56.
[46] Jürgen Habermas, "Der verschleiete Schrecken," *Frankfurter Hefte*, 13 (1958), 530–32.
[47] Dews, *Habermas: Autonomy and Solidarity*, 39, 36.
[48] Jürgen Habermas, "'Ohne Mich' auf dem Index," *Deutsche Studentenzeitung*, 5:5 (1955), 1–2; Arno Klönne, "Ausserschulische Pädagogik 'im Geiste der Jugendbewegung.' Anknüpfungen an jugend-bündische Traditionen nach 1945," in Paul Ciupke and Franz-Joseph Jelich, eds., *Ein neuer Anfang. Politische Jugend- und Erwachsenenbildung in der westdeutschen Nachkriegsgesellschaft* (Essen, 1999), 34.

linked the demand for a new and clean order with the insight into the unique chance of 1945." This chance was the withdrawal of Germany from "world-historical engagement" for "creative retreat": "We would be freed from the pace of events and therewith from the force of routine. We could utilize the potential for unusual experiences for a renewed, western order of life." Reflecting on these dashed hopes, he added: "What disappointment the actual developments brought: the rapidity with which one rehabilitated and continued as before, with which a German future, which was built on the crumbly surface of a past draped in taboos, was once again cast in world-historical categories."[49] His was the resolute "no" to West Germany as an integrative republic, epitomized by Walter Jens's *Nein – Die Welt der Angeklagten* from 1950.

Again like Eppler, Habermas rejected the image of the West offered by the Federal Republican establishment. With its virulent anticommunism, he doubted the authenticity of the talk of "renewing the West," which he called "the appearance of the West." His was a loyalty to "the disinfected West, which is immune to the bacillus of Hispanicization, and that has not already moved into the stage of incubation," by which he apparently meant the process of becoming like Franco's Spain. At the same time, he announced his preference for "republican abstraction," rather than for the concrete, historical nation, even if it was a federal republic. It needed to be cleansed.[50]

But what precisely was this infection? Was it simply the presence of unrepentant Nazis in German society? What precisely did he mean by "Hispanicization"? Evidently, he was referring to processes that transcended Germany. It is necessary to examine Habermas's early cultural-critical writings to elucidate his critique of modernity's relationship to the Nazism. As we will see, redemptive leftists drew system-challenging consequences from the Nazi past. By contrast, liberal commentators who also flagged the problem of unrepentant Nazis and authoritarian popular mentalities, like Kurt Sontheimer and Bracher, were concerned with inculcating the personal dispositions and political culture of liberal democracy. For all their critique, they were integrative republicans because they affirmed the foundation of the state in 1949 and wanted the population to live up to its standards. The system did not need transformation. But for redemptive republicans, the economic and social system as a whole was irredeemably corrupt and polluted by Nazism and the Holocaust. It was necessary, therefore, to set out on a new project.

"Submission to the Higher"

Habermas began his studies in Göttingen in 1949, but he soon moved to Bonn where his main teachers were Oskar Becker and Erich Rothacker. The atmosphere there, he recalled later, was like the 1920s, and although he was

---

[49] Habermas, "'Ohne Mich' auf dem Index," 2.
[50] Jürgen Habermas, "Der Verrat und die Maßstäbe. Wenn Jungkonservative alt werden," *Deutsche Universitäts-Zeitung*, 11:19 (1956), 8–11.

subsequently highly critical of this anachronism, at the time it suited his own psychological and intellectual needs very well. As skeptics of modernity, Habermas's teachers were able to provide the sensitive young man with the tools to challenge the status quo. He completed his 400-page doctoral dissertation – an unusually long work by the standards of the day – on the historical philosophy of Friedrich Schelling in 1954, but he had declared his historical and political concerns beforehand in book reviews and articles in the *Frankfurter Allgemeine Zeitung*. In "Im Lichte Heideggers," the twenty-three-year-old student of philosophy revealed himself as the master's ardent disciple.[51] Heidegger's question, he averred, was the correct one: "the question of Being. It is ... the question of the basis of Western thought since Plato, the essence and depravity [*Wesen und Unwesen*] that has culminated in modern technology." It was the Freiburg professor who unmasked the pretensions of science. "Only Heidegger topples the metaphysical belief in the permanence of a given essence, and he shows that the foundation of the self-empowering and securing subject in scientific certainty is a flight to the apparent certainty of ultimately unbinding truths." Habermas agreed that humans need to learn a "listening countenance" (*vernehmende Haltung*) toward things and that art was the realm where true experience occurred.

Heidegger's well-known critique of technology was only one compelling aspect of his philosophy. The other was its challenge to the philosophical and academic establishment as a whole, which ought to take notice of him, "for a large part of the older professors, who still determine the profile of the universities, seem to need desperately this lesson in order to equip themselves with the tools to engage in a sober discussion with Heidegger." And the aim of such a discussion would be to provoke a "healing crisis" against the "common sense" that held sway in the academy and wider society.

A month later, in June 1952, Habermas found stimulation in Gottfried Benn's latest publication. As with Heidegger, he was still largely ignorant of Benn's commitments in the 1930s and 1940s. He began his review of Benn's book as he began his dissertation – with the words of Leopold von Ranke that each age was immediate to God. Such historical relativism meant that no absolute standards existed. If Benn also renounced transcendental values and sought orientation in the static forms of art, Habermas thought he saw an existentialist answer in his work. The answer was not the art object itself, but the work of the artist as an answer to a destiny – "the voice behind the curtain" – to which each of us was called. "But when the primary imperative is to bear one's destiny, the person can accept it or not. And this 'or' is the measure of all that is good and bad." What this call and its significance were would become clearer several years later.[52]

For the young Habermas, Heidegger and Benn were the radical thinkers of new beginnings who helped him relate his polluted family and national past.

---

[51] Jürgen Habermas, "Im Lichte Heideggers," *Frankfurter Allgemeine Zeitung* (May 12, 1952).

[52] Jürgen Habermas, "Gottfried Benns neue Stimme," *Frankfurter Allgemeine Zeitung* (June 19, 1953), 6.

How disturbing it was, then, when Habermas discovered their recent Nazi past. In his celebrated attack on the former in 1953, he bitterly criticized his philosophical idol for republishing his 1935 lectures on metaphysics without a new preface that withdrew the phrase about "the inner truth and greatness" of National Socialism. Still, the title of his intervention, "Mit Heidegger gegen Heidegger denken" (Thinking with Heidegger against Heidegger) indicated that this incident had not resulted in a complete break with the master. The article revealed the themes that Habermas was treating in his dissertation, and that the interest in Heidegger was driven by his concern to recover a longer "underground" tradition of thought that challenged Western metaphysics: "that peculiarly German thinking...that goes back to Böhme via Schelling, Friedrich Hölderlin, and G. W. F. Hegel."[53]

Why was this "peculiarly German tradition" of interest? For Habermas it recovered and bore witness to the "listening countenance" toward things before it had been replaced by instrumental exploitation. It enabled the realization of the world's fallen state. The recovery of original contact with things when natural life cycles governed experience was made possible by the conservative critique of modernity and industrialization.[54] The Nazi philosopher Ludwig Klages, for example, tapped the "foreign experiences of that underground German philosophy, which flowed over Jakob Böhme, the Swabian pietists, and romanticism into the worldview conditions of the historical school." From his teacher Rothacker, himself a disciple of this school, Habermas learned to appreciate that Klages "unfolded...a myriad of observations that should not be obscured by the veil of an anti-intellectual metaphysics and an apocalyptic philosophy of history: above all, anthropological and speech-philosophical observations that are perhaps untimely, but then in Nietzsche's sense – not superseded, but rather that need to be realized [*einzuholen*]."[55]

> Theoretically [these insights] belong, well before Marx, to the polemical tradition of conservative thinkers since Burke.... Schelling's later writings are deep reflections on this theme, his student Stahl made them politically fruitful. Christian-romantic thought links alienation to the fall through sin.... Nonetheless, this tradition should not be forgotten, because it rescued certain phenomena. And this also includes that whole [*heile*] relationship to things in which openness and intimacy prevail, a contact that is surely more craftsmanlike than organic.[56]

He was of this opinion twenty years later when he wrote that conservative cultural critique "could possess serious theoretical interest" and that the

---

[53] Jürgen Habermas, "Mit Heidegger gegen Heidegger denken. Zur Veröffentlichung von Vorlesungen aus dem Jahre 1935," *Frankfurter Allgemeine Zeitung* (July 27, 1953). Reprinted in his *Philosophisch-Politische Profile* (Frankfurt, 1971), 67–75.

[54] Jürgen Habermas, "Notizen zum Missverhältnis von Kultur und Konsum," *Merkur*, 10 (1956), 212–28.

[55] Jürgen Habermas, "Ludwig Klages – überholt oder unzeitgemäß?" *Frankfurter Allgemeine Zeitung* (August 3, 1956), 8.

[56] Jürgen Habermas, "Die Dialektik der Rationalisierung. Vom Pauperismus in Produktion und Konsum," *Merkur*, 8 (August 1954), 718.

Anglophone "model of representative democracy" and "moderate empiricism" was insufficient.[57]

But in the mid-1950s it was Schelling who held his interest. For Schelling was the first serious philosopher of the nineteenth century who recovered the "underground" tradition of pietism and the kabbalah, a tradition that was revived in the 1920s by Heidegger.[58] The contemporary political implications of this tradition were drawn by the author himself in an important but neglected article on Schelling and "submission to the higher" in the *Frankfurter Allgemeine Zeitung* in 1954.[59] The older Schelling in his *Weltalter* writings, Habermas announced, embarked on a radical new direction in his philosophy after a period of deep depression, an experience of self-emptying, abandonment, and hopelessness. This experience was the basis of the gnostic epistemology that made philosophy an existential rather than theoretical practice. It was how the intellect allowed itself to be transformed by the Absolute.[60] In a veiled reference to the German collapse and the Holocaust, Habermas regarded this experience as a "not-yet-superseded event." It was an experience of self-abnegation that issued in a radical rupture with a corrupt past and that inaugurated a new beginning.

What precisely did the subject see at this point? It saw that the intellect had fouled creation, violated nature, and prevented the culmination of God's development in the world and the restitution of the "original playful feeling" of humans. The experience of self-emptying led to the consciousness of having to realize God's will as a conscious project so that active humanity restored the sundered bond between nature and God, earth and heaven. These were propositions, Habermas repeated, that originated in the "underground canals of the mystical, alchemical, kabbalistic, hermetical, and neo-Platonic traditions and that were carried by Leibniz, Boehme, and Paracelsus."

Why was the intellect the cause of evil for Schelling? Situated between the soul, which was linked to God, and the senses, which were rooted in nature, the intellect had to exist in harmony with the other human elements for an ordered relationship to God and nature. In works of art, the impersonal soul was expressed because the intellect submitted itself to this "impersonal force" that "effaces all human subjectivity." Humans partook in the divine when they produced and maintained the divine order. Where the intellect did not submit itself to the soul, the world became but a resource for its capricious desires. "Falsity always results where the intellect does not want to give up its autonomy." Evil was pure, autonomous intellect, and this insight, Habermas urged,

[57] Jürgen Habermas, "The Intellectual and Social Background of the German University Crisis. Review of F. K. Ringer, *The Decline of the German Mandarins*," *Minerva*, 9 (July 1971), 427.

[58] Jürgen Habermas, "Das Absolute und die Geschichte" (Dr. Phil. dissertation, Bonn University, 1954), 11.

[59] Jürgen Habermas, "Schelling und die 'Submission unter das Höhere,'" *Frankfurter Allgemeine Zeitung* (August 21, 1954).

[60] Josef Kreulatz, *Die verkehrte Welt des Jürgen Habermas*, trans. Inge van der Aart (Hamburg 1995), 51.

was the key to understanding the catastrophes of the recent past and present. "Today we have, in an age of philosophically garbed ideologies and hygienic mass-murders, experienced the truth of this [idea] many times and painfully; we have been taught violently that the most shameless insults against humanity do not emanate from immediate impulses, but come far more from the final workings, and are the product of, thoroughly neutral and perfectly calculated organizations." Here, then, we have an early statement of the now common-place proposition that modernity and the Holocaust are closely linked in a causal nexus.

Habermas regarded Schelling as bearing a message for the Federal Republic by demonstrating the danger of the natural sciences and humanities that ignored the integrity of the subjects they study. If Schelling could educate us to recover the limits of our investigations and tame the intellect, "then he belongs to the philosophers of today." In a review published in the same year, Habermas called for the "radical doubt" that shattered received categories and traditions; it was a "fire of cleansing" that led to a new moral consciousness, akin to a religious conversion. It afforded a new, true perspective.[61] In accordance with this newfound humility, the subject "submits itself to the higher." Here we have the "voice behind the curtain" of which Benn wrote. Habermas uses the terms "turnaround" (*Unwendung*) and "rebirth."

Schelling teaches, as the first step in the "free kingdom of the intellect," the philosophy not of knowing, but explicitly of not knowing, and the renunciation of the self-willedness of the instrumental and forming intellect. At the same time, he teaches that the free decision is not a self-determination or an insurance, but a self-sacrifice, a self-unlocking and an opening to a claim that is never concrete.[62]

Let us be clear about what Habermas was saying. He was not only explaining Schelling's case to contemporary Germans one hundred years after the philoso-pher's death. He was also urging his message as the salvation for Germany and modernity. Finally, he implied that he had undergone a conversion experience himself that afforded him privileged insight. In this new state of self-sacrifice and ego renunciation, he had moved beyond the fixed categories of reason, so that he was receptive to the call of conscience and the radical choices that faced humanity, a choice that led to ethical conflict.

Like Apel, Habermas interpreted the war and Holocaust as world-historical events into which he had "special insight."[63] It was not a matter of discerning the "historical possibilities" open to humanity, as he was to argue later. It was the world-historical mission to make the radical and existential choice open to modern people: either to continue in their sinful ways in a fallen world, or to

---

[61] Jürgen Habermas, "Philosophie als Risiko," *Frankfurter Allgemeine Zeitung* (June 19, 1954).
[62] Jürgen Habermas, "Karl Jaspers über Schelling," *Frankfurter Allgemeine Zeitung* (January 14, 1956). Reprinted in his *Philosophisch-politische Profile*, 97.
[63] Apel, "Zurück zur Normalität?" 94.

renounce this world and set out anew by repairing the sundered bond between God, humanity, and nature.

Habermas called this process "philosophy as risk taking," and this theme arose whenever he expressed dismay at his fellow Germans' failure to use the collapse of 1945 and Auschwitz to reflect critically on their past. For example, in a review of a film about the war, he complained that it did not confront its viewers with the "bitterness and evil" of the past, thereby permitting the pernicious practice of rehabilitating so-called good elements from the past, rather than allowing its viewers to experience the "cleansing" rupture with it. By playing up the fear of "the Russians" and offering "state-guaranteed security," the film downplayed the "personal risk" inherent in the shattering of collective identification, thereby denying them the redemptive republican perspective of the forty-fivers.

The virtues of our fathers need to be broken in the medium of that experience that we had in the historical emergency [of 1945], and that thereby enables us, above all others, to find a current and creative, in any event, appropriate answer. Let us note the experience of the certain tact and the sublime sensibility of the young against the inhuman consequences of collective processes as the most precious. The system that silences the conditions in which these experiences were born demolishes the only effective potential that gives him the chance to live in dignity. It is characteristic of totalitarian systems that they repress the present; how much better is a system that prizes silence about the past so that it is forgotten.[64]

The popular culture of war films and the "system" of Cold War propaganda conspired to prevent other Germans from experiencing what Habermas had: the risk of the self-emptying, cathartic moment that broke one's relationship with the German collective and its past. He had no need to rehabilitate "good aspects" of this past because he thought it was polluted and should be stigmatized. Would that all other Germans do the same.

It was Heidegger, above all, who had failed to make the radical choice. He wanted to see the Nazi period as a chapter in the history of Being rather than in moral terms, Habermas accused, in order to explain away his appalling behavior at the time. But, he demanded, "Is the planned murder of millions of people, about which we all know, explicable as a fateful error in the history of Being? Is it not the actual crime of those who committed them as responsible human beings – and the evil conscience of a whole people? Have we not had eight years to accept the risk of the wrestling with that which we were?"[65] To be sure, Heidegger's interpretation of Nazism as an event in the history of Being did not necessarily mean that he approved of National Socialism, but neither did this interpretation exclude it. At the very best, Heidegger had erred in passively giving himself over to the call of Being. In such circumstances,

---

[64] Jürgen Habermas, "'Morgengrauen' – morgen das Grauen," *Süddeutsche Zeitung* (October 2–3, 1954).
[65] Habermas, "Mit Heidegger gegen Heidegger denken."

"was not a turnaround warranted that as a real act of metonia, conversion, and contrition questions one's own past that still needs an accounting for?"[66]

There is no necessary contradiction between Habermas's point about the omnipotence of modernizing social processes and the importance of individual responsibility. Once individuals recognized the nature of these processes, they were faced with an existential choice about how they were to comport themselves toward them. Habermas had made it his task to tell Germans about this choice and their moral duty. For him, there could be only one choice, and it entailed rejecting any notion of "positive continuities" from the German past. Those who thought they could identify some were not just different, they were perverse. Here was a moralization of a complex political and ethical situation, an absolute claim based on a privileged insight into the truth that did not allow for pluralism or toleration. That was the logic of redemptive republicanism.

The Incubus of Technology and German Tradition

In the early and mid-1950s, Habermas's critique of technology borrowed consciously from the arsenal of conservative cultural criticism, and his newspaper and journal articles of the time are replete with its standard themes: the inner drive of technology to perfectionism and autonomization (*Verselbständigung*) so that it dominated its creators, "dictating what their priorities were." The products of industry were not useful aids for human consumption but the poisoned fruit of a system alienated from human needs. "They are contourless, impersonal, and faceless and make humans strangers in their world, because they exist for purposes to which the authority of technical intelligence submits even though they have not accounted for the practical intelligence of the users."[67] Marx had not appreciated this aspect of technology and consumerism, Habermas argued, because he believed that workers could enjoy the fruits of their labor power after the means of production had been socialized. How impoverished they in fact were by the alienated world of things was evident in the inability of Americans to relax.[68]

Obviously, the task was to resist the "fiery moloch" of technology that had taken on a life of its own, spreading its tentacles around the globe and devouring the delicate life worlds everywhere. The peril to culture was so serious, he thought, that the shortened working day of a worker in the age of mass consumerism was as alienating as the sixteen-hour day of a factory worker at the

[66] Jürgen Habermas, "Freiheit, Anruf und Gewissen," *Frankfurter Allgemeine Zeitung* (August 29, 1953).

[67] Jürgen Habermas, "Der Moloch und die Künste. Gedanken zur Entlarvung der Legende von der technischen Zweckmässigkeit," *Frankfurter Allgemeine Zeitung* (May 39, 1953); Habermas, "Autofahren. Der Mensch am Lenkrad," *Frankfurter Allgemeine Zeitung* (November 27, 1954).

[68] Jürgen Habermas, "Die Dialektik der Rationalisierung. Vom Pauperismus in Produktion und Konsum," *Merkur*, 8 (August 1954), 716; Habermas, "Marx in Perspektiven," *Merkur*, 9 (1955), 994–98.

beginning of the nineteenth century. "Such self-endangering demands a new style-forming answer, the crystallization of a new posture."[69]

It was unclear, however, how this problem related to fascism. Was rampant technology the culmination of fascism, as Heidegger had argued apologetically? Or were particular German elements involved? Habermas seemed ambivalent on the question. At certain points, he wrote of fascism in terms of "the autonomized apparatus," and he considered intelligence tests to be a transnational problem: "The human experiments of fascist doctors demonstrate only too drastically where the inner development of the 'method' leads as soon as it breaks through the alien bonds of piety." The "exact method" of science led to "inhuman consequences," because it objectified people, "that most vulnerable of beings," and because it produced an orientation that prepared the way for political systems "of human contempt."[70]

At other points, he was adamant that a particular German intellectual tradition was at fault. In fact, the problem was the same conservative cultural criticism that provided him with so many insights into the phenomenon of technology. For its mandarin proponents proposed to control technology by appeals to "nature" or "culture," that is, to traditions and ideals that culminated in the conservative revolution of the Weimar Republic with its catastrophic consequences.[71] Fascism was not a perversion of conservative answers to modernity, as some commentators had argued, but its inevitable result: it was the "empirically . . . provided proof that reform plans that revolve around status, inheritance, power, and community, whether sanctioned by a god, Being, or nature, necessarily result in totalitarian practice in the social conditions of the twentieth century."[72] The problem after the war was that the German mandarins, including the outsider Heidegger, did not critically reflect on their cherished "German tradition." According to this exegesis, the cause of fascism was not technology itself, but the irrational myths of social integration that aimed to control technology, like "nature" or the "community," which were particularly prevalent among German intellectual elites. After all, modernity had not resulted in fascism in the Western democracies.

For all that, Habermas's reading of Theodor W. Adorno and Max Horkheimer's *Dialectic of Enlightenment* in 1955 taught him that the myth of reason as absolute domination was the fundamental problem. Here we are back to the problem of the autonomous technology that could obtain in any country. Plainly, he saw both phenomena as deeply problematic. Prewar conservatism, he noted, had been discredited or destroyed, so intellectual conservatives

---

[69] Habermas, "Die Dialektik der Rationalisierung," 719–23.

[70] Jürgen Habermas, "Der biographische Schleier," *Frankfurter Hefte*, 12 (1957), 357–60; Habermas, "Für und wider den Test. Gegen den Geist der Menschenverachtung," *Frankfurter Allgemeine Zeitung* (September 11, 1954).

[71] Jürgen Habermas, "Wider den moralpädagogischen Hochmut der Kulturkritik," *Die Literatur*, 13 (September 15, 1952), 6.

[72] Jürgen Habermas, "Der Verrat und die Maßstäbe. Wenn Jungkonservative alt werden," *Deutsche Universitäts-Zeitung*, 11:19 (1956), 10.

embraced what he called "third-generation conservatism" – that is, neither antimodern resistance to modernity, nor the radicalism of the "conservative revolution," but positivism. Although postwar conservatives decried consumer culture, they actually approved of its compensatory function for "the masses," thereby preaching a new conformism. Consumer culture was now the pernicious myth, rather than the older German legacies.[73]

Even so, Habermas could have been more specific about the difference between these phenomena. On only one occasion was he explicit about the tension in this thinking:

Because today humanity has developed the potential for technical domination and strategic annihilation that surpasses all historical comparison, the essential balance between the impulses of the heart and the capacities of the brain appear to be disturbed. In this regard, it is difficult to say what is politically more dangerous: the most modern means in the naive garb of a traditionally minded orientation – or the autonomous calculation on the rock of which an extinct humanity will be erected.[74]

If he saw the former as fascist, what of the latter? Obviously Habermas did not think the liberal democracies were the same as totalitarian states, despite his critique of mass consumer culture in the Federal Republic and the West. The problem with positivism, then, could not have been that it was fascist itself but that it was an inadequate protection against its recurrence – indeed, that it provoked fascist responses. But this distinction was never clear in his writing, for example, in his first long article, "The Dialectics of Rationalization" of 1954, in which he first outlined his theory of rationalization. Because the end point of technological rationalization was cultural poverty and alienation, he argued, it provoked social rationalization, which was the reappropriation of production by the worker in order to allow him or her to invest some "style" into his or her product. Style was a basic category of Habermas's anthropology, a lesson he learned from Rothacker.[75]

Such a "hygienic process," as he called the cultivation of style, broke the cycle of consumption and advertising by creating goods for a human rather than a technological world. True, such interventions would reduce production by retarding the division of labor, and to that extent social rationalization was economically irrational. But what was truly irrational, he countered, was the cultural impoverishment of humans, and so it was ultimately rational for workers at least partly to control production in order to permit them to become creators of culture.[76] Habermas's answer to rationalization, then, was not to resist it stoically, as the German mandarins had urged, or to control it in the

[73] Jürgen Habermas, "Konsumkritik – eigens zum Konsumieren," *Frankfurter Hefte*, 12 (1957), 641–44.

[74] Jürgen Habermas, "Auf- und Abrüstung, moralisch und militärisch," *Merkur*, 17 (1963), 714–17.

[75] Jürgen Habermas, "Anthropologie," in Alwin Diemer and Ivo Frenzel, eds., *Philosophie* (Frankfurt, 1958), 18–35.

[76] Habermas, "Die Dialektik der Rationalisierung," 720.

name of "substantial communities" like fascism, but to complete the process by democratizing the production and consumption of art and culture.[77]

As always, Habermas posed the German and human situation in existentialist terms. Humans possessed the choice between rejecting consumer culture for a new comportment toward technology or continuing in their fallen ways with the attendant dangers of nuclear war and totalitarianism. But how were they to be made aware of this choice when they were in thrall to advertising? How could social rationalization be implicit in the rationalization process if remnants of the old world were required for the memory of what had gone before? This philosophy of history clearly left unanswered some important questions.

A New Cultural Ideology

In 1956 Habermas, a politically homeless scion of the provincial *Bürgertum*, approached Adorno, who had been impressed by the "Dialectics of Rationalization," about becoming his assistant at the Institute for Social Research in Frankfurt. His application was successful, and he retained the position until 1959. The move to Frankfurt was more than a new intellectual home for the young scholar. Run by the living embodiments of an intellectual tradition with which he could personally identify, the institute offered a project that he could make his life's work. As Albrecht Wellmer (b. 1934) observed of Critical Theory's importance to the "second generation," like Habermas, Ludwig von Friedeburg (b. 1923), and himself, it "was the only position represented in Germany after the war that made conceivable a radical break with fascism without a just-as-radical break with the German cultural tradition, and that meant a radical break with one's own cultural identity."[78] In other words, it was possible to rescue the universalistic dimension embodied in the German Enlightenment in order to purge the country's traditions of its reactionary and fascist dimensions. The Frankfurt School offered a sustainable German identity in the form of a homegrown tradition of universalism for those forty-fivers who were thoroughly alienated from an emphatic particular and national identity.

But that is not all. Because its most famous lights were German Jews, it also offered the leftist forty-fivers the chance to stand with the victims of Nazi persecution. This source of identification was most apparent in Habermas's radio lecture, in 1961, "The German Idealism of the Jewish Philosophers." German idealism was actually indebted to Jewish mysticism because Jakob Böhme had been influenced by the kabbalah, and his Swabian pietism had flowed into the Tübinger seminarians, Hegel, Schelling, and Hölderlin. The content of this mysticism was the human fulfillment of the "new age of the world," the "ancient goal of the redemption of humanity, of nature, and indeed of the God knocked

[77] Jürgen Habermas, "Jeder Mensch ist unbezahlbar," *Merkur*, 9 (1955), 994–98.
[78] Albrecht Wellmer, "Die Bedeutung der Frankfurter Schule heute," in Axel Honneth and Albrecht Wellmer, eds., *Die Frankfurter Schule und die Folgen* (Berlin, 1986), 25–34, 27.

off his throne."[79] It was the interiorization of a mission that was discerned in the external workings of history. It was no surprise, Habermas averred, that the Young Hegelian insight that "the ongoing beginning opens up a view of the still outstanding end" was taken up by Adorno, Horkheimer, Herbert Marcuse, and the early Georg Lukács. "The German idealism of the Jews produces the ferment of a critical utopia."[80] Making no attempt to conceal his views on the success of the controversial "German Jewish symbiosis," Habermas contended that the German spirit and Jewish spirit were mutually dependent, because it was in Germany that Jews were able to emancipate themselves from the ghetto and medieval religion and make Jewish mysticism philosophically reflective. And it was this spirit that would be Germany's salvation after the attempt to exterminate it.

Meanwhile, the question of anti-Semitism itself has been disposed of – *we* have disposed of it by physical extermination. Hence, in our deliberations it cannot be a matter of the life and survival of the Jews, of influences back and forth; only we ourselves are at stake. That is to say, the Jewish heritage drawn from the German spirit has become indispensable for our own life and survival.

Plainly, Habermas was not recommending that Germans embrace Western liberalism. The "critical utopia" that he regarded as the only true lesson of the past demanded much more. The "German spirit" had always struggled against Western liberalism and its technological spirit, so it was necessary to retain this opposition, without, of course, taking the fatal path of its conservative revolutionary representatives.

At the very moment when German philosophers and scientists started to "eradicate" this heritage, the profound ambivalence that so eerily colored the dark ground of the German spirit was revealed as a danger of barbarism for everyone. Ernst Jünger, Martin Heidegger, and Carl Schmitt are representatives of this spirit in its grandeur, but in its perilousness as well. That they spoke as they did in 1930, 1933, and 1936 is no accident. And that this insight has not been realized a quarter of a century later proves the urgency of a discriminating kind of thinking all the more. This has to be one with the fatal German spirit and yet split with it from within to such an extent that it can relay an oracle to it: it must not cross the Rubicon a second time. If there were not extant a German-Jewish tradition, we would have to discover one for our own sakes. Well it does exist; but because we have murdered or broken its bodily carriers, and because, in a climate of an unbinding reconciliation, we are in the process of letting everything be forgiven and forgotten too (in order to accomplish what could not have been accomplished better by anti-Semitism), we are now forced into the historical irony of taking up the Jewish question without the Jews.[81]

Habermas made it his mission to embody this spirit, to pose the Jewish question in a Germany largely bereft of Jews, and to defend it against its enemies,

---

[79] Jürgen Habermas, "The German Idealism of the Jewish Philosophers," in his *Philosophical-Political Profiles*, trans. Frederick G. Lawrence (Cambridge, Mass., 1983), 39.

[80] Ibid., 42.

[81] Ibid.

the former conservative revolutionaries and their postwar successors, the positivists. There could be no compromise with those who had once opposed this spirit and its historical goal.

Habermas's epistemological claims changed after he read *Dialectic of Enlightenment* and joined the institute. He no longer claimed special knowledge based on personal, quasi-religious experience. The dialectic showed the way forward. Accordingly, he now defended Schelling against the accusation that his thinking was "gnostic" or infected by the "spirit of magic" by emphasizing his affinities with the historical rather than existentialist categories. "Do we not find precisely in Schelling and Hegel," Habermas rejoined, "some beginnings of a third, dialectical access to 'transcendence,' more than merely 'enlightening,' and yet not 'gnostic'?"[82] Anticipating Herbert Marcuse's *One Dimensional Man* of 1964, he answered the question about the nature of this access by arguing that the problem with positivism and technology was their failure to recognize the possibility of alternative social arrangements by regarding the existing order superficially as the end of history. It did not understand reality dialectically in terms "of its possibilities."[83]

As the continuing appeal to Schelling indicates, Habermas's invocation of the dialectic retained debts to theology about which he was quite explicit. For dialectical thinking grasped phenomena as a whole, and it made the totality of the world and the historical process the object of thought rather than merely phenomena *in* the world, as positivism did. Dialectical philosophy was based on mythological or religious experiences of "the whole" that it sought to unify after its sundering and development by science or instrumental reason.[84]

Needless to say, Habermas rendered these theological motives in secular terms. The notion of the unity of the world as a theological conception arose in the late eighteenth century and was linked to "objective historical development," namely, the nascent self-consciousness of bourgeois society. It reflected the reality that hitherto humans had not made the world consciously but that they might do so rationally in the future by positing a subject of history – humanity as a whole. Habermas always qualified this belief, referring to the "anticipatory presupposition" of a goal or history as "hypothetical," and the tendencies of historical development as a "fiction." "From the lofty observation post of this fiction the situation is revealed in its ambivalences, which are susceptible to

---

[82] Jürgen Habermas, "Karl Jaspers über Schelling," *Frankfurter Allgemeine Zeitung* (January 14, 1956). Reprinted in his *Philosophisch-politische Profile*, 93–99. In the 1990s, Habermas attacked Böhme and Schelling as anti-Western "German philosophers." See his *Die Normalität einer Berliner Republik*, 16.

[83] Habermas, "Konsumkritik – eigens zum Konsumieren," 644. Habermas was reading Marcuse with critical sympathy in the mid-1950s. See his "Triebschicksal als politisches Schicksal," *Frankfurter Allgemeine Zeitung* (July 14, 1956).

[84] Jürgen Habermas, "Der befremdliche Mythos: Reduktion oder Evokation?" *Philosophische Rundschau*, 6 (1958), 219–21. On the Western Marxist tradition of holism, see Martin Jay, *Marxism and Totality: The Adventures of a Concept from Lukacs to Habermas* (Berkeley and Los Angeles, 1984).

practical intervention, so that an enlightened mankind can elevate itself then to become what up to that point it was only fictionally."[85] In other words, Habermas claimed that this "fiction" was not simply wishful thinking. Nonetheless, while it may be possible to argue that this philosophy of history could be historically located and denuded of its explicitly theological language, there was no doubting that its motivating power retained an explicitly moral dimension. Reason itself did not compel this historical schema: "hope" did, as he admitted and as Ernst Bloch had taught him: "Dialectical theory ultimately recognizes in the positivistic domination of nature . . . that humanity remains delivered up to the forces of nature and does not become rational. The medium of its thought is the *hope* that this insight can be a motivation – despite all."[86] It was essential, therefore, that reason and political commitment were permitted to be rejoined, because an autonomous science uncontrolled by dialectical reason and praxis was akin to the "insanity" of an "exclusively technical civilization."

Today the convergence of reason and commitment, which the philosophy of the great tradition considered to be intimately linked, must be regained, reflected, and reasserted on the level of positive science, and that means carried on through the separation which is necessarily and correctly drawn on the level of technological rationality, the dichotomy of reason and commitment.[87]

Habermas thought that this union of reason and commitment (or hope), theory and practice, was more urgent than ever because humanity was rational enough to manufacture the nuclear weapons to destroy creation but it remained irrational in the conduct of its practical affairs. This situation constituted a world-historical crisis: "Mankind has never before been confronted so sharply by the irony of a capacity to make its own history, yet deprived of control over it, as is the case now that the means of self-assertion by force have developed to such a degree that their deployment for attaining specific political ends has become highly problematical."[88] How did this crisis pertain to the Holocaust? It is not obvious, and Habermas did not clarify the matter by issuing vague warnings: "The demythification which does not break the mythic spell but merely seeks to evade it will only bring forth new witch doctors. The enlightenment which does not break the spell dialectically, but instead winds the veil of a halfway rationalization only more tightly around us, makes the world divested of deities itself into a myth."[89]

[85] Jürgen Habermas, "Between Philosophy and Science: Marxism as Critique (1960)," in *Theory and Practice*, 249–52. To be sure, he later rejected the concept of a historical subject. See ibid. 303–4n67.

[86] Jürgen Habermas, "Ein philosophierender Intellektueller (1963)," in his *Philosophisch-politische Profile*, 184 (emphasis added).

[87] Jürgen Habermas, "Dogmatism, Reason, and Decision: On Theory and Praxis in Our Scientific Civilization" (1963), in *Theory and Practice*, 281.

[88] Habermas, "Between Philosophy and Science," 250–51.

[89] Habermas, "Dogmatism, Reason, and Decision," 281, 267.

In a little-noticed review from 1958 that he did not republish in his essay collections, Habermas gave a hint by distinguishing between two dangers produced by the "halfway rationalization" of technological progress and the disenchantment of the world. Such a rationalization, characteristic of liberalism, dissolved all organic relations in order to prevent a "reversion to barbarism," but it did not go far enough and so delivered up society to the danger of an "administered world." So which aspect of rationalization was responsible for the Holocaust: reactionary German traditions of *Gemeinschaft* (community) and antimodernism, or technological progress? Evidently for Habermas, the Holocaust could be linked to current problems only by seeing the virulent anticommunism of Germany in the 1950s as the wicked incarnation of *both* technology and negative German traditions. When he referred to the "remythologization" of German society, he must have meant the poison cocktail of anticommunism and technological progress as the evil that prevented an honest German reckoning with the past. This connection was confirmed in the person and thought of former fascists, like Hans Freyer, who became postwar positivists. Doubtless, he saw younger positivists in that light, as well.[90]

Either-Or: Another Republican Crisis

During the late 1950s, Habermas and his Frankfurt colleagues Ludwig von Friedeburg, Christoph Oehler, and Friedrich Welz undertook surveys of student political attitudes in order to test their democratic political orientation. The survey results, which were published and interpreted in the well-known book *Student und Politik*, showed that the traditional humanistic culture of *Bildung* had continued largely unchanged since the war.[91] It was precisely this apolitical concentration on private virtues by non-Nazi scholars and students, coupled with a traditional German anticommunism, that had rendered the Weimar university so vulnerable to National Socialism. The authors found that a majority of West German students were not particularly committed to democracy, and they doubted whether the students would defend republican institutions were antidemocratic forces to rise again. The students, Friedeburg concluded, had drawn no implications from the country's experience with National Socialism; they were hostages of "consumer coercion" and were beguiled by the "culture industry." Habermas observed that many students held pragmatic, potentially authoritarian political views devoid of "utopian impulses." It was necessary, therefore, for education to take a "critical" approach.[92]

[90] Habermas, "Der Befremdliche Mythos," 223.
[91] Jürgen Habermas et al., *Student und Politik. Eine soziologische Untersuchung zum politischen Bewußtsein Frankfurter Studenten* (Neuwied and Berlin, 1961).
[92] Ludwig von Friedeburg, "Zum Verhältnis von Jugend and Gesellschaft," in Ludwig von Friedeburg, ed., *Jugend in der modernen Gesellschaft* (Cologne, 1966), 184; Jürgen Habermas, "Zum Einfluß von Schul- und Hochschulbildung auf das politische Bewußtsein von Studenten," in ibid., 430.

But what did Habermas and his colleagues mean by democracy? Habermas wrote the theoretical chapter entitled "On the Concept of Political Participation," which made clear that he opposed the institutionally centered conceptions of democracy of Schumpeter and by, implication, Hennis. In fact, Habermas's vision was diametrically opposed to Hennis's, based as it was solely on the ideal of realizing popular sovereignty in modern conditions.

Habermas's problems with the conservative-liberal model of parliamentary democracy are not difficult to fathom given his suspicions of West German society. The institutional model gave much power to social elites through their control of political parties, consigning the population to passive acclamation of presented options, and thereby preventing the learning process produced by political participation, which he called "human self-emancipation."[93] Such participation dissolved the "irrational" domination (*Herrschaft*) of the state and society over the individual and people that the bureaucracy and capitalist system represented. Drawing explicitly on the Schmittian jurist, Werner Weber, whom, we will recall, Hennis had attacked in 1949, Habermas argued that the parties "mediated" the potentially unified will of the people and in this way prevented it from asserting its will against what he called "totalitarian processes."[94] And the need for public control of politics was greater than ever. The elision of the state and society caused by the state's intervention in the economy to ensure the reproduction of the system meant that private business interests determined government policy. In other words, social power was illegitimately placed in private hands, a dire situation with which the "liberal state of law" was unable to cope.

But it was not just a problem of the illegitimate power of vested interests. These interests, so Habermas maintained with Wolfgang Abendroth, with whom he had gone to Marburg to write his habilitation thesis, were politically dangerous, as they had been at the end of the Weimar Republic and during the Nazi regime. Because there had been no change of elites after 1945, "the impression is not unjustified that the prominent beneficiaries of the reconstituted democracy are not those who would be the first to strike a blow for it [democracy]."[95]

Crisis loomed. The balance of social forces in the liberal state was "highly labile" because of its internal contradictions: the theory of pluralism of social interests concealed the fact that public priorities were determined by private and therefore undemocratic interests at the expense of the original freedoms that the liberal state was supposed to guarantee. This state was faced, therefore, with what Habermas pronounced an "historical alternative": "That sooner or later the liberal state of law fulfills its own intentions in a democratic and social state of law, or reverts against its own inner essence, more or less openly, and assumes an authoritarian form."[96] What this alternative might mean he

---

[93] Habermas et al., *Student und Politik*, 15.
[94] Ibid., 42, 48.
[95] Ibid., 52, 54–55.
[96] Ibid., 42–43.

made clear elsewhere. The danger was "the splitting of human beings into two classes – the social engineers and the inmates of closed institutions."[97] This danger was the nightmare of technocracy, a social system uncoupled from human control that spread its tentacles around the world at the expense of human needs and its environment. What he advocated as an antidote was a change of consciousness on the part of the technocrats. Such a change entailed radical university reform. Only the students could save the people from a possible "authoritarian, fake-parliamentary, status group, party-totalitarian" system of domination.[98]

[97] Habermas, "Dogmatism, Reason, and Decision," 282.
[98] Habermas et al., *Student und Politik*, 126.

6

Theory and Practice

Science, Technology, and the Republican University

"The German university is at core healthy [*im Kern gesund*]," declared the historian and head of the German Rektorenkonferenz (Council of University Presidents) Hermann Heimpel at the education reform conference in Bad Honnef in 1955.[1] The Prussian minister of culture in the Weimar Republic Carl Heinrich Becker had made the same claim in 1919 after the catastrophe of the First World War.[2] The invocation of the German university tradition at times of national trauma had obvious appeal. This tradition had produced internationally famous scientists and thinkers, and served as a model for the world until 1914. Moreover, it was a tradition whose origins lay in the celebrated Prussian revival in the early nineteenth century after Napoleonic armies had vanquished the Prussians in Jena in 1806 and divided much of the kingdom with Russia. One of the few flourishing universities of the Enlightenment, in Halle, was lost, and the king charged the diplomat Wilhelm von Humboldt with renewing education in his shattered realm. Under the sign of German idealistic philosophy, he and his colleagues, the theologian Friedrich Schleiermacher and the philosopher Gottlieb Fichte, produced a model of university education that was incarnated in the Humboldt University in Berlin in 1809.

Its potency as a moral source lay in its institutionalization of a neohumanist anthropology that idealized the classical Greek vision of beauty and the unity of knowledge and culture. This unity was located in the university's philosophical faculty, which was to integrate and synthesize the research of the different disciplines into a coherent worldview. The philosophy of German idealism posited its educational task as the cultivation (*Bildung*) of a universal humanity by internalizing the riches of high culture.

---

[1] Hermann Heimpel, *Probleme und Problematik der Hochschulreform* (Göttingen, 1956), 7.
[2] Carl Heinrich Becker, *Gedanken zu Hochschulreform* (Leipzig, 1919), 17; Guido Müller, ed., *Internationale Wissenschaft und nationale Bildung. Ausgewählte Schriften von Carl Heinrich Becker, 1876–1933* (Cologne, Weimar, and Vienna, 1997).

This vision was a new departure. Hitherto, the Central European universities had provided technical and vocational training, with the disciplines of cameralism, law, medicine, and theology. If this utilitarian tradition continued in the Anglophone countries, the new German university would not follow suit. In the temporary distance to praxis, students would internalize the universal culture of the day, an ideal preparation for the later acquisition of specific skills required for the fulfillment of subsequent duties as administrators in the Prussian provinces. The state would provide financial support but not interfere in the development of science (*Wissenschaft*).

This model had several elements. The new university was to be a corporation of professors who organized themselves into autonomous faculties. Both professors and students were to enjoy academic freedom. Unlike in the Anglophone countries at the time, only mature adults were expected to attend university, which played no quasi-parental role. The students would not enroll in regimented, prestructured courses of study with scheduled examinations. Instead, they would construct their own course of study and attend the lectures and seminars that interested them. These lectures and seminars were not designed to transmit prepackaged knowledge but to expose the student to the latest research findings and interpretations, which they were expected to develop in collaboration and virtual equality with the professors. Teaching thus could not be separated from research. Through the academic freedom to construct their own course of study and by the mutual participation in research – in the quest for "truth" – the students' critical faculties would be awakened and cultivated, and their judgment developed. "The university teacher is no longer a teacher," Humboldt wrote, "the student no longer the learner; instead he researches himself."[3] In theory, the classical German university model possessed no internal hierarchy.

Humboldt's vision was open to rival interpretations as the growth of the state in the nineteenth century led to government attempts to monitor and regulate institutions of higher education. In practice, as might be expected, professors did not regard students as equals, and even liberal professors were appalled at the idea of parliamentary government interference in university affairs. They invoked Humboldt's name to insist on the autonomy and inviolability of the university after the First World War. And Becker did the same in opposing them with his reform agenda of democratic regulation.[4]

These and other issues confronted the Allied powers in the western occupation zones after 1945. What should be the role of the university in the coming democracy? What could be the state's claims on the university? In 1947

---

[3] Wilhelm von Humboldt cited in Gerd Roellecke, "Geschichte des deutschen Hochschulwesens," in Christian Flämig et al., eds., *Handbuch des Wissenschaftsrechts*, vol. 1 (Berlin, Heidelberg, and New York, 1982), 3–36.

[4] Helmut Schelsky, *Einsamkeit und Freiheit. Idee und Gestalt der deutschen Universität und ihrer Reform* (Reinbeck, 1963), 168–69.

the English had formed commissions of inquiry for university reform with German academic and community representation, and in the next year they presented their recommendations, the so-called *Schwalbinger* and *Hamburger Gutachten* (also known as the "Blue Report").[5] They recommended greater contact between the university and the public sphere, a form of general education to counter the specialization of research, and a greater emphasis on teaching. The Americans concurred with these aims.[6] In 1948, the Free University in the west of Berlin was founded by the staff and students of the Humboldt University after its politicization by Soviet authorities became intolerable. Subsequently known as the "Berlin model," it sought to realize Humboldt's ideal of a community of scholars by ensuring direct student representation on university decision-making bodies.[7]

The Humboldt Model and Modernity

Although active students placed enormous hopes in the Blue Report and the "Berlin model," they were rejected by the West German universities, which had soon regained administrative autonomy in accordance with the Allied policy. With vivid memories of Nazi intervention in universities and politicized scholarship, the established professors held fast defensively to the ideals of their autonomy and distance to the world of politics and society. A classic statement of this mandarin ideology was made by the Freiburg historian Gerd Tellenbach (1903–99) immediately after the war. It is so revealing that it is worth examining in some detail.[8]

The point of his intervention was to rescue the "idea of the German university" from implication in the fall of the Weimar Republic and collusion with the Nazi regime.[9] In fact, he insisted, the university had been a victim. "During the Third Reich, the state raped the university in that it tried to make it useful as a political university for its own purposes and thereby exterminate its true aim." True, many students and some professors became Nazis out of a "false nationalist pathos," and others allowed themselves to be called Nazis out of opportunism or delusion, or because they wanted to prevent the worst. But they did not allow politics to interfere with their scholarship and remained essentially uncorrupted. Indeed, Tellenbach continued, "the majority of the professors felt

---

[5] David Phillips, *Pragmatismus und Idealismus. Das "Blaue Gutachten" und die britische Hochschulpolitik in Deutschland bis 1948* (Cologne, Weimar, and Vienna, 1995).

[6] See the comments of James M. Read, head of the Education Section of the American High Commission in Frankfurt in his "Wie steht es mit den Universitäten. Konservativer Lehrkörper – Mangelnder Kontakt mit der Öffentlichkeit," *Deutsche Universitäts-Zeitung*, 6:11 (1951), 6–7.

[7] James F. Tent, *The Free University of Berlin: A Political History* (Bloomington, 1988).

[8] Gerd Tellenbach, "Zur Selbstorientierung der deutschen Universität," *Die Sammlung*, 1 (1945–46), 530–43.

[9] For a case study, see Steven P. Remy, *The Heidelberg Myth: The Nazification and Denazification of a German University* (Cambridge, Mass., 2002).

themselves internally and externally coerced, and they suffered from the attacks and limitations of the National Socialist movement."

He had nothing to say about the failure of German professors to protest against the expulsion of their German Jewish colleagues. Nor did he reflect on the question of the university's share of blame for what had befallen it and the country. In fact, he skillfully interpreted the issue of guilt to his advantage by arguing that the university had failed to live up to its ideal and had lost belief in its special mission, thereby licensing the continuation of the mandarin cultural pessimism and critique of modernity that was common at the time in the bourgeois political class. There had been "insufficient self-clarity and intellectual power, insufficient backbone to form a counterweight against the terribly expanding dangers of the modern world; they [the universities] were weakened by positivism and the spirit of the specialists to oppose mechanization, despiritualization [*Entseelung*], ethical obeisance, and secularism."

Accordingly, he continued, in order to save German and Occidental (*abendländische*) culture, the university now had to be true to its ideal by maintaining a reserved distance to the state and politics, and by prizing its otherworldliness. "It is more true and simultaneously more impressive when universities do not avoid the appearance of strangeness and distance, difficult to approach and strict." The university would fulfill its role in the democratic *Kulturstaat* (state of culture) by serving as a bastion of resistance. In a world in which technology had irreversibly transformed life, only one option remained: "To find and encourage counterweights against the cold, inhuman organizations in which we are caught, and to empower our wills, despite all, to lead a dignified existence."[10]

A consistent trope in the mandarin invocation of the Humboldt ideal was its casting of the German university in feminine terms. It would be no exaggeration to say that it was the functional equivalent of the Virgin Mary: without sin, a source of succor and appeal beyond contradiction. Accordingly, it had to remain "pure" and "inviolate" from penetration from without. Indeed, in the eyes of a Swiss observer, the university did, in fact, fulfill this function.

The lecturer was not just approached as a distant intellectual father; rather for many students, he had suddenly to substitute for the spiritually lost father and collapsed models. The university had suddenly to transform itself from maiden to mother, in whose lap one could find peace and comfort, security and meaning for one's own existence. Since the liberal movement of the first half of the nineteenth century, the German university has not borne the weight of such high expectations, and had so much goodwill, as the intensity of the efforts of the students in 1946.[11]

As this quotation makes clear, a generational rebellion against the older professors was anything but likely. On the contrary, in the immediate postwar years,

[10] Tellenbach, "Zur Selbstorientierung der deutschen Universität," 534–38.
[11] Walter Rüegg, *Humanismus, Studium Generale und Studia Humanitatis in Deutschland* (Geneva and Darmstadt, 1954), 33.

the professors and students relied on one another to rebuild their institutions and search for answers to the "German catastrophe."[12]

There was no fundamental structural reform for other reasons. Most administrators were preoccupied with repairing the physical damage to the buildings.[13] Although some universities, like Tübingen, were spared bombing, some 60 percent of German university infrastructure was destroyed. The first generation of students sat in rudimentary lecture theaters and, as in Münster, actually helped to reconstruct the buildings. Hunger and deprivation were part of student experience at the time. Ivo Frenzel (b. 1924) recalls that, "badly nourished, one studied with little money, without books and heating, and without appropriate lecture theaters, under threat of an electricity outage and *the numerus clausus* [the quotas limiting university entry]."[14]

In the end, however, radical structural reform was rejected because the university leaders of the time considered the mandarin educational ideal to be the appropriate – indeed, the only valid response to the Nazi past and the challenges of an uncertain future. In fact, Tellenbach had observed, if anything, "love" for the university ideal among the professors had intensified during the dark days of the Nazi regime. Rather than experiment and heed the wishes of the Allies, they sought to continue the university they had experienced before 1933. This was indeed a restoration. The historian, Waldemar Besson, gave a balanced assessment of the postwar university in the late 1960s.

This history of the university under Hitler was not an inspiring story. But it was not fully "coordinated" [*gleichgeschaltet*]. It continued to some extent to live its own life, particularly outside the political sciences. Because of this it appeared reasonable to think that the Humboldt tradition still offered a basis for German academic life. The glory of the German university at the end of the nineteenth century was evidence of the fruitfulness of that tradition, and renewed adherence to it seemed to offer the prospect of the revival of this great reputation. Some of its most respected exponents, like Friedrich Meinecke and Eduard Spranger, were still living and their lofty and uncorrupted bearing conferred credit on the old tradition. Immediately after 1945, moreover, the German university felt itself to have been one of Hitler's victims. It took time and hard thinking to realize that the German university belonged at least in part to the anti-democratic mainstream of German history, and that it carried a heavy responsibility for the rise of Nazism.[15]

Where universities did agree with the Allies was in recognizing the problem of the disintegration of the *universitatis litterarum*, the coherent and integrated worldview that a higher education was supposed to provide. Such was the specialization of research and scholarship that no one was able to synthesize them

[12] Carl Christian Kaiser, "Profil einer deutschen Universität," *Deutsche Jugend*, 2 (October 1954), 456–62.

[13] Helmut Becker, "Bildung und Bildungspolitik," in Martin Broszat, ed., *Zäsuren nach 1945. Essays zur Periodisierung der deutschen Nachkriegsgeschichte* (Munich, 1990).

[14] Ivo Frenzel, "Nun tanzen sie wieder," *Deutsche Universitäts-Zeitung*, 11 (April 28, 1956), 3–5.

[15] Waldemar Besson, letter to the editor of *Minerva*, 6:4 (Summer 1968), 614–17.

into the whole to provide much sought-after intellectual orientation. This problem was articulated well by Hans Freyer when he wrote that science "cannot synthesize its findings with claims of finality, and thus it does not offer a world-view or substitute religion."[16] Consequently, some universities instituted the *Studium generale*, often based on different humanist traditions; for example, Roman Catholic regions highlighted Thomism. The *Studium generale* consisted usually of regular lectures on general topics that ran parallel to the regular specialist disciplines. Although these programs were instituted with great hope and enthusiasm in the early 1950s, the students soon lost interest in them.[17] The *Studium generale* was unable to offer the desired integration, and many students no longer cared by the mid-1950s, preoccupied as they were with gaining a degree and entering the work force. Massive increases in student numbers, especially in the age groups born after 1933, made the practical aspect of university study more difficult and increased the length of time for degrees. The specialization of research continued unabated. Confronted with the failure of the *Studium generale* and the gradual fragmentation of the university, Tellenbach could offer only impotent appeals to "intellectual energy."[18]

But not all students were content to view education under the aspect of career advancement. Student leaders in particular regarded the restorative policies of university leaders as a betrayal of the hopes they had entertained and of the solidarity between professors and students after 1945. In those halcyon days, remembered one student leader from Frankfurt in 1954, "the cleverest experiments had been attempted, the most radical reform proposals vigorously discussed. Everything was in flux, the old divisions seemed to be ended, utopian dreams permitted."[19] For these students, the unity of culture and personality in an age of accelerated technological advancement was of particular concern. They linked this problem to the failure of a "new beginning" in the 1940s, and this meant the failure of university reform and the "restoration university."

Hans Heigert (b. 1925) also decried the lack of fundamental reform in post-war universities. In his doctoral dissertation, he had studied the origins of 1930s right-wing student radicalism in the romantic period of the early nineteenth century and, in his capacity as a journalist in Stuttgart, he had attacked the reestablishment of the nationalist fencing fraternities in the 1950s.[20] The big questions of the late 1940s had been wiped from the agenda, he observed

---

[16] Hans Freyer, "Die Wissenschaft des 20. Jahrhunderts und die Idee des Humanismus," *Merkur*, 16 (1961), 101–17. On Freyer in general, see Jerry Z. Muller, *"The Other God That Failed": Hans Freyer and the Deradicalization of German Conservatism* (Princeton, N.J., 1987).

[17] Rüegg, *Humanismus, Studium Generale und Studia Humanitatis in Deutschland*; Gerd Tellenbach, "Aufbau eines Studium Generale," *Deutsche Universitäts-Zeitung*, 9 (1951), 10–11.

[18] Gerd Tellenbach, "Neugestaltung der Universität," *Deutsche Universitäts-Zeitung*, 12 (July 22, 1957), 3–6.

[19] Kaiser, "Profil einer deutschen Universität."

[20] Hans Heigert, "Die Studenten und der deutsche Geist – eine Auseinandersetzung, die noch nicht zu Ende ist," *Deutsche Jugend*, 2 (June 1954), 259–64; Heigert, "Der Selbstmord der deutschen Studentenschaft," *Frankfurter Allgemeine Zeitung* (April 4, 1958).

after the university conference in Bad Honnef in 1955 where Heimpel had pronounced the university's essential health. Sadly, all that remained was the pragmatic reforms that dealt with the pressure of student numbers. But while he saw that the inherited Humboldt model was unable to cope with modern conditions, he rejected the idea of abandoning its humanistic vision to technocratic management. What was required was the kind of reforming vision that Humboldt possessed 150 years before.[21] Manfred Hättich, a leftist Roman Catholic and later director of the Institute for Political Education in Tutzing, who several years earlier had led Freiburg students in protests against the screening of the films of former Nazi director, Veit Harlan, made the same criticisms of the university.[22]

These were sentiments with which Ivo Frenzel, an editor of the *Deutsche Universitäts-Zeitung* and subsequently an important journalist, heartily agreed. "It appears as if the great reformist élan that existed in the first postwar years," he wrote wistfully, "is as spent as the metaphysical appetite of the Germans has in the meantime become satisfied." Noting that Heimpel's declaration was usually interpreted conservatively as a statement of confidence in the university system, he decided to take it at its word. For Heimpel had also said that the Humboldtian idealism was revolutionary at its core. Of course, Heimpel was referring to the revolution that the intellect and personality underwent through the individual's participation in the research process, but Frenzel saw other interpretative possibilities. Did it not entail the implementation of the reforms recommended by the Blue Report: an orientation to social (but not technical) praxis, communication of scholarship to the public, and adult education?

In essence, Frenzel was arguing that the nineteenth-century German university structures needed to be updated to realize their neohumansitic aspiration.[23] Above all, it was necessary to reconfigure the university's relationship to society to regain the unity of knowledge, which meant challenging the mandarin doctrine of the university's autonomy and distance from politics. Already in 1948, Peter van Oertzen had attacked this ideal and lamented that "otherworldliness and specialized narrowness, irresponsibility, and to some extent even dangerous political retardedness dominate in the academic world so much that one cannot expect a self-purification." He called for the social engagement in the same terms as the Blue Report.[24]

This insight was articulated in felicitous terms by Andreas Flitner, professor of education in Tübingen and son of the famous educational reformer, Wilhelm Flitner, when he wrote that

Today the changes in the technical, economic, and social world are so extensive that the education policy makers and professors who call themselves conservative accept the

[21] Hans Heigert, "Die verlorene Hochschul-Reform. Idee und Wirklichkeit der deutschen Universität," *Der Monat*, 8 (May 1956), 23–29.

[22] Manfred Hättich, "Studium Generale?" *Neue Gesellschaft*, 2:3 (May–June, 1955), 58–61.

[23] Ivo Frenzel, "Der Brennpunkt," *Deutsche Universitäts-Zeitung*, 11 (March 22, 1956), 3–4.

[24] Peter von Oertzen, "Reform vor Autonomie," *Göttinger Universitäts-Zeitung*, 6 (1948), 5.

most extreme transformations and alienation of meaning [*Sinnentfremdungen*] where they cleave to the old, whereas others, to be truly conservative, which means to retain what has been passed down and to resurrect the purpose of earlier structures, urge drastic changes.[25]

The conservatives that Flitner attacked for harboring antidemocratic and anti-modern ideas were, of course, the likes of Tellenbach. Flitner added that the source of twentieth-century neohumanism lay in the youth movement before and after the First World War, whose ideals had been perverted by the Nazis. This movement represented the positive legacy of the German contribution to education by which he meant the preservation of the individual against the alienation of bourgeois society. As we will see, this idea would be very important for Habermas.

The Marburg political scientist Wolfgang Abendroth was also of the opinion that the youth movements – he had belonged to its socialist youth branch in the Weimar Republic – offered an important moral resource for the socialist transformation of West Germany. In 1953 he had criticized the university's reversion to an apolitical posture as the incorrect response to the past. Like von Oertzen, he pointed out that social distance had not only failed to protect the university against totalitarianism in 1933 but also concealed the fact that the universities shared the German middle class's vulnerability to National Socialism and its tradition of obeisance to authority. The radical institutional autonomy that the university now demanded was unnecessary in a democratic state. The democratic university had important tasks to fulfill, namely to educate the next generation for key functions in the state, society, and economy. Echoing the rhetoric of Carl Becker, Abendroth called for a new balance between state and university by challenging the taboo that the faculties (the self-governing, intra-university units of full professors) should be able to decide all matters of university policy.

But Abendroth was making more extensive claims for government policy than had Becker. Whereas the Prussian minister did not doubt the ability of the universities to safeguard the unity of knowledge, Abendroth pointed out that now even the universities confessed that they could no longer do so, producing only narrow specialists, which was unsatisfactory for a democratic society, as the "Blue Report" also had argued. Where, then, was "truth" to be found? Political society had its own truth, Abendroth answered. The path to regaining an integrated understanding of the world was for professors and students to reflect on the "concrete function" of their specialties in social life, and on how these functions could contribute to "total knowledge."[26]

[25] Andreas Flitner, "Die gesellschaftliche Krise unseres Bildungswesens," *Universitas*, 20 (1965), 1157.
[26] Wolfgang Abendroth, "Absolute Autonomie. Zur Stellung der deutschen Hochschule im demokratischen Staat," *Deutsche Universitäts-Zeitung*, 8:22 (1953), 6–8.

Hans Tietgens (b. 1922), federal director of the SDS from 1952 to 1954, spelled out the the political implications of Abendroth's line of thinking. He regretted that no "new beginning" had taken place after the war, and he insisted that authentic university reform needed to occur in the context of social "reformation" (*Umgestaltung*). The current university was failing because its much-vaunted academic freedom was vitiated indirectly by the influence of group interests and vocational necessities. Its claim to synthesize knowledge was undermined by research specialization, which mirrored the division of labor in capitalist society. Similarly, individuals had lost touch with "the whole" and stood alienated before ever-changing technological progress that threatened to overwhelm them. Heteronymous social pressures determined scholarship, rather than scholarship providing the perspective with which to steer the "apparatus."

Most Germans, Tietgens observed, had accepted this apparatus because it did not intervene in their private sphere, and this fact meant that the formal structures of the West German state lacked an authentic democratic content. In this context, the university had the role of educating a "new leading strata" that could develop and combine a coherent theory of society with the praxis of policy formulation and implementation. Such a strata would be the bearer of a "social and a democratic social order," which he thought was immanent in the "course of history." In fulfilling this aim, the *Studium generale* was as insufficient as it was superficial. Like Abendroth, Tietgens argued that a synthesis of knowledge and action lay not in the generalist overviews of the *Studium generale*, but in reflection on the connections of the individual disciplines to society and their part in social reproduction. To this end, he recommended a common methodological training of all students in the social sciences that he hoped would guard scholarship and students against what he called "the dogmatization of social life." Should such a reform fail, he added in an ominous warning that would become typical of redemptive republicanism, "all paths would be left open for authoritarian streams." West German democracy was at stake. University reform lay at the heart of new German state in terms of an either-or situation.[27]

Explicit as he was about his political aims, Tietgens remained vague about what he meant by the "dogmatization of life" and the "course of history." Likewise, what did Manfred Hättich mean when he wrote that "we have become slaves" to the technology we have created? And what was Hans Heigert saying when he warned "Whoever wants to retain a free social order cannot encourage those tendencies that incline to transform society into a termite's empire of robots and functionaries?" They were expressing the general anxiety at the time about the fate of "the individual," "personality," and "culture" in the "technological age" that we observed with Habermas. The older generation

---

[27] Hans Tietgens, "Die Hochschule in der modernen Gesellschaft," *Neue Gesellschaft*, 1:2 (September–October 1954), 28–36.

of intellectuals, like Arnold Gehlen, Carlo Schmid, Arnold Bergstraesser, Max Horkheimer, and Theodor W. Adorno, also shared this concern about the end of humanism in an "administered world," notwithstanding their own ideological differences.[28]

At the same time, Hellmut Becker (1913–94), the son of Carl Heinrich, wrote an influential book called *Die verwaltete Schule* (The Administered School) that, in explicit reliance on Adorno, complained about the schools' frictionless integration into its environment. "The school is in danger of producing only functionaries. The educational result of the modern school is gradually becoming conformist, unimaginative, lethargic, coordinatable [*gleichschaltbare*] people, whose knowledge is to be sure broad, but not qualitatively valuable, and therefore easily examinable."[29] His solution was to place more power in the hands of teachers at the local level rather than administrators, parents, and the church. This was not a new idea; it had been popular with the youth movement and *Reformpädagogik* (progressive pedagogy) in the Weimar period, which prioritized the child's developmental needs, shielding it for a time from the instrumental claims of bourgeois society. Becker now added another mission in the context of the Cold War, the culture industry, and the economic miracle: "The attraction of the Western world will be determined by the question whether its education is free. Not the filled shop windows, but the chance for free development is what could be offered to the world beyond the iron curtain. If we want to build a free world, we need above all other schools in which free people can come forth."[30]

Among redemptive republicans, the sense was particularly acute that the "free world" was anything but free. The underlying question was always the same: was the environment in which the school and university existed trustworthy or dangerous? Was it a source of pollution or means of political purification? For the Frankfurt legal historian, Hermann Coing, the university needed to conform to social demands. In a series of much-discussed articles in 1956, he urged increased university funding for extra professors and assistant professors (*Assistenten*) to meet the requirement of a massive rise in student numbers. These were the type of pragmatic reform recommendations that the Wissenschaftsrat, founded a year later to coordinate university policy at a national level, was to make in its first, influential report in 1960. Karl Jaspers and Tellenbach

---

[28] Arnold Gehlen, *Man in the Age of Technology*, trans. Patricia Lipscomb (New York, 1980); Carlo Schmid, *Mensch und Technik. Die sozialen und kulturellen Probleme der zweiten industriellen Revolution* (Bonn, 1956); Arnold Bergstraesser, "Die Technik und das Kulturproblem des 20. Jahrhunderts" (1959), in his *Politik in Wissenschaft und Bildung*, 2nd ed. (Freiburg, 1966), 142–58; Max Horkheimer and Theodor W. Adorno, *Dialectic of Enlightenment*, trans. John Cummings (Boston, 1971 [1944]).

[29] Hellmut Becker, "Die verwaltete Schule," in his *Kulturpolitik und Schule. Probleme der verwalteten Welt* (Stuttgart, 1956), 33–70. Hermann Glaser argues in similar terms: *Gedanken zur Reform der Höheren Schule: Aufsätze zu Grundsätzlichem und Konkretem* (Freiburg, 1963). See the response of Thomas Ellwein, "Die verwaltete Schule," *Das Argument*, 6:4 (1964), 209–19.

[30] Becker, "Die verwaltete Schule," 70.

replied critically to Coing. The university had to remain true to the "intellectual energy" and "spirit" of the Humboldt tradition as the answer to the problems of specialization and overcrowding because it was the principal source of resistance to the modernity they distrusted.[31]

Habermas and the Technocratic University

It was in this context that Habermas, who had read this exchange, intervened and articulated the redemptive position of the forty-fivers. Already in 1956, he had identified the university as the most promising site of opposition to the "totalitarian processes" of technological perfection because, "as places of the residual humanistic tradition, they had resisted the training in isolated disciplines the longest."[32] As already noted in the previous chapter, he had made the argument about rescuing irrational, premodern experiences for progressive purposes several years before. Now he mounted a case to rescue the residues of this tradition by attacking the idealistic position of Jaspers and Tellenbach, as well as the incipient technocratic solution of Coing. All participants in the debate, he wrote, were aware of the problems: the continuing rapid specialization of research made impossible the synthesis of knowledge; the unity of teaching and research was sundered by the development of research institutes and the teaching of prepackaged information and interpretations; students' academic freedom was limited by the sheer amount of material they were expected to master in each field. From the coherence of the early nineteenth century, the university had developed a differentiated spectrum of disciplines and subdisciplines that produced enormous gains in knowledge but, paradoxically, confined individual scholars to narrow limits and alienated students from the research (and consequently the learning) process. The cost of scientific progress was the disintegration of the classical, humanistic university that now threatened to become dispersed into vocational and technological institutes without the synthetic, educative function represented by the Humboldt ideal.

Habermas's innovation was to cast these developments as inner contradictions needing resolution. The inherited structures of the old university could no longer institutionalize Humboldt's vision because they were responsible for the problematic contradictions he had outlined. The traditionalists failed to recognize that the university had become part of the "objective process" of technological development. It was too late to try to isolate the university from society and seek out "administrative free zones," as Jaspers and Tellenbach wished; society had already colonized the university. Uncovering this

[31] Hermann Coing, "Die Lage der deutschen Hochschulen," *Die Gegenwart*, 12 (1956); Coing "Die Lage der deutschen Hochschulen. Abschließende Bemerkungen," *Die Gegenwart*, 17 (1956); Coing, "Die Lage der Hochschulen. Noch eine Nachbemerkung," *Die Gegenwart*, 20 (1956); Karl Jaspers, "Vom rechten Geist der Universität," *Die Gegenwart*, 13 (1956); Tellenbach, "Neugestaltung der Universität."
[32] Jürgen Habermas, "Der Zeitgeist und die Pädagogik," *Merkur*, 10 (1956), 189–93.

dire state of affairs and finding a way out was the task that Habermas set for himself.[33] Only a dialectical solution could revive Humboldt's vision: sublating the gains of specialization and functional differentiation in a higher unity rather than returning to a chimerical unity in the weekly lectures of the *Studium generale*.[34]

For Habermas, the university crisis was a function of the public sphere's decline that he would trace in his habilitation thesis.[35] The social consequences of capitalism in the second half of the nineteenth century had forced the state to intervene in society. At the same time, social groups made claims on the state so that civil society blended into the state. Both the state and the economy had a vested interest in university research, for which they provide appropriate funding and additional support in the training of bureaucrats and professionals. Moreover, the connection of knowledge and technology with social praxis that existed in the medieval university was lost as the philosophical faculty was marginalized by the natural and social sciences, law, and medicine. The knowledge they produced was thereby divorced from unifying conceptions. They produced pure theory, and scholarship became "value neutral." Henceforth, the humanities, which did not fit the positivistic paradigm of an exact science, reacted defensively and became the bearers of cultural protest, which in turn was tamed by its gradual institutionalization in museums and galleries and by an art market – in short, through a "ubiquitous culture industry." Culture was reduced to the function of granting prestige to its holders, who were thereby deemed to possess "personality," a status that Habermas regarded as particularly dubious because real personality consisted in the extension of the self in social and political activity over which the subject exercised essential control.

How could one restore human control over complex social processes and realize the human universality promised by the bourgeois enlightenment? The first task, Habermas continued, was to address the unity of teaching and research, where the problem was the increasing emphasis on transmitting the results of prior research, rather than opening the horizons of students by working with them on current research questions. University teachers no longer offered the key to universality through the participation in critical reflection on some object of inquiry; they passed on prepackaged information for students who regarded the academy as a key to qualifications for careers outside the university. The academy's transformative role "to be a ferment of life" had been lost.

Habermas's aim, then, was to "reactivate the philosophical residues" and "mobilize the best traditions" of the university.[36] True to his dialectical

[33] Jürgen Habermas, "Das chronische Leiden der Hochschulreform," *Merkur*, 11 (1957), 265–84. Reprinted in his *Kleine Politische Schriften, I-IV* (Frankfurt, 1981), 13–40.
[34] Ibid.
[35] Jürgen Habermas, *Die Strukturwandel der Öffentlichkeit* (Darmstadt and Neuwied, 1962).
[36] Habermas, "Das chronische Leiden der Hochschulreform."

premises, he did not recommend a rupture of the university with the surrounding society. If the university needed to continue its new role of reproducing social life by training professionals and conducting scientific research, it also needed to confront the fact that its utilitarian mission contributed to the "immaturity" of students because it did not treat them as mature adults. Addressing this problem meant liberating students from the mass of material and superficial overviews by problematizing omissions in particular bodies of knowledge, as Heimpel had urged. Winning back the unity of teaching and research was possible if the professor explained the reasons for scholarly questions and blind spots, thereby reconstituting the ability of students to make independent judgments.

From this position, Habermas drew the same conclusion that Abendroth and Tietgens had before him: that the path forward was to criticize the relationship of individual disciplines to social reality, and that such reflection led to further criticism of the relationship between science and society. The plausibility of this argument was based on resolving contradictions in a historical process viewed as lopsided rationalization. Thus, he claimed, for example, that the "scientific, newly unfolding productive forces in the parameters of the existing order are obviously bound by irrational relations" because productive rationalization existed in forms "that are as traditional as they are dangerous." Atomic energy had obvious social consequences, for instance, and science needed to abandon its methodological neutrality to reflect on them. A real reform would entail a critique of science and its basic assumptions. Sociology, for example, would have to realize that its absolutization of the quantitative method and functional presuppositions meant that it necessarily presented a harmonious vision of the existing order, that is, that it was unable to critically transcend the "given."

Here Habermas extended the argument of Herbert Marcuse in *One Dimensional Man* and of Adorno in the "Positivism Dispute." Rather than invoking the shallow generalism of the *Studium generale*, he recommended a radicalization of specialization, which entailed reflecting on the phenomena that particular methods were designed to reveal. Where such a reflection would lead in concrete terms he did not say in 1957. What he did say was that theory must not be permitted to collapse unmediated into practice. "Of course, this enlightenment of the enlightened sciences cannot be diverted to a cult of political action or an irrational existence if the university does not want to become, for a second time, the site of a rectoral address and repeat the academic grab for power of 1933," Habermas wrote in a reference to Heidegger. This typically forty-fiver distancing from the spirit of the conservative revolution would be repeated by Habermas and others in their dialogue with the younger generation less than a decade later. The relationship between theory and practice was as complex as it was delicate.

Habermas's article raised the matter of how one would institutionalize the reflection for which he called. Before he could answer this question, he became embroiled in an important controversy with the conservative sociologist Helmut Schelsky (1912–84) about the reform of primary schools. Since the end of the war, the confessional school had been reestablished after its replacement by the Nazi regime. The provincial governments, which retained control of educational matters, had kept the initial common schooling period to a short four years, after which students went either to a grammar school (*Gymnasium*) that led to the *Abitur* and eventually university, or to a high school that led to practical work.[37] At the time, a mere 5 percent of children from working-class families attended universities. The grammar schools were the site where the German elite reproduced itself and cultivated the apolitical habitus opposed by Non-German German redemptive republicans.

The debate about school reform came to a head in 1959 when the German Committee for Education (Deutscher Ausschuß für Erziehungs- und Bildungswesen), the precursor to the Education Council (Bildungsrat), presented its plan for the German school. Although it proposed modest reform, it was met with a hail of criticism from conservative groups, in particular from the grammar school teachers union (Philologenverband).[38] The committee recommended supplementing the four years of common primary school with a two-year "encouragement phase" (*Förderstufe*) in which the suitability of children for different streams of schools would be assessed.[39] Habermas was unsettled by the vehemence of the criticism in which he perceived the defensive reaction of the declining educated elite that opposed the opening up of the grammar school to traditionally underrepresented classes. Although he too was dissatisfied with elements of the plan, Habermas felt obliged to reply to the conservative critics.

He defended the "encouragement phase" in its purpose of compensating for the lack, even in middle-class households, of those cultural goods that inclined children to university study. He thereby anticipated Ralf Dahrendorf's argument about the barriers to education in general, and higher education in particular, especially for rural youth and Roman Catholics. Habermas, like Dahrendorf, was prepared to question the absoluteness of parents' right to decide which type of school their children should attend after the initial, common four-year primary school. "The social basic right for children to an education based on talent today also needs protection against the indifference of their own parents."[40]

But Habermas also had other priorities. Education, he feared, like Becker, would become instrumentalized for competition between the power blocs in the Cold War. It was needed, by contrast, to raise education levels for the sake of democracy itself. For "on the basis of the stupidity produced and maintained by the ruling practice of scientifically directed manipulation of so-called public

---

[37] Ludwig von Friedeburg, *Bildungsreform in Deutschland. Geschichte und gesellschaftlicher Widerspruch* (Frankfurt, 1989), 284–88.

[38] Herbert Enderwitz, "Two German Reform Schemes: *Rahmenplan* and *Bremer Plan*," *Comparative Education Review*, 7:1 (1963), 47–50; Ursula Kirkpatrick Springer, "The *Rahmenplan* for West German School Reform," *Comparative Education Review*, 4:1 (1960), 18–25.

[39] Saul B. Robinson and J. Caspar Kuhlmann, "Two Decades on Non-Reform in West German Education," *Comparative Education Review*, 11:3 (October 1967), 311–30.

[40] Jürgen Habermas, "Konservativer Geist – und die modernistischen Folgen," *Der Monat*, 12 (1959), 41–50. Reprinted in his *Kleine Politische Schriften, I-IV*, 41–57.

opinion, democracy will not be able to reproduce itself over time, at least as democracy."[41] Echoing Hennis's emphasis on the importance of judgment, he pointed out that the problem of political immaturity was especially the case in a modern society, such as West Germany's, where a higher level of judgment was required to understand the abstraction and formalization of the economic processes to which people were subject.

Then there was the distinction between education and training. A majority was condemned to the latter and thereby unable to withdraw from the manipulative "externally guided free-time behavior," and so denied the reflection on the "fulfillment of life." "Should not, to take one example, the mass of the people in the long term be put in the position to be able to choose independently an appropriate book from the mass-produced series of paperbacks?" What Habermas elusively called a "Second Enlightenment" would not occur without an appropriate education system. Such a system would perform two tasks: it would rupture the reproduction of the German elite that he so distrusted, and it would educate the population to enlightened maturity so it could resist the seductions of advertising and consumerism and participate in critical discourse in the public sphere.[42]

An important counterattack was mounted soon thereafter by Schelsky, who advanced many of the arguments that he and conservative forty-fivers would repeat in the 1970s about the alleged "rule of the intellectuals."[43] Schelsky, who, as we know, had lauded the forty-fivers as the "skeptical generation" because they broke with the tradition of the German youth movement, was equally hostile to *Reformpädogik*, which was itself a product of the youth movement's critique of bourgeois society. Schelsky regarded with great suspicion any effort on the part of educationalists to create "free room" for youth; indeed, he opposed the idea of an autonomous stage of development called "youth," which he held to be a dangerous delay from the world of work and "reality." It was, as he himself interpreted his own "totalitarian temptation" in the 1930s, the reality-distant nature of the youth movement and its associated educational philosophy that predisposed young people to fantastical, totalitarian solutions to their self-imposed alienation.

As might be expected, Schelsky attacked Habermas's privileging of the schools' (and thereby the teachers') role in determining the educational direction of students in the proposed "encouragement phase" of the German Education Committee's plan. The title of his polemic, *Anpassung oder Widerstand?* (Conformity or Resistance?), made clear what he thought were the alternative policy options. Either the school would become an "autocracy of parent-free education" in the hands of all-powerful educationalists and teachers, or parents would determine its priorities. Schelsky sided with the parents, whatever

---

[41] Habermas, "Konservativer Geist," 47.

[42] Ibid., 48–51.

[43] Helmut Schelsky, *Anpassung oder Widerstand? Soziologische Bedenken zur Schulreform. Eine Streitschrift zur Schulpolitik* (Heidelberg, 1961).

the aspirations for their children, because their choice of school for their children represented "the free play of social forces" rather than the "socialist" educationalist solution that determined these choices. He even went so far as to call the latter a "danger to civilization."[44]

Schelsky's animus is explicable against the background of his understanding of German society as a whole. He no longer thought it was a classical class society as Habermas and Dahrendorf did. It was rather a *nivillierte Mittelstandsgesellschaft* (flattened out society of the middle orders), a term that described the decline of the educated middle class, rise of the working class, and the evolution of a white-collar class of employees who shared a basic, common life-style through the socialization of luxury goods in consumerism. The society of which these groups were the "bearing strata" was "middle order – petit bourgeois" (*mittelständisch – kleinbürgerlich*). In such a mobile society, the school assumed the crucial function as distributor of life chances and social mobility for families. Schelsky opposed this role because he saw in teachers and educators the remnants of a declining strata of mandarins who claimed to represent a "higher" form of life that he regarded as anachronistic.[45]

The nature of this choice and the source of hostility to this stratum becomes clearer from his analysis of the Humboldtian ideal of humanistic education in his inaugural lecture at the University of Münster in 1960. *Einsamkeit und Freiheit* (Solitude and Freedom), as it was called, was a criticism of this tradition insofar as it was supposed to serve as a model for education reform in West Germany. Here Schelsky's target was conservatives like Heimpel who insisted on university autonomy as well as progressives like Habermas who sought to realize the ideal in radically different circumstances. Schelsky insisted that it was inapplicable because Humboldt and Fichte had proposed a radical distance between the university and bourgeois society. It was not just a matter of academic freedom but also academic isolation. Because this situation was unrealizable today, universities should resign themselves to being solely institutions of training and scientific research. Traditional humanistic *Bildung* would have to occur outside the university, which henceforth would be the preserve of the functional elite rather than the humanistically educated elite. The latter ought to relinquish its social and cultural leadership.[46]

A functional elite would and should assume leadership of the system because, as Schelsky explained in his much discussed lecture a year later, "Der Mensch in der wissenschaftlichen Zivilisation" (The Person in Scientific Civilization), the German tradition of neohumanism tended to cultural pessimism by viewing technology as a nonhuman nature that dominated humanity rather than regarding it optimistically as an extension of human power. Humboldt, he

[44] Ibid., 150, 161–62.
[45] Helmut Schelsky, "Soziologische Bemerkungen zur Rolle der Schule in unserer Gesellschaftsverfassung (1956)," in his *Auf der Suche nach Wirklichkeit* (Düsseldorf and Cologne, 1965), 131–59.
[46] Helmut Schelsky, *Einsamkeit und Freiheit. Zur sozialen Idee der deutschen Universität* (Münster, 1960).

noted, assumed that the world of culture and science was a whole that could be internalized so the individual would become universal. But such cultivation was no longer the case, and so it was impossible to provide a synthesis for an ideology or worldview. Not the wholeness but the openness of a person should be the new anthropological ideal, based on the insight, credited to his former colleague at Leipzig, Arnold Gehlen, that technological advancement issued in a commensurate change in human nature because technology was an extension of human capabilities. Universities should remain places of specialization.[47]

In effect, Schelsky linked the mandarin intellectual class produced by the Humboldtian university to the idea of resistance to bourgeois society and to the intellectuals of the 1920s and early 1930s who had beguiled him. Would the German school orient itself now to society, he asked in *Anpassung oder Widerstand?*, or become an "intellectuals' school" that resisted it? Behind the argument about the "reality" of society lay Hans Freyer's concept of institutions in his *Theorie des gegenwärtigen Zeitalters* (Theory of Current Age). Schelsky maintained that societies reproduced themselves on the basis of the norms embodied in institutions, which could then be adapted and continued by the people who relied on them. This was an orientation he contrasted with the "autocracy of teachers" and "autonomy of pedagogy" that he likened to a church or a religion insofar as they were "an autonomous institution based on an intellectual truth, the bearers of which were the functionaries who alone could recognize and administer it."[48] In other words, Schelsky celebrated the decline and end of the German mandarins.

Redemptive republicans bore the brunt of Schelsky's ire in their aspiration to reform West German society by developing a technology-critical program of education. Accordingly, Schelsky criticized the plans for a new university in Bremen because of the "integrative" role it proposed for social anthropology above the other disciplines, and because of the idea of making it a "people's university" open to adult education and the formation of the broader public (*Volksbildung*). Max Scheler and the youth movement, he noted critically, had proposed such ideas in the 1920s.[49] For Schelsky, this idea smacked of politicization, and he worried that the Bremen plan was popular among "socialists," drawing comparisons with the Nazi instrumentalization of the university. For similar reasons, he attacked the plan to have Christian "ideology professors" (*Weltanschauungsprofessoren*) at the forthcoming new university in Bochum as well as a proposed integrative discipline of "social ethics." Social anthropology or social ethics, he feared, could replace theology or philosophy "to integrate and express the wholeness and essence of modern knowledge." Rather than seek some illusory unity, scholars needed to open themselves to what lay

---

[47] Helmut Schelsky, "Der Mensch in der wissenschaftlichen Zivilisation" (1961), in his *Auf der Suche nach Wirklkichkeit*, 439–80.
[48] Schelsky, *Anpassung oder Widerstand?*, 79, 130, 145.
[49] Helmut Schelsky, "Wie gründet man Universitäten?" *Frankfurter Allgemeine Zeitung* (October 14, 1961).

beyond one's discipline, but interdisciplinary work did not happen in Germany, he regretted. Later in the 1960s, he would propose an interdisciplinary program as the means to winning some overview, especially at Bielefeld University, but there was no going behind the specialization.[50]

None of these objections, however, meant that Schelsky had abandoned humanistic anthropology altogether.

It is about cultivating a highly rational, deemotionalized type who gives himself over to the present while preserving powers of distancing, that mixture of rational precision and intuitive imagination that today determines all essential intellectual production; to show the limits of knowledge and assert them against the will to knowledge is today an act of cultivation; to produce that critical posture and responsibility against the political and social world that, after all, can always free itself from the coercion to act of the social world and withdraw in contemplation. It is about cultivating a person who can incorporate the *suffering of consciousness of the time*.[51]

Humanistic sovereignty, then, remained important for Schelsky, but it was an extra-university, private affair that produced a resigned rather than utopian orientation, that ascribed a compensatory role to the humanities, especially history. Despite his professed opposition to the mandarins, it appears that Schelsky had something in common with them after all, even if he was not hostile to technical civilization.

Habermas replied immediately in the first volume of the reformist-oriented journal, *Die Neue Sammlung*.[52] Naturally he rejected Schelsky's accusation that educationalists sought to instrumentalize the school as an "educational dictatorship," pointing out that Schelsky was himself not "unfriendly" toward the residues of the "real" elite institutions. Habermas was referring to his acceptance of the educated elite's monopoly on the grammar school and the university. This was the monopoly that Habermas wanted to break, and to that end he argued that Schelsky underestimated the social and cultural barriers to education by taking parents' choice at face value. The question was whether the state regarded these barriers as part of the "natural" order, or whether it compensated for the lack of an educational environment in the home by providing it at school. A true liberal orientation, as he argued in *Student und Politik*, would take seriously the promise of equality of opportunity as the legitimization for state interference that for Schelsky smacked of socialism. Schelsky's blind reliance on the sovereignty of the parents, Habermas retorted, smacked of decisionism because it was not normatively grounded.

Habermas revealed his aversion to the social aspirations of the West German "economic miracle" that he perceived Schelsky to be articulating, describing as

---

[50] Paul Mikat and Helmut Schelsky, *Grundzüge einer neuen Universität* (Gütersloh, 1967).

[51] Schelsky, *Anpassung oder Widerstand?*, 80 (emphasis in original). This picture is strikingly similar to that of Gehlen in *Man in the Age of Technology*, 164.

[52] Jürgen Habermas, "Pädagogischer 'Optimismus' vor Gericht einer pessimistischen Anthropologie. Schelskys Bedenken zur Schulreform," *Die Neue Sammlung*, 1:4 (1961), 251–78. Reprinted in his *Kleine Politische Schriften*, I–IV, 58–100.

"truly depressing" an education that based educational aptitude solely "on the dynamic of a motorized ambition of the family." Schelsky, in essence, sought to "make obligatory for the whole society the norms of the petit-bourgeois world-view."[53] For Habermas, these were precisely the norms of a restorative, technologically dominated society that he hoped the school and university could resist. Although he did not use the term, his was an opposition to the *Leistungsprinzip* (achievement ethic) that Marcuse, whose thought especially attracted him at the time, had attacked as the principle of repression that drove industrial production.[54]

At the same time, Habermas's hopes for educational institutions that would unite theory and practice were attacked by liberal critics from two distinct camps. The one was represented by Karl Popper and his continental disciples Hans Albert (b. 1921) and Ernst Topitsch (1919–2003), an Austrian who taught at the University of Heidelberg. Albert and Habermas took up the debate between Popper and Adorno in the so-called Positivism Dispute in Tübingen 1961. So much has been written about the encounter that it is worth considering instead a conflict with the other philosophical camp:[55] the conflict with the neo-Aristotelian school of practical philosophy, especially Hermann Lübbe, based around Joachim Ritter in Münster, which maintained close connections with Helmut Schelsky.

The main collaborator with Schelsky in university politics in the 1960s was Lübbe, who already by 1963 had a reputation in the English-speaking world as a thinker with "democratic and cosmopolitan values."[56] Together they served on the founding committee for the establishment of a university in Bielefeld. Between 1966 and 1969 he was the secretary of state for education in the Social Democratic administration in Northrhine-Westphalia.[57] Lübbe and Habermas were well aware of one another's work, which they cited critically. Habermas regarded Lübbe as one of his primary opponents because Lübbe had political influence and because he advanced a theory of the separation of theory and practice combined with a decisionism that Habermas associated with Carl Schmitt.

In the right-Hegelian interpretation of modernity that Lübbe learned from Ritter, individual emancipation was undercut by modernity itself. If individuals experienced freedom in the replacement of feudalism's estates by equality before the law, the protection of private property, and the emergence of free markets,

---

[53] Habermas, "Pädagogischer 'Optimismus,'" 273–74.

[54] Herbert Marcuse, "Trieblehre und Freizeit," in Theodor W. Adorno and Walter Dirks, eds, *Sociologica*, vol. 1, *Frankfurter Beiträge zur Soziologie* (Frankfurt, 1956).

[55] An example of the literature on the Positivism Dispute is Hans-Joachim Dahms, *Positivismusstreit. Die Auseinandersetzung der Frankfurter Schule mit dem logischen Positivismus, dem amerikanischen Pragmatismus und dem kritischen Rationalismus* (Frankfurt, 1993).

[56] Klaus Epstein, review of Hermann Lübbe, *Politische Philosophie in Deutschland* (1963), in *Review of Politics*, 28 (1966), 112–15.

[57] Hermann Lübbe, "Helmut Schelsky als Universitätsgründer," in Horst Baier, ed., *Helmut Schelsky – ein Soziologe in der Bundesrepublik* (Stuttgart, 1986), 157–66.

the accompanying dissolution of meaning and orientation led to the rise of compensatory totalitarian ideologies.[58] National Socialism and Marxism, of course, were such ideologies, and so too were the infamous "Ideas of 1914" (the German anti-Western ideology in the First World War) because they met his criteria of a totalitarian movement: they provided the means for defining an enemy in a confessional civil war based on a philosophy of history.

The central element of the Enlightenment, then, was the ending of confessional civil wars. Lübbe appealed to Baruch Spinoza for the proposition that political, publicly binding decisions in confessional questions were impossible. Enlightenment was the gradual secularization of the state and the expansion of the freedom of conscience; civil peace was guaranteed by the political indeterminacy of truth.[59] Secularization was the program of the Enlightenment, liberalism, and civilizational progress. National Socialism sought to overcome them. He vigorously opposed the attempts of conservative Roman Catholics, therefore, to blame National Socialism on secularization and the Enlightenment.[60]

Consequently, Lübbe followed Hegel in opposing the politicization of personal political convictions (*Gesinnung*) because such politicization tended to totalitarianism: the attempt to identify an unmediated will of the state with the general will of society. Liberal freedoms lay precisely in the nonidentity of individual and collective. And so he supported the Hegelian and Kantian philosophies of history because they legitimated progress without positing a subject of history like "humanity." "Kantians and Hegelians enjoy the liberal advantage of being permitted to exist 'alienated.'"[61] Totalitarian was the claim to be the subject of history that can demand unlimited power in executing its plan. Freedom could be defended, he added in a reference to the Cold War, against those who pretended to represent "humanity" only by advancing particular interests shorn of a universal mission, that is, those directed to the "classical will to political self-assertion that does not accept the offer of a world civil war."[62]

---

[58] Joachim Ritter, *Hegel und die französische Revolution* (Cologne, 1957). See Lübbe's acknowledgment of the influence in his "Der Weg in die Philosophie kraft Ermunterung, ihn fortzusetzen," in Christine Hauskeller and Michael Hauskeller, eds., ". . . was die Welt im Innersten zusammenhält". 34 *Wege zur Philosophie* (Hamburg, 1996), 40–46.

[59] Hermann Lübbe, "Freiheit und Verbindlichkeit," in Deutsches Institut für Bildung und Wissen, ed., *Wahrheit, Freiheit, Toleranz* (Frankfurt, 1965), 80–87. Reprinted in his *Theorie und Entscheidung. Studien zum Primat der praktischen Vernunft* (Freiburg, 1971), 134–43.

[60] Hermann Lübbe, "Verteidigung der Freiheit als Kampf gegen den Liberalismus," *Zeitschrift für Politik*, 8 (1961), 347–52; Lübbe, "Säkularisierung als geschichtsphilosophische Kategorie" (1962), in Helmut Kuhn and Franz Weidmann, eds., *Die Philosophie und die Frage nach dem Fortschritt* (Munich, 1964), 221–39.

[61] Hermann Lübbe, "Hegels Kritik der politisierten Gesellschaft" (1967), in his *Theorie und Entscheidung*, 93–110.

[62] Hermann Lübbe, "Typologie der politischen Theorie," in Helmut Kuhn and Franz Wiedmann, eds., *Das Problem der Ordnung* (Meisenheim, 1962), 77–94. Habermas answers in "Über das Verhältnis von Politik und Moral," in ibid., 109–11.

What for Habermas were illegitimate social and economic interests, then, were for Lübbe the stuff of interest politics that kept people rooted in the political realm of the possible and prevented the enticement of identifying oneself with some transcendent or universal will. Hegel was not an apologist for Prussian authoritarianism but a founder of pragmatic politics.[63]

Lübbe's liberal Schmittianism is a good example of the integrative republican defense of German national subjectivity. Nazism was not the self-assertion of "Germanness" but a totalitarian ideology in which Germany was to carry out a universal mission for the benefit of humanity. Fichte, he pointed out, argued that the German nation was the sole bearer of genuinely universal ideas, and the same ideas cropped up in the conservative revolution.[64] The problem was not German particularism but the hubris of universalism, a problem that could be projected onto redemptive republicans like Habermas.

Consequently, Lübbe had no time for culturally pessimistic critiques of post-war Germany and modernity. His first target was Schelsky's teacher, Hans Freyer, whose book on technology, *Theorie des gegenwärtigen Zeitalters*, he described as a "defamatory expression of that unease with the modern world that is nourished from the beginning by the cultural criticism of romantic provenance." Many of Freyer's criticisms were the same as Habermas's: the tyrannical independence of the machine, its inner tendency to perfection, the autonomy of human-made things in an alienated "secondary system," the inability of workers to really enjoy their increasing free time because they cannot be full individuals through their consumer formation. Germany's problem, Lübbe concluded, anticipating Schelsky's argument in "Der Mensch in der wissenschaftlichen Zivilisation," was that it took the pessimistic rather than the optimistic interpretation of civilization and progressive philosophy of history. The redemptive posture was one-sided because it did not do justice to the tangible benefits that modernization had brought. Without denying the alienation that the cultural critics observed, Lübbe commented dryly that "far greater than the suffering of those who can't cope with their consumption today is still the number of those who suffer because they have nothing to consume."[65] His posture to this issue could not be more different from that of Habermas who maintained a few years earlier that factory workers today were as alienated in their leisure time as factory workers around 1800 who worked twelve hour days.

Lübbe followed Habermas in seeing the university as a central battleground in the West German culture wars. And like many of his contemporaries, he turned to Max Weber and especially his university address from 1919, "Science

[63] Martin Kriele, "Gesetzprüfende Vernunft und Bedingungen rechtlichen Fortschritts," *Der Staat*, 6 (1967), 45–60; Odo Marquard, "Hegel und das Sollen," *Philosophisches Jahrbuch*, 72 (1964–65), 103–19. See Lübbe's edition of their texts in *Die Hegelsche Rechte* (Stuttgart, 1963).

[64] Hermann Lübbe, *Politische Philosophie in Deutschland* (Basel, 1963).

[65] Hermann Lübbe, "Die resignierte konservative Revolution," *Zeitschrift für die gesamte Staatswissenschaft*, 115:1 (1959), 131–38; Lübbe, *Politische Philosophie in Deutschland*.

as a Vocation," to justify the separation of theory and practice. But unlike the picture of the apolitical and positivist Weber that Talcott Parsons and Reinhard Bendix had popularized in America, Lübbe saw in him a thinker who sought to formulate a political mission for scholarship and the university at a time of bitter ideological conflict. Paradoxically, this mission was to keep its distance from politics and ideology. Weber's context was the clash of the "great ideologies" between 1870 and 1920. Weber had come to realize that rationalization did not dispense with myths: on the contrary, it produced reactions against rationalization that sought to reverse the "disenchantment of the world." He wanted to resist them, which is why he was a scholar, unlike ideologues, such as Marx, who hoped to end human alienation. The "Ideas of 1914" were such a myth, Lübbe continued. Scholarship needed its will to rationality when the social environment was becoming irrational. A bulwark of liberal freedom was the university as an "ideology-free zone," the site of praxis-distant theory. Lübbe was aware of the argument that the university should not be insulated from politics because the Weimar university was so vulnerable to National Socialism. But, he replied, it was ultimately destroyed because it worked with the Nazi state, not against it. Even so, inner-university resistance would have not sufficed. The university must be defended politically by its supporters outside the ivory tower.[66] It was possible for universities to become satellites of totalitarianism in a "declamatory way" by becoming politicized, Lübbe warned. For totalitarianism did not necessarily entail the wielding of state power but the presence of total moral claims that identified and cast out the holders of rival claims as enemies of the common good. Accordingly, "the morality of the university was the ban on scholars' moralizing, and so universities should not be the subject of political will-formation."[67] In this sense, science was the praxis of the scholar and not that of the politician. An example was the issue of mastering the Nazi past. "It is not the *immediate* task of the humanities to undertake this. Its immediate purpose is to make and publish those discoveries and insights that one needs to make possible what one likes to call the mastering of the past."[68]

Underlying Lübbe's conception of the university and its relation to politics was an assumption about the nature of politics and science that was radically different from that of Habermas. Scholarship could be radical only if it did not have to be politically responsible because it needed time to be able to find the reasons for its conclusions. Decisions, by contrast, needed to be made under the pressure of events, lest the state or organization one served be jeopardized by endless debating. The rationality and dignity of a groundless decision lay in the

[66] Hermann Lübbe, "'Politik gehört nicht in den Hörsaal.' Max Weber und der Dezisionismus," *Frankfurter Allgemeine Zeitung* (April 18, 1964).

[67] Hermann Lübbe, "Die Freiheit der Theorie. Max Weber über Wissenschaft als Beruf," *Archiv für Rechts- und Sozialphilosophie*, 48 (1962), 343–65.

[68] Hermann Lübbe, "Reformprobleme der Philosophischen Fakultät," *Pädagogische Rundschau*, 20 (1966), 249–55. Reprinted in his *Hochschulreform und Gegenaufklärung*, 119–30.

real-life need to make a decision even when the reasons did not exist that would end debate.[69] Lübbe took this lesson from his understanding of the weakness of the Weimar Republic. Politics, then, was that realm where groundless decisions were made in the competition of interests. His was the decisionistic model, based on explicit and unapologetic reliance on Carl Schmitt's *Theory of the Political*.[70] Theory could not withstand such political pressure if it wanted to gather the evidence and develop the arguments for its propositions. Decisions may be blind but not irrational.

In this way, Lübbe reversed Schelsky's technocratic argument that posited an end of politics in "scientization" of decision making in the administration of things. Lübbe insisted that ultimately decisions needed to be made when policy was to be implemented because competing interests were often unable to reach agreement about a course of action. But unlike Habermas, Abendroth, and Tietgens, he did not regard interest rivalry as illegitimate or irrational. It was the normal stuff of politics.[71]

Habermas agreed substantially with this analysis but not with the answer. Where Weber and Lübbe want to shield the university from politics and ideology in order to save it from myth, Habermas wanted to cut off the source of myths – the one-sided rationalization process – by continuing the rationalization of science in making the universities political: that is, myths would be banished by citizens' reflecting critically on and controlling the implications of technology. In the end, Habermas was recommending not just reflection on science but also its steering because it was not in fact an "ideology-free zone": the technological process and the history of philosophy that justified it was an ideology.[72] Both thinkers agreed, then, that the rationalization process called for the totalitarian temptation but Habermas saw such ideologies as the result of a lopsided process that needed steering, whereas Lübbe viewed it as a basically sound process that needed defending against the cultural pessimists of the right and the left.

Habermas continued his campaign in an address at the Free University in Berlin in January 1963. The old university model, he contended, had explicit *practical* consequences and was not monastic or otherworldly, as Schelsky

[69] Hermann Lübbe, "Zur Theorie der Entscheidung," *Collegium Philosophicum. Studien. Joachim Ritter zum 60. Geburtstag* (Basel and Stuttgart, 1965), 118–40. Reprinted in his *Theorie und Entscheidung. Studien zum Primat der praktischen Vernunft* (Freiburg, 1971), 7–32.

[70] Hermann Lübbe, "Carl Schmitt liberal rezipiert," in Helmut Quaritsch, ed., *Complexio Oppositorium. Über Carl Schmitt* (Speyer, 1988), 427–40. Reprinted in his *Die Aufdringlichkeit der Geschichte*, 309–22.

[71] Hermann Lübbe, "Zur politischen Theorie der Technokratie," *Der Staat*, 1 (1962), 19–38. Reprinted in his *Theorie und Entscheidung*, 32–53; Lübbe, "Wissenschaftspolitik, Wissenschaft und Politik," in Hans Wenke and Joachim H. Knoll, eds., *Festschrift zur Eröffnung der Universität Bochum* (Bochum, 1965), 136–49, 149, reprinted in his *Hochschulreform und Gegenaufklärung* (Freiburg, 1972), 13–28; Lübbe, "Herrschaft und Planung. Die veränderte Rolle der Zukunft in der Gegenwart," in Heinrich Rombach, eds., *Die Frage nach dem Menschen. Aufriß einer philosophischen Anthropologie* (Freiburg and Munich, 1966), 188–211, reprinted in his *Theorie und Entscheidung*, 62–84.

[72] Jürgen Habermas, *Wissenschschaft und Technik als Ideologie* (Frankfurt, 1967).

especially had portrayed it.[73] The Humboldt model was *not* the isolation of the academy from social praxis because a university education led to the formation of character for action in the real world. To be sure, *Bildung* did not have immediate, practical application; rather, it developed a general "common sense" and norms that superseded tradition for critical application to the life world. "The great emancipation of the neohumanist" formation of norms was based on scholarly reflection.[74] The university, then, was a critical filter that returned the traditions of its environment purified of their caprice and local partiality.

In other words, Habermas argued that the classical Humboldt university mediated theory and practice by providing practical orientation for the development and application of knowledge. In the "classical relationship" between theory and practice, the former guided the latter in its application to prereflexive disciplines based on tradition, like law and medicine. Since the early nineteenth century, however, the disciplines had become "scientized" (*verwissenschaftlicht*) because now they were all rationalized according to their inner logic, which was explicitly not oriented to practical application in the sense of a comprehensive and integrated view of the discipline's purpose.

Today we are dealing with theories that are unpractical applications of technical power, namely that are not explicitly related to the action of social people. To be sure, the sciences provide a specific know-how: but that which they teach is not the same as the ability related to living and acting that one once expected from the scientifically educated.[75]

Habermas wanted to recapture this integrated knowledge or orientation. But how? At this stage, he was unsure. But he was sure about the task:

The retranslation of scientific results is the horizon of the life world that would permit the contents of technical recommendations to be imported into the discussion about what was in the general interest and practically necessary. Today we cannot leave that to the coincidental decisions of individuals or the pluralism of vested interests. It is about not only transmitting the ability and know-how of technically working people, but bringing them back to the ownership of the communicating society. *That* is today the task of academic education that, now as then, must be taken up by one of the disciplines in the position for self-reflection.[76]

It was also the task to end the illusion that the research priorities of universities were somehow unideological if not guided by explicit political priorities. They were not neutral priorities but technocratic ones that reflected the imperatives of vested interests.

[73] Jürgen Habermas, "Vom sozialen Wandel akademischer Bildung," *Merkur*, 17 (1963), 413–27. Reprinted in his *Kleine Politische Schriften, I-IV*, 101–19.

[74] Ibid., 107.

[75] Ibid., 105.

[76] Ibid., 117 (emphasis in original). See also Jürgen Habermas, "Verwissenschaftlichte Poltik und öffentliche Meinung," in Willy Bretscher et al., *Humanität und Politische Verantwortung* (Zürich and Stuttgart, 1964), 54–73. Reprinted as "The Scientization of Politics and Public Opinion," in his *Toward a Rational Society: Student Protest, Science, and Politics*, trans. Jeremy J. Shapiro (Boston, 1971), 62–80.

Until 1965 Habermas was not optimistic about the prospects of his hopes. As he argued in his famous habilitation thesis of 1961, *The Structural Transformation of the Public Sphere*, the public space in which a communicating public could come to consensus over matters of common interest had been severely weakened by its penetration by the state and the dumbing effect of the mass media.[77] Consequently, he advised students, specifically the young members of the SDS, that activism in the service of "responsibility for the whole" was illusory if not linked to broader social movements, by which he meant the SPD. Instead, he entreated them to follow the rather modest strategy of discussion, participation in university politics, and work in the political parties.[78]

Technocratic University Reform

As might be expected, Lübbe's ideas about university reform were very different from those of Habermas. He was acutely conscious that all members of the debate appealed to Humboldt's legacy to legitimize their plans and, like Schelsky, he doubted whether this model had anything to teach people in the so-called scientized civilization (*verwissenschaftliche Zivilisation*). Humboldt's vision was conceived at a time before the explosion of technology and natural science and therefore did not take into account their integration into the *universitatis literatum*. Consequently, Lübbe recommended remembering Wilhelm von Humboldt's scientist brother, Alexander, who arguably had a bigger effect on the German university.[79]

Like Schelsky, Lübbe argued that the university should not try to compensate for the disintegration of specialization with "ideological integration and direct confrontation with the general and the whole." He regarded any attempt to "stop specialization and attempt to heal wounds which specialization has apparently inflicted" as a "serious danger."[80] Again, like Schelsky, he doubted whether an internal reform of the university was possible. Government intervention was necessary, especially after the university's failure to heed the sign of the Wissenschaftsrat's recommendations in 1960.[81]

Wilhelm Hennis presented a contrary voice to such technocratic reformers, arguing that the political potential of the autonomous faculties could be used to invigorate corporate self-government and solve the practical problems that

---

[77] See also Jürgen Habermas, "Wissenschaft und Politik," *Offene Welt*, 86 (Cologne, 1964), 413–23. This is a substantially altered version of "Verwissenschaftliche Politik und öffentliche Meinung."

[78] Jürgen Habermas, "Diskutieren – was sonst?" in Claus Grossner and Arend Oetker, eds., 4 *Daten, Standorte-Konsequenzen* (Hamburg, 1962), 62–63. Reprinted in his *Hochschulreform und Protestbewegung* (Frankfurt, 1968), 83–89.

[79] Hermann Lübbe, "Wilhelm v. Humboldts preußische Universitätsreform," *Deutsches Allgemeines Sonntagsblatt* (June 18, 1967). Reprinted in his *Gegenaufklärung und Hochschulreform* (Freiburg, 1972).

[80] Hermann Lübbe, "Reformprobleme der Philosophischen Fakultät," *Pädagogische Rundschau*, 20 (1966), 249–55. Reprinted in his *Hochschulreform und Gegenaufklärung* (Freiburg, 1972), 119–30.

[81] Eckart Heimendahl, "Das Dilemma der Hochschulen," *Merkur*, 20 (1966), 1171–90.

were plaguing the university. But he was well aware that his older colleagues were not inclined to bring politics and parliamentary-style factions and debates into the faculty meetings.[82] One could not expect initiative from them, Besson observed in 1968, because "The professors formed a highly privileged class which was unable to begin the diminution of its own privileges."[83] Besson also criticized the old Humboldt university's distance to politics and society, and he welcomed the practical and vocational concerns of modern students and their abandonment of the "caste" character of students, who henceforth would be a functional but not humanistic elite.[84]

Consequently, Lübbe's practical reform measures were designed to foster technical development and not to invest in the university an explicit political mission. It was to serve society rather than to critically distance itself from it. Consistent with his technocratic approach, reform was to be pragmatic and solve problems as they arose. To the pressing problem of the university hierarchies of the 1950s when thousands of *Assistenten* (untenured assistant professors) had been appointed to meet the teaching need for the growth in student numbers, Lübbe proposed a rational career path with security and prospects. So did Besson, who thought that they should be granted tenure and given the status of American assistant professors.

Besson also opposed the independent university institutes where "everything was built around individual professors, who acted like demigods."[85] Lübbe wanted to end the institute and faculty structure and replace them with Anglophone-style departments, a concept that was implemented in Bochum and Bielefeld. He also recognized, like Habermas, that the massive increase in teaching load had effectively sundered the link to research. Unlike Habermas, however, he did not seek to restore it, at least not for the mass of students. Again following the example of Anglophone universities, Lübbe proposed restricting the unity of teaching and research to advanced students who would be like Anglophone graduate students. Those students who did not seek an academic future would leave the university earlier. He supported technical universities that were not prestigious in educated German circles but which focused on science, like that at Dortmund. The university's foundation was "pragmatic" not "ideological," in the "spirit of holy sobriety, and this included the opening up of the university to working-class children."[86]

Ralf Dahrendorf, who at this time was usually associated with the left-liberal camp of intellectuals, actually recommended very similar proposals but without the technocratic conception of society of his former teacher Schelsky or

[82] Wilhelm Hennis, "Die Stunde der Fakultäten. Strategische Überlegungen zur Universitätsreform," *Frankfurter Allgemeine Zeitung* (May 13, 1964), 13–14.

[83] Waldemar Besson, letter to the editor of *Minerva*, 6:4 (Summer 1968), 614–17.

[84] Waldemar Besson, "Die Situation des Studenten Heute," in Evangelische Akademie Tutzing, ed., *Student und Gesellschaft* (Munich, 1963), 33–49.

[85] Waldemar Besson, letter to the editor of *Minerva*, 6:4 (Summer 1968), 614–17.

[86] Hermann Lübbe, "Die Universität Dortmund in der Hochschul- und Bildungsplanung des Landes Nordrhein-Westfalen," in Hartmut Rotter, ed., *Technische Universität Dortmund – Hochschulmodell mit Zukunft?* (Dortmund, 1968), 15–25.

Lübbe. He sought to update rather than abandon the Humboldt model, albeit in very different terms from Habermas's.[87] He also agreed that the power of the autonomous faculties needed to be reigned in, and so he readily accepted the invitation of the minister-president of Baden-Württemberg to join his educational "brain-trust" as deputy chair of a planning commission. In the ensuing "University General Plan" of 1967, after spending many months in the Ministry for Culture, he proposed a "differentiated comprehensive university" that would integrate all existing institutions of higher education into a unified system, divided into a "short study" of three years, and a "long study" for a smaller number of qualified candidates for whom traditional research and teaching would be guaranteed. The latter was partly realized in 1966 in the new University of Constance, a small research-focused institution of three thousand students without professional faculties, based on the natural and social sciences.[88]

The education debate was raging by the mid-1960s. The federal chancellor Ludwig Erhard had proclaimed education expansion and access a priority of his inaugural speech in 1963. In the same year, the Max Planck Institut für Bildungsforschung (Max Planck Institute for Education Research) was established in West Berlin.[89] So it was overstated to claim that the issue had been neglected until Georg Picht published a series of alarmist articles in 1964 in the Protestant daily *Christ und Welt* on the chronic lack of school students and graduates. Nonetheless, the title of the ensuing book, *Die deutsche Bildungskatastrophe* (The German Education Catastrophe), captured well the sense that reform of some type was necessary. Ralf Dahrendorf's own newspaper series in *Die Zeit*, based on the empirical research he had conducted in the sociology department at the University of Tübingen, added the social justice dimension.[90] The experience of interest group lobbying in the development and implementation of policy led Lübbe to a life in politics itself, and after 1967 he stood for candidacy for a Bundestag seat for the Free Democrats.

The year before, the Wissenschaftsrat had presented another set of recommendations very similar to the reform conceptions of Dahrendorf and Lübbe. They sought to limit study to four years of regimented courses with an automatic cancellation of student enrollment after that time. As might be expected, the conservative Rektorenkonferenz opposed them for their putative infringement of academic freedom and pedagogization of undergraduate teaching.[91] Now students, especially at the Free University in Berlin, became active. They opposed the recommendations for precisely the same reason, denouncing it as

[87] Ralf Dahrendorf, "Starre und Offenheit der deutschen Universität: die Chance der Reform," *Archives Européenes de Sociologie*, 2 (1962), 263–93.

[88] Ralf Dahrendorf interview with *Der Spiegel* (October 9, 1967), 54–62.

[89] Christoph Führ, *Deutsches Bildungswesen seit 1945. Grundzüge und Probleme* (Neuwied, 1997), 7–24.

[90] Ralf Dahrendorf, *Bildung ist Bürgerrecht. Plädoyer für eine aktive Bildungspolitik* (Hamburg, 1965).

[91] Wolfgang Schöne, "Universität oder Berufsschule?" *Der Monat*, 18 (December 1966), 38–46. See also his *Kampf um die deutsche Universität* (Hamburg, 1966); G. Kloss, "University Reform in West Germany. The Burden of Tradition," *Minerva*, 6:3 (Spring 1968), 323–53.

"technocratic" university reform. This was on the eve of what later would be called "1968."

A telling salvo was fired by Werner Hofmann (1922–69), Abendroth's former collaborator in Marburg. His arguments were basically simplified versions of those advanced by Habermas for the past decade, but he was less hesitant in naming a subject of redemption from the current malaise of the technocratic university. The savior would recognize the "possibilities of society" as the "final value criteria" in scholarship. And this meant those at the level of "intellectual illiteracy," by which he meant the majority of the population, could not lead reform. Unless scholarship related to the burning questions of the day, it would be "purely affirmative," as was the case in West Germany. Postwar developments had led to a profound crisis of orientation. If universities did not become politically relevant, "other powers" would take the initiative, he averred ominously. "In a time of elementary self-threat and self-destruction of our entire culture, civilization, and ethics, every individual stands in for that which once was historical hope for all."[92]

Habermas had little different to say but went into greater detail about the problems of the reform. The rigid stratification of courses of study and cap of four years, as was the case in many Anglophone universities, would prevent the "healthy problematization" of academic questions that cultivated critically minded students and which was "politically necessary." West Germany, he argued, could not afford to copy other countries until it had learned to master the practical consequences of technical progress.[93] As might be expected, by this vague formulation he meant the danger of nuclear war because atomic technology was misused by Cold War anticommunism. "New potentials for expanded power of technical control make obvious the disproportion between the results of the most organized rationality and unreflected goals, rigidified value systems, and obsolete ideologies."[94] The proposed university reform threatened to hinder the formation of the only group in German society that could challenge the hegemony of technological development and its ideological apologists, the positivists. The German university needed, so to speak, to move forward to its best traditions, and only the students could effect this move: they represented "what the German university once wanted to be."[95] Habermas spoke about the necessity of subjecting technology to open discussion, but he did not mean for

---

[92] Werner Hofmann, "Die gesellschaftliche Verantwortung der Universität," *Marburger Blätter* (January 1968). Reprinted in his *Universität, Ideologie, Gesellschaft. Beiträge zur Wissenssoziologie* (Frankfurt, 1968), 35–40.

[93] Jürgen Habermas, "Zwangsjacke für die Studienreform. Die befristete Immaktrikulation und der falsche Pragmatismus des Wissenschaftsrates," *Der Monat*, 18 (November 1966), 7–19. Reprinted in his *Hochschulreform und Protestbewegung*, 92–107.

[94] Jürgen Habermas, "Technischer Fortschritt und soziale Lebenswelt," *Praxis*, 1–2 (1966), 217–28. Reprinted as "Technical Progress and the Social Life-World," in his *Toward a Rational Society*, 50–61.

[95] Jürgen Habermas, foreword to Wolfgang Nitsch et al., *Hochschule in der Demokratie* (1965). Reprinted in his *Hochschulreform und Protestbewegung*, 90–91.

the process to be open-ended. He knew what the answer should be, just as he and other redemptive republicans knew what the answer to the Nazi past was. In the mid-1960s, no republican consensus based on an open dialogue about the meanings of the past was possible. As we will see in the next chapter, such was the political and ideological polarization of the time that a consensus was in fact inconceivable.

7

The Crisis of the Republic, 1960–1967

The 1960s in West Germany are commonly seen as the decade of cultural awakening, political progress, and social dynamism, indeed as the breakthrough to reform and innovation after the stifling conservatism and stagnation of the 1950s. In fact, most West Germans experienced the time as one of deep crisis. Historical accounts of the period that concentrate on the socioeconomic indicators of material progress and declare it to be the way station to the "social-liberal era" of the 1970s miss the point that the consciousness of contemporaries ran in the opposite direction.[1] The historian Lutz Niethammer is on target in his categorization of the 1960s as the Federal Republic's first "orientation crisis."[2] He does not say why this change in political discourse and consciousness occurred, but there are good reasons to think that it has much to do with that society's first major generational shift. If the democracy was open to redefinition, it was because in the late 1950s and early 1960s, the forty-fivers were between thirty and forty years of age and were entering the key institutions of cultural transmission, namely, the universities and the media. In the case of the independent writers, they published their first well-known works: Martin Walser his *Ehen in Philippsburg* in 1957, Günter Grass his *Blechtrommel* in 1959, and Rolf Hochhut *Der Stellvertreter* in 1963. Virtually all forty-fivers, irrespective of their varying political commitments, rejected the pragmatic "chancellor-democracy" of Konrad Adenauer. What would replace it? A consensus obtained that it must be democratic and republican, but these words permitted a wide variety of options. Conservatives, liberals, and leftists made their respective cases for a particular vision of the republic, and as in other

[1] Klaus Schönhoven, "Aufbruch in die sozialliberale Ära. Zur Bedeutung der 60er Jahre in der Geschichte der Bundesrepublik," *Geschichte und Gesellschaft*, 25 (1999), 123–45.
[2] Lutz Niethammer, "Stufen der historischen Selbsterforschung der Bundesrepublik Deutschland. Ein Forschungs-Essay," in Deutsches Institut für Fernstudien, Universität Tübingen, ed., *Nachkriegsjahre und Bundesrepublik Deutschland. Deutsche Geschichte Nach 1945*, part 1 (Tübingen, 1985), 23–34.

Western countries of the time, the key issues were (anti)communism and the role of intellectuals, issues with domestic as well as foreign policy implications.

Unique to West Germany was the role that the Nazi past played as a discrete political issue and as a source of moral energy for the respective intellectual protagonists. This past and the fact that the West German population of 1960 was largely the same population that had waged "total war" fifteen years earlier was also a condition for the relative openness of the political situation. For the liberal and leftist intellectuals of this generation, in particular, it was readily apparent that the majority of their fellow citizens had no affective relationship to the new republic, as the American political scientists Gabriel Almond and Sidney Verba concluded in their well-known study about civic consciousness in 1959.[3] Consequently, both leftist and liberal intellectuals regarded themselves as a beleaguered minority, bearers and guardians of the republican ideal. The early 1960s was not the highpoint of the New Left. It was a time, at least initially, of an alliance of leftist and liberal intellectuals against a predominantly "old right." Redemptive and integrative republicans of the forty-fivers often found themselves on the same side of the burning issues of the day because they were united against a common enemy: an illiberal right-wing tradition.

A very public aspect of this past was the series of trials of concentration camp guards and Nazi figures in the early and mid-1960s. Already in the winter of 1959–60, the issue had made headlines and gained international notoriety after youths defaced synagogues with Nazi symbols.[4] Only now, almost two decades after the end of the war, did the extent of the German crime become publicly visible. The expression "mastering the past" became the standard term with which to refer to the continuity of Nazi symbols, mentalities, and personnel.[5] The 1960s was the first time in West Germany that the traumatic recall of the Nazi past played a major political role. It did so by framing key issues in terms of the "Weimar syndrome": whether "Bonn was Weimar" and whether the country's second republic was on the brink of collapse. This fear was a product of the mutual suspicion with which the contending parties of the republic regarded one another's ambitions. The escalation of political rhetoric and intensification of a crisis of consciousness was programmed into the structure of the discourse itself. Indexed to rival versions of the recent past, the competing republican visions were symmetrically opposed to each other so that the gains of one were necessarily interpreted as the realization of the other's worst fears.

If a feature of the 1960s was the fragile and temporary alliance between leftist and liberal intellectuals, their philosophical differences led them to divergent reactions to the student movement. Redemptive republicans worried about the

[3] Gabriel Almond and Sidney Verba, *The Civic Culture: Political Attitudes and Democracy in Five Nations* (Princeton, N.J., 1963).

[4] Rebecca Elizabeth Wittmann, *Beyond Justice: The Auschwitz Trial* (Cambridge, Mass., 2005); Devin O. Pendas, *The Frankfurt Auschwitz Trial, 1963–1965: Genocide, History and the Limits of Law* (Cambridge, 2005).

[5] Harold Marcuse, *Legacies of Dachau: The Use and Abuse of a Concentration Camp, 1933–2001* (Cambridge, 2001).

weakness of social and political opposition to the "system," while hoping for an "alternative" or third way. Liberals fretted about the passivity of civil society and the population's commitment to parliamentary democracy. For their part, conservatives were anxious about the weakness of the state in relation to the parliament and political parties. The story of the 1960s is the crystallization and disintegration of a tenuous and loose left-liberal alliance.

The Intellectuals and Republican Resistance, 1959–1962

The election victory of the conservative Chistian Democratic Union (CDU) in 1957 with an absolute majority was a crushing blow not only for Social Democats. For the "nonconformist" intellectuals, the continuing conservative hegemony marked the unqualified triumph of the "economic miracle" and the anticommunist worldview that, as Wolfgang Abendroth scornfully put it, "afforded the opportunity to obtain the acclamation of the majority of the population for this 'Western' system and to further depoliticize the masses of the workers."[6] Some of these intellectuals saw in the new prosperity a crass materialism, individualism, and renunciation of spiritual goals with a right-wing twist.[7]

As we saw in the case of the young Habermas, the redemptive republicans hoped for a third way between the fronts of the Cold War and the limitations of parliamentary democracy, and they felt unable to identify closely with the Social Democratic Party, which they regarded as an organization of functionaries that had failed in 1933 and offered no way out of the impasse of modern technology. For all its shortcomings, though, the party's Marxist-inspired party program and distance from the Western alliance made the Social Democrats the only mainstream political force with which intellectuals could associate. Thus, in 1958, intellectuals and the SPD shared a platform against the nuclear armament ambitions of the federal government, and especially those of the defense minister, Franz Joseph Strauss (1915–88), who had made a belligerent speech in the Bundestag in early 1958 that was heavily criticized by the Social Democratic deputies.

In a major article in the SPD newspaper *Vorwärts* in April 1958, Hans Werner Richter announced the renewed faith of writers and intellectuals in the party. "In the moment that the party with full force and without tactical considerations sets itself against atomic armament, all reservations will disappear and become... secondary."[8] Three demands made the SPD the "rallying point" for the "liberal and socialist camps": its opposition against atomic armament in general, and against atomic weapons for the Bundeswehr (West German army)

---

[6] Wolfgang Abendroth, "Aufgaben einer deutschen Linken," in Horst Krüger, ed., *Was ist Links? Thesen und Theorien zu einer politischen Position* (Munich, 1963), 130–57.

[7] On Sieburg, see Elliot Y. Neaman, *A Dubious Past: Ernst Jünger and the Politics of Literature in West Germany* (Berkeley and Los Angeles, 1999), 85–88.

[8] Hans Werner Richter, "Die Intellektuellen und die Sozialdemokratische Partei," *Vorwärts* (April 4, 1958), 4.

in particular, as well as its struggle for an atomic-weapon-free zone in Europe. This program was not a tool of pragmatic politics for interest group gain, he pointed out: it was designed to avoid the apocalypse. For Richter, as for the left and many liberals, the escalation of the government's Cold War rhetoric not only meant the fatal possibility of nuclear war but also possessed ominous domestic implications, namely that "all reactionary, chauvinistic, indeed fascist forces of the past again could raise their heads." These were the forces that would destroy those domestic freedoms the conservatives claimed to defend against the communists. Insofar as the SPD did not subordinate universal principle to party egoism, he concluded, it stood a chance of regaining its original moral energy and the support of intellectuals, the party of humanity.

But to their bitter disappointment, the SPD made two fundamental decisions in the next year that once again put the intellectuals at a distance from mainstream politics: the party finally acceded to the government's foreign policy position, and it abandoned its Marxist program, exchanging its identity as a class party for a "people's party" (*Volkspartei*) at the famous Bad Godesberg party conference. The left-wing Social Democratic forty-fivers, like Jürgen Seifert (b. 1928), and the student wing of the party, the SDS, were expelled from the party in 1961 for their opposition to this "conformist" course, while other Marxists like Peter von Oertzen, who had been a member of the provincial parliament in Lower Saxony in the mid-1950s, tried to keep alive the so-called ideology discussion from within its ranks. Jürgen Habermas's assistant, Oskar Negt, left the party out of protest. Habermas and Abendroth subsequently mentored the young exiled SDS intellectuals.[9]

The SPD had abandoned its idealism and had accepted the division of the country and the fronts of the Cold War to win votes, intellectuals complained. Henceforth, the SPD did not represent a fundamental "alternative," as Fritz J. Raddatz (b. 1931), Hans Magnus Enzensberger (b. 1929), and Martin Walser (b. 1927) lamented in their contributions to the collection of statements by intellectuals just before the federal election in 1961.[10] This collection, tellingly entitled *Die Alternative oder brauchen wie eine neue Regierung?* (The Alternative or do we need a new Government?), edited by Walser, proclaimed the writers' allegiance to the French tradition of public intellectuals "from Voltaire to Zola until Jean-Paul Sartre." Having lost faith in the Social Democrats as a party of democratic socialism, they now supported it reluctantly as the only political force that could prevent yet another conservative administration.

Three aspects of these essays are striking. In the first place, fifteen of the twenty writers were forty-fivers. The voice of protest was now being carried by

---

[9] Willy Albrecht, *Der Sozialistische Deutsche Studentenbund (SDS). Vom parteikonformen Studentenverband zum Repräsentanten der Neuen Linken* (Bonn, 1994).

[10] Fritz J. Raddatz, "Analyse, kaum Therapie," in Martin Walser, ed., *Die Alternative oder brauchen wir eine neue Regierung?* (Reinbeck, 1961), 81–84; Hans Magnus Enzensberger, "Ich wünsche nicht gefährlich zu leben," in ibid., 61–6; Martin Walser, "Das Fremdwort der Saison," in ibid., 124–30; Jürgen Habermas, "Die Bundesrepublik: Eine Wahlmonarchie?" *Magnum*, 36 (June 1961), 26–29.

this generation, led by older figures like Richter, Erich Kuby, Dirks, and Andersch. Second, there was their sober realization of the political and moral state of the country, combined with a suspicion that the Christian Democrats were tolerating, indeed, reviving fascist tendencies. Although not one of the nonconformist intellectuals, the liberal contemporary historian Waldemar Besson captured this sense of moral dismay well when he wrote of the virulent public reaction to his own television documentaries of the early 1960s about the Nazi period: they "opened the abyss. The fundament of inhumanity in our society became openly visible."[11] Third, they were dismayed at domestic developments during the 1950s and were unremittingly gloomy about the republican future.

Wolfdietrich Schnurre, a founding member of the Gruppe 47, was incensed by the "satanic success" of Adenauer's "rendering harmless and diminishing Nazi inhumanity," because he paid off "the active big Nazis with massive pensions while thousands upon thousands of Jewish people still wait for the so-called reparations." In Adenauer's infamous support of his cabinet secretary Hans Globke (1889–1973), who had written an official commentary on the 1935 Nuremberg racial laws, Schnurre saw a vile attempt to make "inhumanity openly acceptable."[12] Raddatz wrote of the "political corruption of this people" that did not permit the word Auschwitz to pass its lips.

These intellectuals resorted to the rhetoric of pollution and cleansing. Heinz von Cramer (b. 1924) also focused on the problem of the Nazi past and its presence in the conservative government. What was necessary was a "full cleansing of political life from the dirt of a thoroughly infamous and compromised past. For this reason alone, we need a new government, because the old one is irredeemably permeated with elements of this past: with persons, whose names and duties are much too closely linked with the time of the Nazi regime."[13] As Franz Schonauer put it: "Full of hope and promise the house was begun in 1949, but it has become a dirty nest."[14]

Their point was not just that the continuity of former elites into the Federal Republic and the absence of a cathartic foundation were moral problems. It was that this continuity put the state in real danger. The integrative republic, they argued, was too tolerant of right-wingers, while it persecuted the leftists and intellectuals who had opposed Nazism. Von Cramer spoke for many when he observed that this continuity "always drew our state into a dangerous proximity with those most oppressed countries of Franco, Salazar, and the South American dictators, which rob the West's rhetoric of freedom of so much credibility."[15] It was easy to pour scorn, as Abendroth did, on the rhetoric of the

[11] Waldemar Besson, "Wie ich mich geändert habe," *Vierteljahreshefte für Zeitgeschichte*, 19 (1971), 401.
[12] Wolfdieter Schnurre, "Das falsche Gleis," in Walser, *Die Alternative*, 68–69.
[13] Heinz von Cramer, "Est ist so spät wie es schon einmal war," in ibid., 85–96.
[14] Franz Schonauer, "Das schmutzige Nest," in ibid., 73–75.
[15] Von Cramer, "Es ist so spät wie es schon einmal war," in ibid., 85–96.

"free West," even before the American involvement in Vietnam. As we will see, the fear that the Western democracies in general, and the Federal Republic in particular, would degenerate into the kind of states with which they were allied played an important role in alienating redemptive intellectuals from the state and preventing a republican consensus.

Gerd Hirschauer (1928–2007), who, with Carl Amery represented the left-Catholic position, worried about the new clericalism of his church, which he called "Counter-Enlightenment clerical absolutism," a judgment only topped by the secular humanist Gerd Szczesny's angry denunciation of a "Christian totalitarianism" that attacked liberalism and intellectuals in the name of "German-Occidental" culture, a syndrome that reminded him of National Socialism itself.[16] Less sanguine, Hirschauer saw the current government as a danger because its style of administration was more suited to authoritarian, indeed, fascist regimes, rather than democratic ones.[17]

All writers concurred on the concrete issues that threatened the constitution: the militaristic strivings of Strauss and the army, the desire of leading conservatives like the Bavarian vice-president of the Bundestag Richard Jäger (1913–98) to introduce the death penalty, and that of the minister for the interior Gerhard Schröder (1910–89) to introduce draconian "emergency laws," the attempt of Adenauer to control the media by establishing a state television station, his courting of the veterans' associations and the irredentist claims of the refugees' organizations, and finally his shameful denunciation of the SPD chancellor candidate and mayor of West Berlin Willy Brandt for his emigration to Norway in 1933 and subsequent service in the Norwegian army during the war. As Gerhard Schoenberger (b. 1931), the author of *Der gelbe Stern* (The Yellow Star) and organizer of a prominent exhibition of the Nazi persecution of Jews, observed, the government's democratic credentials were dubious because by instrumentalizing the population's "brown resentment" to chase votes, "it betrayed the foundations on which the state was built."[18] By playing up the external communist threat, the authors of *Die Alternative* feared, the conservatives would justify their hard line against its domestic opponents while courting former Nazis and fellow travelers, with anticommunism serving as the functional equivalent of the anti-Semitism of the 1930s.

Habermas also saw a fatal social psychological mechanism at work that was analogous to the anti-Semitism of the prewar period. The appeal to nationalism satisfied collective narcissism, which placed the group above all moral standards, leading to the dubious identification of the population with state authorities and the projection of social aggression and anxiety onto minorities like intellectuals, homosexuals, and pacifists. Because "future pogroms" were made of this volatile cocktail, it was fatal to marginalize certain groups as "inner enemies" lest they be targets of this social-psychological condition that

[16] Gerhard Szczesny, "Humanistische Union," in ibid., 26–43.
[17] Gerd Hirschauer, "Brauchen wir eine neue Regierung?" in ibid., 14–24.
[18] Gerhard Schoenberger, "Die Zerstörung der Demokratie," in ibid., 137–45.

mobilized moral indignation in a reactionary manner.[19] It was with this mechanism in mind that Habermas responded to the attack of the government minister Dufhues on the Gruppe 47, which he denounced as the West German equivalent of Goebbels's Imperial Chamber of Culture (*Reichskulturkammer*).[20] He would likewise use the term "pogrom" in relation to the atmosphere of the "German Autumn" of 1977 in which intellectuals were publicly attacked for their alleged responsibility for the terrorism that plagued the Federal Republic in the 1970s.

Democracy seemed under threat. Schonauer warned that another CDU victory would represent a "great danger" for the democratic constitution. Erich Kuby was concerned it would mean another German "special path" of aggression against the East that would end in nuclear war.[21] Von Cramer and Richter were just as pessimistic, the former writing that it "would mean the end of all democratic endeavors." He elaborated: "It is not a matter of realizing nice political utopias, but simply of saving what can be saved. It is at least as late as it was at the beginning of the thirties; only that this time no Hitler threatens, but rather a refined form of dictatorship, more suited to the times, beneath a democratic mask – which could (if it began to be active) mean all our deaths in atomic war."[22] Richter pointed out that if the government gained a two-thirds majority in the lower house of parliament, it could change the constitution, in which case there would be no limits to the power of men like Strauss who stood behind the aged Adenauer. As far as Richter was concerned, the relevant decisions to change the system in an authoritarian direction had already been made: "The agony of democracy has begun."[23] Such was the gloomy and fearful assessment of the Federal Republic by its leftist intellectuals on the eve of the fourth elections in 1961. Not for them the reassurance of the Swiss journalist Fritz Allemann that "Bonn is not Weimar": the beginning of the beginning of the end was underway.[24]

Liberal Critiques

The liberal intellectuals shared a language of critique but differed from redemptive republicans as well as among themselves in important respects. It is instructive to compare them so that the area of overlap and point of difference in their common front against the "old right" in the early 1960s can be appreciated. The reactionary polemics of the Roman Catholic writer Josef O. Zöller, who wrote for the CDU organ *Die Politische Meinung* (The Political Opinion), and whose

[19] Jürgen Habermas, "Auf- und Abrüstung, moralisch und militärisch," *Merkur*, 17 (1963), 714–17.
[20] Jürgen Habermas, "Parteirügen an Schriftsteller – hüben und drüben," *Merkur*, 17 (1963), 210–12.
[21] Erich Kuby, "Und ob wir eine neue Regierung brauchen!" in Walser, *Die Alternative*, 145–54.
[22] Von Cramer, "Es ist so spät wie es schon einmal war," in ibid., 96.
[23] Hans Werner Richter, "Von Links in die Mitte," in ibid., 115–23.
[24] Fritz Allemann, *Bonn ist nicht Weimar* (Cologne, 1956).

screed *Die Irrlehren der Gegenwart* (The Heresies of the Present Day) was published in 1960, presented a good common target. Zöller coupled his attack on
the Enlightenment and liberalism, which he saw as materialistic philosophies
that culminated in National Socialism – this was a common interpretation
among Christian Democrats in the 1950s[25] – with a condemnation of intellectuals as the "executors" of these "errors": "Among the most difficult problems
of the unmastered present belongs the alienation from the state and political
homelessness of the intellectuals."[26] He denounced them as "sectarians" stuck
in the pubescent stage of truculent rebellion and individualist self-absorption,
who therefore were unable to recognize the greater truths represented by the
Roman Catholic Church and the necessity of the state's authority.[27]

Walter Dirks's spirited reply in the election year of 1961 contains the key
elements of the leftist assessment of the time.[28] "Something is brewing," he
observed, identifying tendencies –the government's equation of itself with the
state and its concomitant criminalization of the opposition – that did not augur
well for democracy. Everything had deteriorated after the great hopes in 1949.
Zöller's invective against intellectuals, he pointed out, was the same as that of
the Nazis, and Zöller was too naive to realize this continuity.

Representing the integrationist liberal camp, Hermann Lübbe took issue with
Zöller as well.[29] Like Dirks, he noted that the new democracy was not anchored
in the population as an "ethical substance" (*sittliche Substanz*) that could be
"unreflectedly taken for granted." But unlike the leftist critics, he did not find
this situation surprising in view of Germans' totalitarian commitment in the
recent past and the weak, native democratic tradition. In fact, Lübbe went so
far as to write that it was by no means certain whether the new democracy was
secured against another "totalitarian temptation." It was all the more important, he wrote, to reflect consciously on the foundations of democracy, and
for this reason, he found Zöller's "slander of the Enlightenment" so objectionable. For the Roman Catholic polemicist had attacked precisely those features
of modernity that were the preconditions for liberal democratic government:
Renaissance individualism, the Enlightenment, and, above all, the secularization of the state that guaranteed its citizens were not obliged to follow a particular confession or ideology. Consequently, Lübbe argued, such regimes must tolerate "error" (as Zöller denounced pluralism) so long as it did not impinge upon
the rights of others. Regimes that did not permit such toleration, he continued,

---

[25] Maria Mitchell, "Materialism and Secularism: CDU Politicians and National Socialism," *Journal of Modern History*, 67 (June 1995), 278–308.

[26] Josef O. Zöller, "Heimatlose Kritik. Versuch einer Begriffsbestimmung des Intellektuellen," *Die Politische Meinung*, 4:41 (October 1959), 43–50. This article appeared as the chapter "Die intellektuellen Vollstrecker" in his book, *Irrlehren der Gegenwart* (Osnabrück, 1960).

[27] Zöller, *Irrlehren der Gegenwart*.

[28] Walter Dirks, "Heilige Allianz. Bermerkungen zur Diffamierung der Intellektuellen," *Frankfurte Hefte*, 16 (1961), 23–32.

[29] Hermann Lübbe, "Verteidigung der Freiheit als Kampf gegen den Liberalismus," *Zeitschrift für Politik*, 8 (1961), 347–52.

were authoritarian as the Spanish and Portuguese examples demonstrated, or totalitarian as in eastern Europe. Democracy needed to be defended against Zöller and his ilk, who interpreted its history as an illegitimate rebellion against the "authority of God and his church."[30]

It is important to remember in this context that religious pluralism was not yet a taken-for-granted right by the Roman Catholic Church, which, according to Pius XIII's statement of 1953, still taught that heresy possessed no objective right of existence. The Roman Catholic Ernst-Wolfgang Böckenförde, too, doubted whether the church's emphasis on an objective order of natural law at the expense of personal freedom was compatible with democracy.[31] Although he did not consider himself one of the "nonconformist intellectuals," Lübbe took their side by pointing out that Zöller established the dangerous anticommunist criteria by which their persecution could be considered a "state-political necessity," as he put it. Ultimately, Zöller did not grasp that National Socialism was "in no way" a child of the Enlightenment, and that on the contrary "Nazism undertook the same denunciation [*Verketzerung*] of the Enlightenment and its intellectual executors as he does." His position was similar to that of the Munich-based political scientist Paul Noack (1925–2003) who argued that despite their evident negative one-sidedness, the intellectuals represented an important bulwark against authoritarianism, and that the government's colors were revealed in its inability to deal with their criticism.[32]

What was liberal about Lübbe's defense of the redemptive intellectuals was his model of the state. Like his colleagues from Münster's Ritter school of neo-Hegelianism, he saw the essence of liberal republicanism in the neutrality of the state, which needed to be strong enough to withstand its capture by ideologically committed interest groups like the Roman Catholic Church. The individual conscience could remain free only in such a polity. His targets, therefore, were those who challenged this conception of the state, whether from the right as with Zöller or on the left as with his Marxist opponents. What was integrative about this theory was that the ideological neutrality of the state meant that it tolerated ex-Nazis and reactionaries so long as they obeyed the law. The new republic was a learning process that gave its citizens the time and space to distance themselves from their pasts but did not pry into their consciences.

A rival liberal republicanism was centered around the German Jewish émigré political theorist of pluralism Ernst Fraenkel (1898–1975) of the Otto Suhr Institute at the Free University in Berlin. It included figures like Kurt Sontheimer (1928–2005), Karl Dietrich Bracher (b. 1922), Thomas Nipperdey (1927–92), Alexander Schwan (1931–89), and Gerhard A. Ritter (b. 1929). It overlapped with members of the so-called Freiburg School of political philosophy that had been centered around another émigré, Arnold Bergstraesser, until his untimely

[30] Ibid., 351.
[31] Ernst-Wolfgang Böckenförde, "Das Ethos der modernen Demokratie und die Kirche" (1957), in his *Die deutsche Katholizismus im Jahre 1933* (Basel, 1981), 21–38.
[32] Paul Noack, *Die Intellektuellen. Wirkung, Versagen, Verdienst* (Munich, 1961).

death in 1964. Its members included Sontheimer, Schwan (before they moved to Berlin), Hans Maier (b. 1931), Hans-Peter Schwarz (b. 1934), Manfred Hättich (1925–2002), and Dieter Oberndörfer (b. 1929).[33] These figures had opposed right-wing politics in the 1950s. Fraenkel was a key figure in the campaign against the reintroduction of men's fraternities at the Free University, while Hättich had led student demonstrations in Freiburg against the films of the Nazi director Veit Harlan, who enjoyed an immense popular following after the war.

Unlike redemptive republicans, however, these liberals did not think that the answer to the Nazi past should be an alternative social or political system. Regardless, their analysis shared much with that of leftist intellectuals and demonstrated less patience with the residues of Nazism than did Lübbe. The slogan of "mastering the past," Sontheimer noted in 1961, had become popular in the late 1950s when it was apparent that "the turning away from the old had not occurred so decisively and unanimously after all, [and,] as symptoms of a wanting, mastering of the past became visible."[34] Such a mastering now had to entail asking how and why the Weimar Republic had collapsed, and inserting National Socialism into the continuum of German history. Above all, the past should be used to help form a better future. Because it was no great achievement that the Federal Republic was better than the Nazi regime, it was too soon to end the talk of the past, as conservatives advocated. "Had the past occurred as it appears in the current justificatory efforts of many Germans." Sontheimer noted sardonically, "the Third Reich would be at the most something like a friendly children's home with a concealed compulsory character," adding that many were unhappy "to be reminded of the deeds of the Eichmanns and their helpers." This discomfort was hardly surprising. "Many civil servants, judges, professors, and officers served Hitler and are still active today for the Federal Republic."[35]

Karl Dietrich Bracher made a similar analysis. He had vigorously opposed neo-Nazi parties in the 1950s, and in the early 1960s observed with concern the revival of the right-wing student fraternities at the universities and the continuing apolitical orientation of other West Germans, citing with approval Habermas's study of Frankfurt students in *Student und Politik*. Politics may be plain sailing in West Germany, he conceded, but there were reasons to harbor doubts: "To this day, one can hear the voices of those who think that there was something to National Socialism."[36] Then there was the "tireless activity" of

[33] Horst Schmitt, *Politikwissenschaft und freiheitliche Demokratie: Eine Studie zum "politischen Forschungsprogramm" der "Freiburger Schule" 1954–1970* (Baden Baden, 1995). Although he did not undertake his training with either Fraenkel or Bergstraesser, Hennis is often associated with both schools because of his extensive contact with Fraenkel, his presence in Freiburg, and the congruence between his practical philosophy and the Freiburg School's engaged liberalism.
[34] Kurt Sontheimer, "Pfahl im Fleisch – die deutsche Vergangenheit," *Magnum*, 19 (July 1961), 29.
[35] Ibid.
[36] Karl Dietrich Bracher, "Wissenschaft und Widerstand. Das Beispiel der 'Weißen Rose'" (1963), in his *Deutschland zwischen Diktatur und Demokratie* (Bern and Munich, 1964), 273–97.

a small neo-Nazi minority that found resonance in the "thoughtlessness and comfortableness of wide circles of the population," a lamentable situation that issued from the lack of attention to the historical reality of National Socialism in the public sphere. Much education needed to be undertaken with a population the majority of which, as opinion polls at the time revealed, affirmed the proposition that Hitler would have been one of the great German statesmen but for the war, that thought it was better that the country had no Jews, that was opposed to the resistance to Hitler, and that opposed the naming of new schools after its members, while only a quarter of which said that it would oppose a new National Socialism.[37] The counterforces against the right were not stronger in the early 1960s than in 1933, he warned, so there was much to do, especially in view of the nationalist resentment Germans expressed privately. "Therefore we cannot allow ourselves comparisons and excuses by reference to the mistakes and crimes of others, nor can we tolerate the numbers game that downplays the millions of murdered Jews." How would such a population behave in a time of crisis? He saw his own role as a university professor to be a "guardian of our Res publica" by warning of dangers to the constitution.[38]

A background fear for liberals like Bracher was the end of the Fourth Republic in France in 1958. An ineffective regime of parliamentary democracy had been quickly replaced by a presidential regime headed by the strongman de Gaulle who appealed successfully over the heads of the parties to the population for plebiscitary approval. For a right-wing commentator like Armin Mohler, a newspaper correspondent in Paris at the time who identified with the German *Volk* and disliked party politics, "Gaullism" was manna from heaven.[39] But if, like most of the forty-fivers, one did not identify with the political views of most Germans and hoped that they would finally come to terms with political parties, it was a dangerous model indeed. At the time, the right-wing publicist Winfried Martini, who argued that the Weimar Republic lasted only as long as it did because of, not despite, the wide presidential powers of rule by decree in article 48, was a popular speaker before Bundeswehr officers.[40] And the more sophisticated jurist and former student of Carl Schmitt, Ernst Forsthoff, decried the two-party parliamentary system as typically English and saw the pernicious hold of the parties over the state only combatable by a public opinion that could be tapped as a plebiscitary source of power.[41] Bracher's fear of the future was cast against these statist positions: "Precisely the power increase of the executive, the predominance of the bureaucratic administrative state, the retreat of parliament with the plebiscitary prioritization of elections ... works against the political participation of the citizens and prepares the way again,

---

[37] Karl Dietrich Bracher, "Zeitgeschichte und Rechtsradikalismus," in ibid., 298–312.
[38] Ibid.
[39] Armin Mohler, *Die Fünfte Republik. Was steht hinter de Gaulle?* (Munich, 1963).
[40] Winfried Martini, *Freiheit auf Abruf: Die Lebenserwartung der Bundesrepublik* (Cologne and Berlin, 1960), 221–24.
[41] Ernst Forsthoff, *Strukturwandlungen der modernen Demokratie* (Berlin, 1964), 7.

in the case of a crisis, for the danger of the alienation of the citizen from the democratic representatives."[42]

Similar as their analysis of the situation was to that of leftist intellectuals, Sontheimer's and Bracher's model of mastering the past put them in the liberal integrationist camp because they did not entail system-changing transformations and a "third way." Sontheimer advocated an "inner mastering" of the past: "It presumes decency [*Lauterkeit*], openness to the truth and self-contemplation [*Selbstbesinnung*]. Only the individual can undertake it, for himself alone in his heart." Bracher similarly emphasized such a transformation. The sign of an "inner" commitment to liberal democracy was the support, rather than the condemnation, of the German resistance, about which he wrote with such great pathos, enjoining his countrymen to be inspired by their stirring example. Ultimately, for liberals the unmastered past was a moral and political rather than systemic problem. There was no sense of insecurity about the incubus of technology, as was the case with Habermas and the redemptive left. Germans needed to grow up by accommodating themselves to the modern world.

To be sure, moral change would take time, and Sontheimer warned against placing too much hope in sudden transformation. "A politically doleful people, such as the Germans had been since the middle of the last century," he continued, "a people that in its majority willingly and without many scruples served the National Socialist regime, would not be transformed into a politically mature and democratically acting people by the experience of the catastrophe alone." For that development to occur would require a longer and "crisis-tested" continuity of a free and democratic form of life.[43] For all that, Sontheimer cautioned against the "hopelessly black prognoses" of the redemptive republicans.[44] The basic difference between redemptive and integrative republicans among the forty-fivers was that for the former the liberal freedoms were a necessary but insufficient condition for a qualitatively different political and social system. But at the time when such liberal freedoms were not to be established securely in the Federal Republic, leftists and liberals stood on the same side of the fence against an illiberal government and its supporters. But, unlike the leftists, there was no sense of anything but basic opposition to Eastern communism, even if the domestic problem was on the right rather than the domestic left.

The liberals from the Berlin and Freiburg schools and the leftists faced a common dilemma. As democrats, they needed to appeal to "the people" as a source of legitimacy against antidemocratic and illiberal German traditions of authoritarian statism, just as they knew that large numbers of the German

---

[42] Karl Dietrich Bracher, "Die zweite Demokratie in Deutschland – Von Weimar nach Bonn (1963)," in his *Deutschland zwischen Diktatur und Demokratie*, 109–38.

[43] Sontheimer, "Pfahl im Fleisch – die deutsche Vergangenheit."

[44] Bracher, "Zeitgeschichte und Rechtsradikalismus."

people remained in thrall to such traditions and had no desire to confront the Nazi past. Paradoxically, the left continued to keep faith in them. Thus, in 1961 Habermas attacked the political parties for their "depoliticization" and "conformism" in maintaining certain "structures of communication" (i.e., anti-communism) and preventing the articulation of opposition "from below," an argument reminiscent of Abendroth's conviction that reactionary elites rather than the people were to blame for fascism.[45] Liberals, for their part, purported to speak in the people's name when invoking democratic legitimacy.

Perhaps the more realistic position was presented by Lübbe who maintained that in light of the recent past it was impossible to base a new German patriotism on historical continuities or to expect an inner conversion or radical democratic challenge to technology. A democracy without tradition had to be won from a future that prevented a Nazi revival. "The democracy that we have offers good conditions for this prospect, and to this extent that determination means above all the political determination for this democracy. The commitment to it dominates publicly, and even its opponents can be effective only if they hide behind this commitment."[46] He argued, in effect, that it would take time for the "ethical substance" of democracy to take root in a liberal system that was confessionally neutral. But would such a substance develop simply over the course of time? The danger in Lübbe's sober assessment of the Nazi legacy in the 1950s and 1960s was that his integrative patience meant that many morally sensitive Germans remained indignant about the prosperity of former-Nazis and found it difficult to support the new order, which they could view as a right-wing cartel, the "true" ugly face of which could emerge anytime from behind the democratic facade to lash out at its enemies.

The Spiegel Affair and the Conservative Backlash, 1962–1965

That ugly face seemed to make a dramatic appearance in the form of the defense minister Strauss in late 1962. After the influential news magazine, *Der Spiegel*, run by its colorful editor Rudolf Augstein (1923–2002), published an article by Conrad Ahlers (1922–81) using classified documents on the lack of preparation of the German defense forces for nuclear war, Strauss ordered their arrest, going so far as to have Ahlers tracked down in Spain where he was vacationing. For the government, as for conservatives in general, the journalists had acted treasonously in a time of heightened international tension during the Cuban missile crisis. But for both liberals and leftists, the government had gone too far. Freedom of the press is a basic tenet of parliamentary democracy, and it was on this issue that a broad, self-conscious oppositional coalition could form for the first time in West German history. It was, according to the young sociologist

---

[45] Habermas, "Die Bundesrepublik: Eine Wahlmonarchie?"; Abendroth, "Aufgaben einer deutschen Linken," 152.

[46] Lübbe, "Verteidigung der Freiheit," 350.

M. Rainer Lepsius (b. 1928), the birth of the critical public sphere in the Federal Republic.[47]

Yet even within this coalition, there were noticeable differences in interpretation that foreshadowed a later split. For liberals, like Hennis and the Münster neo-Hegelians, the main issue was the apparent illegality of the government's drastic measures and Strauss's dishonesty in the Bundestag when he lied about his involvement in the arrest of Ahlers. In their newspaper statements, petition campaigns, and various public appearances, they demanded that the government respect the constitution and that Strauss resign.[48] Redemptive forty-fivers read more into the scandal. The government's action confirmed their fear that anticommunism and Strauss's ambition of West German nuclear armament would lead to internal repression, indeed to a police state. Only a year earlier, *Der Spiegel* had predicted such a scenario in a vitriolic attack on the defense minister, accusing him of desiring to establish a new dictatorship.[49] Determined always to resist the vicelike grip of international and domestic Cold War politics, members of the Gruppe 47 issued a manifesto declaring that "At a time in which war as a means of politics has been rendered redundant, it regards the instruction of the public about the so-called military secrets to be an ethical duty that should be fulfilled at all times."[50]

Karl Dietrich Bracher was particularly active against the government, and because the Spiegel affair coincided with the historiographical Fischer controversy about German war aims in the First World War, he was about to fight the battle on two fronts. His target in both theaters was the older historian Gerhard Ritter, who supported the government's actions and who attacked the Hamburg historian Fritz Fischer (1913–99) for his claims about Germany's primary responsibility for the outbreak and escalation of war in 1914. Bracher was appalled at Ritter's salvos against "younger historians" (i.e., forty-fivers) for their apparent "darkening of German historical consciousness."[51] Imanuel Geiss, who was working with Fischer, also rushed to the defense of his teacher.[52]

The Spiegel affair and Fischer controversy both destabilized the conservative hold on the public debate and control of the symbolic politics of West Germany by establishing academics, writers, and journalists as an autonomous force against the state and its foreign and domestic policy designs. And this coalition

---

[47] M. Rainer Lepsius, "Kritik als Beruf. Zur Soziologie der Intellektuellen," *Kölner Zeitschrift für Soziologie und Sozialpsychologie*, 16 (1964), 75–91. This article was first delivered as a habilitation lecture in Munich in July 1963.

[48] Jürgen Seifert et al., eds., *Die Spiegel Affäre*, vol. 2, *Die Reaktion der Öffentlichkeit* (Freiburg, 1966), 22, 165, 175.

[49] *Der Spiegel* (April 4, 1961).

[50] Seifert et al., *Die Spiegel Affäre*, 184.

[51] Karl Dietrich Bracher, "Vorspiel zur deutschen Katastrophe," *Neue Politische Literatur*, 7:6 (1962), 472–82; Gerhard Ritter, "Eine neue Kriegsschuldthese," *Historische Zeitschrift*, 194 (1962), 646–68.

[52] Imanuel Geiss, *Der Monat*, 171 (December 1962), 58ff.

had proved its power, forcing Strauss to resign. Ironically, Habermas published his bleak assessment about the decline of the public sphere at this time, but conservative commentators were convinced that they were losing ground.[53] Speaking before the Protestant working group of the CDU in 1964, the philosophical anthropologist Arnold Gehlen (1908–75), who had received a professorial chair for his support of the Nazis during the war and afterward had taught in the comparative obscurity of the Technical University in Aachen, turned his attention to "The Engagement of the Intellectuals in Relation to the State."[54]

This much-cited article is significant in a number of respects. For one, it did not mention the Spiegel affair or the Nazi past, which were, as we have seen, the intellectuals' prime matter of concern. Their posture and influence, he implied, must be accounted for by reasons other than those relating to these uncomfortable issues. Gehlen resorted to a general theory of modernity that perceptively laid bare the self-understanding of intellectuals, although, of course, he judged it in negative terms unlike Paul Noack, who had expressed remarkably similar ideas three years earlier.[55] The world had become so complex, maintained Gehlen, that it was impossible to experience its entirety, leading to the frustration of those (i.e., intellectuals) who aspired to understand and steer social processes. The success of emancipation had resulted in rough economic equality and a "most radical democracy," denying intellectuals a historically meaningful mission. And so, frustrated and bitter, they reverted to pure negativity and an "antitraditional" ethic of universal solidarity that reflected the "abstract world intercourse" of modernity. The engaged publicists thus had a "broken relationship to the state's institutions," which were administered by their rivals, the technocrats, whose expertise they lacked but whom they moralistically upbraided for not measuring up to abstract standards of justice.

It was because former radical conservatives like Gehlen made such arguments after 1945 that Habermas could identify positivism as the new conservatism. Gehlen saw the principles of abstract universalism and concrete particularism as a world-historical contest on German soil, just as Habermas did. Their categories were the same even if their judgments differed. It was necessary, Gehlen concluded, to form institutions that integrated the intellectuals "to help detoxify [*entgiften*] the public atmosphere, which we Germans need all the more because we don't possess the positive cohesion that characterizes the great nations."[56]

On this view, the missing republican consensus was the result of modernization processes. But, if so, why did "the great nations" not also have such a poisoned public atmosphere? This hole in Gehlen's argument was his failure

---

[53] Jürgen Habermas, *Strukturwandel der Öffentlichkeit* (Darmstadt und Neuwied, 1962).

[54] For a brief overview of Gehlen, see Jerry Z. Muller, *The Other God that Failed: Hans Freyer and the Deradicalization of German Conservatism* (Princeton, N.J., 1987), 395–99.

[55] Noack, *Die Intellektuellen*.

[56] Arnold Gehlen, "Das Engagement der Intellektuellen gegenüber dem Staat," *Merkur*, 18 (May 1964), 401–13. Reprinted in his *Einblicke* (Frankfurt, 1975), 9–24.

to address adequately the specifically German situation. To the extent that he did, he resorted to the canard of blaming all on the resentment of intellectuals. He did not see that part of the problem was the integration of ex-Nazis like himself into the new order. Little wonder that so many found West German institutions difficult to trust. In fact, Gehlen went a step further and implied that intellectuals who tried to politicize the masses and demand of them decisions on issues about which they had little knowledge were responsible for Nazism. This slander may have been a displaced reference to his own past but served conveniently to deflect the causes of Nazism onto those who fought its legacy in the Federal Republic.[57] Finally, the article was significant because of its argument about the alienation of intellectuals from the majority of West Germans. Gehlen naturally sided with the majority because it represented the concrete particularity of a historical nation against the abstract universalism of the intellectuals.

At the same time as Gehlen addressed Protestant Christian Democrats, their Roman Catholic counterparts in Bavaria were hearing Armin Mohler's analysis in Munich. It was little different from that of Gehlen in the dismay at leftist negativity and commitment to abstract values. The principal difference lay in Mohler's acute observation that intellectuals were not "free floating" and therefore alienated from institutions. On the contrary, they had in fact become "institutionalized." Indeed, they dominated public debate to the extent that they had alienated themselves from the population, as Gehlen had also noted. "All over the Federal Republic," Mohler wrote in a telling revelation of his view about the Nazi past, "the opinion of the people regarding the one-sided persecution of exclusively German war crimes is clearly different from that which can be read in newspapers and heard on the radio."[58] In a country whose population was considered suspect, whose traditions were broken, and whose political system necessarily required the mediation of the "general will," cultural and political elites possessed enormous symbolic power.

Unlike Gehlen, Mohler recognized that the consensus of the 1950s was unable to meet the challenges of the 1960s. So what kind of republic, he asked, did the Basic Law intend? This was the salient question, and his answer echoed the general conservative paranoia about the power of the press and the public sphere. "Finally, one begins to see that the really serious enemies of this state will not march up in a brown shirt or even with a red cockade; they could more likely be those who use the Basic Law."[59] Such people were "that leading strata [*Führungsschicht*] that, next to the political elites, had experienced the most radical change in personnel after 1945," by which he meant the professors in the new disciplines of contemporary history, political science, media studies, and sociology and, of course, the critical writers like Grass. Viewing himself

---

[57] Gehlen, "Das Engagement der Intellektuellen gegenüber dem Staat," 405.
[58] Armin Mohler, "Die institutionalisierte Linke," *Die Politische Meinung*, 9 (July–August, 1964), 42.
[59] Ibid., 45.

as member of a tiny minority despite the conservative domination of German government, Mohler called upon the politically passive administrative strata to develop "civil courage" – a term usually used by the left to mobilize resistance to the state – to win back the political agenda from "aggressive leftists."[60]

These conservative interventions provoked a considered but energetic response from liberals and leftists and revealed three basic positions among the forty-fivers. In the middle, Ralf Dahrendorf berated Gehlen's vilification of critique without which no liberal society could exist, although he conceded the point that equality had become normative and that much of the Enlightenment program had become hegemonic.[61] The problem in Germany was that there remained distrust in the idea that permanent critique or opposition was the precondition for progress, as Hennis had also complained. "The conviction still reigns that strength lies in unity, so every critique counts as evil and fundamental and understands itself as such."[62] But Dahrendorf also renounced utopian socialism and the nascent "New Left," as he put it, which was historically spent, reminding his readers that the first leftists were liberals. The task was not to construct socialism but to resist "the steady expansion of power of private and public authorities in modern society. There is much that can and must be done to cap this power." The "search for new ways to secure the individual" was the task he set for what he called a "new liberal left."[63]

Augstein took the utopian view that Dahrendorf regarded as superseded. Naturally, he defended critique. It was necessarily destructive, as Gehlen argued, because it heralded "utopia." Gehlen was also correct in identifying the "hatred" of intellectuals in their frustrated ambitions and their broken relationship to institutions, which Augstein thought warranted little trust.[64] Was Germany really such a free country when its politicians were reluctant to tell the population the truth about the reasons for the division of the country? Dahrendorf would not have disagreed with such sentiments, but Augstein took the leftist position further by arguing that the restrictive, anticommunist, ideological "closedness" of the country, which could lead to nuclear war, should be replaced by one of fundamental openness to the East.[65] By this aspiration he did not mean simple détente. The West should give up its claim to moral and political superiority by not insisting that parliamentary democracy be the aim of reform in communist countries. After all, were there really free elections in the West under the cartel of political parties, he asked, reminiscent of Werner Weber's and Jürgen Habermas's hostility to the mediating role of these organizations?[66]

[60] Ibid., 47.
[61] Ralf Dahrendorf, "Angst vor den Hofnarren?" *Merkur*, 18 (July 1964), 663–67.
[62] Ralf Dahrendorf, "Links in der Bundesrepublik," in Krüger, *Was ist Links?* 35–43.
[63] Ibid., 43.
[64] Rudolf Augstein, "Schwärmer, noch zu besänftigen," *Merkur*, 18 (July 1964), 655–56.
[65] Rudolf Augstein, "Chancen des Intellektuellen zu einer Gestaltung der Wirklichkeit," *Der Spiegel* (June 2, 1965), 3–28.
[66] Rudolf Augstein, "Geht in die Parteien," in Claus Grossner and Arend Oetker, eds., *4 Daten. Standorte-Konsequenzen* (Hamburg, 1962), 44.

Nor did he think that the current system was reformable. Foreshadowing the SPD's Ostpolitik policies of the 1970s, he argued for the coexistence of the communist and capitalist systems, going so far as to write that "we should construct the world with the communists," as the "differences between communists and noncommunists will perhaps be smaller than between the rich and poor." Here was the desire for a pacifist Europe beyond the frontiers of the Cold War, a dream kept alive in the face of a German population two-thirds of which believed Hitler was the lesser evil to communism. Intellectuals needed to preach against their people like the prophet Amos.[67]

The political publicist Rüdiger Altmann (1922–2000), representing the moderate right-wing position among the forty-fivers, was significant because he was a major political adviser to Adenauer's successor as chancellor, Ludwig Erhard. He had written his doctoral thesis with Wolfgang Abendroth on the concept of the public sphere and was well aware of the arguments that circulated about the role of intellectuals in West German society. He was far more prepared than either Gehlen or Mohler to concede the brokenness of German tradition and the moral obloquy of the older generation, which could not be a viable example for the younger generation.[68] And he was happy to admit that the literary intellectuals of the Gruppe 47 had revitalized the country's literature by rescuing it from provincialism and shielding the "weakened domain of the human" that was "overcome by the terrible philistine pragmatism."[69]

But like the older two conservatives, he thought that the intellectuals overplayed their hand and existed in a disordered relationship to the rest of society. More than in other countries, they had taken on the role of conscience of the nation in the name of "mastering the past," which was used occasionally in a denunciatory way. "They have no right to disport themselves as moralists and to benefit their own reputations in the shadow of the truth."[70] Altmann's argument was an extreme example of integrative conservatism, which recognized the truth of the Nazi past and that therefore considered its thematization to be a threat to the stability of the country. As Mohler argued at the same time, he thought that political leaders neglected the tasks of public interpretation of collective meaning and social goals, thereby leaving a vacuum for the redemptive intellectuals who exercised political authority illegitimately because they had no expertise and no intention of actual involvement in public administration.[71] Altmann, it appears, therefore assumed that a republican consensus based somehow on the popular spirit would emerge were it not prevented by the moralizing intellectuals. Consequently, he opposed the considerable efforts of contemporary historians and political scientists (like Bracher and Sontheimer)

[67] Augstein, "Chancen des Intellektuellen zu einer Gestaltung der Wirklichkeit," 26.

[68] Rüdiger Altmann, "Verstehen wir unsere Geschichte?" in Grossner and Oetker, 4 *Daten. Standorte-Konsequenzen*, 47–48.

[69] Rüdiger Altmann, "Das intellektuelle Niveau der Politik," *Merkur*, 18 (July 1964), 667–70.

[70] Ibid., 669.

[71] Rüdiger Altmann, "Eine literarische Partei?" *Merkur*, 19 (1965), 770–73.

to engage in "political education" (*politische Bildung*), which was the liberal program of forging a republican consensus. Like Werner Weber, he placed his faith in the instincts of the "the German people" and regarded with suspicion any attempts to mediate, divide, or thwart its potential united will. But unlike political thinkers further to the right, he rejected the political system in Portugal because the Portuguese people were manifestly politically *un*conscious. Strange as it may seem, Altmann must have thought that "political education" in the Federal Republic was analogous to the efforts of the Portuguese state to keep its population docile and governable.[72]

This interpretation recommends itself when we consider the program for which Altmann is best known: his vision of the "formed society" (*formierte Gesellschaft*). In 1964, a year after Erhard became chancellor, he had already lamented the state's inability to make decisions (*Entscheidungsunfähigkeit*) in the face of strong interest groups.[73] In his programmatic essay a year later, he specified his target: an "overdeveloped pluralism." Pluralism, we will recall, was the democratic theory of the liberal Berlin School around Ernst Fraenkel. Reflecting the state-oriented Münster School of thought, Altmann argued that the state needed the capacity to make rational budgetary decisions free from the need to opportunistically satisfy vested interests. Echoing Werner Weber's hostility to political parties and organized interests, he asserted that a society would be unreformable if the state were unable to extricate itself from it.[74] Here was a version of technocratic conservatism, reflected in the opening statement of Roman Schnur (1927–96) in the first issue of the new Münster-based journal of political theory, *Der Staat* (The State), and supported by Altmann's close collaborator and admirer of de Gaulle, Johannes Gross (1932–99).[75]

Interestingly, Altmann's arguments about the instability of a state in thrall to organized business interests bore a striking resemblance to those of Habermas in *Student and Politik*. Both men advocated the separation of the state and civil society, the former in the name of a strong state, and the latter in the name of civil society and the critical public sphere. The key difference between them was Altmann's traditionally German conservative position that a strong state above society best represented, served, and governed "the people," paradoxically coupling democracy and authoritarianism. Habermas, for his part, thought that the unified will of the people which could steer or at least limit social processes and government policy must be deliberatively formed in open discussion in the public sphere, thereby avoiding the decisionism implicit in Altmann's Schmittian model of plebiscitary acclamation.

---

[72] Altmann, "Verstehen wir unsere Geschichte?" 48.

[73] Rüdiger Altmann, "Der Kompromiß" (1964), in his *Abschied vom Staat. Politische Essays* (Frankfurt and New York, 1998), 49–60. For a leftist critique, see Reinhard Optiz, "Der große Plan der CDU: Die 'Formierte Gesellschaft,'" *Blätter für deutsche und internationale Politik*, 10:2 (1965), 750–76.

[74] Rüdiger Altmann, "Die Formierte Gesellschaft" (1965), in his *Abschied vom Staat*, 61–70.

[75] Roman Schnur, "Einleitung," *Der Staat*, 1:1 (1964); Johannes Gross, *Lauter Nachworte. Innenpolitik nach Adenauer* (Stuttgart, 1965).

Nonetheless, despite these differences, the congruence between these positions was a feature of political debate in West Germany in the mid-1960s, and they were nowhere more evident than in Karl Jaspers's famous best-selling jeremiad against its political culture, *Wohin treibt die Bundesrepublik* (Wither West Germany?), which elicited spirited replies from the forty-fivers and laid bare the political-intellectual camps.[76] The occasion for Jaspers's intervention was the Bundestag debate in 1965 about the statute of limitations on Nazi crimes. He was appalled by what he perceived to be the moral blindness of its participants from all parties, a blindness that bode ill for the future of the republic. Although not a member of the German left, Jaspers's republicanism was redemptive because, with his existentialist and Protestant categories of "conversion" (*Umkehr*), which the young Habermas shared, he viewed the West German state as the opportunity for Germans to break from their past and commence a qualitatively new polity. But, alas, they had failed to recognize the fundamental criminality of the Nazi regime by continuing to rehabilitate elements of prewar German culture. "The insight into the necessity of an ethical-political revolution since 1945, the unlimited will for a rupture with the continuity with the criminal state, the recognition and will for a new foundation – all this is the condition for us if we want to have a future."[77] The problem lay in the nature of the foundation in 1949, which was imposed by the Allies rather than determined by Germans themselves. Security rather than freedom had been the priority.[78]

Such sentiments were standard fair for redemptive republicans. What made this book significant was not only the moral authority of its author but its unrelenting critique of the West German political system. For Jaspers held responsible the "party oligarchy" of the political establishment, whom he had watched debate the urgent moral issues in the limitations debate in parliament, for the apathy and moral turpitude of the majority of Germans. They could not be educated by such leaders, he declaimed. In fact, the people were being corrupted further by the men in Bonn who appealed to their worst nationalist instincts to win votes. Jaspers viewed the whole political system as a conspiracy to prevent the moral growth of his fellow citizens, and consequently this system needed to be reformed to allow those Germans who knew better to register their protest. Such Germans were the representatives of intellectual spirit (*Geist*) who constituted the "democratic public sphere." For this reason, he painted a dark picture of the plans for "emergency laws" that he thought would stifle public demonstrations against the nuclear war he so feared. Would not the government have used such draconian laws in 1962 against the *Spiegel* protesters had they existed then, he asked?

Then there was the presence of recalcitrant ex-Nazis in all walks of life who hindered the necessary *Umkehr*. Their integration had been a fatal condition of

[76] Karl Jaspers, *Wohin treibt die Bundesrepublik?* (Munich, 1966).
[77] Ibid., 22.
[78] Ibid., 176.

the new state, Jaspers maintained. He did not pose the question of the necessity of integrating such people – after all, some 8 million Germans had been members of the Nazi Party – because he demanded an inner *Umkehr* of them. He therefore felt licensed to make the most damning of parallels: "The consciousness that we are heading toward a catastrophe is today the dark background of our feeling of life. What will come? 'It must be different' in order to hinder the catastrophe. One can compare the circumstances with those of the 1920s before Hitler's seizure of power."[79]

As might be expected, Habermas praised the book in *Die Zeit* in May 1966 and adjudged Jaspers's warning about the danger of another authoritarian seizure of power "not to be incorrect." Interestingly, however, he held the Basel-based philosopher to have overstated his criticism of political parties, which showed him to be the captive of traditional German cultural criticism.[80] For all that, Habermas had similar things to say of the German parties in relation to the Grand Coalition between the CDU and SPD only eight months later.

A tension with the leftist forty-fivers can be observed between those like Habermas who remained an external observer to the political system and those like Erhard Eppler who worked within the SPD. The latter were far harder on Jaspers. While regarding his analysis of debate on the statute of limitations as worthy of reflection and agreeing with his negative judgment on Adenauer's domestic effect, Eppler was uncomfortable with the pessimistic, even apocalyptic tone of the book. Above all, he attacked Jaspers's caricature of the political system that for him smacked of the traditional German prejudice against party politics. Jaspers was also wrong in relation to the emergency laws, because he polemicized against plans that the government had given up in the face of the SPD's opposition. In any event, could one attribute dictatorial motives to Social Democratic figures like Willy Brandt? Parts of the book, Eppler concluded, could have appeared in the right-wing press, which railed against the "enslavement" of the people to the parties.[81] Dahrendorf agreed, describing the book as "unfortunate" in its attack on parties as "fundamentally corrupt." Jaspers's warned of a right-wing seizure of power, but it was he who was stuck in the political discourse of the Weimar Republic.[82]

Sontheimer was far more vitriolic. Although he also shared the disappointment in the level of the debate on the statute of limitations and noted that the politicians "were mostly interested in reflecting the unclear desire of the people not to be held responsible for the past," the author of *Antidemocratic Thinking in the Weimar Republic* could not countenance Jaspers's "Rousseauean vulgar democratism," which (as Hennis had said) always made the German

[79] Ibid., 161–71.
[80] Jürgen Habermas, "Über den moralischen Notstand in der Bundesrepublik" (1966), in his *Philosophisch-politische Profile* (Frankfurt, 1971), 113.
[81] Erhard Eppler, "Wohin treibt Karl Jaspers?" *Die Zeit* (July 22, 1966), 3.
[82] Ralf Dahrendorf, "Das Ende eines Wunders," in Freimut Duve, ed., *Die Restauration entläßt ihre Kinder oder der Erfolg der Rechten in der Bundesrepublik* (Reinbeck, 1968), 90–96.

relationship to a liberal representative constitution more difficult. "I can't help but say this: Jaspers's antiparty orientation is, in this form, nothing less than an unhappy new edition of the party critique of the Weimar Republic" reminiscent of that of Carl Schmitt. "His high aristocratic ethical sense prevented him from seeing what was politically possible in a difficult situation." "In my judgment," concluded Sontheimer, "the Federal Republic is neither a party-oligarchy nor on the way to a dictatorship. It is a moderately well-functioning mass democracy of an ethical-political *passive* welfare society with all the problems that democratic institutions have elsewhere, but – and here one can agree with Jaspers – with undeniable authoritarian-restorative tendencies."[83] All forty-fivers were suspicious of conservative revolutionary moments in their elders, and as we will see, they were also suspicious of such thinking in their students.

The parallel between redemptive republicanism and the right-wing conceptions of people like Altmann become readily apparent if one considers the liberal critique of the Schmitt school. Sontheimer's broadside against Münster's conception of a strong state was essentially the same as his reply to Jaspers. It was time, he argued, to relinquish the typical German conceptual distinction between the state and civil society and embrace the Anglo-Saxon openness to the pluralism of social and political interests. The state should not be fetishized: it existed to secure the rights of individuals and groups that comprised society.[84] But "the will of the people" should not be fetishized either. Echoing Hennis, he wrote that a democracy without governance (*Herrschaft*) was a myth. Popular sovereignty needed to be mediated by interests and political parties, and state authority was legitimized by the people through representative institutions. The lesson of the Weimar Republic, after all, was that this popular will could not determine the content of democracy. People were integrated into the state – Sontheimer appealed explicitly to Smend – by involvement in the intermediate institutions of the family, churches, and clubs, where they could realize a democratic form of life.[85]

In making such arguments, however, he found himself facing the same legitimacy dilemma as Hennis and other liberals. For only a few years earlier in 1961, he had written how the popular milieux remained in thrall to nationalist resentment for the loss of the war, the division of Germany, and the imposition of the party system. It was difficult to recommend liberal institutions to a population that regarded them with suspicion, and to redemptive republicans who distrusted the instincts of that society's elites and citizens.

Such distrust was evident with the sociologist Christian Graf von Krockow (1927–2002). Educated in Göttingen with the German Jewish émigré Helmut

[83] Kurt Sontheimer, "Menetekel über die Bundesrepublik," *Der Monat*, 18 (July 1966), 72–79; Sontheimer, *Antidemokratisches Denken in der Weimarer Republik. Die politischen Ideen des deutschen Nationalismus zwischen 1918 und 1933* (Munich, 1962).

[84] Kurt Sontheimer, "Staatsidee und staatliche Wirklichkeit heute," *Aus Politik und Zeitgeschichte*, 16 (April 15, 1964), 3–10.

[85] Kurt Sontheimer, "Vom Staatsbewußtsein in der Demokratie," *Frankfurter Allgemeine Zeitung* (June, 1962), 11.

Plessner, von Krockow painted a far blacker picture of West German democracy than did Sontheimer. Von Krockow accused the Münster School of implicitly supporting the Gaullism he saw entertained in sections of the CDU, and he pointed out that "substantial groups in the justice and administrative bureaucracies, in the middle strata [*Mittelstand*] and the rural populations, in the churches, and educational institutions, and elsewhere are at least reserved toward the democratic constitutional idea."[86] All this represented an "authoritarian potential" that could be released at a time of crisis. The difference between this redemptive republican fear and Sontheimer's integrative republicanism was the assessment of a coming crisis.

The Coming Crisis, 1965–1967

The Federal Election in 1965 reproduced the same anxieties among "nonconformist" intellectuals that it had in 1961, mainly because the same restorative, indeed, reactionary figures sat as prominent members of the ruling party. Richard Jäger, for example, echoed Zöller's praise of religion and authority in his party's column in the *Münchner Abendzeitung* where he complained that "in certain German circles it is considered modern to turn up one's nose at Spain and Portugal. But a glance over the Pyrenees could convince every German which crises of the Western world have been spared through the firm leadership of Franco."[87] During the election campaign, the CDU once again resorted to personal attacks on the SPD chancellor candidate, the mayor of West Berlin, Willy Brandt, by criticizing his wartime service for Norway, a tactic that led Brandt's press secretary Egon Bahr (b. 1922) to accuse it of endangering the republic by its opportunism.[88] In his controversial speech upon receiving the Georg Büchner Prize from the German Academy for Speech and Poetry, Günter Grass pointed angrily at the hypocrisy of criticizing Brandt while welcoming men like Hans Globke into the echelons of power, a posture that poisoned the state.[89]

  The failure of the SPD to win government naturally delighted conservative commentators who took the opportunity to pour scorn on their opponent, *Spiegel* editor Rudolf Augstein. He was a "sect leader," wrote one, while the former leader of the conservative revolutionary *Tat-Kreis*, Hans Zehrer (1899–1966), who had forged an influential career as the chief editor of the conservative daily *Die Welt*, cited Armin Mohler's article to support his proposition that

[86] Christian Graf von Krockow, "Staatsideologie oder demokratisches Bewußtsein. Die deutsche Alternative," *Politische Vierteljahresschrift*, 6 (1965), 118–31.
[87] Cited in Hans-Joachim Lieber, "Totalitarismus – Aspekte eines Begriffes" (1962), in his *Philosophie – Soziologie – Gesellschaft* (Berlin, 1965), 227. In *Die Zeit* (October 29, 1965), he averred that a "state of law was possible without democracy."
[88] Egon Bahr, "Emigration – ein Makel? Das geistige Gift der Hitler-Jahre wirkt noch immer nach," *Die Zeit* (October 29, 1965), 44.
[89] Günter Grass, "Rede über das Selbstverständliche," *Süddeutsche Zeitung* (October 16–17, 1965).

the intellectuals had become institutionalized. Why, then, did they not succeed in electing the SPD? Because, he continued, of their distance from the people. "The people...don't want to be criticized for twenty years, beaten and punished, and then from an intelligentsia whose opponents are dead [he meant Hitler and his henchmen], who have nothing more to risk and whose criticisms on the current reality on the nether side of the iron curtain is too soft. They want to be redeemed, freed, and healed, and critique cannot do this."[90]

Like Gehlen, Zehrer did not see that the suspicion of redemptive intellectuals was not of dead Nazi satraps but of those who had supported them, even if temporarily, and now occupied influential positions in the new republic. People like himself! But it was not just redemptive republicans who were worried by sentiments like Franz Josef Strauss's praise of South Africa and his links with Mohler.[91] The rector of the Free University, the sociologist Hans Joachim Lieber (b. 1923), who would later clash bitterly with the student protestors, also discerned dangerous elements in the CDU and German society. Hysterical anticommunism, he wrote, represented a "pretotalitarian potential" because it once again set the Germans a world-historical mission that linked with their traditional ambitions in the East and that divided the country into two camps.[92]

Critical opposition was therefore as necessary as ever, but for redemptive republicans the survival of democracy itself was now at stake. So they were appalled when the SPD decided to enter into a Grand Coalition with the CDU at the expense of the Free Democrats (FDP). Grass, for example, wrote a vitriolic open letter to his friend Brandt.[93] But that was not all. During the year that the Grand Coalition took office, in 1966, the far-right-wing party, the Nationale Partei Deutschlands (NPD), gained unexpectedly high returns (between 7 and 10 percent) in state elections. Both liberals and leftists were shocked and disturbed by this development, but they interpreted it in different ways. The former saw it as the effect of a mild recession on a socially conservative and politically reactionary minority of the population. The latter perceived the beginning of the incremental "fascistization" of the country.[94]

This was the year in which the effects of a mild recession – especially higher unemployment – made themselves felt, and a growing sense of insecurity was reflected not only in the voters' support of an extreme party but also in the

[90] Ludwig Pesch, "Naziß in Utopie. Rudolf Augsteins gnostischer Intellektualismus," *Christ und Welt* (July 16, 1965), 18; Hans Zehrer, "Das Volk und die Intelligenz," *Die Welt* (September 25, 1965), 1–2.
[91] Kurt Lenk, "Armin Mohler oder die Sinngebung der Bundesrepublik," *Tribüne*, 6:22 (1967), 23–32.
[92] Lieber, "Totalitarismus – Aspekt eines Begriffes," 225.
[93] Günter Grass, "Diese neue Regierung," *Die Zeit* (December 9, 1966), 17.
[94] Dahrendorf, "Das Ende eines Wunders," 95; Erwin Scheuch, "Rückschlüsse von den Wahlergebnissen der NPD auf die Wähler in der Bundesrepublik," *Die Neue Gesellschaft* (July–August 1967); Kurt Sontheimer, "Die Wiederkehr des Nationalismus," *Tribüne*, 18 (June 1966), 1916–34; Werner Hofmann, "Der Rechtsextremismus in der Bundesrepublik und seine Quellen," in his *Abschied vom Bürgertum. Essays und Reden* (Frankfurt, 1970), 140–7; Hofmann, "Der neue Nationalismus," in ibid., 148–52.

political elites' desire to cooperate in managing the "crisis." Redemptive republicans had no truck with the perceived opportunism and cowardice of the SPD, which they thought might have soon shared power with the FDP and now had to share the cabinet table with Strauss, who had come back in from the cold after the Spiegel affair. Their profound disappointment with the SPD led them to view the new government as even more dangerous than its predecessor. Habermas wrote in the student newspaper of Frankfurt University that "we have grounds to fear the regime more than the old one," because the SPD was prepared to make any deal to gain power. There would be foreign policy adventures and perhaps a crackdown on unions. Repression was in the air.[95]

Above all, Habermas feared the plans for the Grand Coalition for the so-called emergency laws that were eventually passed in 1968. For him, they represented the mechanism for the suppression of domestic dissent and the path to an authoritarian regime in the mold of Spain or Portugal that redemptive republicans had always feared. This was the beginning of the "Hispanization" of the country he had warned against since the late 1950s. Redemptive republicans were adamantly against the laws, but so were integrative republicans like Bracher, and he appeared with Habermas, Seifert (who made his reputation with several prominent publications on the laws), Werner Hoffmann, and Abendroth at podium discussions in university towns to campaign against the laws.[96] Significantly, other leftists, like Hennis's student friend Horst Ehmke, who was Augstein's lawyer during the Spiegel trial and who was later to play an important role in Brandt's federal cabinet, supported the laws because of his SPD membership. Insiders like Ehmke, Lepsius, and Eppler did not see fascism waiting in the wings. Neither did Bracher after the SPD had diluted the government's powers under the laws. The trade-union movement, after all, had waged a bitter campaign against them ever since they were proposed in the late 1950s.

On the eve of the student movement's radicalization in 1967, the stage was set for a further polarization of German intellectuals. As we will see, the nature of student protest was such as to drive a wedge not only between redemptive republicans and integrative ones like Lübbe, who early in the decade had supported their protest. Even figures like Bracher and Sontheimer eventually came to see that the danger no longer came from the right but from the left. No republican consensus was possible while the intellectual generation of 1968 distrusted the state's institutions. But in 1967 Bracher still thought the danger came from the right and he asked whether "Bonn was in fact Weimar?" "The unpolitical posture of self-pity, so characteristic for the atmosphere of the Weimar Republic, is returning in the slogans of the right of original homeland [*Heimatrecht*],

[95] Jürgen Habermas, "Thesen gegen die Koalition der Mutlosen mit den Machthabern," *Diskus*, 16 (December 1966), 2.
[96] Neue Kritik, ed., *Demokratie vor dem Notstand. Protokolle des Bonner Kongresses gegen die Notstandsgesetze am 30. Mai 1965* (Frankfurt, 1965); Jürgen Seifert, *Gefahr im Verzuge. Zur Problematik der Notstandsgesetzgebung* (Frankfurt, 1963); Seifert, *Der Notstandsausschuss* (Frankfurt, 1968).

the complaint about the undeserved packhorse fate of the Germans, in the talk about the isolation, indeed encirclement of the Federal Republic, in the tabooization of the consequences of the defeat." The attacks on the "corrupting intellectuals" continued, for democracy had not taken root in a country held together by only anticommunism and the popularity of the patriarch Adenauer. In 1967, he wrote, the country's special situation had ended, and West Germans needed to make their own decision on what kind of democracy it would be.[97] The student movement and "1968" would make this question more acute than ever.

[97] Karl Dietrich Bracher, "Wird Bonn doch Weimar?" *Der Spiegel* (March 13, 1967), 60–88.

8

1968 and Its Aftermath

Student and youth rebellions broke out across the world in the middle and late 1960s, and the West German experience certainly shared common features with them.[1] The Nazi past, however, was a distinguishing feature, adding an intensified measure of distrust of West German institutions and older West Germans for the sixty-eighters. The danger of integrating the ex-Nazis about which Kurt Nemitz had warned in 1955 had come to pass. "The cooperation of the young people under the auspices of the state-bearing organizations and groups will not be possible through political arguments alone; ultimately, the young generation will be convinced only through the radiance, example, and integrity of the leading personalities of our democracy. Here lies the greatest danger that can grow from the renazification."[2] Students had been concerned by the presence of ex-Nazis among the German professorate, and it was often on student initiative that the well-known public lecture series on the German university under Nazism in the mid-1960s were organized and published.[3]

It was no surprise, then, when Helmut Schelsky observed with trepidation in 1965 that "judging by its literary expressions, it appears that for the current academic youth the year 1933 is closer than the year 2000."[4] Two years later, the politically active students on the left shared the fears of the redemptive republicans among the forty-fivers that the absence of an effective parliamentary opposition, the proposed emergency laws, and technocratic university reform signaled the beginning of the end for German democracy.[5] Images of the

---

[1] Carole Fink, Philipp Gassert, and Detlef Junker, eds., *1968: The World Transformed* (Cambridge, 1999); Gerard J. De Groot, ed., *Student Protest: The Sixties and After* (London and New York, 1998).

[2] Kurt Nemitz, "Das Regime der Mitläufer. Soziologische Notizen zur Renazifizierung," *Neue Gesellschaft*, 11:3 (May–June 1955), 45.

[3] See, for example, Andreas Flitner, ed., *Deutsches Geistesleben und Nationalsozialismus: Eine Vortragsreihe der Universität Tübingen* (Tübingen, 1965).

[4] Helmut Schelsky, "Unbewältigte Zukunft," *Der Spiegel* (July 28, 1965), 77.

[5] Antonia Grunenberg and Monika Steffen, "Technokratische Hochschulreform und organisierter Widerstand," *Neue Kritik*, 53 (April 1969), 41–53.

Nazi period and Holocaust led the sixty-eighters and leftist forty-fivers to view West German elites as fellow travelers and harbingers of fascism. At the same time, the radicalism and tactics of the sixty-eighters protest triggered traumalike experiences for liberals and conservatives among the forty-fivers who saw in the activists of the younger generation the enemies of democracy against which they had struggled in their youth. No republican consensus could develop while West German intellectual and political elites portrayed one another as very incarnations of the fascist or totalitarian threat that had overwhelmed German democracy once before.

Ludwig von Friedeburg made clear where he and Habermas, who were in close communication with the SDS leadership in Frankfurt and West Berlin, stood. In the foreword to the second edition of *Student and Politik* in 1967, the former wrote:

Whereas in the fifties, silent conformism was characteristic of the behavior of students regarding the university and society, not only in the Federal Republic but in all developed industrial nations, so the current, much-discussed student protest shocks the public. The genuine democratic potential of a once very small democratic minority has increased and found resonance. The critical engagement against a social development is that which Jürgen Habermas analyzed in his introductory thoughts on the concept of political participation.[6]

This was the "democratically engaged minority," as von Friedeburg put it, that Horst Ehmke called "the generation for which we have been waiting" at the SPD party congress in 1968.[7] Leftist and some liberal forty-fivers saw in the sixty-eighters images of themselves and the opportunity to realize those ambitions that had been thwarted since 1945.

The radicalization of the students can be dated to the fatal police shooting of Benno Ohnesorg at a demonstration in Berlin on June 2, 1967, coinciding as it did with great anxiety over the emergency laws under consideration by the Grand Coalition government in Bonn. By the late 1960s, the university became as much an object of student attention as outside political issues like the Vietnam War and the conservative Springer press that vilified student protestors. Many junior academics – the assistants – were also active, and their organization, the Bundesassistentkonferenz (BAK), understood itself as the "motor of university reform."[8] Democratization of the university had long been the aim of the students and assistants. Their program usually took the form of *Drittelparität*, a system of co-determination in which the "estates" of students, assistants,

---

[6] Ludwig von Friedeburg, foreword to Jürgen Habermas et al., *Student und Politik. Eine soziologische Untersuchung zum politischen Bewußtsein Frankfurter Studenten* (Neuwied, 1961), 8.

[7] Horst Ehmke, "Die Generation, auf die wir gewartet haben" (1968), in his *Politik der praktischen Vernunft* (Frankfurt, 1969), 187–207.

[8] Johannes T. Theissen, "Die Rolle der Interessenverbände im Hochschulbereich unter besonderer Berücksichtigung von 'Bund Freiheit der Wissenschaft' und 'Bund Demokratischer Wissenschaftler'" (Dr. Phil. dissertation, University of Bonn, 1984), 69.

and professors would share the administration of the university, although it was unclear whether a literal trifurcation of power was envisaged in all places: sometimes other ratios were considered.[9] Forms of *Drittelparität* were implemented in various Social Democratic provincial governments during the late 1960s and early 1970s.

After mid-1967, the humanities and social science departments in many German universities were taken over by students who proclaimed the inauguration of the "critical university," as in Berlin, or the "political university," as in Frankfurt.[10] Some of the occupiers were simply enthusiastic reformers who sought to integrate the learning process more closely with their most pressing political concerns, as Habermas, Hofmann, and others had recommended. Others were more radical and, according to one historian, adopted a "guerrilla strategy," wanting to "set up bases at the universities that would offer a collective opportunity to discover and develop long-term social-revolutionary strategies for the cities."[11] By 1969 these students came to dominate the SDS, and they called for an instrumentalization of scholarship for political ends or simply for its abolition altogether.[12]

In these circumstances, the forty-fivers had mixed relations with the student movement. Its rhetorically radical and at times violent nature certainly concerned all forty-fivers, but many of them nonetheless remained positively disposed to the younger generation at least for several years after 1968. All the same, in the subsequent decade of campus radicalism and terrorism, the loose left-liberal alliance of the early and middle 1960s disintegrated and was replaced by a loose coalition of liberals and conservatives that the redemptive republicans called "neoconservatism."[13] The polarization of the academy and political culture reached its pinnacle in 1977 with the so-called German Autumn, represented by the clash between Habermas on the one side and Lübbe and Sontheimer on the other. The move of critical support for the West German state to its unqualified affirmation in the face of a perceived leftist onslaught was indicative of the Fraenkel school of liberalism in particular, which had sided with the redemptive republicans in the 1960s. This chapter does not reconstruct the events of "1968," nor give an account of student movement and the New Left. It briefly maps out the reactions to them of the various generational

---

[9] Christoph Oehler, *Hochschulentwicklung in der Bundesrepublik seit 1945* (Frankfurt and New York, 1989).

[10] See the documentation in Wolfgang Kraushaar, ed., *Frankfurter Schule und Studentenbewegung. Von der Flaschenpost zum Molotowkocktail, 1945 bis 1995*, 3 vols. (Hamburg, 1998); Detlev Claussen and Regine Dermitzel, eds., *Universität und Widerstand. Versuch einer Politischen Universität in Frankfurt* (Frankfurt, 1968).

[11] Rolf Wiggershaus, *The Frankfurt School: Its History, Theories, and Political Significance*, trans. Michael Robertson (Cambridge, Mass., 1994), 632–33.

[12] Ibid., 635.

[13] Jerry Z. Muller, "German Neoconservatism and the History of the Bonn Republic, 1968 to 1985," *German Politics and Society*, 18:1 (2000), 1–32.

units of the forty-fivers between the "red decade" of 1967 and 1977 in order
to lay bare the difficulties of developing a republican consensus because of the
"Weimar syndrome": the tendency of redemptive and integrative republicans
to view one another as the incarnation of Germany's fatal path to fascism or
totalitarianism.

The Forty-fivers and the Sixty-eighters

The alliance of the redemptive republicans among the forty-fivers with the
sixty-eighters was rendered increasingly difficult and at times impossible by the
escalation of the student movement in mid-1967. The violence of police against
peaceful protestors in West Berlin and Frankfurt had provoked a discussion
about the efficacy of violence among sections of the protest movement, which
signaled the development in the SDS of a Jacobin revolutionary consciousness
and a willingness to engage in provocation in order to escalate a potentially
violent situation.[14] It was at this point, in the winter of 1967–68, that leftist
forty-fivers like Habermas drew the line. At the SDS conference in Hanover
on June 9, 1967 – one week after Ohnesorg's death – he used the infelicitous
term "leftist fascism" to characterize the mentality and strategy of actionism.[15]
His reaction underscored the common posture of all forty-fivers to revolutionary rhetoric, whether of the left or the right. Their commitment was to the
Federal Republic as a project of reform, either radical or conservative; having
witnessed it in their youth, blind actionism was an anathema. Thus Günter
Grass condemned the violence and confrontational posture of the SDS, saying that "The slogans 'Ban the SDS' and 'Expropriate Springer' are written in
the same authoritarian ink."[16] Peter von Oertzen, in taking issue with Habermas's controversial term and in distancing the students from fascism, had to
admit that one had to regret "the actionism of the radical wing of the rebelling
students, and criticize most harshly their partly irrational character, lack of
tactical wisdom, their strategic aimlessness, and often bitter intolerance."[17]
And in his criticism of the conservative reaction to the students' call for the
democratization of society, Hartmut von Hentig had to refer disparagingly to
the left's program as "either breathtakingly naive or ideologically strained."[18]
Ralf Dahrendorf famously crossed swords with the SDS leader Rudi Dutschke
on the roof of a van before thousands of students in Freiburg in 1967. Like

[14] Richard L. Merritt, "The Student Protest Movement in West Berlin," *Comparative Politics*, 1
(July 1969), 516–35.

[15] Jürgen Habermas, "Diskussionsbeiträge," in his *Protestbewegung und Hochschulreform* (Frankfurt, 1969), 148. He later regretted and withdrew the term.

[16] Günter Grass, "Gewalt ist wieder Gesellschaftsfähig," *Der Spiegel* (May 6, 1968), 57.

[17] Peter von Oertzen, "Was ist eigentlich Linksfaschismus?" *Süddeutsche Zeitung* (January 13–14,
1968).

[18] Hartmut von Hentig, "Das Sache und die Demokratie," *Die Neue Sammlung*, 9 (1969), 121;
von Hentig, "Die grosse Beschwichtigung," *Merkur*, 22 (1968), 385–400.

Hans Albert, he had no truck with the New Left, utopianism of any sort, and criticism of representative democracy.[19]

Nonetheless, despite the violence and revolutionary rhetoric of key student leaders, redemptive republicans continued to support their aims insofar as they coincided with their own. West Berlin professors and writers were more worried about the escalation of the street clashes, and especially by what they called the "pogrom atmosphere" among the population and the police. "The disturbance of the youth is justified," they wrote in an open declaration in *Die Zeit* that was probably penned by Habermas, because the parliaments were not discussing the pressing issues like Vietnam.[20]

Such support was not surprising. What was significant was that many liberals also affirmed the movement after 1968 despite the radicalization. Figures like Sontheimer, Bracher, and Alexander Schwan who are today thought of as antistudent neoconservatives were among these liberals. Typical was Horst Krüger's reaction. Though highly critical of the radical wing of the student movement, he argued that one should not reduce the protest movement to this dimension. On the whole, the protest movement was effecting a liberalization of society, and the sooner some of its members abandoned revolutionary activity and devoted themselves to concrete matters, like anti-authoritarian kindergartens, reformed medical and legal practices, and so on, the better. "The option [*Kreuzweg*] between romanticism and reality, between anarchy and social engagement, is still open."[21] Writing in 1969, Bracher had no doubt that the danger to the republic still came from the right. He remained disturbed by the passive character of the population regarding the state, and the "frighteningly little" identification with its democratic institutions. "Here also lie the constructive aspects of the current 'disturbances' insofar as they are directed toward inner reform and the recognition of the GDR."[22]

The analysis of the chief editor at the *Norddeutscher Rundfunk* radio network and later antileftist editor of the conservative *Frankfuter Allgemeine Zeitung* newspaper, Joachim Fest (1926–2006), followed similar lines. In "The Dilemma of Student Romanticism," he argued that the Federal Republic had not used the opportunity to develop a state consciousness. Its creaking structures and stagnant public life had been embarrassingly exposed by the students, and the political elites were unable to furnish them with a legitimating rationale for

[19] Ralf Dahrendorf, "Aktive und passive Öffentlichkeit," *Merkur*, 21 (December 1967), 1109–22; Dahrendorf, "Sozialismus oder Liberalismus," *Die Zeit* (November 21, 1969), 59–60; Hans Albert, "Plädoyer für kritischen Rationalismus," *Die Zeit* (December 5, 1969), 63–68.

[20] "Appell an den Berliner Senat," *Die Zeit* (March 8, 1962), 6. The signatories included Wolfgang Abendroth, Theodor W. Adorno, Richard F. Behrendt, Dieter Claessens, Wolfram Fischer, Otto Flechtheim, Ludwig von Friedeburg, Günter Grass, Jürgen Habermas, Werner Hofmann, Walter Jens, Walter Killy, Alexander Kluge, Christian Graf von Krockow, Werner Maihofer, Fritz Raddatz, Hans Werner Richter, Wolfgang Schnurre, Jakob Taubes, and Harald Weinrich.

[21] Horst Krüger, "Wohin treibt die Protestbewegung?" *Merkur*, 23 (September 1969), 883–86; cf. Golo Mann, "Hört auf, Lenin zu spielen," *Die Zeit* (April 26, 1968), 3.

[22] Karl Dietrich Bracher, "Die zweite Demokratie," *Die Zeit* (December 12, 1969), 54–57.

the system. "Their [the students'] legitimate need for suggestive future options have been neither recognized nor addressed for twenty years."[23] Unbridled utopianism, revolutionary rhetoric, and violence were the fruit of such neglect. The student movement's inability to articulate coherently its demands and utopian vision merely reflected the muteness of the establishment. The one-sidedness of both parties, Fest suggested, put the republic in danger. "What the younger generation does not want to learn from history is that which the elder one evidently did not consider or share in learning: that it is possible to ruin [*verhunzen*] the regime and undermine it through a false understanding of its foundations."[24] One of the roots of student irrationality was what he called "the denial of history." They were able to lash out at surrounding conditions unencumbered by historical consciousness or guilt: burning newspapers and destroying television sets evoked no uncomfortable associations. They were unable to see that their ideas – the totalitarian smell of their utopianism and uncompromising approach – paralleled those of the enemies of Germany's first republic.[25] It was not possible, therefore, to take seriously the students' own proposals.

For all that, they had rattled the cage of the "democracy of notables" and thereby created reform energy and opportunities: the students had unintentionally given the republic some "enlightened impulses." The way forward was liberalization and democratization, and so, Fest argued, the real problem was the German prejudice against the left. The danger lay in the traditional German "reaction schema" by which the population fell into the arms of the right when it took fright from the left. "Not in student annoyance, in their lack of respect and call to action, but in the authoritarian reaction against it, lies – and this point is well founded – what will be essentially the real test for the Federal Republic in the near future."[26] M. Rainer Lepsius made precisely the same point.[27]

Sontheimer was even harder on the establishment. The threat continued to come from the right, he argued in 1968, because the conservative establishment could not distance itself satisfactorily from the far right, sharing as it did an ensemble of dubious concepts and categories. To be sure, the extraparliamentary opposition (*ausserparlamentarische Opposition*: APO) had some antiparliamentary streams, but it presented no danger and was a salutary challenge to the regime.[28] Like Fest, he insisted that the real danger to the republic did not come from a revolutionary but essentially isolated and impotent group of

[23] Joachim Fest, "Das Dilemma des studentischen Romantizismus," in Hans Dollinger, ed., *Revolution gegen den Staat? Die ausserparlamentarische Opposition-neue Linke* (Bern, 1968), 225.

[24] Ibid., 239.

[25] Ibid., 226.

[26] Ibid., 232.

[27] M. Rainer Lepsius, "Unruhe als Studentenpflicht?" *Stimmen der Zeit*, 180 (1967), 299–310.

[28] Kurt Sontheimer, "Antidemokratisches Denken in der Bundesrepublik," in his *Antidemokratisches Denken in der Weimarer Republik. Die politischen Ideen des deutschen Nationalismus zwischen 1918 und 1933* (Munich, 1968), 317–47.

students but from the latent authoritarian, indeed fascist sentiments they may evoke in the population. The electoral success of the NPD should be a lesson to politicians that only through the true grounding of democracy in public institutions would the country be rendered immune from such threats in the future.[29] The alarmist "Cassandra calls" of conservative professors that students were paralyzing the universities were understandable, he agreed, for it was true that some of them had resolved to use the campuses as launching pads for revolution. But the professors had to realize that the student push for a direct, plebiscitary input into university decision making represented a frustrated reaction to stalled university reform.[30] It was essential, therefore, not to hold fast defensively to the discredited old university structures but to exploit the opportunity for reform that the students had unintentionally created. Successful university reform could serve as a model for general social democratization. "In that realm we call academia, where discussion is oriented to truth, good, and justice and must be domination-free, only the argument and not social position is decisive."[31]

As late as 1970, Alexander Schwan was hopeful of a successful democratization of the Otto Suhr Institute, despite the reaction of conservatives and revolutionaries.[32] And Walter Rüegg, the Jewish Swiss rector of Frankfurt University who was known as a dangerous liberal by his conservative colleagues, argued that while the university needed to resist SDS provocation, the demonstrations had opened the possibility of real reform, because the attention of the public sphere had been gained. While he did not support Habermas's democratization plans, he did want student participation of some kind.[33]

But older German Jews who had experienced persecution in the 1930s by Nazi students were not so understanding, and none more so than the paradigmatic liberals of the Otto Suhr Institute, Ernst Fraenkel and Richard Löwenthal, the philosopher Helmut Kuhn, and Hennis's mentor Siegfried Landshut.[34] Their common observation was that the students' utopianism, dogmatism, and gnostic insights into the nature of reality possessed the inner structure of a religion that threatened the efficacy of a liberal public sphere. Richard Löwenthal argued in his much-cited *Der romantische Rückfall* (The Romantic Reversion) that the

[29] Kurt Sontheimer, "Gefahr von rechts – Gehahr von links," in Sontheimer et al., eds., *Der Überdruss an der Demokratie: Neue Linke und alte Rechte – Unterschiede und Gemeinsamkeiten* (Cologne, 1970), 1–43.

[30] Kurt Sontheimer, "Die Demokratisierung der Universität," in Alexander Schwan ed., *Reform als Alternative. Hochschullehrer antworten auf die Herausforderung der Studenten* (Cologne, 1969), 63–73.

[31] Kurt Sontheimer, "Die Universität als Modell für die Demokratie," in Dollinger, *Revolution gegen den Staat?*, 59–62, 62.

[32] Alexander Schwan, "Macht Demokratisierung die Universität unregierbar?" *Frankfurter Hefte*, 25 (1970), 259–67.

[33] Walter Rüegg, *Die studentische Revolte gegen die bürgerliche Gesellschaft* (Zürich, 1968).

[34] Ernst Fraenkel, *Universität und Demokratie* (Stuttgart, 1967); Richard Löwenthal, *Studenten und demokratische Öffentlichkeit* (Berlin, 1967); on Landshut, see Rainer Nicolaysen, *Siegfried Landshut. Die Wiederentdeckung der Politik: Eine Biographie* (Frankfurt, 1997), 424–21.

students' moral sensitivity was affronted by the hypocrisy of the older generation that had not lived up to the ideas for which the Federal Republic stood,
resulting in a utopian despair and cynicism regarding Western civilization itself.
The disorientation of the students was also the result of the evaporation of those
social adhesives, religious faith and national feeling, that hitherto had guaranteed a sense of common purpose.[35] Kuhn thematized his experience as someone
who had been "forced to undergo a rupture in his life," and he attacked Habermas's criticism of the Wissenschaftsrat's recommendation in 1967. Habermas,
he wrote, "had been long recognized by the students as a *spiritus rector*," and
his conception of university reform repeated the mistakes of the conservative
revolutionaries of the 1930s by politicizing higher education.[36] Hellmut Becker,
who sympathized with the students, was appalled that such men as Fraenkel,
and even Adorno in Frankfurt, would become targets of student harassment.[37]
He recalled a particularly egregious incident from 1968.

One day in 1968 the leader of the ASTA [the student parliament] visited me, because he
rightly assumed that I sympathized with much [of his agenda]. At the time, there was
here a lecture boycott against a Jewish academic. I told this ASTA leader, whom I later
befriended, that "I don't like his scholarship either, but this man once had to wear a
Jewish star while I was quite well as a young man. Consequently, I find it impossible
to humiliate him in this way." The ASTA leader replied: "Yes, that is your hopeless
liberalism."[38]

That such men with impeccable liberal credentials who had suffered before at
the hands of German students in the 1930s became victims of the student protest
three decades later outraged and inspired those forty-fivers who viewed the students in the same terms. Two of the most significant of their criticisms were
Erwin Scheuch's *Die Wiedertäufer der Wohlstandsgesellschaft* (The Anabap-
tists of the Welfare Society) and Wilhelm Hennis's *Die deutsche Unruhe* (The
German Unrest). Scheuch's main point was much the same as Löwenthal's: the
students and New Left had imported the intellectual currents of the 1920s into
the 1960s. The essence of the intellectual currents of the 1920s was the proposition that truth was beyond academic proof and scrutiny. This was the ideology
in which the crimes of the twentieth century had been committed, and it was
typical of youth movements that possess a precritical desire for total explanation in the manner of theology or philosophies of history. Scheuch went so far

---

[35] Richard Löwenthal, "Unreason and Revolution," *Encounter*, 33:5 (November 1969), 30–34.
This article was first delivered as a paper in English before a Rand Corporation audience in late
February 1969 while its author was on leave at Stanford University. It was reprinted in German
as the first chapter of *Der romantische Rückfall* (Stuttgart, 1970).

[36] Helmut Kuhn, "Studentenrevolten diesseits und jenseits des Ozeans," *Merkur*, 21 (November 1967), 1001–12; Kuhn, *Jugend im Aufbruch. Zur revolutionären Bewegung unserer Zeit*
(Munich, 1970).

[37] "Of Barricades and Ivory Towers," interview with T. W. Adorno, *Encounter*, 23:3 (September
1969), 63–9; see, most recently, the correspondence between Adorno and Marcuse about the
occupation of the institute by students in *New Left Review*, 233 (1999), 118–35.

[38] Hellmut Becker, *Aufklärung als Beruf. Gespräche über Bildung und Politik* (Berlin, 1992), 186.

as to lend academic credibility to the popular canard that linked the left-wing students to right-wing Nazi students from the 1930s by employing the term *"linke Leute von Rechts"* (leftist people from the right). Not for nothing did he think that the students reincarnated the Anabaptist religious chiliasm of the radical Reformation.[39]

With the sixty-eighters he contrasted his own generation, born mainly between 1925 and 1932 – that is, forty-fivers – who were replacing the reconstruction generation whose work it viewed "mostly with critical distance." The main conflict between the generations, however, was not between the sixty-eighters and the reconstruction generation, but between the sixty-eighters and what Scheuch called his own "middle generation." The latter were appalled by the ideological protest of the New Left unlike some members of the older generation such as Ernst Bloch and Abendroth who had a certain sympathy with the students. Why did the forty-fivers find the emphasis on political spirit and orientation (*Gesinnung*) so disturbing? "This generation remembers its elementary experiences that in modernity all the great crimes were committed by people and groups who asserted that the content of their politics was an ideology and that their spirit and orientation could not be questioned. The *Gesinnungskriminelle* of politics is the typical arsonist and murderer of great magnitude of this century."[40]

This was precisely the argument made by Hermann Lübbe in the early and middle 1960s, and not surprisingly his assessment of the younger generation was the same as Scheuch's. He thought that the student generation of the 1920s and the culture of the First World War experience had been replicated in the 1960s and 1970s by a "worldwide student-intellectual partisan cult." It represented a "flight from reality" indicative of those who had been unable to stabilize their identities due to the pace of the modernization process. As a result, they exhibited a sectarian worldview well known since the nineteenth-century as "partisan romanticism." In short, the students were the apogees of the counter-Enlightenment because they "rediscovered the old political 'truths' that not only decisive arguments but violence also cuts the Gordian knot, clarifies situations, and simplifies everything."[41] This was the argument about the "second student movement" (the first being the turn-of-the-century movement that fed into right-wing student radicalism in the Weimar Republic) made popular by Rudolf Krämer-Badoni.[42] The radical wing of the student movement represented precisely the totalitarian agent that many of the Münster liberals and conservatives feared: a social group that identified its own interests as

---

[39] Erwin Scheuch, "Zur Einleitung," in Erwin Scheuch, ed., *Die Wiedertäufer der Wohlstandsgesellschaft. Eine kritische Untersuchung der 'Neuen Linken' und ihrer Dogmen* (Cologne, 1967), 7–13.

[40] Ibid., 11.

[41] Hermann Lübbe, "Das Elend der Universitäten" (1970), in his *Hochschulreform und Gegenaufklärung* (Freiburg, 1972), 62–64.

[42] Rudolf Krämer-Badoni, "Die zweite Jugendbewegung," *Aus Politik und Zeitgeschichte*, 44 (1967), 3–16.

universal and which justified itself by appeal to a philosophy of history. The antidote was to protect the state from a totalitarian seizure of power.

Hennis analyzed the situation by mobilizing his arguments about the causes of right-wing thinking in German history that he first expressed in his dissertation. He had argued, we will recall, that Germans had a disturbed relationship to politics and an affinity to extremism. Contrary to the arguments of Bracher and Dahrendorf, Hennis claimed that activism rather than passivity was the dangerous German contribution to Western political culture.[43] Consequently, the country did not need more activism but the development of a civic-bourgeois tradition that was anything but passive. Hennis observed that, for some students, activism had become a life-style and end in itself. Most of them would languish in resignation, he observed presciently, but "an anarchistic group that does not shy away from anything will certainly remain behind." Like his colleagues, he saw a dangerous parallel between such students and young Nazis. "Back then one also wanted to have a revolution, sweep away the existing order, and destroy the decayed bourgeois state."[44] Again like Scheuch he contrasted the sixty-eighters with the forty-fivers. "Was not the pragmatism of the generation that returned from war in 1945, a generation that had seen where pure idealistic activism leads, one of the great hopes of the German postwar development? Did not here, after generations of German politicians had confused themselves through self-deception, a little sobriety finally enter German thinking and activity?"[45]

The SDS-Nazi analogy was popular in these circles. Moderate students were entreated to resist the attempts of the SDS to democratize and politicize scholarship. These attempts were akin, one commentator argued, to Goebbels's attempts to control university life in the Third Reich.[46] Christian Democrat Anton Böhm warned that the current skepticism about parliamentarism recalled that of the young members of the SS and SA.[47] And Ernst Topitsch, who had spent the 1950s and 1960s campaigning against conservative clericalism, argued that the students' claim to a privileged insight into truth was just the latest in a long line of threats to academic freedom that went back through the Nazis to the church.[48] These provocative analogies drew a sharp response from leftists and some liberals. Peter Glotz thought the comparison "unbearably tasteless,"[49]

---

[43] Wilhelm Hennis, *Die deutsche Unruhe: Studien zur Hochschulpolitik* (Hamburg, 1969); Hennis, "Die deutsche Unruhe," *Merkur*, 23 (February 1969), 103–20; Hennis, "Die Stunde der Studenten," *Frankfurter Allgemeine Zeitung* (January 30, 1968), 10.

[44] Hennis, "Die deutsche Unruhe," 118–19.

[45] Ibid., 118.

[46] Karl Willy Beer, "Die Demokratie in Gefahr," *Die Politische Meinung*, 13:122 (1968), 3–6.

[47] Anton Böhm, "Was haben wir denn falsch gemacht?" *Die Politische Meinung*, 13:123 (1968), 5–9.

[48] Ernst Topitsch, *Die Freiheit der Wissenschaft und der politische Auftrag der Universität*, 2nd ed. (Neuwied, 1969).

[49] Peter Glotz, "Die bündischen Professoren," *Süddeutsche Zeitung* (November 18, 1970), 8.

while the historian Helga Grebing wrote a book that aimed to invalidate the equation of left- and right-wing radicalism.[50]

The Berlin historian Ernst Nolte wrote the he felt obliged to defend a university that had elevated him to the status of professor – no mean feat in Germany for a schoolteacher from the lower middle class – and that was threatened by a politically engaged ideology like Marxism.[51] The disturbances on the campuses, he averred, could not be explained solely by internal university problems: they were ideologically driven. "Never in its centuries-old history has the German university been so externally humiliated like today; smeared with ideological slogans and obscene language, its lecture theaters [are] the marketplace of emotions." German universities had become "jungles." What had happened between 1966 and 1969 was a sign of the "deep weakness of the state." As we will see, Nolte was determined to strengthen it.[52]

The growing frustration with the students was evident in the rejection by the political scientist Hans Maier of "reform without consensus, facilitated solely by an enlightened despotism of those few with the 'correct consciousness' [and] reform as the product of an educational dictatorship." Here Maier was expressing not only the complaints of mandarin professors unused to student participation in the learning process but also exasperation with some of their classroom tactics. Maier represented the trend toward conservative stonewalling with his warning that were it impossible to reach agreement on university organization, it would be better to retain the "known and publicly accepted 'good old ways.'"[53]

While the analysis of such liberals and conservatives highlighted disturbing aspects of the student movement, they equated the part with the whole and thereby failed to see its significance as a symptom of the state's legitimacy dilemma. Accordingly, their analyses were blind to the reasons for the suspicion that the sixty-eighters had for West German institutions. Anton Böhm is a good example. A reform conservative and editor of *Die Politische Meinung*, he lamented the fact that the caesura of 1945 had cut off a generation of fathers from their sons, making impossible peaceful generational change. This failure of cultural transmission had been compounded by youth's "separation from history." The lack of a "historical consciousness," Böhm thought, produced a denuded "state consciousness" that issued in a revolutionary rather than reformist mentality. The student generation was reacting against a sterile political order that had failed to instill the proper, active political instinct in the population and left it vulnerable to the overtures of demagogues and ideologues.

---

[50] Helga Grebing, *Linksradikalismus gleich Rechtsradikalismus. Eine falsche Gleichung* (Stuttgart, 1971).

[51] Ernst Nolte, *Sinn und Widersinn der Demokratisierung in der Universität* (Freiburg, 1968), 11–12.

[52] Ibid. Ernst Nolte, ed., *Deutsche Universitäten 1969. Berichte und Analysen* (Marburg, 1969).

[53] Hans Maier, "Reform in der Demokratie," in Alexander Schwan, ed., *Reform as Alternative: Hochschullehrer antworten auf die Herausforderung der Studenten* (Cologne, 1969), 12; also see Hans Maier and Ulrich Matz, "Grenzen der Demokratisierung," *Die Politische Meinung*, 2 (1969), 42–78.

The values of the constitution – "social justice, freedom and human dignity" – had been preached rather than practiced during the 1950s, he conceded, and for too long intellectuals had been marginalized by the establishment. Germany was now paying the price for its complacency. Reform, Böhm suggested, especially greater democratization, was necessary, but he could not understand the historical reason for the redemptive republican consciousness of indignation at the pollution of German national identity.[54]

The same can be said of Konrad Repgen (b. 1923), a conservative Roman Catholic historian. His attack on the student movement focused solely on its extreme expressions and did not ask what had caused the escalation, like the brutal tactics of the police and the shooting of the harmless bystander Ohnesorg, the blame for which the Berlin press had lain cynically at the feet of the protestors themselves. In condemning student violence, Repgen signally failed to go further when he mentioned the attempted assassination of Dutschke in April 1968, nor did he mention the press campaign against the student leader to which the shooting on a Berlin street was obviously related, as the subsequent statements of the perpetrator indicated.[55]

Hans Schwab-Felisch's criticism of Hennis at the time made telling points in this vein. Hennis had nothing to say about the pressing problems that outraged the consciousness of younger Germans, above all the eight-month silence of the Berlin city government about the shooting of Ohnesorg, and establishment's exaggerated outrage about a few thrown rocks and protests.[56] The conservative interpretation ignored the specifically German circumstances. As much as the disorientation of modernization and rapid social change experienced by all modern countries may have been a factor in the phenomenon, the rejection of the Federal Republic's institutions by the sixty-eighters was also a result of the pollution represented by the integration of ex-Nazis and the absence of a redemptive republican foundation in 1949.

Rarely was this issue thematized, and when it was, the moral blindness of integrative republicanism became most apparent. Hans Buchheim (b. 1922), the political scientist and contemporary historian at the Institut für Zeitgeschichte (Institute for Contemporary History) in Munich who had written early books on the Nazi regime, addressed the redemptive arguments explicitly. "Its arguments are based substantially on an identification of our society and its state with 'fascism.' The Federal Republic is seen as a continuity of the Third Reich with other means."[57] The students failed to realize the important difference between the Nazi regime and liberal *Rechtsstaat*, thereby condemning liberal democracy in the same way as the Nazis had. Moreover, their promiscuous use of the term "Nazi" to denounce anyone peripherally associated with the regime misunderstood the way in which totalitarian regimes implicated everyone

[54] Böhm, "Was haben wir denn falsch gemacht?"
[55] Konrad Repgen, "Staatskrise?" *Hochland*, 60 (1967–68), 474–77.
[56] Hans Schwab-Felish, "Versuch einer Replik," *Merkur*, 23 (February 1969), 121–24.
[57] Hans Buchheim, "Der Protest aus falsch bewältigter Vergangenheit," *Frankfurter Allgemeine Zeitung* (March 6, 1968), 2.

in their crimes. In a notably unguarded statement, Buchheim went so far as to argue that the older generation (the forty-fivers and older Germans) were being condemned by the sixty-eighters in terms of the same group thinking as Jews were in the 1930s and 1940s.[58] Here was another classic example of the Weimar syndrome haunting the analyses of otherwise sober social scientists among the forty-fivers.

The Dogmatization of the Student Movement

The transmogrification of the antiauthoritarian student movement after 1970 into a radically reformist generation of young academics and public servants on the one hand, and into a number of campus-based dogmatic, quasi-revolutionary, Marxist groups on the other, profoundly altered the Federal Republic's political culture, effecting a deep political realignment: the political spectrum extended far further to the left than it had in the 1950s and early 1960s, and liberals and Social Democrats were caught in the middle.

When the SDS abolished itself in the 1970s, many of the students joined one of the variety of campus-based Marxist groups that ran the gamut from the New Left to dogmatic and authoritarian revolutionaries like the Spartacists (Spartakus). They made the universities their home and dominated student governments. In the winter semester of 1972–73, for example, leftists held 1,242 of the 2,033 student government seats at the sixty German institutions of higher education. Of these, Spartakus had 164 seats, its ally the Sozialist-ische Hochschulbund held 291, a cluster of Maoist groups had 140, the Social-ist Bureau–affiliated Sozialistische Front and Sozialistische Hochschulgruppen had 120, and another 352 were in the hands of a plethora of independent *Basis-gruppen* and cells.[59] One student was so bold as to publicize the tactics that he and his comrades employed. It was imperative, he stated, to separate clearly those who had succumbed to the "pressure of bourgeois society" from those who had not. "Argumentation, active adjustment, dialogue are in any case not possible, because they imply two, prepared 'dialogue partners.'" Typically an apolitical, "naive liberal professor" was singled out for "confrontation." In the ensuing intimidation, he would be revealed as a closet conservative. In this way, explained the student, a process of mutual clarification took place. Ultimately, the liberal-conservative professor must be replaced by "one of our people."[60] These were precisely the kind of tactics that had shocked Fraenkel, Scheuch, and other liberals.[61]

---

[58] Ibid.

[59] Horst Mewes, "The German New Left," *New German Critique*, 1 (Winter 1974), 22–41, 24n10; Gerd Koenen, *Das rote Jahrzehnt. Unsere kleine deutsche Kulturrevolution. 1967–1977* (Cologne, 2001).

[60] Bernd Güdter, "Wir Linken sind besser," *Die Zeit* (May 26, 1972), 15.

[61] Martin Kriele, "Wenn Studenten stören, dürfen Professoren schweigen," *Vorwärts* (February 2, 1972). First published in *Zeitschrift für Rechtspolitik* (February 1972).

In May 1972, the assistant professors' organization (BAK) reconstituted itself as a self-conscious "Marxist *Kampfverband* [fighting organization]."[62] Professorial complaints that some students waged the class struggle on campus, it seemed, were not without foundation. The reaction of the Czech conservative philosopher Nikolaus Lobkowicz, president of Munich University from 1973 to 1984, was typical.

During the next few years [after 1970], the character of the "revolution" began to change. The discussions became increasingly more dogmatically ideological; the radical movement took on more and more Leninist features. There emerged a generation of radical functionaries no longer interested in theoretical discussions but demanding the participation of students in all academic bodies and meetings. Often discussions were deliberately used to disrupt classes. Around 1970, it was already obvious to me that my initial sympathy with this unruly generation which, in fact, desperately looked for an authority imbued with some wisdom, could not be extended to the "red cells" and other well-organized Leninist groups.[63]

This culture persisted well into the 1970s. According to Ernst Nolte, "The worst years of the German university, and especially of the Free University of Berlin, were 1976 and 1977, when many institute buildings were regarded by the radical students as 'liberated territories.' No official of the government, and certainly no policeman, dared to enter these buildings."[64] Little wonder, then, that certain liberal professors viewed university democratization less as the institutionalization of communicative reason than a naked power grab. In their eyes, Habermas's ideas were as much *Kampfbegriffe* (concepts for battle) as explicit Leninist rhetoric. Topitsch's response, remarkable for its hysterical tone, reflected the campus atmosphere:

In the name of the slogans like "rational discussion" and "domination-free dialogue" that originated in the Frankfurt School, assistants and lecturers at many German universities are being subjected to interrogation by the men of the new inquisition; in the name of "democratization," a terror of conviction [*Gesinnungsterror*] is spreading that exceeds what the author knew during his student days under the National Socialist regime; behind the veil of "emancipatory" phrases an unfreedom is being established compared with which the relations in an institution of higher learning in the GDR appear almost as a liberal idyll.[65]

The hostility that many students and leftist intellectuals exhibited toward the Republic and German culture left some forty-fivers and older liberals in a quandary. They were old enough to remember National Socialism and the war years: liberal institutions, feeble as they sometimes appeared, were a painfully

---

[62] Theissen, "Die Rolle der Interessenverbände," 69.

[63] Nikolaus Lobkowicz, "Reflections on Eleven Years as President of a German University," *Minerva*, 22:3–4 (Autumn–Winter 1984), 370–71.

[64] Ernst Nolte, "Thoughts of the State and Prospects of the Academic Ethic in the Universities of the Federal Republic of Germany," *Minerva*, 21:2–3 (Summer–Autumn 1983), 169.

[65] Ernst Topitsch, "Machtkampf und Humanität," *Frankfurter Allgemeine Zeitung* (November 28, 1970).

won gain that were not to be jeopardized. Moreover, because they themselves represented positive continuities in German history, they were irritated by the younger generation's root-and-branch vilification of the entire German past.

Gradually, some of them moved from a progressive to a defensive posture. Some went sooner than others. Sontheimer and Imanuel Geiss hung on much longer. The central interpretive shift was to begin to see the left as a greater threat than the right. This did not necessarily mean believing that Bonn would go Weimar's way rather than associating the leftist campus milieu with terrorism and the destabilization it caused. This opinion became increasingly plausible if controversial when after 1970 the NPD collapsed, campus-based Marxist groups became more active, a large university counterculture was consolidated, and left-wing terrorism punctuated German public life with bombings and assassinations. Fest typified the defensive liberal reaction. Already by 1971 his reform rhetoric had been replaced by alarm at leftist extremism.

> The leaders of the protest movement in all its varieties are all convinced that they are the defenders of human autonomy, and they claim to be undermining the authoritarian potential. The question, however, is whether it is not they who constitute precisely that potential. Historical experience inclines one to skepticism, for it tends to confirm the theory that everything romantic works in the service of other, very unromantic forces.[66]

He began to see that the students were engaging in Germany's second romantic, counter-Enlightenment revolt this century against technological civilization. Despairing of the future, they engaged in antics that expressed a "collective narcissism" and "rhapsodic irrationality." Although the students were not themselves fascists, the structure of their psychological response to, and their critique of, modernity evidenced a "close, basic, kinship" with the fascist mentality and tradition of cultural pessimism.[67] Before 1970 Sontheimer did not deny the totalitarian ambitions of some student groups, but he thought that vilifying the left served to obscure the right-wing threat. But by the mid-1970s, he had changed his focus and devoted his polemical attention to left-wing intellectuals and the leftist campus milieu.[68] So did Hans Heigert, who had spent the 1950s opposing right-wing student fraternities.[69]

---

[66] Joachim Fest, "The Romantic Counter-Revolution of Our Time," *Encounter*, 36:6 (June 1971), 61.

[67] Ibid., 61. See also Gerd Langguth, "Die Entwicklung der Protestbewegung und ihre gesellschaftspolitische Bedeutung in der Bundesrepublik," in Konrad Adenauer Stiftung, ed., *Die studentische Protestbewegung: Analysen und Konzepte* (Mainz, 1971), 51–76.

[68] Kurt Sontheimer, *Das Elend unserer Intellektuellen. Linke Theorie in der Bundesrepublik* (Hamburg, 1976).

[69] Hans Heigert, "Wie die politische Moral verdirbt," *Süddeutsche Zeitung* (January 29–30, 1972), 4.

The Liberal-Conservative Rapprochement:
The Origins of Neoconservatism

"Is one today permitted to be conservative?" asked Dolf Sternberger, who led the liberal school of political theory at Heidelberg, in 1970. The question needed to be posed, he explained, because the appellation "conservative" had become a term of abuse and derision (*Spott- und Schimpfwort*) employed by radicals to discredit their opponents.[70] Topitsch agreed. "The reproach of conservatism," he wrote in 1973, "is an abusive term, indeed, a weapon with which to render [*vernichten*] the accused to the category of an unperson."[71] In the early 1970s, Geiss had berated his party for the controversial *Berufsverbot* (ban on extremists in the public service begun in 1972) and advised them that only socialist reform would stabilize the republic.[72] But a decade later he had adopted a new tone. His home university at Bremen, he wrote, "had been overwhelmed and perverted by cultural revolutionary forces, so that here 'progressive forces' among professors, students, and staff dominate the tone." And he added bitterly: "Whoever refuses the youngest cultural revolutionaries is counted automatically as a 'conservative' or 'reactionary.'"[73] Even the Social Democrat Iring Fetscher published his "Conservative Reflections of a Non-Conservative" in 1973.[74] And a year later, Sontheimer cautiously welcomed the work of the young and ambitious conservative theorist Gerd-Klaus Kaltenbrunner with the words that "certainly there are good grounds in our current situation for an enlightened conservative orientation."[75] Sternberger explained that "those who had understood themselves their entire lives as liberals, democrats, indeed as socialists, find themselves marked in one group with the conservatives." This meant, he added, that "the front lines [of political division] seem to have fundamentally shifted."[76]

And yet if some leftists and liberals were pushed from their accustomed place on the political spectrum, they could certainly not make common cause with a conservative tradition. Where were they to go? The answer, Topitsch suggested, was not to rehabilitate the old conservatism, "but to give it a new

---

[70] Dolf Sternberger, "Darf man heute konservativ sein?" *Frankfurter Allgemeine Zeitung* (October 7, 1970), 1.

[71] Ernst Topitsch, "Aufklärung als konservative Aufgabe," *Frankfurter Allgemeine Zeitung* (July 21, 1973).

[72] Imanuel Geiss, "Warning an die SPD," in Freimut Duve, ed., *Aufbrüche: Die Chronik der Republik, 1961 bis 1986* (Hamburg, 1986), 253–56; Geiss, *Was wird aus der Bundesrepublik? Die Deutschen zwischen Sozialismus und Revolution* (Hamburg, 1973).

[73] Imanuel Geiss, "Die hausgemachte Bildungskatastrophe," in Horst Albert Glaser ed., *Hochschulreform – und was nun?* (Hamburg, 1982), 191–203, 193.

[74] Iring Fetscher, "Konservative Reflexionen eines Nicht-Konservativen," *Merkur*, 27 (October 1973), 911–19.

[75] Kurt Sontheimer, "Der Konservatismus auf der Suche nach einer Theorie," *Merkur*, 28 (July 1974), 688.

[76] Sternberger, "Darf man heute konservativ sein?"

content and new importance." In other words, the task was to take up the
challenge of the left's accusation of conservatism and make a virtue of the vice:
that is, transform conservatism into an enlightened defense and promotion of
liberal values and institutions in the manner of Anglo-Saxon democracies.[77]
Sontheimer agreed in adding that "the development of societies regularly needs
a conservative corrective if stability, order, freedom, and human dignity, are to
be protected."[78] But nobody articulated the relationship between the experience
of the Nazi past and the perceived current threat from the left as clearly as
Sternberger when he wrote that "whoever has the experience of the 'national
revolution' in his bones, precisely he must today be conservative – namely
constitutionally conservative, rights-conservative, freedom-conservative, even
state-conservative."[79] This was the integrative republican catchcry and self-
understanding of the 1970s, and it was the experiential matrix out of which a
renewed discourse of German conservatism emanated.

The Federal Republic's principal representative and articulator of the conservative tradition, Armin Mohler, was dismayed by the liberals' attempt to appropriate conservative rhetoric.[80] Far from genuinely joining the fold, Mohler
feared that the "renegades from the center" would poison the well of true
conservatism with the liberalism that he thought was actually the cause of the
cultural revolution in the first place. After all, Waldemar Besson had called for a
"German Edmund Burke" while expressing his dislike of the term conservatism
in the German context because he did not wish to be associated with the likes
of "Martini and Mohler."[81]

Mohler's prediction that they would revert to their usual centrist posture
when the political situation changed was confirmed by the positional changes
of Sternberger, Fetscher, Topitsch, and Sontheimer later in the 1970s.[82] The
first two were never associated with a conservative movement of any kind,
and the latter pair, while labeled as neoconservatives by their opponents on
the left, certainly kept their distance from conservatism of the Mohler variety.[83] They always understood themselves as liberals who moved against the
political current of the day in order to stabilize the ship of state. But however
much some liberals like Sontheimer and Richard Löwenthal drifted away from

---

[77] Topitsch, "Aufklärung als konservative Aufgabe." See also Peter Graf Kielmansegg, "Versuch
   über den Gegensatz 'fortschrittlich-konservativ,'" Merkur, 9 (1975).
[78] Sontheimer, "Der Konservatismus auf der Suche," 689.
[79] Sternberger, "Darf man heute konservativ sein?"
[80] For an account of Mohler in relation to Ernst Jünger, see Elliot Y. Neaman, A Dubious Past:
   Ernst Jünger and the Politics of Literature after Nazism (Berkeley, 1999), 70–73.
[81] Waldemar Besson, "Um einen deutschen Edmund Burke bittend," Der Monat, 22 (October
   1970), 81–84.
[82] Armin Mohler, "Die Kerenskis der Kulturrevolution. Zur Invasion APO- geschädigter Liberaler
   ins konservativer Lager," Criticon, 4 (1974), 23–25.
[83] For example, Ernst Topitsch, "Aufgeklärter und unaufgeklärter Konservatismus," Criticon, 39
   (1977), 9–13; Topitsch., "Ideologie von rechts. Warnung von einer Restauration der Restauration," Deutsche Zeitung, 15 (April 7, 1978), 2; Kurt Sontheimer, "Flächendeckender Konservatismus," Merkur, 37 (September 1983), 710–13.

their defensive positions of the early to mid-1970s, a neoconservative discourse was generated that survived and was sustained as much by a committed, core group of proponents as by its vociferous opponents. The latter coined the term "neoconservative" to situate the former in the dubious tradition of German conservatism. For Peter Glotz and Jürgen Habermas, "neoconservatism is the net into which the liberal can fall when he begins to fear his own liberalism."[84]

Neoconservatives regarded themselves in the Enlightenment tradition as thoughtful reformers.[85] Leftist critics considered them sophisticated purveyors of counter-Enlightenment. Neoconservatives denied associations with traditional German conservatism and with conservative revolutionary politics. Their opponents thought the continuities as strong as the discontinuities. They maintained that neoconservatives had abandoned their liberalism, but the high-profile Hermann Lübbe replied that neoconservatives were "worried liberals" rather than "disillusioned liberals."[86] Neoconservatism was the form that integrative republicanism took in reaction to the New Left and the success of the redemptive republican language in the 1970s.

Victory of the Redemptive Republicans?

"Nineteen sixty-eight," Habermas's former doctoral student Hauke Brunkhorst has written, was the "hour of the intellectuals." For the first time in German history, the socially critical role of intellectuals, as opposed to quiescent one of "mandarins," was institutionalized.[87] Henceforth, politically committed professors and graduates in education, the media, and cultural life generally were in a position to effect the political culture of the Federal Republic and make it live up to the ideals contained in the Basic Law. Habermas concurred with this view, understanding the student movement and its consequences broadly as a movement of enlightenment.[88] There are few today who would disagree with this analysis, but only if it is considered as part of the story. For it does not account for what might be called the "dark side" of the student movement.

---

[84] Jürgen Habermas, "Neo-Conservative Culture Criticism in the United States and West Germany: An Intellectual Movement in Two Political Cultures," *Telos*, 56 (Summer 1983), 78. See Hermann Lübbe's reply: "'Neo-Konservative' in der Kritik," *Merkur*, 37 (September 1983), 622–32.

[85] Odo Marquard, "Aufklärer ohne Exaltation. Der besonnene Mahner. Zum 60. Geburtstag des Philosophen, Hermann Lübbe," *Frankfurter Allgemeine Zeitung* (December 12, 1986).

[86] Lübbe, "'Neokonservative' in der Kritik," 627; Hauke Brunkhorst called Lübbe "intellectually the most prominent and perspicacious of the neoconservatives." *Der Intellektuelle im Land der Mandarine* (Frankfurt, 1987), 104. According to Hans-Ulrich Wehler, he is "one of the most clever neoconservative commentators on the times." See his *Entsorgung der deutschen Vergangenheit? Ein polemischer Essay zum "Historikerstreit"* (Munich, 1988), 249n110. "The most outstanding proponent of West German neoconservatism." Thus Claus Leggewie in his *Der Geist Steht Rechts. Ausflüge in die Denkfabriken der Wende* (Berlin, 1987), 73.

[87] Brunkhorst, *Die Intellektuelle im Land der Mandarine*, 131.

[88] Jürgen Habermas, "Die Zweite Lebenslüge der Bundesrepublik: Wir sind wieder 'normal' geworden," *Die Zeit* (December 11, 1992).

Peter Sloterdijk, writing from a sympathetic distance to the students and to Critical Theory with which they were rightly or wrongly associated, has identified two moments or stages of enlightenment critique (used as a synonym for Critical Theory). The first proceeded along the lines advocated and represented by Habermas: the attempt to discover and disseminate truth by means of uncoerced dialogue on the basis of the most compelling argument. When, however, the enlighteners discovered that the holders of power and cultural authority resisted their arguments or refused to engage in dialogue, the second moment ensued. The discourse model that recognized the integrity of the dialogue partner was replaced by a "combative stance" and critique became a "theory of struggle." Former dialogue partners became objects of analysis, suffering from false consciousness or repression. Enlightenment became a "war of consciousness" as strategic considerations replace peaceful discussion. "Ideology critique means the polemical continuation of the miscarried dialogue through other means."[89] Sloterdijk was describing the kind of inner cleansing in which the redemptive republican consciousness can engage.

Both these moments characterized the student movement and New Left. When Habermas referred to the student movement era in general terms, he means the first moment (notwithstanding his own reservations about some student behavior), and he resisted the argument that the students were organically linked with the second. When conservatives remembered the period, they pointed to the second moment, and attempted to link it to the project of emancipation. This was the basic pattern of ideological polarization during the 1970s.

Sloterdijk's analysis of the two moments of enlightenment were borne out by the behavior of the radicalized students and by Habermas's response to them. Habermas consistently and steadfastly combated these tactics by recommending a democratization that maintained the distinction between theory and practice. It was central to the concept of co-determination, he argued, that the lines of communication remained open and strategic action was eschewed.[90] He was as well aware as the neoconservatives that the students had retreated "into the ghettos of dogmatism or alternative life-styles," and that they "achieved with the self-appointed guardians . . . a notion of democracy that is more militarist than defensible." With language reminiscent of neoconservative polemics, Habermas criticized the students' "delusive autarchy of their own private milieu" and "paths of irrelevance" that had divided "cities such as Frankfurt and Hamburg no less effectively than the Berlin Wall."[91]

---

[89] Peter Sloterdijk, *Critique of Cynical Reason*, trans. Michael Eldred, foreword Andreas Huyssen (Minneapolis, 1983), 14–16.

[90] Jürgen Habermas, "Demokratisierung der Hochschule – Politisierung der Wissenschaft," in his *Kleine Politische Schriften, I–IV*, 190; Habermas, "Seminarthesen," in ibid., 261–64.

[91] Jürgen Habermas, introduction to his *Observations on the "Spiritual Situation of the Age,"* trans. Andrew Buchwalter (Cambridge, Mass., 1985), 7–9. See also Peter Glotz's considered views on the problem of the university subculture, its alleged relationship with terrorism, and the inability of the SPD to make an impression on it: "'Jeder fünfte denkt etwa so wie Mescalero,'" *Der Spiegel* (October 3, 1977), 49–63.

It is curious, therefore, that Habermas was surprised by the nature of neo-conservative mobilization. On one page he bemoaned the spread of a "new dogmatism" in leftist student circles during the 1970s, and on the next he berated neoconservatives for conceiving of public discourse "as something of a paramilitary operation at the front of a semantic civil war."[92] When he did ask why liberals "began to fear their own liberalism," his answer was that they opposed the "consequences of cultural modernity."[93] How could he argue this? Surely he could not mean that the separatist-campus counterculture, of which he himself was critical, was the fruit of cultural modernity. Were that the case, then the neoconservative mobilization might appear legitimate. He failed to make the connection either for polemical reasons or because he had something else in mind when he referred to "the consequences of cultural modernity."

In his writings of the late 1960s on the student movement, Habermas distinguished between the actionistic and irrational minority, of whom he disapproved, and a majority of reformist students who, in his eyes, represented the authentic fruit of cultural modernity and the hope of the future.[94] They were the students who became progressive teachers, journalists, and so on during the 1970s, and who contributed to the communicative rationalization of the political culture. Presumably Habermas had them in mind when he refers to "cultural modernity." But he also repeatedly rejected neoconservative descriptions of the 1970s as a period dominated by a "new class" of leftist intellectuals, teachers, and journalists.

Without doubt, the conservatives' claims were exaggerated, but others on the left like Oskar Negt were more confident that leftists *had* indeed won substantial gains in the decade after 1965. He interpreted the neoconservative mobilization as a *defensive* gesture to recapture a lost cultural hegemony. Talk of a new class was not right-wing fear mongering, he implied: it reflected a changed power constellation in culturally significant areas of the Federal Republic.[95] And this is, of course, what Brunkhorst meant by the successful institutionalization of the role of intellectuals.

The Bund Freiheit der Wissenschaft

Many liberals and conservatives reacted to this changed constellation. The origins of the largest and most influential organization of such intellectuals, the Bund Freiheit der Wissenschaft (Federation for Freedom of Scholarship: BFW) reveals this process very clearly. Over the course of the 1970s, the BFW united

---

[92] Habermas, introduction, 13–14.
[93] Habermas, "Neo-Conservative Cultural Criticism in the United States and West Germany," 78.
[94] Habermas, *Toward a Rational Society: Student Protest, Science, and Politics*, trans. Jeremy J. Shapiro (Boston, 1970).
[95] Oskar Negt, "Terrorism and the German State's Absorption of Conflicts," *New German Critique*, 12 (Fall 1977), 16–17.

liberals and conservatives in defense of a positivist and technocratic university settlement (one that rejected tying scholarship explicitly to political goals), as well as affecting to speak on a wide range of educational matters pertaining to all levels of the system. In this way it became a neoconservative organ and primary articulator of the neoconservative integrative position.

On November 18, 1970, some 1,500 people – about half of whom were professors, some assistants, students, and private citizens – gathered in Bad Godesberg for the founding congress of the BFW. Of the 4,849 *Ordinarien* (senior professors) in German Universities, 2,000 who could not attend sent their regrets. The meeting received considerable media coverage and a hostile response from the progressive and radical representative organizations of students and assistants. For the latter, the BFW was a conservative, even reactionary *Kampfbund* (fighting organization): the gathering of right-wing, antireformist elements in the university and society.[96] All in the educational world saw the formation of the BFW as marking a new chapter in the politics of German university reform.

But if the appearance of the BFW meant that the warring parties had drawn their respective lines in the sand, it did not mean that the battle lines in what Dolf Sternberger called the "university *Kleinkrieg* [small war]"[97] had not already taken shape. In fact, the movement against the direction of university reform and the activities of radical students had been gaining momentum for some two years. Already in April 1968, 1,618 university teachers signed the Marburg Manifesto that had been drawn up to publicize misgivings about the direction of university democratization and proposals for *Drittelparität*. State-government-imposed reform, the professors complained, was politicizing scholarship by giving students and assistants an overweighted determination in university affairs. In their comparison of the German university with the Chinese cultural revolution, the authors of the manifesto exhibited a hint of hysteria that reflected the growing polarization of the Federal Republic.[98] Kurt Sontheimer thought the manifesto's arguments "reactionary."[99] At least a quarter of the manifesto's signatories joined the BFW.[100]

There was local activity, too. In the same year, a group of about twenty professors at the University of Frankfurt began meeting to discuss the predicament of scholarship. Known as the Frankfurt Circle, the group was initiated by the sociologist Friedrich H. Tenbruck (1919–94) and university rector Walter

---

[96] See, for example, Herbert Claas, "'Bund Freiheit der Wissenschaft,'" *Blätter für deutsche und internationale Politik*, 16 (February 1971), 148–57; Reinhard Kühnl, "'Bund Freiheit der Wissenschaft' und sein Standort im politischen Spektrum der BRD: Ein Gutachten," *Blätter für deutsche und internationale Politik*, 11 (November 1973), 1202–15.

[97] Dolf Sternberger, *Frankfurter Allgemeine Zeitung* (November 28, 1981), 1.

[98] Hilke Schlaeger, "Ein Viertel nur...," *Die Zeit* (June 28, 1968), 10; Thiessen, "Die Rolle der Interessenverbände," 73–74.

[99] Kurt Sontheimer, "Die Demokratisierung der Universität," in Schwan, *Reform als Alternative*, 67.

[100] Thiessen, "Die Rolle der Interessenverbände," 75.

Rüegg. Rüegg, who was then president of the West German rectors' conference, later resigned his Frankfurt post in protest against the Hessian university reform.[101] In January 1969, the group was formally founded as the Scientific Society (Wissenschaftliche Gesellschaft) and included among its members future BFW leaders Hennis, Maier, and Nolte.[102] Of the society's forty-seven members, twenty-nine joined the BFW, and until 1972 the society served as its secretariat. The society was also instrumental in establishing the BFW in the first place. It organized the conference in June 1970 that was the prelude to the BFW's founding congress in November. It was at the midyear meeting that Nolte suggested Bund Freiheit der Wissenschaft as the name of the projected, permanent, and united association.[103] Some of the more significant among the hundred or so participants were the historian Andreas Hillgruber, Alexander Schwan, Richard Löwenthal, Scheuch, and the philosopher, and then Social Democratic state secretary of Northrhine-Westphalia, Hermann Lübbe.[104]

Meanwhile in Berlin, like-minded professors had organized themselves into the "Emergency Community for Academic Freedom," as a direct response to Berlin University Law of August 1969 and the election of Rolf Kreibich, who was suspected of intending to politicize the university in a leftist direction, to the presidency of the Free University. The community was also influential in founding the BFW and proved to be its strongest branch, providing leading figures such as the historian Thomas Nipperdey, Topitsch, and jurist, and future president of the republic, Roman Herzog (b. 1930).[105] In Bonn, the "Society for Freedom in the University" became an associate organization of the BFW, while the members of the Bonn-based, CDU-related "Thursday Circle" all joined. The founding of the BFW served to unite and coordinate the spontaneously arisen, liberal-conservative resistance groups under an executive on a federal basis, served by a secretariat and various journals and publishing houses.

Six hundred joined the BFW at its inaugural congress in November 1970, and by the end of the year 2,500 members were on the books, with some 4,000 in 1972, peaking with 5,200 in 1975. About half the members were private citizens, 35 percent professors, and the balance assistants and students. With these numbers, the BFW felt able to speak in the name of academic freedom. Its declared aims were essentially that of the Marburg Manifesto – to oppose the state-imposed "democratization of the university" and the aspirations of the radical students for co-determination in university affairs. These developments, the BFW claimed, were politicizing scholarship giving Marxist students and assistants the opportunity of linking teaching and research to explicitly

---

[101] Nina Grunenberg, "Die Prügelknaben schlagen zurück," *Die Zeit* (August 7, 1970), 31–32.
[102] Ibid.
[103] Ernst Nolte, "Was kann getan werden?" in Hans Maier and Michael Zöller, eds., *Gegen Elfenbeinturm und Kaderschmiede. Die hochschulpolitische Tagung in Bonn am 22. Juni 1970* (Cologne, 1970), 36.
[104] Theissen, "Die Rolle der Interessenverbände," 76–82.
[105] Ibid., 79–80.

political goals.[106] It was also a question of morale. According to Hans Maier, co-determination had "made professorial majorities ineffective," although students were technically in a minority. "At the universities," he added, "there reigns... an atmosphere of massive intimidation and corresponding fear."[107]

In rallying reformers and conservatives under the banner of "rational educational reform" and "value freedom," the BFW claimed to represent the middle ground.[108] And it appealed to the public and government for help in reforming the reformed universities. Like the Marburg Manifesto, the BFW's declarations had the air of alarmism. Its central claim was that the radical students viewed the university as the soft underbelly of "late capitalism" and that they intended to undermine the "free, liberal-democratic order" from the campus. Nobody doubted that this indeed was the ambition of radicalized portions of the student movement and that they had paralyzed parts of the universities. This claim was not the invention of the professors.[109] But the BFW alienated many potential supporters by seeming to believe the hopeful illusion of the revolutionary students: that the integrity of the Federal Republic was in fact threatened by a few thousand disaffected campus radicals. By exaggerating the magnitude of the crisis and becoming fixated with "Marxist students," the BFW gave the impression that it expressed the views of a defensive professorate and the technological, positivist university ideal rather than the general interest of reform. Far from overcoming the polarization, the BFW appeared to be a symptom of it. As Nina Grunenberg, the education correspondent of the liberal weekly, *Die Zeit*, put it, "With the foundation of the Bundes 'Freiheit der Wissenschaft' the polarization of the universities continues. The middle path and voice of reason will become even more difficult."[110]

It is not surprising, therefore, that BFW's critics were unconvinced by its rhetoric of impartiality and that they doubted its claim to represent the middle ground. They pointed to the presence of prominent business figures and the overwhelming preponderance of CDU politicians on the membership list, as well as to the minuscule numbers of assistant professors and students. There was considerable evidence for these accusations. While there were, in fact, some high-profile Social Democrats in the BFW, they did not last long. Prominent BFW members like Alexander Schwan and Hennis left the SPD, the latter promptly joining the CDU. Less than a month after being elected to the executive of the BFW in November 1970, Maier resigned to become minister for culture and education in the conservative Bavarian CDU/CSU administration.

[106] Hans Maier and Michael Zöller, eds., *Die andere Bildungskatastrophe. Hochschulgesetze statt Hochsculreform* (Cologne, 1970).

[107] "'Professoren sind nicht mutiger als Andere': Gespräch mit Hans Maier über den 'Bund Freiheit der Wissenschaft,'" *Der Spiegel* (November 23, 1970), 115.

[108] Hans Maier and Michael Zöller, eds., *Bund Freiheit der Wissenschaft. Der Gründungskongress in Bad Godesberg am 18 November 1970* (Cologne, 1970).

[109] Peter Glotz, for example, agreed that the BFW's anxieties about *Drittelparität* in research questions and its concerns about the "Leninist oriented student minority" were well placed: Glotz, "Die bündischen Professoren."

[110] *Die Zeit* (November 27, 1970).

Maier was also one of the three BFW members on the Presidium of the Central Committee of German Catholics.[111] Hermann Lübbe, by contrast, resigned his ministerial post in Northrhine-Westphalia after his education reform proposal was amended against his will.[112]

Despite their opposite trajectories, the political meaning of Maier's and Lübbe's career moves was clear: the BFW had little or no affinity with the SPD. Prominent CDU figures like party General Secretary Bruno Heck were BFW members, as were conservative university rectors like Nikolas Lobkowicz of Munich, who in 1984 became president of the clerical Roman Catholic University in Eichstätt, Bavaria. As one commentator pointed out in early 1971, the Social Democrat Richard Löwenthal was "in the role of odd man out; the only leftist in a circle of rightists."[113] In fact, seven years later Löwenthal left the BFW claiming that it had degenerated into "the educational-political front organization of the CDU."[114] Contemporaries were not unjustified, therefore, in understanding the BFW as a *Professorenbund* (federation of professors) opposed to "progressive," if often poorly conceived and executed, university and social reform. But the accusation of the BAK that the BFW was a fascist organization was seen rightly by all as well off the mark, and it indicated more about the worldview of some assistants than it did that of the BFW.

Educating Non-German Germans: The High School Curriculum Reform Controversy

With the victory of the SPD in the federal elections of 1969, many liberals and leftists hoped for radical reform, especially with regard to the recognition of East Germany and to education. The program for the latter, especially at the state level, caused as much controversy as Brandt's and Egon Bahr's Ostpolitik, because it represented a policy of cultural engineering to make good the missed opportunity of 1949 to "start again" by diluting the emphatically national identity of young West Germans. The form of this innovation was new high school curricula in several West German provincial states controlled by the SPD, particularly Hessia and Northrhine-Westphalia. Their general orientation was based on the Frankfurt School critique of mass culture that had found its way in a new brand of critical educational theory, especially via forty-fiver educationalists like Hartmut von Hentig, Arno Klönne, and Wolfgang Klafki.[115]

---

[111] Theissen, "Die Rolle der Interressenverbände," 120.

[112] "Alte Absicht," *Der Spiegel* (November 23, 1970), 115.

[113] Rudolf W. Leonhardt, "Professoren Bund rückt nach rechts," *Die Zeit* (January 22, 1971), 13; Herbert Claas described Löwenthal as a "*bekehrte Sozialist*" in "'Bund Freiheit der Wissenschaft.'" See also the polemical exchange between Löwenthal and Alexander Mitscherlich: Löwenthal, "Lernprozess in der Hochschulpolitik?" *Die Zeit* (December 11, 1970); Mitscherlich, "Vor bösen Buben bangen," *Die Zeit* (December 11, 1970); Mitscherlich, "Bund gegen studentische Untaten," *Die Zeit* (January 22, 1971), 14.

[114] Cited in Theissen, "Die Rolle der Interressenverbände," 165–66.

[115] For a good overview of this literature and field generally, see Wolfgang Klafki, "Erziehungswissenschaft als kritische-konstruktive Theorie: Hermeneutik – Empirie – Ideologiekritik," *Zeitschrift für Pädagogik*, 17:3 (June 1971), 351–85.

The curricula possessed two characteristics that were bound to cause controversy. First, they abolished the traditional focus on content in curricula and replaced it with controversial, "learning goals." The Hessian one – Hessische Rahmenrichtlinien – made its leading goal the "ability for self- and co-determination."[116] The aim was to produce Non-German Germans. As might be expected, this aim was understood by German Germans in terms of the language that the students and New Left used in university battles. Co-determination was seen as a synonym for "emancipation" – the desire for a "domination-free" institutionalism. If there were to be no authority in the schools, what had things come to? Critics felt their suspicions confirmed by the principal learning goal of Northrhine-Westphalia, which was simply "to place young people in the position, either to freely and naturally recognize the given social norms, or to decline to follow them and decide upon others."[117] What and where precisely this "position" was, and how schoolchildren would be "placed" there, aroused a great deal of mistrust. The new curricula's purpose, it was feared with a gesture to the problems on the country's campuses, was to "educate for protest."[118] As might be expected, integrationist liberals objected to the attempt of redemptive republicans to distance children from their social and cultural environments. They had accurately seen the purpose of the curricula to effect a cultural "new beginning" with the younger generation via the education system. For redemptive republicans, the national culture was polluted and students needed to be able to emancipate themselves from it. For integrative republicans, students should be encouraged to trust the traditions in which they and their parents had been raised.

The second problem for neoconservatives was the curricula's absorption of "history" and "geography" into the new subject of "social studies" and the abolition of the canon of German literature in German classes. Henceforth, the authors of the curricula stated, history was to be drawn upon only insofar as it related to present-day issues and events. This move reminded many observers of the "Wozu noch Geschichte?" (What is the Point of History?) debates that had recently taken place in academic circles in response to neo-Marxist criticisms that historical studies should be replaced by sociology because they were not oriented to practical questions of political reform.[119] Matters stood the same with German classes, which were designed to increase communicative competence rather than expose students to "classic texts."[120]

These reforms provoked a storm of protest from German Germans. The BFW became involved by organizing an oppositional parent group that waged a

[116] "Erziehung zum Klassenkampf? Die Autoren Ingrid Haller and Harmut Wolf über die Richtlinien für Hessens Schulen," *Der Spiegel* (March 26, 1973), 149–57.

[117] Cited by Hermann Lübbe in "Wie mann es lernt, sich zu distanzieren," *Frankfurter Allgemeine Zeitung* (June 26, 1974).

[118] Schelsky used the phrase in a review of a book by Hartmut von Hentig, an influential "critical" educational theorist. See his "Erziehung zum Protest?" *Der Spiegel* (December 9, 1968), 202–3.

[119] Reinhart Koselleck, "Wozu noch Historie?" *Historische Zeitschrift*, 1 (February 1971), 1–18; Jürgen Kocka, "Wozu noch Geschichte?" *Die Zeit* (March 3, 1972), 52.

[120] Ludwig von Friedeburg, *Bildungsreform in Deutschland* (Frankfurt, 1989), 454.

high-profile and damaging publicity campaign.[121] The curricula were discussed at all levels from newspaper columns to scholarly journals. They were interpreted by all as a test case of what the generation of 1968 that had *not* joined the separatist-university counterculture would do when it held the reins of power. The relevant minister in Hessia was Ludwig von Friedeburg, head of the Institute for Social Research in Frankfurt. The ideas animating the reforms were therefore thought to be fairly transparent. A rowdy and lengthy (lasting over seven hours) televised public meeting in Frankfurt on November 5, 1973, featuring a panel of seven experts, including Habermas, von Hentig, von Friedeburg, and Golo Mann, did not allay the fears of conservatives.[122] The *Frankfurter Allgemeine Zeitung* thought the new curricula to be a manifestation of "vulgar Marxism."[123] Neoconservative intellectuals were a little more subtle. Mann, for example, thought them Deweyan rather than Marxist in their future and antibourgeois orientation. Marx, he said, would not have thrown out the entirety of Western culture. He suggested that they may have been useful in the languid climate some twenty years earlier but in the current situation they were disastrous. The German literary canon was already in decline and historical consciousness on the wane. He rejected the Hessisiche Rahmenrichtlinien as a legitimate implementation of lessons from the Nazi past. In the name of learning from the past, he wrote, a "[cultural] *theft* from youth was being planned":

Goethe could not prevent the Nazis. This argument is impressive on the first glance, but on the second it is without substance. Music, too, could not prevent the Nazis. Nor love, sport, eating or drinking. Were we to abolish everything that did *not* prevent the Nazis, then we would have to abolish ourselves, or better still, our planet.... What does he [the German] not *throw out* when he wants to be progressive: literature, we are assured by the curricula, only has a new value. It has it – in the dustbin.[124]

Mann obviously thought the rush to be "progressive" an odious threat to the continuum of German culture. The real threat was not tradition but the "new age of capitulation" to the spirit of "progress." And then he added darkly: "In *this* relation at least, are our current times reminiscent of those before the *Machtergreifung* [Nazi seizure of power] of 1933?"[125] Like others in the debate, Mann was suffering from the Weimar syndrome.

Hermann Lübbe and Thomas Nipperdey, who in 1973 were still publicly identified as members of the SPD, submitted a joint critique of the Hessian curriculum. Both publicized their views in newspaper and journal articles, and

---

[121] Theissen, "Die Rolle der Interessenverbände," 121–22.
[122] "Meinungspatt auf dem Hessen-Forum," *Süddeutsche Zeitung* (December 8–9, 1973).
[123] Kurt Reumann, "Girgensohn stellt Friedeburg in den Schatten," *Frankfurter Allgemeine Zeitung* (August 18, 1973), 2.
[124] Golo Mann, "Wenn der Deutsche progressiv sein will...," *Süddeutsche Zeitung* (June 2–3, 1973).
[125] Ibid.

Nipperdey even wrote a book on the reforms.[126] Lübbe agreed with Mann that the curricula were less Marxist indoctrination than a "programmed decultivation" that issued from the student-based "cultural revolution."[127] The potential results were no less explosive. The aim of the curricula, as he rightly interpreted it, was to instill in high school students a critical distance to their society. The development of a critical disposition was considered, quite understandably, to be a corrective of the national *Obrigkeitskultur* (culture of authoritarianism). As Lübbe viewed them, however, they went much further. By abolishing history as a discrete subject and by invoking the past only in relation to practical concerns of the present, the curricula aimed to develop a hypercritical disposition that would issue in the Spartakus rather than democratic citizenry. Hans Maier made precisely the same point.[128] Spartakus had evidently become the catchall term for the campus counterculture. High school students were taught, the neoconservatives thought, that history, society, and reality were at their disposal and to be altered according to their will. It was in this light that the learning goal of the Northrhine-Westphalia was interpreted as so radical. Indeed, that particular formation ("to place young people in the position . . . ") and the Hessian controversy became lore in neoconservative circles and were still quoted years later as examples of leftist cultural experimentation.[129]

But how was this education supposed to result in a revolutionary consciousness? The radical distancing from one's own culture and history, Lübbe argued, could not be sustained in the long run because it undermined one's identity and provided no substantive replacement. The adolescent would inevitably seek a compensatory new identity, and there would be little doubt as to its nature. "It will be that which, free from self-doubt, offers a program to change the world, whose nature one has exposed, in such a way that one can end the frustrating distance toward it." The Hessian curricula reform, he continued, "in their ultimate effect are curricula for the creation of a hunger for a restabilizing political, redemptory certainty."[130] The historian Michael Stürmer made much the same point in his criticism of the Hessian reforms. A decade later, he joined Helmut Kohl's political staff in an effort to undo the damage.[131]

Terrorism and the "Unintended Consequences" of Critique

The liberal and conservative intellectuals were well aware that Adorno, Habermas, and even Marcuse were no advocates of actionistic behavior, let alone

---

[126] Thomas Nipperdey, *Konflikt – Einzige Wahrheit der Gesellschaft? Zur Kritik der hessischen Rahmenrichtlinien* (Osnabrück, 1974).

[127] Hermann Lübbe, *Unsere stille Kulturrevolution* (Zürich, 1976), 12.

[128] Hans Maier, "Die Schule ist eine Vor-Gesellschaft," *Die Zeit* (December 7, 1973), 21.

[129] For example, see Peter Graf Kielmansegg, *Nachdenken Über die Demokratie: Aufsätze aus einem unruhigen Jahrzehnt* (Stuttgart, 1980), 118.

[130] Lübbe, *Unsere stille Kulturrevolution*, 12.

[131] Michael Stürmer et al, "Hessische Gesellschaftslehre," *Das Parlament* (July 7, 1973), 6, 9.

violence. Adorno, in particular, offered anything but practical recommendations. Neoconservatives recognized that the critical philosophers had spoken
out against the irrationality and dogmatism of some students groups and their
revolutionary delusions. It was Habermas, after all, who to his cost had coined
the term "leftist fascism." Yet the neoconservatives held redemptive republicans
at least partly responsible for what they termed the campus-based "nihilistic
counterculture" and what they saw as its poison fruit – terrorism. This association or attribution of guilt took two forms.

On the first reading, "unintended consequences" flowed from the activists'
vulgarization of Critical Theory. Bracher complained that the "Habermas-
wave" had been "eagerly adopted and vulgarized" by young radicals, who had
collapsed knowledge into interest, and society into the state.[132] Hans Maier
thought that the youth movement's "vulgar brand of actionistic Marxism" was
becoming increasingly embarrassing for Adorno and Habermas.[133] Writing in
1976, Lobkowicz agreed that Habermas's influential *Knowledge and Human
Interests*,[134] in whose central thesis he recognized the critical theorist himself
as having by then largely abandoned, had nevertheless "become, in varying
degrees of vulgarization, an article of faith for many self-styled critical academic politicians and theoreticians."[135] The experience of having the vocabulary of "emancipation," "democratization," and, above all, "domination-free
consensus" serve as *Kampfbegriffe* in university power struggles had led the
philosopher Robert Spaemann from the Münster School of neo-Hegelianism, in
his public correspondence on the subject with Habermas, to write "that in your
mouth [at least], the talk of domination-free discourse is not a weapon to end a
real discussion in an authoritarian manner or to disqualify the doubter."[136]
Only with Habermas, it appeared, was the concept used as its maker
intended.

On the second reading, neoconservatives argued that "unintended consequences" inhered in the logic of Critical Theory itself. Already in 1967,
Hans-Georg Gadamer had maintained that the arguments for an emancipatory consciousness made in Habermas's *Knowledge and Human Interests*
basically "have in mind the dissolution of all authority, all obedience. This
meant, the hermeneuticist continued, "that unconsciously the ultimate, guiding image of emancipatory reflection in the social sciences must be an anarchistic

---

[132] Karl Dietrich Bracher, *Schlüsselwörter in der Geschichte* (Düsselldorf, 1978), 28.
[133] Maier, "Reform in der Demokratie," 26.
[134] Described by *Der Spiegel* in the following manner: "No work by a German philosopher over
the past decade has found as much international resonance...," in "Immer Diskutieren," *Der
Spiegel* (March 28, 1973), 141.
[135] Nikolaus Lobkowicz, "Erkenntnisleitende Interessen," in Kurt Hubner et al., eds, *Die politische
Herausforderung der Wissenschaft. Gegen eine ideologisch verplante Forschung* (Hamburg,
1976), 55.
[136] Robert Spaemann, "Die Utopie der Herrschaftsfreiheit," *Zur Kritik der politischen Utopie*
(Stuttgart, 1977), 135. The exchange with Habermas first appeared in *Merkur*, 26 (December
1972).

utopia."[137] Or, as Bracher put it, the socialist critique "culminated in a socio-logically and psychologically founded emancipation protest against society *as such*, against its values and taboos, and ultimately as political criticism of the system generally."[138] Spaemann argued similarly that the logical conclusion of Habermas's idea of "domination-free discussion" was in fact, paradoxically, unlimited and uncontrolled domination. The problem of left-wing extremism, he declared, did not issue from *any* political theory but from one that was unable to justify authority short of the ideal speech situation.[139] Accordingly, Harald Weinrich agreed that the problem with discourse theory was that it contained no guidelines for ending discussion short of an authentic consensus. As a theory of establishing norms that was oblivious to the conditions under which practical decisions were actually made, discourse theory was more suited to a "very academic utopia." Its problems lay, first, in the fact that an iconoclastic student movement used the theory and, second, that the relevant topic of discussion was always more complex than the discussion was long. One danger was not securing a consensus of the compelling argument but one of simply agreeing to continue discussion, which became a "dictatorship of perseverance [*Sitzfleisch*]." The second danger was the masking of one's basic interests through a facility with the topic's complexity. This tactic was "domination through complexity." These dangers, he added, were a possible but not necessary reading of discourse theory, "and certainly not one wished by Habermas."[140]

Hermann Lübbe, too, argued against the conflation of the practical (or ideal) and social grounding of norms. But his conclusions were more sinister than Weinrich's because he thought the conflation contained the basic structure of totalitarian domination and terrorism. Grounding norms on the basis "of the most compelling argument" did not lead necessarily to extremism, he implied. Its "political meaning" was extremist, however, when this abstract grounding of norms was combined with what he called the "terroristic imperative" – the identity of the empirical subject (an individual or a party) with the transcendental. A group was in thrall to the "terrorist imperative" when it considered itself in possession of norms that were more "real" (i.e., true and just) than the extant social and political norms. The inevitable consequence was the transition of the terrorist imperative into terrorist action. Lübbe did not go so far as to name which individuals or groups were possessed by the "terrorist imperative" (other than the terrorists themselves, of course), but his use of the Habermasian vocabulary in the context of the public attack on the Frankfurt School in the fall of 1977, no doubt left his readers with a clear picture of whom he had

---

[137] Hans-Georg Gadamer, "On the Scope and Function of Hermeneutical Reflection," in his *Philosophical Hermeneutics*, trans. and ed. David E. Lange (Berkeley, 1976), 42.

[138] Karl Dietrich Bracher, *The Age of Ideologies: A History of Political Thought in the Twentieth-Century* (New York, 1984), 213.

[139] Spaemann, "Die Utopie der Herrschaftsfreiheit."

[140] Harald Weinrich, "System, Diskurs und die Diktatur des Sitzfleisches," *Merkur*, 26 (August 1972), 809–10.

in mind.[141] Prominent conservative politicians like Franz Joseph Strauss and Hans Filbinger (the latter of whom was later disgraced by revelations of his activities as a Nazi judge) publicly laid the blame for terrorism at the feet of the Frankfurt School, who, they claimed, were the terrorists' "spiritual fathers." Habermas responded in turn.[142]

Habermas reminded everyone that he and other leftist intellectuals had been among the first to criticize what Adorno called "student activism." He himself had referred to "leftist fascism" because the ideology of radical voluntarism and violence reminded him of the German conservative revolutionary professors of his youth, Carl Schmitt and Martin Heidegger. This was his generational experience speaking. The conservative argument that the Frankfurt School was somehow "objectively responsible" for the terrorism, he pointed out, was the kind of argument Stalinists used in another context. Invoking the specter of Weimar, Habermas suggested that Strauss wanted to impose "Franco's legacy" in the Federal Republic.[143]

The attack on redemptive republicans continued unabated. Although the likes of Sontheimer and Löwenthal were critical of Helmut Schelsky, they would have probably concurred with his following judgment:

The so-called Frankfurt School was certainly not an association for class war in academic garb, but it had class war effects. The speech norms that authors like Adorno, Habermas, and Marcuse formulated and that have been taken up by countless authorized and unauthorized students, and employed in the intellectual class war, have been used for anything but "domination-free discussion"; on the contrary, they have been used to choke sober [*sachlich*] discussion, and to further group power. That this was not the intention of the authors, that in particular it could never be an issue to these academic teachers in their academic seminars because they opposed such speech and argumentation abuses in their 'ex cathedra' statements, cannot hide the fact that this domination-intended communication cessation was done in their name.[144]

The effect of the redemptive critique, maintained neoconservatives, was to destabilize West Germany society. Some, like Schelsky, believed seriously that the students and intellectuals were a new class that possessed the cultural influence to threaten the state.[145] Others observed that the republic's

---

[141] Hermann Lübbe, "Freiheit und Terror," *Merkur*, 31 (September 1977), 819–29.

[142] Jürgen Habermas, "Probe für Volksjustiz," *Der Spiegel* (October 10, 1977), 32, reprinted in English in *New German Critique*, 12 (Fall 1977), 11–3. For a contemporary defense of the Frankfurt School, see Rolf Wiggershaus, "Die Geschichte der Frankfurter Schule," *Neue Rundschau*, 89:4 (1978), 571–86.

[143] Habermas, "Probe für Volksjustiz," 32. For a contemporary defense of the Frankfurt School, see Rolf Wiggershaus, "Die Geschichte der Frankfurter Schule," *Neue Rundschau*, 89:4 (1978), 571–86.

[144] Helmut Schelsky, *Die Arbeit tun die Anderen. Klassenkampf und Priesterherrschaft der Intellektuellen* (Opladen, 1975), 239.

[145] Helmut Schelsky, "Macht durch Sprache," *Deutsche Zeitung*, 15 (April 12, 1974), 2.

ethical substance (*Sittlichkeit*) had been seriously weakened, rendering it divided and vulnerable. Hans Maier lay somewhere between these two views. "The charge of those who want a 'new Republic' is limited for the time being," he admitted in 1972. "But the ideological potency and the determination of aggression are not to be ignored, and I must agree...that the defensive capacities are in no way greater, in fact weaker, than in the years before 1933."[146]

Sontheimer criticized Schelsky for confusing social power with intellectual influence. But this influence, he maintained, did have a negative impact. Characterizing the Bonn Republic in terms of "structural" or "objective violence," he pointed out, logically implied a utopian state of equality, the unrealizability of which issued in terrorism.[147] The analogy had unnecessarily accentuated nagging doubts about the system and had thereby destabilized its institutions. Left-wing theory that had its origins in the systemic social crisis only served to worsen it. The tragedy of leftist theory lay in the betrayal of its enlightened aims:

Its bewildering appeal for our already unstable identity consciousness lies in its attempt to realize those universal ideas that since the French Revolution have constituted the content of our enlightened political rhetoric: freedom, equality, fraternity. Yet precisely in its inability to remain faithful to them on the path to their putative implementation – in the absence of the readiness not to abandon them in the process of practically realizing the great aims – lies the dilemma of leftist theory. It breaks what it wants to bring to fullness.[148]

Habermas claimed that neoconservative intellectuals (and here he set aside the critiques of Sontheimer and Richard Löwenthal, whom, he claimed "did not set the tone")[149] considered the legitimation problems of the Federal Republic simply the result of leftist-intellectual troublemaking.[150] This may have been true of Schelsky, but it did not apply to Lübbe. Like Sontheimer, he acknowledged that behind the social crisis were systemic problems related to the pace of modernization. "Naturally the current political crisis consciousness among us and elsewhere is not groundless."[151] Consequently, he did not believe that the legitimacy crisis could be alleviated by a change of consciousness: "Such

---

[146] Hans Maier, "Die Sprache der Neuen Linken verhindert den Dialog," *Frankfurter Allgemeine Zeitung* (July 13, 1972), 8. This essay, first delivered as a speech at the "Bergedorfer Gesprächkreis" on May 29, 1972, was reprinted in many places, including in Gerd-Klaus Kaltenbrunner, ed., *Sprache und Herrschaft: Die umfunktionierten Wörter* (Munich, 1975), 55–69.

[147] Kurt Sontheimer, "Gewalt und Terror in der Politik," *Neue Rundschau*, 1 (1977), 1–12.

[148] Sontheimer, *Das Elend unserer Intellektuellen*, 278, 289.

[149] Habermas, "Neo-Conservative Cultural Criticism in the United States and West Germany," 80.

[150] Habermas, introduction, 11.

[151] Hermann Lübbe, *Endstation Terror: Rückblick auf lange Märsche* (Stuttgart, 1978), 10.

crises of consent," he wrote, "are not amenable to cure by means of decree."[152] His point, made persistently in many newspaper articles and pamphlets, was that the system managed to reproduce itself by relying on the "commonsense," unreflective basic trust of ordinary citizens in culture and institutions. Against redemptive republicans who suspected that German culture itself was the problem, Lübbe regarded its *Sittlichkeit* (customary norms) as the bulwark against totalitarianism. West Germany's systemic crisis was exacerbated when these unreflective strategies were called into question by left-wing theorists. This was the root of terrorism. "The matter is simply that the thesis of the 'simply formal' or 'repressive' character of liberal-rights-institutions has been an especially effective means of destroying the sense of political worth of a civil order and its liberal constitution, and nobody becomes a terrorist unless beforehand this sense was destroyed."[153] Like Sontheimer, he did not believe that a handful of terrorists represented any danger to the republic. But because their activities triggered a massive display of self-doubt in the consequent debate about the Republic's "fundamental values," they showed that the "cultural revolutionary" denunciation of the system had destabilizing effects.[154] As with their analysis of the student protest of the 1960s, the integrative republicans were blind to the specific German problems that led to the alienation of the redemptive republicans from Federal Republican institutions.

The "German Autumn" of 1977

For neoconservatives, living proof of the fruit of the "cultural revolution" was the leftist milieu on the campuses.[155] During the notorious fall of 1977 when numerous terrorist attacks provoked a mood of hysteria among middle-class Germans and the state took extraordinary security measures that were interpreted by many as a resurrection of authoritarianism, the campuses were targeted as the breeding ground of the so-called terrorist sympathizers. Peter Glotz estimated that about 15 to 20 percent of students (about 140, 000 to 170, 000) agreed with the student author of a notorious article who admitted he had experienced "clandestine joy" at the recent assassination of the Federal prosecutor Siegfried Buback.[156] This shared joy was evidence enough for Sontheimer and others that the left as a whole was responsible for the terrorist disaster. Sontheimer, explicitly eschewing the reductionist conclusion of positing a causal

---

[152] Hermann Lübbe, "Fortschritt als Orientierungsproblem im Spiegel politischer Gegenwartssprache," in P. G. Podewils, ed., *Tenendzwende? Zur geistigen Situation der Bundesrepublik* (Stuttgart, 1975), 20.

[153] Ibid., 8. This was also the position of Bracher, *Schlüsselwörter in der Geschichte*, 104–5.

[154] Lübbe, "Fortschritt als Orientierungsproblem," 173.

[155] Jeremy Varon, *Bringing the War Home: The Weather Underground, the Red Army Faction, and Revolutionary Violence in the Sixties and Seventies* (Berkeley, 2004).

[156] "'Jeder fünfte denkt etwa so wie Mescalero,'" 54.

nexus between leftist theory and terrorism[157] (as CDU politicians like Alfred Dregger did), made the same, more general point as Lübbe: "The political terrorism that we have since the student revolt in Germany cannot be adequately explained without the radical polarization of the student movement, without the factor of the prepared, intellectual background of leftist theory, and without the fermented weariness and unease with our political relations induced by the new critical consciousness."[158]

Habermas naturally rejected Sontheimer's Weimar analogy only to substitute it with one of his own. The *Berufsverbot* was akin to Bismarck's *Sozialistengesetz* (antisocialist laws) a century later. The only progressive element in the Republik, its intellectuals, was once again being demonized. Old authoritarian traditions were rearing their ugly heads. The real threat was not the left but the establishment, which was able to use terrorism to identify an internal enemy (the left) and thereby stifle any critique. "Only a state that makes the fascist self-understanding of Carl Schmitt its own, needs internal enemies that it can fight, as is the case with foreign enemies during war."[159] Whereas Habermas saw a "pogrom" atmosphere in the population directed against the tradition for which he had devoted his life – the German Jewish tradition of critique – Lübbe saw the population's revulsion at terrorism and contempt for redemptive republicans as the sign of a healthy *Sittlichkeit*: unlike the 1950s and 1960s, the institutions of the republic were anchored firmly in the West German population and they instinctively turned on those who threatened them.

The notorious "German autumn" of 1977 marked the high point of intellectual and political polarization in the Federal Republic. It continued into the 1980s, but, as the Historians' Dispute of the mid-1980s showed, a new alliance between redemptive leftists and liberals was still possible with which to construct a republican consensus. Yet it was not until the end of the Cold War in 1989–90, when redemptive republicans had to relinquish their plans for a socialist democracy, that a liberal republican consensus could be forged.

[157] Sontheimer was not so tactful when he was not arguing directly with Habermas. See especially his "Gewalt und Terror in der Politik," 8.
[158] Kurt Sontheimer, "Um eine Basis der Gemeinsamkeit," *Süddeutsche Zeitung* (November 26–27, 1977). This was published as part of an ongoing dialogue on the subject with Habermas.
[159] Jürgen Habermas, "Verteuflung kritischen Denkens," *Süddeutsche Zeitung* (November 26–27, 1977). For an attack on Habermas's case in this article, see Golo Mann, "Über die Denkkunst des Professors Jürgen Habermas," *Neue Rundschau*, 89:1 (1978), 142–47.

9

The Structure of Discourse in the 1980s and 1990s

So much has been written about the historical disputes of the 1980s – museum exhibitions, film, and television dramas about the Nazi past, Ronald Reagan's visit to the Bitburg war cemetery in 1985, and above all the Historians' Dispute in the middle of the decade – that there is no need to recount their well-known details.[1] The same can be said of similar disputes in the 1990s: the Goldhagen Debate and the controversies about the Exhibition of Crimes of the German Army in World War II, the intellectual assistance rendered by prominent historians to Nazi imperialism, and the Berlin Memorial to the Murdered Jews of Europe.[2] Rather than trace the supposed "development of German memory" – whatever that may mean – the next three chapters highlight the polarized terms of its underlying structure. This short chapter briefly sets out the terms of the debate and relative locations of the contending positions in the intellectual-political field in the 1980s and 1990s.

By early 1982, when the Christian Democrat Helmut Kohl became chancellor of the Federal Republic, leftist and left-liberal intellectuals had gained significant beachheads in the media, universities, school, museums – in other words, in the commanding heights of the public institutions of cultural transmission. Challenging this perceived hegemony of political correctness was a

---

[1] H. Glen Penny, "The Museum für Deutsche Geschichte and German National Identity," *Central European History*, 28 (1995), 343–72; Alon Confino, "Edgar Reitz's Heimat and German Nationhood: Film, Memory, and Understandings of the Past," *German History*, 16:2 (1984), 185–208; Geoffrey H. Hartman, ed., *Bitburg in Moral and Political Perspective* (Bloomington, 1986); Ilya Levkov, ed., *Bitburg and Beyond: Encounters in American, German, and Jewish History* (New York, 1987); Richard J. Evans, *In Hitler's Shadow: West German Historians and the Attempt to Escape from the Past* (New York, 1989); and Charles S. Maier, *The Unmasterable Past: History, Holocaust and German National Identity* (Cambridge Mass., 1988).

[2] Geoff Eley, ed., *The "Goldhagen Effect": History, Memory, Nazism – Facing the German Past* (Ann Arbor, 2000); Bill Niven, *Facing the Nazi Past: United Germany and the Legacy of the Third Reich* (London and New York, 2002); Siobhan Kattago, *Ambiguous Memory: The Nazi Past and German National Identity* (Westport, Conn., 2001).

mission of the Kohl government, which had signaled its intention to inaugu-
rate a "spiritual-moral change" (geistig-moralische Wende) in order to repair
the cultural damage of "1968." The polarized cultural-political terms of German identity were evident in the redemptive republican reaction to this conservative project. Leftist and left-liberal intellectuals, for whom Cold War and
nationalist rhetoric evoked bad memories of the 1950s and early 1960s, mobilized themselves in the 1980s against this conservative counterpolitics of memory. They did so in a spectacularly successful way in the Historians' Dispute
by agreeing with Western intellectuals that the Holocaust was a singular or
unique event, above all in relation to Stalinist crimes. In other words, with
the backing of American, English, and Israeli historians, these Non-German
German intellectuals were able to render the Holocaust an internationally recognized stigma. They became managers of this stigma by excoriating anyone
who doubted the Holocaust's uniqueness. Because so much of the public culture
reproduced this identity, Non-German Germans became attached to its institutions of cultural transmission, especially after 1990 when the (re)unification
of East and West Germany placed the national question back on the table.
The sixty-eighters were learning to trust at least parts of the society that they
had helped transform. In an interview in 1988, Habermas even admitted that
"Today there are majorities in Germany that we don't have to be afraid of."[3]
A republican value consensus around a liberal rather than socialist democratic
Germany was developing because the "Weimar syndrome" led each wing of
the intelligentsia to defend the system against the perceived threats of the
other.

The (re)unification of Germany in 1990 intensified this process because the
stakes were higher. Throughout that momentous year, Germany's neighbors
expressed anxiety about the prospect of domination by the new colossus.[4] Neo-
Nazi violence against resident foreigners and asylum seekers, and the electoral
success of right-wing parties, sparked fears of a reemergent German nationalism.[5] Paradoxically, Germany's ambivalent role during the first Gulf War a year
later provoked concern that it would abjure participation in international peace-
keeping in favor of "checkbook diplomacy" and the tending of its own garden.
Since the Maastricht Settlement of January 1992, nobody had been counting
on European integration in the near future, making it harder for German policy

---

[3] Jürgen Habermas, The New Conservatism: Cultural Criticism and the Historian's Debate, trans.
Shierry Weber Nicholsen (Cambridge, Mass., 1994), 194.
[4] Dirk Verheyen and Christian Soe, eds., The Germans and Their Neighbors (Boulder Colo., 1993);
Roland Dumas, "Angst vor den Deutschen?" Die Zeit (September 14, 1990).
[5] See, for example, "A Worry for Germany: Resurgent Nationalism," New York Times (July 27,
1991); "German Vote Raises Foreigner's Fear," New York Times (October 8, 1991); "When Will
Germany Draw the Line?" Times (London) (November 24, 1992); Colloquium, "The Growth
of Aggressive Nationalism: Foreigners and Anti-Foreigner Attitudes in Germany," German Historical Institute, Washington, D.C., February 5, 1993, convened by Hartmut Keil and Dietmar
Schirmer.

makers to pursue the common European good as an end of German foreign policy.[6]

In the context of nationalist revivals in Central and Eastern Europe, commentators began to talk about the "return to the nation-state" as the paradigm of international relations. Above all, there was a growing appreciation in Germany and Europe of the enormous importance of what was decided in Bonn (and eventually Berlin) for the "common European house." The German question was far more important in the 1990s than it was during the 1980s. With its population of almost 80 million, its dynamic economy, and its strategic position in the center of Europe, some even suggested that Germany was the third most potent nation in the world.[7] Not for nothing did the former chancellor Helmut Schmidt remind Germans on the day of their reunification that "the question about our own understanding of our future role will not be asked just in Dresden but throughout Europe."[8]

It followed that the two great questions of German national identity were: how would it use its great power status (i.e., foreign policy), and who would be permitted to belong to the German nation-state (i.e., citizenship)? These were the two sides of the national identity coin. They caused as much tension in Germany as trepidation in Europe. Nor did a consensus exist in the political class about the future of the country. In answering these questions, certain interpretations of the national past were thought to inform particular national identities, as Ernst Nolte noted at the time: "The question of German history is fundamental for the question of identity. But 'history' is not a viewable entity; rather it is present only in specific forms that we call paradigms, of which only a limited number exist. From each paradigm follow different judgments about German history and, with that, different concepts of German identity."[9]

Books hit the streets with titles like *Which History Should We Choose?*, indicating how conscious Germans were of their history's pervasive hold on the present and significance for the future.[10] And, as usual, memory of the Holocaust and the Nazi regime framed the debate. Left-liberals asserted that Germany's "Western," liberal political culture was inextricably tied to its consciousness of responsibility for Auschwitz. To diminish this memory or to relativize the singularity of the Holocaust threatened this painfully won political "normality" of the 1980s. Conservatives retorted that the memory had become a dogma and a taboo that amounted to destructive collective obsession with

---

[6] A good example of this problem was the dispute with Great Britain in late 1993 over the negative impact of German monetary policy on the value of the pound.

[7] Fritz Stern, "Freedom and Its Discontents," *Foreign Affairs*, 72 (September–October), 108–23; Christoph Bertram, "Der Riese, der ein Zwerg sein möchte," *Die Zeit* (April 26, 1991).

[8] Helmut Schmidt, "Deutschlands grosse Chance," *Die Zeit* (October 3, 1990).

[9] Ernst Nolte, "Identität und Wiedervereinigung," *Die Politische Meinung*, 277 (December 1992), 37.

[10] Antonia Grunenberg, ed., *Welche Geschichte wählen wir?* (Hamburg, 1992).

guilt and that prevented the development of a "normal" national identity like that of "Western" powers. The question of Auschwitz that lay at the heart of the spiteful Historians' Dispute was yet to be resolved. The dilemma that determined the structure of postwar German subjectivity and memory was best articulated by the historian Saul Friedlander: "The Nazi past is too massive to be forgotten, and too repellent to be integrated into the 'normal' narrative of memory."[11] This dilemma was now more acute than ever because Germany was expected to perform the international responsibilities of any "normal" nation-state – indeed, to lead the reconstruction of Central and Eastern Europe – while continuing to acknowledge responsibility for its disastrous history.

An Ethnic Nation

Non-German German's intense anxiety about the conservative identity project is explicable only when that project's ethnically nationalist basis is fully appreciated. Kohl's policy of "spiritual moral change" was the culmination of some ten years of reaction to the cultural transformations wrought by the sixty-eighter generation. By the mid-1970s, commentators in Germany identified a mood shift in the German population that became known as the *Tendenzwende* (ideological change of current). They interpreted the growing preoccupation with local history, museums, memorials, the renovation of villages and the medieval areas of cities, neighborhood festivals, and even the growing ecological consciousness as disillusionment with the promises of progress. The concept of *Heimat* once again became a popular metaphor to describe the desire for feelings of rootedness and the thirst for memory.[12] Conservatives had become excited, regarding the disenchantment with social aspirations as a confirmation that men and women did not live by bread alone, as the "materialistic" Social Democrats believed. The moment was ripe to rehabilitate the vocabulary of national transcendence not heard for decades – the language of *Vaterland*, *Volk*, and nation.[13]

This reinvocation of traditional German political language was not the simple rearticulation of an unconscious conservatism that had survived on the margins in its original instinctive, pre-1960s form. It was rather, much as Karl

---

[11] Saul Friedlander, "Some German Struggles with Memory," in Geoffrey H. Hartmann, ed., *Bitburg in Moral and Political Perspective* (Bloomington, 1986), 27.

[12] "Heimat – unter grüner Flagge," *Der Spiegel* (July 23, 1979), 134–36; Wilfried von Bredow and Hans-Friedrich Foltin, *Zweispältige Zufluchten. Zur Renaissance des Heimatgefühls* (Berlin, 1981); Gerhard Paul and Bernhard Schossig, eds., *Die andere Geschichte* (Cologne, 1986). One perspicacious observer called these desires "Der Griff nach der Vergangenheit" (The Grasp for History), Werner Weidenfeld, "Geschichte und Politik," in Werner Weidenfeld, ed., *Geschichtsbewusstsein der Deutschen* (Cologne, 1987), 7.

[13] Bruno Heck, foreword to Klaus Weigelt, ed., *Heimat und Nation. Zur Geschichte und Identität der Deutschen* (Mainz, 1984), 9–14.

Mannheim wrote in relation to the conservative romantics of the early nineteenth century,[14] traditionalism raised to the level of reflection by ideological challenge, systematized, and then employed by a political party – in this case, the CDU – in a rescue operation of those virtues, habits of mind, and, above all, the strong national identity that it regarded as essential for the German character. Conservatives were not so much enjoining a continuation of tradition as its revival, not a heightening of historical consciousness as its rehabilitation, not just a greater love of nation but its restoration as the principle source of personal and collective orientation.

For conservatives, attachment to the cultural nation was simultaneously the source of the unanimity and those virtues that the Federal Republic now needed to overcome its bitter domestic divisions, especially those occasioned by the peace movement, which was seen as the culmination of 1960s and 1970s leftism. An influential conservative historian of the day, Michael Stürmer, even went so far as to argue that "The pluralism of values and interests, when they no longer share a common ground, nor can find one, and when they are not mitigated due to the assumption of [Nazi] guilt, will sooner or later lead to a social civil war, like at the end of the Weimar Republic."[15] Leading CDU right-winger Alfred Dregger announced before the Bundestag that Germany needed a revival of those Prussian virtues that had forged prosperity from the ashes of defeat in the 1950s and early 1960s – duty, hard work, self-sacrifice for the common good, and responsibility before God and Man. Without them, democracy and freedom, particularly in view of the communist threat, could not survive. Democracy must be nationalized to be able to reproduce itself.[16] The real caesura in recent German history was not 1945 but 1968, after which radical professors and the new universities corrupted a generation of youth.[17]

As we see in Chapter 11, one of the battlefronts for the conservatives was historical consciousness. Stürmer, who took time off from his University of Erlangen professorship to work directly for Kohl, even referred to this "ideological battle" as a *Historikerstreit* a full three years before the eruption of the public dispute of that name in 1986.[18] His target was the *Sonderweg* (special path) thesis of the Social-Democratic-oriented Bielefeld School of historians that

---

[14] Karl Mannheim, "Conservative Thought," in his *Essays on Sociology and Social Psychology* (London, 1953), 115. I am not arguing that 1980s neoconservatism was the same as that of the early nineteenth century. Rather, I am drawing on Mannheim's description of how a conservative ideology can be mobilized.

[15] Michael Stürmer, "Kein Eigentum der Deutschen: die deutsche Frage," in Werner Weidenfeld, ed., *Die Identität der Deutschen* (Munich, 1983), 84.

[16] Alfred Dregger, "Rede vor dem Deutschen Bundestag," in *Texte zur Deutschlandpolitik*, 3rd ser., vol. 1, October 13, 1982–December 30, 1983 (Federal Ministry for Inter-German Relations), 168.

[17] Ludolf Herrmann, "Hitler, Bonn und die Wende: Wie die Bundesrepublik ihre Lebenskraft zurückgewinnen kann," *Die Politische Meinung*, 28 (July–August 1983), 17.

[18] Michael Stürmer, "Kein Eigentum der Deutschen: die deutsche Frage," in Weidenfeld, *Die Identität der Deutschen*, 84.

accounted for Germany's catastrophic twentieth-century experience by arguing that the nation's development had deviated from the Anglo-American norm of modernization, and that German normality – the attainment of liberal, capitalist democracy – had been achieved only during the postwar era in the decisive break with those antidemocratic and illiberal German traditions that had hitherto held the nation back. This view, which stigmatized the German history as abnormal, was challenged from a number of quarters, but in particular by the conservative historians on the grounds that its political meaning, as they saw it, wrote-off the entirety of prewar German history as saying that "all roads led to Hitler."[19]

Conservative policy was no less nationalist in relation to immigration and citizenship. "Germany is not an immigration country,"[20] announced Kohl indignantly in February 1991 in response to criticism of his country's citizenship laws and the violence against foreigners. As might be expected, this statement provoked considerable protest from the government's opponents. After all, had not the Federal Republic been an immigration country since its foundation? Twelve million refugees and expellees from Central and Eastern Europe settled in the country after the war. And could one not refer to the 5 million foreign workers and their families who live permanently in Germany as immigrants? And what about the status of those nonethnic German refugees who had been granted asylum?[21]

Germany was not an immigrant nation, Kohl and his supporters maintained, because the postwar refugees and expellees were ethnic Germans (*Volksdeutsche*), as were the more than 1 million Germans (*Aussiedler*) who had come to the Federal Republic since emigration from communist countries was liberalized in the late 1980s. Classical immigration meant, they argued, inviting foreign nationals to settle within one's own national community in order to add to its evolving culture as well as contribute to its economic life. Such an aim bespoke a fundamentally different self-understanding from countries with historically established cultures such as Germany. Foreigners (*Ausländer*) who found their way into Germany and who satisfied the required criteria could join this objectively given, finished culture.

The bearers of traditional, German nationalism and conservatism in postwar Germany were the well-organized associations of Germans who were expelled or fled westward after the war from their long-time *Heimats* in the former eastern German territories and elsewhere in Central and Eastern Europe. As the Parliamentary State Secretary Ottfried Hennig put it in June 1983, they

---

[19] Andreas Hillgruber, *Die Last der Nation* (Düsseldorf, 1984); Michael Stürmer, "Die Deutsche Frage als europäisches Problem"; Weigelt, *Heimat und Nation*, 286–302; Dregger, "Rede vor dem Deutschen Bundestag," 171.

[20] Helmut Kohl quoted in *The Week in Germany*, 1 (February 1991), 1.

[21] Klaus Bade, ed., *Deutsche im Ausland – Fremde in Deutschland: Migration in Geschichte und Gegenwart* (Munich, 1992); Bade, *Vom Auswanderungsland zum Einwanderungsland: Deutschland, 1880–1980* (Berlin, 1983); Heiner Geissler, ed., *Ausländer in Deutschland: Für eine gemeinsame Zukunft*, vol. 2 (Munich, 1982).

"understand themselves ... as islands of rescued *Heimat*."[22] In 1987 they composed about 20 percent of the West German population.[23] Prewar identities were kept alive in these tight-knit circles, which defined the nation in relation to a special temporality. Time was experienced spatially unlike with progressives, for whom the present was the beginning of the future. For the expellees, by contrast, the present was only the latest point reached by the past rather than the springboard for the future and its possibilities of normative change.[24] The legacy of the past was the German cultural nation into which they were born, and with which they felt themselves entrusted to perpetuate. To identify oneself in the objectively given cultural transmission process was to be a member of the 1,000-year-old German nation, the source not only of one's identity but also of many of Europe's most enduring cultural achievements.

Ardent conservatives held Poland up as the great example of the nation that survived long partition. Some of the more ardent CDU leaders referred to the GDR as "Middle Germany" and the lost eastern territories (e.g., East Prussia, Silesia) as "Eastern Germany."[25] That the German Democratic and German Federal Republics would eventually be reunited was apparently of existential importance for many conservatives. Kohl himself said, "Without this historical posture, without memory ... we could not live."[26] Another put it this way: the division of Germany meant that he was a "divided German."[27]

Conservatives opposed multiculturalism because they insisted that states existed as ethnic nation-states. Multinational states had existed, to be sure, but they were burst asunder by the political aspirations of the nationalities within them. All the trouble spots around the world – in Ireland, Turkey, Lebanon, Spain, Sri Lanka, and elsewhere were evidence for the inherent instability of multicultural societies. Germany ought not to import its own nationality problem by facilitating the growth and consolidation of foreign ethnic communities within its borders.[28] The direct personal experience of the German expellees, of course, confirmed this view.

[22] Ottfried Hennig, "Verpflichtung zur Bewahrung der Einheit der deutschen Kultur," in *Texte zur Deutschlandpolitik*, 3rd ser., vol. 1, October 13, 1982–December 30, 1983 (Federal Ministry for Inter-German Relations), 107–16, 109; On the expellees, see Marion Frantzioch, *Die Vertriebenen: Hemmnisse und Wege ihrer Integration* (Berlin, 1987).

[23] Gerhard Reichling, "Deportation, Flucht und Verteibung in Zahlen," in Marion Frantzioch et al., eds., *40 Jahre Arbeit fuer Deutschland – die Vertriebenen und Flüchtlinge* (Frankfurt, 1989), 33.

[24] Mannheim, "Conservative Thought," 111–12.

[25] Dregger, *Freiheit in Unserer Zeit* (Munich, 1980), 83; Helmut Kohl, "Innerdeutsche Beziehungen und Geschichtsbewusstsein," *Texte zur Deutschlandpolitik*, 3rd ser., vol. 3, *January 1, 1985–December 30, 1985* (Federal Ministry for Inter-German Relations), 539.

[26] Helmut Kohl, *Zwischen Ideologie und Pragmatismus* (Stuttgart, 1973), 47.

[27] Alexander Demandt "Geschehene und Ungeschehene Geschichte. Historische Perspektiven zur deutschen Frage," *Die Politische Meinung*, 30 (May–June 1985), 23.

[28] See the comments of Dr. Olderog (CDU) in *Verhandlungen des Deutschen Bundestages*, 11 Wahlperiode, 88 Sitzung, June 24, 1988, 6048; Edwin Faul, "Gegen die Multikulturisten," *Die Politische Meinung*, 268 (March 1992), 9.

There were a number of basic assumptions that the redemptive republicans targeted in their response: the world was divided into cultural nations, and everyone was born into one;[29] cultures and nations were fixed in space;[30] they were nurtured and formed in a particular environment, and consequently memory of Germany's historical eastern lands should not be forgotten; and the Federal Republic should act as a representative and home state of all dispersed and oppressed Germans in Central and Eastern Europe, just as Israel did for oppressed Jews.[31]

A Multicultural Society?

If the consciousness of larger national unity was a priority, then protecting the national character at home was as well. In a remarkable article of 1980, the secretary-general of the German Red Cross, Jürgen Schilling, declared that the hope of German unity was being dissipated by the growing presence of foreign workers and their families, who were ethnically dividing the two Germanys and who enfeebled the will of West Germans to overcome the barriers with their eastern brothers and sisters.[32] He was referring to the so-called guest workers and their families who had been actively recruited by German governments in Mediterranean countries between the mid-1950s and early 1970s and who were not, as anticipated, returning to their countries of origin. In fact, despite, and perhaps because of the end of their recruitment in 1973, those who remained commenced building tight-knit communities and, with the declining German birthrate, began to increase as a proportion of the population. In the late 1970s and early 1980s, it became clear that Germany was to have a permanent and perhaps growing foreign (i.e., non–Northern European) population of at least 4 million people.[33]

Germany's citizenship laws, which dated (with amendments) from 1913, did not make their naturalization very easy. Turks and other *Ausländer* could become citizens only through a demanding process requiring, among other things, ten years' residence, after which its conferral was still discretionary. Their German-born children, who numbered some 2 million, did not receive automatic citizen rights and also had to endure this process.[34] Attaining

---

[29] Dregger, for example, spoke of Europe as a *Völkerfamilie*: "Heimat, Vaterland, Europa," in his *Einigkeit und Recht and Freiheit* (Munich, 1993), 125–37.

[30] Hennig, "Verpflichtung zur Bewahrung Einheit der deutschen Kultur," 112.

[31] Dregger, "Rede vor dem Deutschen Bundestag," 167; "Im Jahr 2000 ein türkischer Kanzler," *Der Spiegel* (February 13, 1989), 26.

[32] Jürgen Schilling, "Einwanderung und Staatsidee," *Deutschland Archiv*, 12 (February 1980), 158.

[33] Hermann Korte, "Guestworker Question or Immigration Issue? Social Sciences and Public Debate in the Federal Republic of Germany," in Klaus Bade, ed., *Population, Labour and Migration in 19th- and 20th-Century Germany* (Leamington Spa, 1987), 163–88.

[34] Barbara John, "Wer ist ein Deutscher?" *Neue Gesellschaft/Frankfurter Hefte* (October 1990), 890.

citizenship was supposed to be difficult because it represented more than just the right to participate in the political affairs of the state. It meant becoming German. Concessions in citizenship, it was argued, would encourage only the partial assimilation of *Ausländer* communities because they could enjoy many political rights without needing to make an irrevocable commitment to Germany. It would only encourage the consolidation of ethnic minority group identities in Germany, and thereby perhaps pose a threat to domestic harmony some time in the future. As CDU politician Herr Dr. Olderog told the *Bundestag* in arguing against a liberalization of the citizenship law, "ethnic, religious, and cultural 'closed-ness' [*Geschlossenheit*] facilitates the foundational consensus of a people. Ethnic minorities and religious and cultural differences create tensions that all too often lead to explosive situations and bloody conflicts, which then add to the flow of refugees."[35] As another conservative commentator put it, "we cannot allow German citizenship to simply fall in their laps."[36]

The situation was quite different with the *Aussiedler*.[37] The 1953 law relating to postwar refugees and expellees was still in force, and under it the *Aussiedler* were granted citizenship as members of the cultural nation. Many could not speak German, said the government's opponents, particularly the Greens, who accused it of employing racial criteria in its citizenship laws.[38] As the joke went, What is the difference between a Turkish Berliner and an *Aussiedler*? The former can speak German.[39] It was true that some had lost the German language, replied the government, but only because they had been culturally oppressed in the lands whence they came. They were owed a moral obligation of respite because they suffered for their nationality after the war far more than Germans in the West.[40] Germans should "open our hearts and doors" to them, as the government advertisement put it. Germans were enjoined to "celebrate" the return of their putative countrymen and women.[41] In any case, they were easily integrated into the country, as the experience of the 12 million postwar refugees and expellees showed. Unlike other refugees, they came as Germans to be German, not as those in search of a materially better life.[42] So, unlike *Ausländer*, *Aussiedler* could be trusted with dual citizenship.

Accordingly, it was possible to discern three limbs to the CDU's citizenship policy since it came to power in coalition with the liberal Free Democrats in

---

[35] In *Verhandlungen des Deutschen Bundestages*, 88 Sitzung, 6048.
[36] Ludolf Herrmann, "Hoffnung Statt Getto," *Die Politische Meinung*, 27 (November–December 1982), 51.
[37] For an excellent introduction, see Klaus J. Bade, ed., *Neue Heimat im Westen. Vertriebene, Flüchtlinger, Aussiedler* (Münster, 1990), and Siegfried Schwab, *Deutsche unter Deutschen: Aus- und Übersiedler in der Bundesrepublik* (Pfaffenweiler 1990).
[38] See *Verhandlungen des Deutschen Bundestages*, 11 Wahlperiode, 102 Sitzung, October 26, 1988, 7007–8.
[39] John, "Wer ist ein Deutscher?" 888.
[40] See comments of CDU speakers in the Bundestag debate on the matter. *Verhandlungen des Deutschen Bundestages*, 102 Sitzung, October 26, 1988, 7003–19.
[41] Thomas Darnstaedt, "Deutsches Blut, fremde Folter," *Der Spiegel* (November 7, 1988), 123.
[42] Faul, "Gegen die Multikulturisten," 8.

1982:[43] first, to retard the increase of the local *Ausländer* population from their countries of origin by making family reunions more difficult; second, to encourage those who want to return home to do so through financial incentives;[44] and, third, to accept that some accidental "immigration" had taken place in the case of the guest workers and therefore to assimilate them as far as possible into the life of the nation. These measures were necessary, explained the then minister for the interior Franz Zimmerman, to "preserve German national character."[45]

In the explanation of his administration's aims in the Bundestag in October 1983, Kohl, who had always sympathized with the expellees and refugees, committed himself to realizing the preamble of the Basic Law – the reunification of the entire, that is, prewar, German nation, in a free, democratic state. This aim meant thwarting the development of an incipient Federal republican identity that had been growing during the 1970s, particularly among the young.[46] "I have no wish to become a Federal Republican," announced former CDU party secretary and East Prussian expellee Rainer Barzel defiantly.[47] Kohl agreed that West Germany always had to be seen as a provisional state. The citizens' loyalty should be gained by its teleological representative function for the entire cultural nation, rather than as an end in itself.[48]

In the next chapter, we see how redemptive republicans reacted to the ambitious identity project of integrative republicans.

[43] For a good summary, see Jürgen Fijalkowski, "Nationale Identität versus multikulturelle Gesellschaft. Entwicklungen der Problemlage und Alternativen der Orientierung in der politischen Kultur der Bundesrepublik in den 80er Jahren," in Werner Süß, ed., *Die Bundesrepublik in den achtziger Jahren* (Opladen, 1991), 235–52.

[44] Heiko Körner, "Das Gesetz zur Förderung der Rückkehrbereitschaft von Ausländern vom 28. November 1983 – Eine kritische Bilanz," in Heiko Körner and Ursula Mehrländer, eds., *Die "Neue" Ausländerpolitik in Europa: Erfahrungen in den Aufnahme-und Entsendeländern* (Bonn, 1986), 65–73.

[45] "Zuwanderung von Ausländern abwehren," *Der Spiegel* (April 18, 1988), 23; Dr. Kappes (CDU) told the Bundestag that: "I don't distance myself from the proposition that the maintenance of national identity is a legitimate goal of every people"; *Verhandlungen des Deutschen Bundestages*, 88 Sitzung, 6053–54.

[46] As Gebhard Schweigler put in 1984, "West Germans are increasingly losing their all-German national consciousness and developing a strictly West German one instead"; *West German Foreign Policy: The Domestic Context*, Washington Papers, vol. 12, no. 106 (New York, 1984), 45.

[47] In Clay Clemens, *Reluctant Realists. The Christian Democrats and West German Ostpolitik* (Durham, 1989), 248.

[48] Kohl, *Zwischen Ideologie und Pragmatismus*, 44.

10

History, Multiculturalism, and the Non-German German

The leftist intellectuals and many left-liberals were by no means overjoyed by German (re)unification. Some were offended by "capitalist" triumphalism and dismayed that a democratic socialist "third way" was not given a chance after November 1989. Others were more perturbed by what they saw as the one-sided nature of the unification process in which the East Germans were treated more as objects of West German policy than as equal partners in a common project.[1] A shared fear of all left-of-center intellectuals in the Federal Republic was that the new order would provide an impetus for a revision of the nascent Non-German German consensus that they and others had forged in the 1980s.[2] The fear of a resurgent conservatism after 1990 led redemptive republicans to emphasize continuities with the political culture of the old Federal Republic while confirming their distrust of large sections of the population – in particular, East Germans who had not been exposed to West Germany's postnational culture. The attempt to produce a population of Non-German Germans was redoubled. But what kind of relationship with the memory of the Holocaust's victims did such an identity imply? This question is taken up in the last section of this chapter.

---

[1] Günter Grass, *Two States – One Nation?*, trans. K. Winston and A. S. Wensinger (San Diego, 1991); Grass, "Wider den Einheitsstaat," in Ulrich Wickert, ed., *Angst vor Deutschland* (Hamburg, 1990), 61–72. For a critique of left-wing intellectuals' reactions to reunification, see Lewis H. Gann, "German Unification and the Left-Wing Intelligentsia: A Response," *German Studies Review*, 15 (February 1992), 99–110. See also Klaus Hartung, "Wieder das alte Denken," *Die Zeit* (May 10, 1991); Klaus Hartung, "Wieder den Linken Alarmismus," *Die Zeit* (November 20, 1992); Helmuth Kiesel, "Die Intellektuellen und die deutsche Einheit," *Die Politische Meinung*, 264 (1991), 49–62; Alison Lewis, "Unity Begins Together: Analyzing the Trauma of German Unification," *New German Critique*, 64 (Winter, 1995), 135–59.

[2] Jürgen Habermas, "Die andere Zerstörung der Vernunft," *Die Zeit* (May 10, 1990); Volker Ulrich, "Die Neue Dreistigkeit," *Die Zeit* (October 20, 1992).

Reinscribing Stigma

Twenty years after it had started as the critical revisionism of the 1960s, the Non-German German interpretation of nineteenth- and twentieth-century German history had gained substantial ground, at least in public discourse.[3] The historians and social theorists who were then at the forefront of challenging conventional wisdom and forging a critical, social-scientific understanding of German society and its past took pains to ensure that the gains of the past quarter century were not wiped away. In a series of articles in the liberal weekly *Die Zeit*, a number of them reinscribed a stigmatized interpretation of German history by restating the various versions of the *Sonderweg* thesis for public consumption.[4]

In his account of the tortuous development of the German state since 1871, Heinrich August Winkler reminded his readers of the traditional obstacles to liberal democratic development – the nationalism and anti-Catholicism of the Prussian liberals, the transition of the national ideal from the left to the right, and the persistent suspicion of Social Democrats and Roman Catholics into the Weimar period when the nation considered that its will was distorted by parliamentary institutions. So the Nazis replaced them with a system that reflected the true will of the people: a plebiscitary-legitimated *Führerstaat* (state of dictatorial leadership). Germany was the only highly industrialized country that, during the Depression, rejected its democratic system in favor of a totalitarian one. This *Sonderweg* was inexplicable without the long tradition of authoritarian government and delayed democratization. In a forthright reply to his English critics teaching at American universities, he wrote: "To be sure, there is no 'normal' development to liberal democracy, and in that sense all history is a history of *Sonderwege*. But upon reflection on the German development, one may add that this *Sonderweg* is more special than the others." The deep rupture of 1945 explained, to a large extent, why Bonn has not become Weimar.[5]

The historian Jürgen Kocka concurred, warning that the new eastern states were more German than those in the west, and therefore its citizens had not undergone the learning processes of West Germans. Would their admixture to the population change the nation's Western political culture? Reunification should be thought of more as an opportunity to extend the

---

[3] For postwar developments in German historiography, see Georg G. Iggers, *The Social History of Politics: Critical Perspectives in West German Historical Writing* (Leamington, Spa, 1985); Hans-Ulrich Wehler, "Historiography in Germany Today," in Jürgen Habermas, ed., *Observations on the Spiritual Situation of the Age* (Cambridge Mass., 1984), 221–59; Volker R. Berghahn, "Die Fischer-Kontroverse – 15 Jahre danach," *Geschichte und Gesellschaft*, 6 (1980), 403–19.

[4] These historians have many differences with leftist literary figures like Günter Grass and Heiner Müller. However, in their assessment of German history and the lessons it taught, they were in broad agreement.

[5] Heinrich August Winkler, "Mit Skepsis zur Einigung," *Die Zeit* (September 28, 1990). The principal document of British criticism of the *Sonderweg* thesis is David Blackbourn and Geoff Eley, *The Peculiarities of German History* (Oxford, 1984). See also leading *Sonderweg* thesis proponent Hans-Ulrich Wehler, "Wider den falschen Apostel," *Die Zeit* (November 9, 1990).

pluralistic-democratic system to hitherto dictatorially ruled parts of Germany than as the rehabilitation of the German nation-state. The 1990 merger was no convergence of, or compromise between, east and west. The new Federal Republic had to be the continuation of its Western-oriented predecessor.[6] The stigma, so cultivated in West Germany, had to persist.

The principal Non-German German voice was that of Jürgen Habermas. Since the 1980s, above all, during the Historians' Debate and unification discussions in the early 1990s, Habermas attacked conservative memory politics that he saw running counter to his postnational philosophy of history and the lessons of Auschwitz. His redemptive German philosophy of history now took the following form. The central event of modernity was the French Revolution because it actualized a new principle of sovereignty, the nation rather than the dynastic monarch. This historical progress brought its own problems because the "nation" – hitherto the appellation for a prepolitical ethnic community – became the defining term of citizenship within the state. At the same time, the "nation-state" provided the legal forum for its democratization, although this process occurred at the expense of ethnic minorities because a "sovereign people" presupposed a common will and therefore a homogeneous population. From its inception, then, the nation-state contained the contradictory principles of the prepolitical attachment to particular ethnic and cultural life forms (which restricts full membership to its own), and the universalistic implications of a democratic constitutionalism (which conceives of the nation as a community of citizens, that is, citizenship is conferred on those who consent to certain procedures and processes of government irrespective of their ethnic or cultural background).[7]

The historical process in Western Europe since the French Revolution, Habermas continued, has been constituted by the untangling of these contradictory ideas of the nation. The German problem was that this process had been retarded: ever since the so-called Wars of Liberation, the nationalist principle had dominated the democratic one. National Socialism was the ultimate apotheosis of the nation conceived in prepolitical, racial terms. Germany was able to develop into a *staatsbürgerliche* (civic) community only after experiencing a radical caesura with its past in 1945, by abandoning the romantic tradition with its anti-Semitism, obscurantism, and national narcissism for the universalism of the Western Enlightenment.[8] Indeed, the conclusion that Habermas drew from Auschwitz was "that the Germans have forfeited the right to base their political identity on grounds other than the universal principles of citizenship in whose light national traditions are no longer unscrutinized but are appropriated only critically and self-critically."[9] Since the Holocaust, Germans could

---

[6] Jürgen Kocka, "Nur keinen neuen Sonderweg," *Die Zeit* (October 19, 1990).

[7] Jürgen Habermas, "Citizenship and National Identity: Some Reflections on the Future of Europe," *Praxis International*, 12:1 (1992), 2–3.

[8] Jürgen Habermas, *Die nachholende Revolution* (Frankfurt, 1990), 99, 162.

[9] Ibid., 220; Habermas, "Historical Consciousness and Post-Traditional Identity," in his *The New Conservatism: Cultural Criticism and the Historians' Debate*, trans. Shierry Weber Nicholsen

not "rely on the continuities of history" for national orientation.[10] The identity they should retain – a constitutional patriotism – was one that registered ambivalence toward every tradition. The constitutional patriot's reading of the past was necessarily critical, he or she appropriating those traditions consistent with democratic constitutionalism.[11] Only a constitutional patriotism, with its renunciation of the German *Sonderweg* – that is, with a stigmatized identity – could ensure the country's continued attachment to the Western community of values. And such a patriotism could be secured only by placing consciousness of Auschwitz at the center of collective identity because it was the thorn in the flesh that provokes critical reflection and dissolution of the collective "we."[12]

To be effectively normal for redemptive republicans, it was imperative to consolidate the critical culture that broke through with the Historians' Dispute, the controversy that embedded the proposition in public culture that the Holocaust is unique. Jürgen Kocka expressed this position in 1988 with his paradoxical formulation that, "This break [from German tradition] stands at the center of our [Federal Republican] tradition."[13] The problem with (re)unification in 1990, he and Habermas feared, was that it threatened to undermine this nascent culture of contrition that Non-German Germans had developed in the Federal Republic. He was referring to the antinationalism that had emerged in West Germany since the 1950s, which had culminated in the country as a "civilian power" and "human rights society" committed to demilitarization and multilateralism.[14]

The lesson that these Non-German Germans drew from the past was that German nationalism, however tempered, was in the long term incompatible with European peace. The nation's size and economic power would eventually

(Cambridge, Mass., 1994), 259: "Every identity that establishes membership in a collectivity and that defines the set of situations in which those belonging to the collectivity can say 'we' in the emphatic sense seems to be part of an unquestioned background that necessarily remains untouched by reflection."

[10] Jürgen Habermas, "Der DM Nationalismus," *Die Zeit* (March 30, 1990); Habermas, "Die zweite Lebenslüge der Bundesrepublik: wir sind wieder 'normal' geworden," *Die Zeit* (December 11, 1992); Habermas, "Historical Consciousness and Post-Traditional Identity," 255. For commentary on Habermas and unification, see Howard Williams, Catherine Bishop, and Colin Wright, "German (Re)unification: Habermas and His Critics," *German Politics*, 5:2 (1996), 214–39.

[11] Jürgen Habermas, "On the Public Use of History: The Official Self-Understanding of the Federal Republic Is Breaking Up," in *Forever in the Shadow of Hitler? The Original Documents of the Historikerstreit*, trans. James Knowlton and Truett Cates (Atlantic Heights, N.J., 1993), 166.

[12] Jürgen Habermas, "A Kind of Settlement of Damages: The Apologetic Tendencies in German History Writing," in ibid., 43; Habermas, "Historical Consciousness and Post-Traditional Identity," 264.

[13] Jürgen Kocka, "Deutsche Identität und historischer Vergleich: Nach dem 'Historikerstreit,'" *Aus Politik und Zeitgeschichte*, 40–41 (September 30, 1988), 28.

[14] Habermas, *Die nachholende Revolution*, 159, 215; Hanns W. Maull, "Germany and Japan: The New Civilian Powers," *Foreign Affairs*, 69:5 (1990–91), 91–106; Hans Karl Rupp, *Politik nach Auschwitz: Ausgangspunkte, Konflikte, Konsens* (Münster, 2005), 5. See also Timothy Garton Ash, *In Europe's Name: Germany and the Divided Continent* (London, 1994).

manifest itself in military terms. Should an unproblematic relationship to the past develop, they feared, it would only be a matter of time before the old German policies reemerge.[15] Here the left-liberals curiously seemed to agree with conservatives in arguing that Germany's geopolitical circumstances were the decisive factor in determining its *Spielraum* (room to maneuver) as a nation-state. In contradistinction to intellectuals on the right, however, their answer was that Germany must *self-consciously* abandon the nation-state rather than rehabilitate a more sober version. "Our goal must be first, to overcome the nation-state – in all of Europe. The hope of the future does not lie in nation-states; not in the compromiseless representations of particular self-assertions, nor in the vain jockeying for national profiles. It lies in combination and cooperation, in the progressive abandonment of national sovereignty to supranational institutions in common issues."[16]

It was up to Germany to continue taking the lead in the new style of diplomacy based on socioeconomic achievement, cooperative security and peacemaking, rather than power politics and military coercion. The new paradigm of international relations must be the merging and identification of national interests with the collective goals of allies and partners in international organizations. European nation-states would become absorbed into the United States of Europe for which Germany must strive. The older nation-states, France, England and the United States, were certainly not models to follow. German consciousness must become European consciousness, Non-German Germans insisted. The country had been leading the continent in this direction for some time; it must not revert to the bad old ways. The success of "the policy of the good example," as it was termed by former foreign minister Genscher, and the degree of European integration even led one sympathetic scholar to go so far to as to suggest that "in many ways it no longer makes sense to talk about Germany as a distinct national unit."[17] To this extent, Non-German Germans gave up on the nation-state as a constructive vehicle for individual and collective human aspirations and as a source of orientation. It was too small to effectively address large issues and too large to solve small ones.[18] Germans had learned that their national consciousness was particularly dangerous. Overcoming the paradigm of the nation-state was all that prevented it from becoming a danger to itself and its neighbors. Indeed, history had appointed Germany to lead Europe to a postnational consciousness and a united and fully integrated Europe.

---

[15] Theo Sommer, "Keine Sehnsucht nach Stahlgewittern," *Die Zeit* (August 31, 1990); Peter Glotz, "Wieder den Feuilleton-Nationalismus," *Die Zeit* (April 19, 1990). Eberhard Jaeckel's reading of European history led him to much the same conclusions. See his essay "Deutschland zwischen Geschichte und Zukunft," in Hartmut Wasse, ed., *Deutschland in der internationalen Politik* (Weingarten, 1992), 87–103.

[16] Sommer, "Keine Sehnsucht nach Stahlgewittern."

[17] Maull, "Germany and Japan," 105; Maull, "Zivilmacht Bundesrepublik Deutschland. Vierzehn Thesen für eine neue deutsche Aussenpolitik," *Europa Archiv*, 10 (1992), 269–78.

[18] Jürgen Habermas, "Gelähmte Politik," *Der Spiegel* (July 12, 1993), 54.

From this perspective, it was entirely logical, although not without some irony, that Germany possessed a special mediating role in Central and Eastern Europe to protect Western values from the West, especially from the Americans. A vision of a German-led, neutral, united, and democratic socialist Central Europe had been articulated by sections of the German left since the early postwar years. Unilateral disarmament and the ending of the NATO and the Warsaw Pact security alliances were advocated as a prelude to German and European unification. As one perspicacious commentator observed, "To be a good European once meant to favor the integration of the West. By the 1980s, it meant to call for a reunited continent."[19] Accordingly, Europe must move beyond the divisive paradigm of the nation-state. Germany, in particular, could not rehabilitate its nation-state, "but must overcome it in Europe" (i.e., the European Community).[20]

Habermas's views characterized the leftist intelligentsia generally. The writer Günter Grass famously pronounced that Auschwitz had disqualified Germany from having a united nation-state, while the Social Democratic chancellor candidate Oskar Lafontaine said that such an ideal was historically superseded.[21] Social Democrats agreed. The politician and editor of *Die Neue Gesellschaft/Frankfurter Hefte*, Peter Glotz, and editor of *Die Zeit*, Theo Sommer, both based their recommendations for "overcoming the nation-state" foursquare on Habermas's intellectual edifice. For Glotz, Sommer, and other leftist intellectuals, "the West" had a double meaning. On the one hand, it was a synonym for the universalism of the Enlightenment that they saw themselves as defending. On the other hand, it referred to the *Western powers*, the imperialist, capitalist nations of whom Germany should be as suspicious as they were of the communist powers to the east. As Glotz made clear in his analysis of communism's demise: "The West has won. But will 'Western values' win, too?"[22] Far from the Federal Republic becoming more like the Western powers, its postnational consciousness must be hailed as a step in the direction of overcoming the nation-state.[23] Sommer denounced the "fictitious community of values" of the Western powers because they hypocritically supported the dictators Salazar in Portugal and Papadopolous in Greece. Preferable is the "real, universal community of values evidenced in the East during the revolutionary year of 1989."

Habermas put such anxieties in historical context. Fearing the return of a distinct consciousness of Mitteleuropa that viewed the years 1917 to 1989 as an abnormal era of world wars and the Nazi period as merely one episode among

[19] H. Stuart Hughes, *Sophisticated Rebels: The Political Culture of European Dissent, 1968–1987* (Cambridge Mass., 1988), 150.

[20] Theo Sommer, "Unser nunmehr fertiges Vaterland," *Die Zeit* (June 29, 1990).

[21] Jochen Fischer and Hans Karl Rupp, "Deutsche Vereinigung und NS-Vergangenheit," *Aus Politik und Zeitgeschichte*, 40 (2005), 41.

[22] Peter Glotz, "Europa nach der Revolution," *Aus Politik und Zeitgeschichte* (January 31, 1992), 52.

[23] Glotz, "Wieder den Feuilleton-Nationalismus."

others, he invited Germans to believe that the former Federal Republic's history had more in common with Italy, France, and the United States than the former German Democratic Republic. "Their [East Germany's] history is not our History."[24] What mattered was the universalist political principles of democratic constitutionalism, not the prepolitical bonds of ethnicity or culture. For this reason, he viewed German (re)unification in 1990 as an exercise in extending liberal democracy and civil rights to unfree lands rather than politically realizing "the pre-political unity of a community with a shared common historical destiny."[25] A standard leftist argument during the 1980s, therefore, had been excising the preamble from the Basic Law that posited the Federal Republic as a provisional state pending the political unification of the entire German people.[26] An ethnic German identity, stigmatized by its association with Nazism, needed to be dissolved in a new, multicultural Non-German Germany.

Multiculturalism for a Postnational Germany

The fantasy of a Non-German Germany drove the leftist discussion of immigration and multiculturalism in the 1990s. Redemptive republicans like Habermas argued for a purely *ahistorical political* identity. Once Germans had realized the criminality of their history, political consciousness could only be procedural, enabling a tolerant pluralism of other, non-German cultures. "[This identity] exists *only* in the method of the public, discursive battle around the interpretation of a constitutional patriotism, which must be concretized in particular historical circumstances."[27] The influx of ethnic Germans from Eastern Europe after 1990 was therefore a problem: the "repressed feeling that Germany is becoming more German has a paralyzing effect."[28] The less German Germany became, the better.

Such intellectuals advanced two arguments against a national basis for political identity, one pragmatic, the other normative. First, the objective situation obtaining in Europe would not allow it: the continued immigration of needed labor, and the continued influx of refugees from the east and southeast ensured that no country would be homogeneous. All countries had and would continue to contain a variety of minorities. Nation-states, resting as they did on the myth of cultural homogeneity, were a political ideal of the past. The only possible policy was that of a culturally neutral state.[29] Trouble spots of ethnic conflict, often cited by conservatives as an argument against immigration and multiculturalism, were not evidence of the inevitable struggle for cultural mixing but

---

[24] Jürgen Habermas, "Die andere Zerstörung der Vernunft," *Die Zeit* (May 10, 1990).
[25] Habermas, "Citizenship and National Identity," 2–3.
[26] Micha Brumlik, "Patriotismus, Verfassung und verdrängte Geschichte. Diskussion zwischen Micha Brumlik und Hermann Lübbe," *Neue Gesellschaft/Frankfurter Hefte* (May 1989), 409.
[27] Habermas, "Der DM Nationalismus" (emphasis added).
[28] Habermas, "Gelähmte Politik," 54. Curiously, this quotation does not appear in the English translation of this essay: "Afterword (May 1993)," in Habermas, *The Past as Future*, 143–65.
[29] Theo Sommer, "Europa zwischen Mythen und Zeiten," *Die Zeit* (January 1, 1993).

the results of assimilationist ambitions by one or the other of the groups in a state.[30] The German definition of its nation-state – as originating in the pre-political concept of *Volk* – meant that the nation-state must be abandoned.[31] Detaching national identity from citizenship would pry open German society and prevent its citizens from becoming "wolves."[32] The age of the nation-state was being replaced by regional and supranational allegiances. As Peter Glotz put it, "the future of Europe lies in guaranteed communal rights for minorities, in open borders, and manifold, regionally specific cultures."[33] Others urged the establishment of Swiss-style multiculturalism forthwith.[34]

The second reason was couched in terms of normative political theory. It held that because the principles of democratic constitutionalism and human rights enshrined by the Basic Law possessed a universal potential, the nexus between cultural and political nation was necessarily unstable. The state was not in fact the political manifestation of a *Volk* but was established according to universally acceptable norms of common life. The state therefore should not privilege one cultural life form over another. Its aim was simply to help civil society reproduce itself rather than protect, nurture, and foster the prepolitical ethnic-cultural community that may have originally established the state. As the realm of spontaneous, self-interested activity, civil society would be regulated by laws to which all could assent – this was its universalistic dimension – and that allowed a high degree of cultural autonomy. In the political process, citizens likewise would be required only to commit themselves to institutions that embodied universally legitimate processes of procedural justice, rather than the historical destiny of the German people.[35]

This much was clear: only the universalistic political cultural dimensions of any particular culture (i.e., German) possessed a claim on immigrants or resident foreigners. The state was a guarantor of a liberal democratic political culture to which all were committed. Different communities were free to pursue their own ends.[36] "Germanness" was only one of many cultures and ought not receive privileged status, even within Germany.[37] To this extent, immigrants would have to accustom themselves to democratic ways and eschew any cultural practices inconsistent with individual autonomy and dignity. That is, they would have to pledge allegiance to the constitution – hence the term constitutional

---

[30] Daniel Cohn-Bendit and Thomas Schmid, *Heimat Babylon: Das Wagnis der multikulturellen Demokratie* (Hamburg, 1992), 318.

[31] Peter Glotz, *Der Irrweg des Nationalstaats* (Stuttgart, 1990), 10; Cohn-Bendit and Schmid, *Heimat Babylon*, 321; Habermas, "Citizenship and National Identity."

[32] Cohn-Bendit and Schmid, *Heimat Bablyon*, 321.

[33] Peter Glotz, "Das Multikulturelle Abandland," in Michael Kloecker and Udo Tworuschka, eds., *Miteinander – Was Sonst? Multikulturelle Gesellschaft im Brennpunkt* (Cologne, 1990), 68.

[34] Heiner Geissler, "Die Multikulturelle Gesellschaft," in Heiner Geissler, *Zugluft: Politik in stürmischer Zeit* (Munich, 1990), 177–218.

[35] Jürgen Habermas, "Die Festung Europa und das neue Deutschland," *Die Zeit* (June 4, 1993).

[36] Habermas, "Citizenship and National Identity," 7, 17.

[37] Ibid., 17.

patriotism. But a society had the right to demand only political integration, not cultural assimilation. It was not permissible to require *Ausländer* (foreigners) to abandon their previous history and subjectivities in order to become members of their new host community.[38] It was intolerable, redemptive republicans argued, that about 6 million people were shut out of the political process, most of whom had lived in the country for more than ten years, and many of whom were born there. German laws asked too much in return for citizenship. They should be asked to join the political community, not the cultural one. Moreover, what they required of the immigrants was also demanded of the native Germans, who needed to radically change their understanding of what it meant to be German. Germany was no longer a nation, with all the historical orientation that the term entailed, but a *demokratischer Rechtsstaat* (democratic state of laws).

A Non-Identity Identity

For all that, Habermas was well aware that Germans could not cut themselves off from the national past even though the Federal Republic marked a radically new and positive departure in German history. Although not directly culpable of the Nazi misdeeds, Germans could not wash their hands of the past with the excuse of their "late birth" used by Chancellor Helmut Kohl. Much like Karl Japsers's argument in *The Question of German Guilt*, Habermas thought they were collectively liable for what happened by the prepolitical bonds of history and culture:

Our own life is linked to the life context in which Auschwitz was possible not by contingent circumstances but intrinsically. Our form of life is connected with that of our parents and grandparents through a web of familial, local, political, and intellectual traditions that is difficult to disentangle – that is, through a historical milieu that made us what and who we are today. None of us can escape this milieu, because our identities, both as individuals and as Germans, are indissolubly interwoven with it.[39]

There was a glaring contradiction in his approach, symptomatic of the impossibility for the Non-German German subjectivity to be conceived in isolation from the society it sought to transform. On the one hand, Habermas asked Germans to remember their continuing responsibility for Auschwitz, which meant demanding that they understood themselves historically as a prepolitical national community. But, on the other, he was insisting that Germans should understand themselves politically as an ahistorical, democratically self-willed, political collective. Alternatively: Germans were held responsible (guilty?) for the Holocaust because of their national-family connections, but they were forbidden to experience other (positive?) national feelings and ascribe political relevance to them. Not for nothing did the political scientist Walter Reese-Schäfer point out that such a paradoxical anti/post-nationalism contained a religious

---

[38] Cohn-Bendit and Schmid, *Heimat Babylon*, chap. 1.
[39] Jürgen Habermas, "On the Public Use of History," in *The New Conservatism*, 233.

dimension. Habermas wanted to maintain national consciousness (i.e., belonging to descendants of perpetrators) as the occasion for its political enervation and eventual disappearance in postnational consciousness. Proscribing national feelings as a form of historical punishment – a permanent hair shirt – made sense only to those for whom the nation mattered.[40]

To be sure, Habermas linked national and postnational consciousness by arguing that Auschwitz reminded Germans that they could not build their political identity on the former, but who or what was the "we" that was supposed to do the remembering in the long run? The community of penance was bound to disappear with the multicultural future he envisaged for Germany. Then what? Germany would be populated by people(s) who bore no affective or effective relationship to the past commemorated in camps and monuments around the country.[41] Ultimately, Habermas's was an entreaty for the self-liquidation of the German nation via critical self-reflection and immigration in the same way as the Non-Jewish Jew would mean the end of the Jewish people if all Jews adopted this identity.[42] After all, the Palestinian intellectual Edward Said claimed that he was "the last Jewish intellectual."[43] Like the Non-Jewish Jew, then, the Non-German German subjectivity was predicated on the continuity of the nation or people it wanted to transform. National life was transmitted by those with national identity. That is the contradiction in the postnational perspective.

The rage that Habermas felt against the stubborn self-pity of his compatriots, which had alienated him from German nationality as a youth after the war, was shared by his friends, the psychoanalysts Alexander and Margarethe Mitscherlich. In their famous 1967 book, *The Inability to Mourn*, they told Germans that the "guilt feelings at the horrors that were committed, at murder on a scale which we can only know objectively, but are incapable of re-enacting in our imagination, can no more be eliminated from the German unconscious awareness than can the shame of having lost face as a civilized nation."[44] But the Mitscherliches were not simply reminding Germans of their pariah status

---

[40] Walter Reese-Schäfer, "Universalismus, negativer Nationalismus und die neue Einheit der Deutschen," in Petra Braitling and Walter Reese-Schäfer, eds., *Universalismus, negativer Nationalismus und die neue Einheit der Deutschen* (Frankfurt, 1991), 39–54.

[41] Turkish German authors disclaim feeling part of the German coming to terms with the past and enjoin a less ritualized comportment to the past that excludes them. See Leslie A. Adelson, "The Turkish Turn in Contemporary German Literature and Memory," *Germanic Review*, 77: 4 (2004), 326–38.

[42] See Jürgen Habermas, *Theory of Communicative Action*, vol. 2, trans. Thomas McCarthy (Boston, 1987), 77, where he argues that the "linguistification of the sacred" entails making "symbolically mediated to normatively guided action." In the national context, this means that the prepolitical bonds of ethnicity are supplanted by the communicative community of those committed to the procedures of constitutionally secured political deliberation.

[43] Said is quoted in Ari Shavit, "My Right of Return," *Ha'aretz* (August 18, 2000). Cited in Ephraim Nimni, "Wada'an to a Jewish Palestinian," *Theory and Event*, 7:2 (2004).

[44] Alexander Mitscherlich and Margarete Mitscherlich, *The Inability to Mourn – Principles of Collective Behavior*, trans. Beverley R. Placzek (New York, 1975), 65–66.

in the eyes of the world. Their solution to overcoming the "ideals of the Nazi regime" was to cultivate a radical sense of guilt by internalizing the trauma of its victims: "We Germans should extend our introspection so that we can at least recognize ourselves in such scenes as that of the German officer in the Danish café, and those appalling occasions when one hundred, five hundred, or one thousand bodies lay in front of us, bodies of people we had killed." They continued that "This would imply a compassionate and poignant acknowledgement of the victims long after the time of horror."[45]

In fact, it implied the eventual dissolution of the German group self. For if the Holocaust was the unprecedented evil and trauma the Non-German German claimed, how could it be bearable, let alone compatible with the continuity of the German self deemed responsible for its commission? That is a question that Habermas neither posed nor answered. Instead, he wrote that Germans should say "'never again' to ourselves," and embrace the Holocaust as an "element of a broken national identity" that is "branded [*eingebrannt*] as a persistent disturbance and warning."[46] This notion was taken a step further by Habermas's younger colleagues Hajo Funke and Dietrich Neuhaus, who went so far as to say that "a German identity after 'Auschwitz' can only be a NONIDENTITY."[47] Habermas's unconscious historical fantasy, then, was not only the end of Germany as a nation-state but also the end of the German people as a "community of destiny" (*Schicksalsgemeinschaft*), a hope shared by German Jewish intellectuals as well.[48]

Sacrifice and Redemption

To turn the moral disadvantage of this nonidentity into a moral advantage, the Non-German German had to represent himself or herself as untypically German to the international public. This transformation necessarily enlisted the victims of the Holocaust into a historical drama in which their murder by the Nazis became the occasion for the founding moment of a new polity and a new German subjectivity. The only way by which to remember the murdered Jews of Europe for such an identity is a sacrificial one. Remembering the Holocaust redeems those Germans prepared to identify with the victims rather than the perpetrators. By seeking forgiveness from the world public sphere and demonstrating that they have atoned for the Holocaust and changed for the better, these Germans cast Jews in the role of the sacrificed Jesus in a secularized

---

[45] Ibid., 67.
[46] Jürgen Habermas, "Der Zeigefinger: Die Deutschen und ihr Denkmal," *Die Zeit* (March 31, 1999).
[47] Hajo Funke and Dietrich Neuhaus, "Einleitung: Nationalismus, Antisemitismus, Demokratie – Beobachtungen zu einem gespannten Dreieckverhältnis," in Hajo Funke and Dietrich Neuhaus, eds., *Auf dem Weg zur Nation? Über deutsche Identität nach Auschwitz* (Frankfurt, 1989), 8 (capitalization in original).
[48] Dan Diner, "Nation, Migration, and Memory: On Historical Concepts of Citizenship," *Constellations*, 4:3 (1998), 305.

christomimesis, only now the Christ killers are not the Jews but the Nazis.[49] Such Germans have left their sinful selves behind and walk in grace.

Of course, Non-German Germans do not regard themselves as having killed the Jews so that a redeemed Germany could be born. The chronological unfolding of the Holocaust is inconsistent with the redemptive logic of this modality of German remembrance. Yet despite this temporal aporia, this memory is based on a substitutionary theology in which the Jews were killed so that a new Germany can be born. For Non-German Germans, the Berlin memorial thus works as stigmata, the divine sign of grace and of Jesus's sacrifice, rather than as a stigma, a source of shame. Moreover, the sinful but repentant community needs to keep resacrificing the Jews in regular, national rituals in the same way as Christians regularly celebrate the Eucharist. The memory of the murdered Jews thereby serves as a permanent resource for collective regeneration. So where Christians are redeemed by identifying with the sacrifice of Jesus rather than with the figure of Pilate or the ancient Jews who called for his execution – the so-called Christ killers who have been the staple of anti-Jewish prejudice through the ages – the post-Holocaust German community is redeemed by remembering the death of the Jews and excoriating their killers, the Nazis. The sacrifice is, in the words of Bruce Lincoln, a "transformative negation" because one entity is given up for the benefit of another.[50]

The link between the victims of the Holocaust and the crucified Jesus has recurred in postwar Germany. Eugon Kogon used a poem of Werner Bergengruen that makes this equation in his famous book, *Der SS-Staat*.[51] And it is made by the premier intellectual who defended the Berlin memorial, Jürgen Habermas, who referred to the crucifixion scene depicted in the famous Isenheim altarpiece by Matthias Grünewald (c. 1513–15). Jesus is on the cross, at his feet is the lamb holding a cross, the symbol of the sacrifice for humanity's sins, and John stands behind the lamb, Bible in hand, pointing to Jesus. Habermas explained its contemporary meaning for Germans. "The pointed finger of a [Holocaust] museum or memorial pedagogy is different than that of John in the altar picture of Matthias Grünewald."[52] Germans were not being collectively accused because John is not pointing at those who executed Jesus but at Jesus himself. Germans need not feel the memorial is an embodiment

---

[49] Giesen notes the elements of christomimesis in the German and indeed developing international "politics of apology," but does not identify the sacrificial object in the contemporary German case, namely, Jews: Giesen, "The Trauma of the Perpetrators," in Jeffrey C. Alexander et al., *Cultural Trauma and Collective Identity* (Berkeley, 2004), 133, 147. For notions of "Jews on the Cross," see David Roskies, *Against the Apocalypse: Responses to Catastrophe in Modern Jewish Culture* (Cambridge, 1984), 258. I am indebted to the theologian Greg Zuschlag for insights into Christian theories of atonement.

[50] Bruce Lincoln, *Death, War, and Sacrifice: Studies in Ideology and Practice*, foreword by Wendy Doniger (Chicago and London, 1991), 204.

[51] Eugen Kogon, *Der SS-Staat* (Falkenhaus, Taunus, 1946). For commentary, see Y. Michael Bodemann, "Eclipse of Memory: German Representations of Auschwitz in the Early Postwar Period," *New German Critique*, 75 (Autumn 1998), 65.

[52] Habermas, "Der Zeigefinger."

of their disgrace, a *Schandmal*, as Hohmann and Augstein contended. Rather, Germans could build a tolerant, diverse – that is, less German – society if they identified with the Jews of the Holocaust in the same way as Christians identified with the victimized Jesus. The U.S.-based German historian Michael Geyer also entreated Germans to regard the Holocaust in this manner.

> What do Germans need (now that it is entirely in their hands), in view of the war and genocide they caused, in order to live with themselves and the world in the future? That is the problem of self-realization in historical consciousness today. My response is that this renewal of civilization requires a national history that in the historical reflection on war and annihilation will do justice to the need for self-recognition among later generations.

German memory had to make the murdered Jews the center of its historical consciousness; "remembrance of the dead" was essential for its social transformation.[53] Like the Zionist interpretation of the meaning of Israel's foundation, Germany was moving from destruction to rebirth.[54]

This enlistment of the Holocaust had social consequences because sacrifice is an exchange between a deity and sacrificer, and communication between sacred and profane, as Henri Hubert and Marcel Mauss pointed out in their ground-breaking essay on the subject in 1898.[55] Like their contemporary Emile Durkheim, with whom they collaborated, Hubert and Mauss saw society as the hidden God to whom sacrifice was made. Not only was the sacrificer transported momentarily into a sacred realm, but social solidarity was fostered by the sacralization of altruistic, communal norms that transcended the egoistical interests of the bourgeois self. This line of argument was continued by the sociologist of religion Hans Mol who regarded religion as sacralized identity. By objectifying the sacred into a system of symbols, focusing emotional attachments on this system through sacrifice, and institutionalizing the sacred in rituals and rites, collective identities were anchored and lent a sacred aura.[56]

Discursive taboos – which are identifiable when questions are prohibited and cannot be answered by rational argument – accompany such a sacralized identity.[57] Since the Historians' Dispute, an important taboo in Non-German German circles had been to compare Nazi and communist crimes. Those who

---

[53] Michael Geyer, "The Place of the Second World War in German Memory and History," *New German Critique*, 71 (Spring–Summer, 1997), 10.

[54] Dalia Ofer, "The Strength of Remembrance: Commemorating the Holocaust during the First Decade of Israel," *Jewish Social Studies*, 6:2 (2000), 24–55.

[55] Marcel Mauss and Henri Hubert, *Sacrifice: Its Nature and Function* (Chicago, 1964). For skepticism on the notion of a unitary concept of sacrifice, see Marcel Detienne, "Culinary Practices and the Spirit of Sacrifice," in Marcel Detienne and Jean-Pierre Vernant, eds., *The Cuisine of Sacrifice among the Ancient Greeks*, ed. and trans. Paula Wissing (Chicago, 1989), 1–20.

[56] Hans Mol, *Identity and the Sacred* (Oxford 1976), 206–46. Mol also stipulates myth and theology as the fourth element of sacralization, but notes that they are less common in modern societies.

[57] Jeffrey K. Olick and Daniel Levy, "Collective Memory and Cultural Constraint: Holocaust Myth and Rationality in German Politics," *American Sociological Review*, 62:6 (1997), 921–36.

did, like Ernst Nolte, were effectively purged from much of intellectual life, and even became stigmatized persons. To be accused of arguing "like Nolte" became a knockout putdown in sections of the German intelligentsia in the mid-1980s. This taboo was challenged from the outset by conservative writers but later also from within leftist circles in the debate about the *Black Book of Communism*, which appeared in Europe in 1998.[58] Thus the editor of the *taz* newspaper Stephen Reinecke mocked the Marxist historian Wolfgang Wipperman's "prayer-wheel-like" insistence that the Holocaust was unique compared to Stalinist crimes.[59] Another leftist journalist Reinhard Mohr decried the "taboo guards" protecting the record of communist regimes, while Social Democratic historian Heinrich August Winkler, who moved away from his earlier skepticism of reunification, also said the time had come to end the taboo on associating communism and fascism.[60]

All three critics also noted how the taboo sacralized a certain type of anti-German identity. The Holocaust was used for the "negative creation of meaning" (*Sinnstiftung*), Reinecke observed in an article tellingly entitled "Don't Touch My Holocaust."[61] Winkler followed him in ascribing the prohibition on comparison to the left's "negative nationalism," which he thought was "no less pseudoreligious than 'real' nationalism."[62] For Mohr, the taboo was part of a "catechism" of the "leftist petit-bourgeois" (*linken deutschen Spießers*): "The only remaining issue we are dealing with is the sulking intellectual ego, the very last stage of a gradually fading, inner-worldly redemptive religion: the negative utopia of *Furor teutonicus*."[63]

But who was the god to whom Non-German Germans were making a sacrifice? It was the world public sphere whose recognition of a nonstigmatized identity they sought. The variety of sacrificial practices worldwide, however, indicated that they need not be directed to a god; they could also be addressed to ancestors. The impulse to engage in expiatiation – to propitiate gods or ancestors – derived from the need to conceal from the community the fact that its existence was based on a founding act of violence that needed to be commuted and ascribed to another source. This concealing function of sacrifice was likewise evident in Germany. Non-German Germans could believe that the Jews died for "our" sins because they no longer identified with the "perpetrator generation," their own ancestors.[64] Political emotions and political theology were enmeshed to release religious-like energies of identity reconstruction enabled by

---

[58] Stefan Courtois, ed., *The Black Book of Communism: Crimes, Terror, Repression*, trans. Jonathan Murphy and Mark Kramer (Cambridge, Mass., 1999).

[59] Stefan Reinecke, "Don't touch my Holocaust," *taz* (June 25, 1998).

[60] Reinhard Mohr, "Die Wirklichkeit ausgepfiffen," *Der Spiegel* (June 29, 1998), 176–77; Heinrich August Winkler, "Lesarten der Sühne," *Der Spiegel* (December 24, 1998), 180–81.

[61] Reinecke, "Don't touch my Holocaust."

[62] Winkler, "Lesarten der Sühne," 181.

[63] Mohr, "Die Wirklichkeit ausgepfiffen."

[64] Katharina Vester, "Reducing the Holocaust to 200,000 Square Feet of Cement," *Jewish Bulletin of Northern California* (October 21, 2005).

the hyperidentification with the terrible fate of the Jews. The sacrificial modality of memory inhered in the fact that it concealed from Non-German Germans that they were effectively engaging in a form of ancestor worship – the murdered Jews become their functional ancestors. And the ancestors – and Jews today – were bidden to accept the sacrifice and sanctify the sacrificer.

The proposition that Non-German Germans made victims of the Holocaust their ancestors is supported by Freud's commentary in his *Moses and Monotheism*. After the Israelites murdered Moses, they reverted to their old polytheistic religion until finally turning to Moses' monotheism. The perpetrator collective experienced a trauma of its own, but it was only much later, when the descendants of the killers realized what their ancestors had done. They responded by devoting themselves to Moses' law.[65] In fact, this train of events can be rendered in sacrificial terms. Because the sacralization process takes time to unfold, a sacrificial rendering of events may occur only generations later, as was the case with Jesus's execution.[66] Certainly, the sacrificial memorialization of the murdered took more than forty years to develop in West Germany, and it has produced a new self in a regenerated and sanctified Non-German German community committed to human rights. The German participation in NATO's attacks on Serbia in Kosovo in 1999 was justified by reference to Auschwitz.[67]

Ancestor worship entailing veneration and homage was linked to yet another dimension of sacrifice: the consumption of the offering. It is with a certain bewilderment that foreign observers of Germany note "a sort of Jewish chic among non-Jewish Germans that manifests itself in the massive proliferation of klezmer bands featuring non-Jewish Germans as producers and consumers to a degree that exists nowhere else in the world, including the United States and Israel."[68] These energies were also evident in efforts to revive Jewish culture in Germany, an exemplary act of anamnesis like the Eucharist for Christians. Just as Christ is re-presented to the community of believers so it may be redeemed, so German culture after the Holocaust was supposed to be regenerated after its moral bankruptcy by re-presenting the Jewish body in regular public commemorative rituals. Thus former foreign minister Joschka Fischer saw the redemption of Germany in the revival of Jewish life there. It was all the more necessary to ensure that Jews could live in safety in Germany again. Germany today

---

[65] Richard Bernstein, *Freud and the Legacy of Moses* (Cambridge, 1998); Cathy Caruth, ed., *Trauma: Explorations in Memory* (Baltimore and London, 1995), 153; Jan Assmann, "Tagtraumdeutung," *Frankfurter Allgemeine Zeitung* (July 1, 1999), 48. As Dominick LaCapra puts it: "an event becomes traumatic retrospectively when it is recalled as a later event." See his "History and Psychoanalysis," in his *Soundings in Critical Theory* (Ithaca, N.Y., 1989), 35.

[66] Mol, *Identity and the Sacred*, 243.

[67] Christine Achinger, "Evoking and Revoking Auschwitz: Kosovo, Remembrance and German Identity," in Ronit Lentin, ed., *Re-Presenting the Shoah for the Twenty-first Century* (New York and Oxford, 2004), 227–52; Frank Schirrmacher, ed., *Der westliche Kreuzzug: 41 Positionen zum Kosovo-Krieg* (Stuttgart, 1999).

[68] Andrei S. Markovits, "A New (or Perhaps Revived) 'Uninhibitedness' toward Jews in Germany," *Jewish Political Studies Review*, 18 (2006), 1–2, viewed at www.jcpa/phas/phas-markovits-s06.htm. See details at Peck, *Being Jewish in the New Germany*.

possessed a "second chance" for the German-Jewish symbiosis even if the return of Jewish soul to Germany was impossible. "Today there is once again Jewish life in Germany and this is certainly one of the most important victories won over Hitler and National Socialism."[69]

The community was regenerated not only by expiation but also by cleansing. Anyone who reminded Non-German Germans of their inescapable membership of the perpetrator collective disturbed the sacrificial logic of their identity and had to be expelled. Whereas for the Nazis the Jews were stigmatized and considered unclean by polluting German blood, for Non-German Germans it was the former Nazis and nationalists who were stigmatized and who contaminated the new republic. Whereas the Jews were sacrificed by Nazis after 1933 so that Germany could be reborn, afterward Germany could emerge phoenix-like from the ashes of another defeat by its ritual purification through cathartic expulsion or banishment of ex- and neo-Nazis and garden-variety nationalists who did not share their view of Holocaust memory. René Girard was right to identify the purgative function of sacrificial rites; they enable communal purification by casting out defiling elements. He was wrong in claiming that modern societies were unstable because they no longer possessed sacrificial rites: Germany certainly did.[70]

Consider the case of the speaker of the West German Bundestag Philip Jenninger, who in 1988 was forced to resign his post after delivering what was considered a taboo-breaking speech on the fiftieth anniversary of the November 9, 1938, pogrom. Rather than focus on the suffering of the Jews, he attempted to explain (though not excuse) the racist behavior of his compatriots, thereby distinguishing clearly between "we Germans" and Jews in contemporary Germany. Many of the Green and Social Democratic deputies of the sixty-eighter generation felt increasingly uncomfortable during the speech and even left the chamber in protest. When the dust settled after Jenninger tendered his resignation and his speech was read in the cold light of day, many wondered what the fuss had been about. Jenninger's ideas were based on the latest research but had been delivered in such a clumsy manner that he was interpreted as sympathizing with the anti-Semitic views he was explaining. For some, he was seen as having

---

[69] To be sure, Fischer regards this as a Sisyphean project: "Yet we sense there is something irreparably broken, a gap that can never be filled"; Joschka Fischer, "A Second Chance? Germany and the Jewish Community Today," speech at the annual meeting of the American Jewish Committee (May 3, 2001), Washington, D.C., www.germany-info/relanch/politics/speeches/050301. html, viewed January 15, 2005; *Spiegel* Forum with Joschka Fischer and Heinrich August Winkler, "How Normal Is Germany," *Spiegel Online International* (May 2, 2005), http://www. spiegel.de/international/spiegel/0,1518,354746,00.html, viewed January 15, 2005; speech by Federal Foreign Minister Joschka Fischer on the occasion of receiving the Leo Baeck Award, Berlin (May 10, 2005), http://www.auswaertiges-amt.de/www/en/ausgabe_archiv?archiv_id= 7193, viewed January 15, 2005.

[70] René Girard, *Violence and the Sacred*, trans. Patrick Gregory (Baltimore, 1997). Drawing on Girard, La Capra sees a sacrificial dimension in scapegoating and victimization of minorities treated as impurities or contaminations. LaCapra, *Representing the Holocaust: History, Theory, Trauma* (Ithaca, 1994), 172.

broken a taboo, but actually he had not properly played his priestly role in the sacrificial drama. In fact, he had reversed its meaning by reminding the younger parliamentarians that they were still members of a stigmatized people rather than of a redeemed community.[71] Observers of the leftist scene, like the writer Peter Schneider, were not blind to the purgatory logic inherent in the constitution of its nonstigmatized identity. "A cathartic exercise takes place: a competition for the true, the most radical antifascism in which the victor is awarded the crown of innocence. The best way of achieving a clear conscience is to detect elements of fascist ideas in others. The way to avoid accusations of misusing the Auschwitz is to accuse others of misusing it."[72]

The rage against the "perpetrator generation" and the stigmatized collective self it bequeathed younger leftists was split off and projected onto others who represented "bad" Germans and the sinful nation, which acted as reservoirs or containers that served as enduring objects of scorn.[73] This mechanism of projective identification allowed Non-German Germans simultaneously to disavow their own national selves and excoriated the national selves of their compatriots, while converting the stigma into stigmata. Once again, Bauman's observations of the social psychological pressures on German Jews in relation to immigrants from the east in late nineteenth century Germany could have been made about Non-German Germans.

They would forever remain on guard against those hidden aspects or their own selves which they now regarded as outmoded, disgraceful, and therefore shameful. And they would be eager to displace, project, and exteriorize again the harrowing experience of ambivalence: they would forever obsessively scrutinize and censure other bearers of the hereditary stigma they wished to obliterate.[74]

As the anthropologist Victor Turner observed of the social purpose of sacrifice, it is an important means of unblocking the "great circulation of thoughts, feelings and goods," because it destroys "that part of the self which impedes the flow" in an act of "social surgery."[75] Reversing this type of surgery was the aim of German Germans, as we see in the next chapter.

---

[71] Elisabeth Domansky, "'Kristallnacht,' the Holocaust and German Unity: The Meaning of November 9 as an Anniversary in Germany," *History and Memory*, 4 (1992), 60–94.

[72] Peter Scheider, *Vom Ende der Gewißheit* (Reinbeck bei Hamburg, 1994), 117, quoted in Christian Jennerich, "Discomfort, Violence, and Guilt," *Debatte*, 8:1 (2000), 62; Domansky, "'Kristallnacht,' the Holocaust and German Unity," 76–77.

[73] For the Kleinian background for this conclusion, see Marcelo M. Suarez-Orozco and Antonius C. G. M. Robben, "Interdisciplinary Perspectives on Violence and Trauma," in Marcelo M. Suarez-Orozco and Antonius C. G. M. Robben, eds., *Cultures under Siege: Collective Violence and Trauma* (Cambridge, 2000), 28–31; and Robert M. Young, "Psychoanalysis, Terrorism, and Fundamentalism," *Psychodynamic Practice*, 9:3 (2003), 307–24.

[74] Zygmunt Bauman, *Modernity and Ambivalence* (Oxford, 1991), 135. I am not suggesting any other parallels between these two cases.

[75] Victor Turner, "Sacrifice as Quintessential Process: Prophylaxis or Abandonment?" *History of Religions*, 16:3 (1977), 207.

11

German Germans and the Old Nation

The persistence of national-oriented German Germans is not difficult to fathom: they did not wish to endure a nonidentity. Most people are not intellectuals or educators for whom daily reflection on the meaning of the Nazi past constitutes their habitus. Moreover, populist journalists and politicians defend the population's intuitive national identity against Non-German German efforts to promote the national stigma and consequent transformative culture of contrition. Until the 1980s, they still denounced those who dredged up the past as *Nestbeschmutzer* (foulers of the nest) – those who defecate on and thereby pollute the family and nation.[1] The problem for conservatives was that the national ideal had been stigmatized by its association with National Socialism. The issue was how to separate them. Some argued that the Nazis abused and perverted the idea of the nation,[2] while others contended that the two concepts were in fact unrelated. National Socialism's biological puritanism was a twentieth-century concept dialectally united in its supranational aims with its mortal enemy – the international class war of Bolshevik Russia. The idea of the nation had no necessary unsavory implications, and National Socialism had no specific German roots. Moreover, conservatives continued, the Nazi phenomenon possessed no metahistorical significance but was explicable in terms of the pressures brought to bear on Germany during the Weimar Republic. And German history had trajectories that reached beyond the twelve dark years of Nazi rule.[3] The point was not to judge the crimes by moral criteria today but to understand how people could have legitimated them at the time.[4] German history, conservatives concluded, was not irredeemably contaminated. There was

[1] Ira Brenner, "On Confronting Truth about the Third Reich," *Mind and Human Interaction*, 2 (1991), 97.
[2] Bruno Heck, *Auf festem Grund* (Stuttgart, 1977), 11.
[3] A good discussion of this problem is in Konrad Jarausch, "Removing the Nazi Stain? The Quarrel of the German Historians," *German Studies Review*, 11 (May 1988), 293–97.
[4] Hermann Lübbe in "Patriotismus, Verfassung und verdrängte Geschichte. Diskussion zwischen Micha Brumlik und Hermann Lübbe," *Neue Gesellschaft/Frankfurter Hefte* (May 1989), 415.

no reason why it could not provide the same unifying point of reference once provided by religion.[5] Such strategies permitted Germans to feel good about, or at least not crippled by, their national identity despite the insistence that it was stigmatized. Germans could trust their traditions, integrative republicans told them. But what was the cost of such displacements?

Rejecting Stigma

The conservative interpretation of German history represented the other half of the rigidly symmetrical German approach to its collective memory. The project of conservative historians throughout the 1980s was to destigmatize the national past. Indeed, it was Ernst Nolte's reinterpretation of the Holocaust through its comparison with other acts of genocide that, with Habermas's vigorous rebuttal, inaugurated the first *Historikerstreit*. Habermas sensed concerted revisionist apologetics in the effort of some German historians and the well-known Kohl agenda to revivify the German self-image.[6] Such suspicions seemed plausible in view of the presence on the chancellor's personal staff of Michael Stürmer, the conservative Erlangen historian. His call in 1986 for German historical writing that balanced the needs of national orientation and the demythologizing of the past did not gel well with the political smell of his admission that "in a land without history, the future is controlled by those who determine the content of memory, who coin concepts and interpret the past."[7]

The German government's perceived vacillation in response to the first Gulf War in 1991, and the discovery that most Germans desired the international profile of neutral Sweden or Switzerland, prompted many conservatives to pick up their pens in defense of the German sword. Once again, the past was invoked to legitimate present and future policy. Stürmer, in *Die Grenzen der Macht* (The Limits of Power) asked, "How should our thinking about the past instruct or inform our insight into the future?" And Gregor Schöllgen, in *Die Macht in der Mitte Europas* (The Power in the Middle of Europe) declared that, at this time of international uncertainty, "a historical review affords the opportunity of political orientation."[8] What, then, did German history have to teach?

---

[5] Michael Stümer, *Dissonanzen des Fortschritts. Essays über Geschichte und Politik in Deutschland* (Munich, 1986); Ernst Nolte, "Revolution im 20. Jahrhundert," *Frankfurter Allgemeine Zeitung* (January 29, 1983).

[6] Richard J. Evans, "The New Nationalism and the Old History: Perspectives on the West German *Historikerstreit*," *Journal of Modern History*, 59 (1987), 761–97; Charles S. Maier, "Immoral Equivalence: Revising the Nazi Past for the Kohl Era," *New Republic* (December 1986), 36–41; Volker R. Berghahn, "Geschichtswissenschaft und Grosse Politik," *Aus Politik und Zeitgeschichte*, 11(March 13, 1987), 25–37.

[7] Ernst Nolte, "Between Historical Legend and Revisionism? The Third Reich in the Perspective of 1980," in *Forever in the Shadow of Hitler? The Original Documents of the Historikerstreit*, trans. James Knowlton and Truett Cates (Atlantic Heights, N.J., 1993), 1–16; Michael Stürmer, "History in a Land without History," in ibid., 16–17.

[8] Michael Stürmer, *Die Grenzen die Macht. Begegnung der Deutschen mit der Macht* (Munich, 1992), 10; Gregor Schöllgen, *Die Macht in der Mitte Europas. Stationen deutscher Aussenpolitik*

One of the themes of Stürmer's and Schöllgen's account of the German past was the importance of the correct historical consciousness in conducting foreign policy. Its absence in the past lay at the bottom of many disasters of history. For Stürmer, the victors of the First World War did not realize that the Weimar Republic was a "homage to Western values" and the only guarantee of freedom in Germany and Europe. France and England permitted resentment to get the better of their judgment, persecuted the hapless Germany, and thereby destabilized European diplomacy. "Before Hitler triumphed, Europe became a victim of its history and old demons."[9] Today, however, it was Germany whose judgment was impaired by an obsession with the past.

German history should not be stigmatized. All large nations had breached the "limits of power" at some time, Germany in a particularly violent way, but German history as a whole was not to blame. Considering all that had befallen the nation between the First World War and the early 1930s, when else "was the time so ripe for a hellish messiah?"[10] To be sure, an authoritarian regime probably would have replaced the Weimar Republic, but were the Second World War, Auschwitz, Germany's political and moral destruction, and subsequent division inevitable? Hitler was the wild card. None of these cataclysmic developments were immanent in German history. His worldview was not of the pre-1914 world but originated in the trauma of the trenches, the Bolshevik victory, and the "revolt against modernity." The tragedy was that the German present was tainted by Hitler as well as its past, for all elites were seen to have helped him in some way, although his support was actually among the masses. While the establishment certainly wanted to use him for its ends, it was not to blame for what ensued. Hitler was a radically untraditional ruler who breached all the limitations on power of the nation's institutions and political culture. German traditions were essentially sound. Indeed, far from being a litany of disasters, twentieth-century German history contained many redeeming features of progress – trade unions, the tradition of corporatism, and so on.[11]

Stürmer's message was clear: Hitler was a freak accident in an otherwise healthy German past. All the misfortune that had befallen the nation was not implicit in the national tradition. Germans had no reason to be neurotic about their heritage. What about the Holocaust? Did it mark the nation as special as the left maintained? Stürmer did not think so. The nation would develop a national consciousness like that of other "normal, Western" nations even while consciousness of Auschwitz would not be diminished: "The shudder in front of one's mirror will remain for the Germans." But like the young German law

von Friedrich dem Grossen bis zur Gegenwart (Munich, 1992), i; Karlheinz Weissmann, *Rückruf in der Geschichte* (Berlin, 1992); Gregor Schöllgen, *Angst vor der Macht: Die Deutschen und ihre Außenpolitik* (Berlin, 1993).

[9] Stürmer, *Die Grenzen der Macht*, 107.
[10] Ibid., 114.
[11] Ibid., 110–21.

student, Kathi-Gesa Klafke, he added, "but not them alone."[12] With this tantalizingly brief reference to the vexed question of the singularity of Auschwitz, he characterized German fascism as just one of so many nations' breaching of the "limits of power" over the centuries. This was the lesson of the past.

What did this conclusion mean for the new Germany? For one thing, it would allow Germans to perceive clearly their current predicament. They would learn that they had reverted to the traditional German condition of Mitteleuropa (the dominant power in Central Europe). The Berlin Republic was not a larger version of West Germany. The nation had reunited at a time of international transition and volatility, especially in the East. The nonpolitical existence between two power blocs was over. Alone in the middle of Europe, the Federal Republic's interests had changed fundamentally. The nation was not strategically part of the West, and to this extent it was in the same position as it was in 1871. In this context, the salutary lesson of history was that Germany could never again afford to isolate itself from its neighbors. As Schöllgen put it, "Germany is not part of the West. But Germany will never be able to do without it."[13] At the same time, these intellectuals enjoined European integration and the strengthening of security ties with the emerging treaty organizations in much the same terms as their opponents. Indeed, conservatives repeatedly emphasized the pro-European nature of their stance, which was supposed to prevent another German *Sonderweg*.[14]

As might be expected, these conservatives entertained different visions of Germany's relations with the European Community. Redemptive republicans, for their part, wanted to use Europe to overcome the nation-state by uniting them as much as possible in the European Community and having their populations think of themselves first and foremost as Europeans. Until the United States of Europe came to pass, Germany in particular ought to identify its essence with Europe: the German interest was the European interest. Conservatives, by contrast, saw the European Community in purely instrumental terms, as a means to an end – solving those policy problems (the environment, asylum laws, trade, etc.) that were more efficiently addressed at the supranational level. There was no philosophical commitment to the European ideal. Because it was doubtful whether the interests of nations could ever be harmonized, it was unlikely that nation-states would incrementally wither away.[15] Europe remained a continent of competing nation-states, much as De Gaulle

---

[12] Ibid., 124.

[13] Schöllgen, *Die Macht in der Mitte Europas*, 184–85; Stürmer, *Die Grenzen der Macht*, 246–48.

[14] According to Hans-Joachim Veen (Konrad Adenauer Foundation) the distinction between the CDU and the right-wing Republicans is "the isolationist, anti-Western nationalism of the Republicans as opposed to the Western-integration orientation of the CDU since the end of the 1940s.... No party is so vigorously active for European integration as the CDU," in a discussion in 1989 organized by the Evangelischen Akademie Hofgeismar, *West-Deutsch-National?* (Hofgeisamer, 1990), 92.

[15] Michael Stürmer, "Globale Aufgaben und Herausforderungen: Die Schwierige Suche nach Weltordnung," *Aus Politik und Zeitgeschichte*, 15–16 (April 9, 1993), 5.

envisaged. Such intellectuals enjoined German enlightened self-interest rather than the recklessly pursued self-interest of the prewar Germany. Reunification was the nation's second chance.

National sovereignty had foreign policy implications. Because the European Union and other organizations were simply vehicles for national interest, Germany must cease conducting its foreign policy as if it and other supranational organizations were the objects of the ultimate good. Germany was the only nation-state that conducted its foreign policy in this way. "It can get lonely and desperate on the moral high ground." In the future, Germany would no longer be judged by "moral criteria, but by its ability to plan and be decisive."[16] In a bold defense of *Realpolitik*, the security policy correspondent of the conservative *Frankfurter Allgemeine Zeitung*, Karl Feldmeyer, urged Germany to abandon the "politics of principle." This policy change did not mean relinquishing all principles, he argued, but recognizing that international relations were played according to certain rules that made no exceptions for the Federal Republic's noble intentions. Sounding like North American neoconservatives of the twenty-first century, they argued that Germany should disabuse itself of those illusions it gained during the unusual circumstances of 1949–90: that violence and war were no longer a means of policy; that peace was humanity's natural condition; that responsible, principled policy and the pursuit of national interest were contradictory; and that the pursuit of such interests, like the pursuit of power, were in themselves objectionable.[17]

Germans needed to appreciate the nation's sovereignty, understand its interests, and the best means of their attainment. The danger of hubris had passed: the nation knew the temptations of power, and it has learned this lesson well. Nobody advocated a Prussian revival, the conservatives said. Germany's problem was that it has gone from one extreme to another, from *Machtbesessenheit* (obsession with power) to *Machtvergessenheit* (forgetting of power), and now the nation had been tamed, to use the much-quoted terminology of conservative historian, Hans-Peter Schwarz.[18] If the nation was to remain open to alliances and eventual "integration" in Europe, it had to develop a new consciousness. A fully self-conscious Germany would realize that it could survive only by strategically working through supranational organizations and, further, that it could permit itself the claims considered obvious for any other "normal" nation.[19] Ultimately, what the conservatives recommended was a transformed national consciousness. Germans must reverse Thomas Mann's dictum: they had to be Germans first and Europeans second. The implicit message, then, was that history demanded the nation pursue its own interests, but this time it

[16] Ibid., 8; Stürmer, *Die Grenzen der Macht*, 248–49; Eckhard Fuhr, "Melancholie und Gereitzheit," *Frankfurter Allgemeine Zeitung* (November 10, 1992).
[17] Karl Feldmeyer, "Deutschland sucht seine Rolle," *Die Politische Meinung*, 287 (October 1993), 21.
[18] Hans-Peter Schwarz, *Die gezähmten Deutschen. Von der Machtbesessenheit zur Machtvergessenheit* (Stuttgart, 1985).
[19] Schöllgen, *Die Macht in der Mitte Europas*, 178.

should do so prudently. To be prudent meant "Germany must overcome its false guilt."[20]

Conservatives did not deny the enormity of the Holocaust. Neither did they during the *Historikerstreit*. The question, they asserted, was what Auschwitz and the course of German history meant for Germans today. They denied Auschwitz amounted to a stigma because they also rejected the redemptive attachment to Enlightenment optimism and progress, which they caricatured as a naive faith in a utopia, the "perfectibility of man."[21] The Holocaust was one of humanity's less edifying moments, to be sure, but these occurred periodically in history. It had no metahistorical significance. Other "normal" nations regularly reassessed their past in light of contemporary circumstances. It was time Germans did the same, that they put Auschwitz in perspective, and addressed the pressing questions of the day unencumbered by guilt.

While Schöllgen, Stürmer, Feldmeyer and others typically highlighted the primacy of foreign policy for Germany's destiny, other conservatives attended to domestic matters. As mentioned earlier, the most explosive domestic issue since reunification was the asylum law and related violence against asylum seekers and resident foreigners. The question of Germany's ethnicity-based immigration law had also been raised in this regard. There was talk of a national crisis, and Chancellor Kohl even mooted a state of emergency as right-wing thugs terrorized city streets.[22] Hans-Joachim Veen, a specialist on domestic affairs with the Konrad Adenauer Foundation, assured readers that these were merely symptoms of transition and did not evidence a general antidemocratic turn. After all, the Berlin Republic was not Weimar. But then came his discreet admission of Germany's special character. "On the other hand, the reunified Germany will not also be the ultraclean model democracy any longer; rather, it will have an ambivalent normality in relation to the Western European states."[23]

Chancellor Kohl made his views clear while condemning violence against foreigners, affirming his party's and government's commitment to the right of asylum, and assuring all that Germany was an *ausländerfreundliches Land* (a country friendly to foreigners). There was no mention in this context of any change in citizenship laws, or even a consideration of the issue. There was a need for a common European policy on asylum, he argued. Germany was bearing the burden of the refugee problem. But there was no thought that the problem could be addressed in part, at least, by adopting the citizenship laws of other European Community members. Kohl generously acknowledged the

---

[20] Stürmer, "Globale Aufgaben und Herausforderungen," 8.

[21] Ibid., 4; Joachim Fest, "Encumbered Remembrance: The Controversy about the Incomparability of National-Socialist Mass Crimes," in *Forever in Hitler's Shadow?*, 63–71; Hartung, "Wieder das alte Denken."

[22] Marc Fischer, "Kohl's 'Emergency' Suggestion Raises Questions, Draws Criticism," *Washington Post* (November 3, 1992); Gunter Hofmann, "Hilflos vor dem Fremdenhass," *Die Zeit* (October 3, 1991).

[23] Hans-Joachim Veen, "Ein Jahr vor der Wahl," *Die Politische Meinung* (September 1993), 9.

contribution to German prosperity of *Gastarbeiter* but not the aspirations of their German-born children to a real stake in the life of the nation.[24]

The rehabilitation of the *Volk* continued with maverick Berlin historian Ernst Nolte who employed his controversial interpretation of twentieth-century European history as a springboard for some reflections on the German identity debate. National identities could be sustained by allegiance to the categorical imperative, he wrote caustically, but must be nourished by an attachment to the past. The past, however, can be interpreted in different ways, each version informing a particular idea of national identity. Nolte analyzed briefly the central claims of each of the prominent schools of German historiography. He rejected the interpretation of those who view the past as the "struggle for mastery over Europe" (Stürmer, Schöllgen, Schwarz, Feldmeyer, Arnulf Baring).[25] The Nazis were more than a "hegemonical power," and Hitler was not a parallel figure to Philip II or Napoleon. Inadequate as well was the "fundamental revolution" interpretation that saw a process of progressive individual and national emancipation occurring through the great revolutions in which National Socialism was the high point of resistance (i.e., Habermas). For reunified Germany, the inference was that it had finally joined the posthistorical world and that it must renounce its historical identity, "which ought not to be difficult because it is doubtful whether in posthistorical civilization it is possible to speak about particular national identities at all."[26] Then there was the anti-German *Sonderweg* posture of the Fritz Fischer school and the subsequent social science historians who spoke of the missing revolution, premodern continuity, and who laid the blame for the First World War firmly at Germany's feet. These historians, who saw 1933 and Auschwitz at the end of every development, did not realize that they stigmatized Germans as "perpetrators and criminals" in the same way as the Nazis spoke of the Jews. Finally, the theory of totalitarianism, which attempted to demonstrate the essential similarity between terrorist one-party regimes, was no longer widely accepted.[27]

Unsatisfied with them all, Nolte proceeded to his own well-known interpretation of twentieth-century history as a "European civil war," and, after 1945, as a "world civil war." The greatest threat to all national identities was the utopian determination of the Bolsheviks to construct a "world civilization" (the "melting together" of all peoples and races) through world revolution. The Weimar Republic found itself in a unique situation as the object of a concentrated attack by the largest communist party outside the USSR. Had it been successful, the German identity would have disappeared. The Nazis were the

[24] Throughout his speeches, Kohl referred to *Gastarbeiter* in the second person plural indicative. Helmut Kohl, *Der Kurs der CDU. Reden und Beiträge des Bundesvorsitzenden, 1973–1993* (Stuttgart, 1993), 391–92, 425–26.

[25] Arnulf Baring, *Deutschland, was nun?* (Berlin, 1991).

[26] Ernst Nolte, "Identität und Wiedervereinigung," *Die Politische Meinung,* 277 (December 1992), 39; Nolte, *Streitpunkte. Heutige und künftige Kontroversen um den Nationalsozialismus* (Berlin, 1993).

[27] Nolte, "Identität und Wiedervereinigung," 40.

only party willing and able to oppose the communists. "With that they were not unjustified in an extreme 'do or die' battle situation that the communists were first to postulate." The characterization of the Nazis simply as a racially fanatical, anti-Semitic party, he insisted, failed to recognize its self-perception as the last bastion against Bolshevism.[28] It was in this light that we must understand Martin Heidegger's association with the Nazi government in the early years, as Nolte argued in a recent biography of his former teacher.[29] The tragic reversal of the Nazis' defensive posture consisted in the fact that, "despite its national point of departure, it [the Nazi Party] had to become a supranational 'racist' party, and thereby was led to make an identity-destroying identity claim." Their unjustified attribution of collective guilt to the Jews meant that the Nazis bore a greater burden of historical guilt than the communists of the time. In this way, the era became the era of fascism when it was also, just as much, the era of militant, organized communism.

For all that, Nolte pleaded a special case for fascism. Because nobody doubted that a rational core of utopianism drove communism, why not Nationalism Socialism, too? "It should be becoming just as clear today that the question must be asked whether National Socialism also possessed a rational core, that is, the self-assertion of a national identity against an antinational 'world civilization.'" The value of his interpretation, he argued, was that it pointed in the direction of a national identity that no longer struggled against world civilization but constituted a specific "superstructure" over a generic "substructure."[30] This argument was the latest installment in his long campaign to normalize the German past. During the 1970s and 1980s, he advocated the historicization of the Holocaust through a strategy of spurious comparisons with other genocidal experiences.[31] Now in classical historicist manner, he invited readers to empathize with the intentions of National Socialism. He could also rescue the national ideal, because he attributed the excesses of the Nazis to the fact that they became a *"supranational, 'racist' party."*[32]

How were Germans supposed to forge a positive identity from these attempts to destigmatize their past? One way of finding out was to read the *Frankfurter Allgemeine Zeitung*. Its senior journalists wrote articles recommending that

---

[28] Ibid., 41. For a defense of Nolte's interpretation by a young German conservative historian, see Rainer Zitelmann, "Nationalismus and Antikommunismus. Aus Anlass der Thesen von Ernst Nolte," in Uwe Backes, Eckard Jesse, and Reinhard Zitelmann, eds., *Die Schatten der Vergangenheit. Impulse zur Historisierung des Nationalsozialismus* (Frankfurt, 1990), 218–42. The same collection also contains a self-defense by Nolte himself: "Abschliessende Reflexionen über den sogenannten Historikerstreit," 83–109.

[29] Ernst Nolte, *Martin Heidegger: Politik and Geschichte im Leben und Denken* (Berlin, 1992).

[30] Nolte, "Identität und Wiedervereinigung," 42.

[31] These efforts led American scholars to complain well before the *Historikerstreit*. See Felix Gilbert's review of Nolte's *Deutschland und der Kalte Krieg*, in the *American Historical Review*, 81 (June 1976), 618–20; and the exchange of author and reviewer in the same journal, 82 (February 1977), 235–36; See also Peter Gay's indignation in his *Freud, Jews and Other Germans: Masters and Victims in Modernist Culture* (Oxford, 1978), xi–xiii.

[32] Nolte, "Identität und Wiedervereinigung," 42 (emphasis added).

the German government no longer contribute funds to American Holocaust museums because they did not also highlight brighter spots in the recent German past.[33] The former Federal Republic was regarded in almost pathological terms as an abnormal, provisional period of *halbsouveräne Vergangenheit* (semisovereign past) that was happily ended by reunification and the decision to move the capital back to Berlin.[34] They gave the impression that the problem with violence against foreigners was the foreigners themselves.[35] These sentiments struck a chord with many Germans who believed that the nation ought to "finally bring the past to a close."[36] To them, the conservative revision of the nation's history made sense because there were indeed many continuities with the Bismarckian state. But what about the political emotions of German Germans? To understand their economy, we need to single out one figure for focused attention.

Dramatizing the German German

The writer Martin Walser (b. 1927) is an ideal subject because he was usually considered a former leftist, a Non-German German even, who in the 1990s "moved to the right" by embracing the national cause and attacking Holocaust memory. Critics saw his notorious 1998 Paulskirche speech, with its rhetoric of intellectuals wielding the Holocaust as a "moral cudgel" with which to intimidate Germans, as part of a trend that culminated in his supposedly anti-Semitic novel, *Tod eines Kritikers* (Death of a Critic) four years later.[37] On closer inspection, a consistent theme of national identification in a complex relationship with Holocaust memory was evident in his many reflections on the subject since the 1960s. Walser was always a "German German," as were many leftists of his generation. The group self has not been polluted by the Nazi deeds, nor ought it be stigmatized, they effectively insisted. Unlike Habermas, Walser thought the nation was redeemable, indeed, that it warranted basic trust. An examination of his relevant writings reveals the development of his efforts to rescue the national ideal in relation to the changing status of Holocaust commemoration and discourse in the Federal Republic.

Walser always saw himself as speaking on behalf of the silent majority of compatriots, the provincial nonelites looked down on by the powerful, the

---

[33] Günter Gillessen, "Bedenkliche Art der Erinnerung," *Frankfurter Allgemeine Zeitung* (August 4, 1992).

[34] Fritz Ulrich Fack, "Eine Historische Entscheidung," *Frankfurter Allgemeine Zeitung* (June 22, 1991).

[35] Klaus-Dieter Frankenburger, "Protest der 'Kleinen Leute,'" *Frankfurter Allgemeine Zeitung* (October 1, 1991).

[36] According to a *Spiegel* survey, 62 percent of respondents agreed with this statement. Reported in "Jews in the New German Society," *Washington Post* (January 20, 1992).

[37] Elke Schmitter, "Der Ewige Flakhelfer," *Der Spiegel* (September 5, 2005), 176. On the novel, see Bill Niven, "Martin Walser's Tod eines Kritikers and the Issue of Anti-Semitism," *German Life and Letters*, 59:3 (July 2003), 299–311.

fashionable, and the worldly.[38] This orientation was in keeping with his analysis of National Socialism, which was close to that of the writer Peter Weiss, who shared his proximity to the German Communist Party (DKP) in the 1970s. Weiss's controversial play about the Frankfurt Auschwitz trials, *Die Ermittlung* (The Investigation), which linked the Holocaust to capitalism rather than to anti-Semitism, mirrored Walser's 1960 novel, *Halbzeit* (Half-Time), in which a company executive, a former senior officer of the Nazi security service, engaged in marketing with the same rhetoric of aggression and efficiency of the Nazi regime.[39] Influenced by Bertolt Brecht, Weiss and Walser held the population less criminally culpable than misled and betrayed by corrupt elites.[40] For these and other intellectuals, the technocratic and capitalist system that had wrought Auschwitz was running the Federal Republic.

Three years later, Walser continued this critical tradition in the article "Our Auschwitz," a scathing commentary on the media coverage of the trial of Auschwitz guards in Frankfurt between 1963 and 1965.[41] The enduring themes of his essays on the Holocaust and national identity are all on display: a leftist critique of bourgeois society, especially its egoism and hegemonic media; a subtle defense of national solidarity; and the emotional abyss separating the Holocaust's victims and perpetrators and their descendants. Thus he rejected a moralistic interpretation of the Nazi past that led to affirming the status quo. "If the concentration camp trials . . . are to be proof that we don't shy back from 'mastering' our past, then they have to have some kind of political effect."[42] He was pessimistic of such enlightenment, however, given the media's sensationalist reporting of the guards' crimes. What bothered him most was the individualistic, indeed, anarchic, consciousness of bourgeois Germans that permitted a distancing from the Holocaust. The media's singular focus on the gory details of the camp guards' specific crimes aided this exculpation.[43] By distancing themselves from the guards with whose spectacular crimes they had nothing in common, and by claiming lack of direct involvement, the average German could disavow any relationship of significance to Auschwitz, or indeed to Nazi Germany. Reported as a gross mass murder committed by demons and

---

[38] Jan-Werner Müller, *Another Country: German Intellectuals, Unification and National Identity* (New Haven and London, 2000), 152.

[39] Robert Cohen, "The Political Aesthetics of Holocaust Literature: Peter Weiss's *The Investigation* and Its Critics," *History and Memory*, 10:2 (1998), 43–67; Martin Walser, *Halbzeit. Roman* (Frankfurt, 1960).

[40] Hellmuth Karasek, "Der Ewige Antisemit?" *Die Welt* (July 30, 2005).

[41] Martin Walser, "Unser Auschwitz," in Ingrid Karsunke and Karl Markus Michel, eds., *Bewegung in der Republik, 1965 bis 1984*, 2 vols. (Berlin, 1985), 1:13–22. Originally published in *Kursbuch*, 1 (1965). For commentary see Michael Töteberg, "Walsers Stücke im Kontext der Zeit," *Text und Kritik*, 41–42 (2000), 91–109.

[42] Walser, "Unser Auschwitz," 18. Two recent books on the trial follow Walser on this point: Rebecca Wittmann, *Beyond Justice: The Auschwitz Trial* (Cambridge, Mass., 2005), 246; Devin O. Pendas, *The Frankfurt Auschwitz Trial, 1963–1965: Genocide, History, and the Limits of the Law* (Cambridge and New York, 2006), 245, 294ff.

[43] Walser, "Unser Auschwitz," 17.

sociopaths, Auschwitz would recede into oblivion like other crimes, an event of no particular consequence for the country.

What is more, Walser thought he detected cheap emotional identification with the victims as the means by which Germans avoided affective ties with the perpetrators. Yet all that separated contemporary Germans from them, he said, were contingent life narratives. Were we not all potential camp guards? At the very least, all Germans had enabled the persecution of Jews in the 1930s as passive bystanders.[44] One could avoid these connections only by emotionally and imaginatively standing with the victims, whose experiences were actually incomprehensible to everyone but themselves. "Only through the hapless attempt to place ourselves on the side of the victim as much as possible, at least to imagine how terribly they suffered, only with this participation does the perpetrator become so contemptible [*verabscheuungswürdig*] and brutal, as we need him for our reality-distant but momentarily intense feeling."[45]

To tie Germans to Auschwitz – to make it "Our Auschwitz" – Walser argued that the individualistic imagination of the bourgeois German needed to be replaced by a social one of the humanist. In a move that would become more important in future decades, he linked Germans in collective political guilt to the Holocaust through national membership. If the problem was that Germans have lost any residual "national solidarity with the perpetrators," then it was important to force Germans to associate themselves with the crime by highlighting their national connection. Although he disclaimed feelings of guilt or shame, he saw himself "implicated in the great German crime"[46] The distinction between implication and guilt was how Walser was able to reconcile his nationalism and imperative to feel connected to the Holocaust. And this distinction was how he came to different conclusions from those of Habermas, with whose premise about prepolitical connections between Germans across the generations he agreed. Another key difference with Habermas was that Walser suspected the media's representation of the crime. His argument was communitarian; the collective preceded and enabled the individual.

But if the *Volk* and state still retain meaning for a polity, that is, for a collective that appears in history, in whose name justice could be spoken or broken, then all that occurred was determined [*bedingt*] by this collective, and the reasons for everything are to be sought in this collective. No act was just subjective. Auschwitz was a pan-German issue. Everyone belonged to some part of the causes of Auschwitz. It would be a task for everyone to find his or her part. One need not have been in the SS.[47]

[44] Ibid., 19. Here his argument is close to that of Daniel J. Goldhagen, *Hitler's Willing Executioners: Ordinary Germans and the Holocaust* (New York, 1996). I analyze his methodology in "Structure and Agency in the Holocaust: Daniel J. Goldhagen and his Critics," *History and Theory*, 37:2 (1998), 194–219.
[45] Walser, "Unser Auschwitz," 17.
[46] Ibid., 19.
[47] Ibid., 21.

Two years earlier, he had reflected more specifically on the dilemmas of German identity after Auschwitz in terms redolent of socialist humanism and national self-determination of the Schumacherian type. His generation was the first raised as emphatically national, he observed, not mediated by regional bonds that characterized the world of his grandfather. But because of what Germans did to "finally become conscious of our individual nature [*Eigenart*]," he continued, "one prefers forever not to be German."[48] In fact, he lamented, "Today Germany no longer exists," referring to the country's division, and to the ostracization of those, like him, who advocated reunification in freedom and peace. Directing his hostility to Konrad Adenauer, he excoriated the bourgeoisie's political immaturity in succumbing to the fantasy of inner enemies, the French and socialists before the First World War, then the Jews, and now the communists.[49] In this way, Walser narrated himself as a leftist patriot into a story of bourgeois-elite oppression of the little people in which the fate of the Jews was included.

Feeling increasingly alienated from the Federal Republican consensus that accepted the country's division, he announced in 1977 that we can "defend ourselves" (*uns wehren*) against the seemingly immutable outcome of the history of World War II. His declarations were existential rather than discursive; they stated his political emotions with disarming honesty: "I find it unbearable that German history – as bad as it ultimately unfolded – has to end as a product of catastrophe [*Katastrophenprodukt*]," "Germany cannot be removed from my consciousness," "We have to keep the wound called Germany open." He mourned for the German nation and imagined it in terms of the leftist nationalism of the 1950s.

I refuse to participate in the liquidation of history. In me, Germany still has another chance. One, namely, whose socialism is not imposed by the victorious powers, but rather is allowed to develop on its own; and one whose development toward democracy does just not exclusively stumble along the capitalist crisis rhythms. This other Germany, I believe, could be useful today. The world would not need to shy away any longer from such a Germany.[50]

As in the 1960s, he coded National Socialism as a German form of fascism that represented a degenerate potential in all capitalist societies. To overcome the past entailed not chipping away at national traditions, but raising awareness

---

[48] Martin Walser "Ein deutsches Mosaik" (1963), *Werke*, vol. 11 (Frankfurt, 1997), 51–52. Walser was not alone in making such observations. Thus Golo Mann wrote in 1968 that in Germany "History no longer forms the public conscience.... The past has ceased to determine the identity of democratic society": Golo Mann, *The History of Germany since 1789*, trans. M. Jackson (New York, 1968), 528. Cf. Hans Magnus Enzensberg, "Bin ich ein Deutscher?" *Die Zeit* (June 12, 1964).

[49] Walser "Ein deutsches Mosaik," 71.

[50] Martin Walser, "Über den Leser – soviel man in einem Festzelt darüber sagen soll" (1977), *Werke*, 11:569, 571.

that, in the terms of Adorno and Brecht, "We still live under the conditions that can produce fascism," namely the hyperegoism of liberal capitalism.[51]

Where did Auschwitz and the Jews fit in here? Already in 1979, Walser explained his position in terms no different from those he expressed nearly twenty years later in his Paulskirche speech. As he did in 1998, he noted the temptation to avert his gaze from images of Auschwitz: "One can't live with such pictures." And he admitted that "We are all tempted to defend ourselves against Auschwitz" (*uns gegen Auschwitz zu wehren*).[52] The Holocaust seemed incompatible with German national subjectivity. So how were Germans to comport themselves to this historical trauma? With humility, he effectively argued. Such was its excess that no one could gain a firm epistemological foothold from which to pronounce confidently about its meaning. There was no mastering of Auschwitz. The problem, as he argued in "Unser Auschwitz," was that Germans as individuals could not bear the guilt of the Holocaust, and therefore dissociated themselves from it and the nation in whose name it was perpetrated. The modern bourgeois, the relaxed and "critical" (Non-German) German whom Walser lampooned, was possible only by renouncing the collective that had committed the crime. "Today's individual has emancipated itself from the nation." Confronting the past was delegated to others, to officialdom.[53]

Walser's suspicion of official ritualization of the Holocaust in public life grew with this hostility to what he saw as the moralization of the Nazi past aimed against the German national ideal in the 1980s: that West Germany was still suspected by some to contain a fascist potential, even that "Germans are all Nazis." Such rhetoric evidently triggered intense anxieties in him. Throughout history, he complained, Germany, which once was little more than a plethora of small states, had been subject to persecution that questioned its survival, as in the Treaty of Versailles.[54] That German division was punishment for its sins, he understood. "But surely not forever. Punishment serves not contrition, but surely resocialization. Don't we feel resocialized?" he asked. Here were the first signs of concern about the stigmatization of Germany, a mark that led, he thought, to the feeling of one author that East Germany was as foreign to him as Mongolia.[55] That an innocent (*unblamiertes*) Germany still existed – a Germany in which basic trust could be placed – was evident in an East German poet who wrote in primal German traditions untainted by subsequent international literary trends about politics or morality. Such poetry's virtue lay in its isolation from what he called the "conscience industry" (*Gesinnungsindustrie*) that purveyed antinational ideas against the people's instincts.

---

[51] Martin Walser, "Unsere historische Schuldigkeit" (1978), *Werke*, 11:608–10.
[52] Martin Walser, "Auschwitz und kein Ende" (1979), *Werke*, 11:632.
[53] Ibid., 635.
[54] Michael Walser, "Über Deutschland reden" (1988), *Werke*, 11:899–900.
[55] Ibid., 901, 905.

The binary relationship between innocent *Volk* and corrupt elites was thereby mapped onto literary production.[56]

As might be expected, no one was happier than Walser when the Berlin Wall came down in late 1989. The people had spoken against the elites on both sides of the border who had accepted the nations' division. It was time for West Germans to show solidarity with East Germans and rejoice. "Now is the time to be happy, and to delight in the fact that history will work out once for the Germans, too."[57] But his emotions were mixed, for the unification was accompanied by vocal opposition from Non-German Germans, who expressed disdain about the desire of East Germans to join West Germans in one country. "Whoever says *Volk* instead of *society* may, no, must, be howled down [*niedergeschimpft*]," he complained. The end of German division did not mean the end of his critique of cultural elites hostile to national rhetoric. On the contrary, it increased it.[58] Walser's imperative now was to rescue the nation from its criminalization by intellectual elites. And the problem was the media and leftist intellectuals. His identification with the nation intensified as his impatience with intellectuals grew; after the collapse of socialism, only the nation remained as the ideal of collective life. The stigma against it had to be removed. One way was to imagine historical continuities whose teleology was not genocide.

One cannot study this all-inclusive historical narrative [about the military assassination attempt on Hitler] without again and again developing the hope that this time Hitler would not escape, that the war would stop before it could manifest its worst consequences. In order not to suffocate in hopelessness [*Ausweglosigkeit*] and fatalism, one probably needs a factual narrative that permits us to think constantly that the outcome might have been different. I am embittered by little so constantly as every assertion that Hitler and thereby Auschwitz were unavoidable, that German history runs into nothing but Hitler and Auschwitz.[59]

This aim collided with the alarm about German nationality that emerged in the wake of arson and other attacks on foreigners living in Solingen, Mölln, and Rostock between 1991 and 1993. The radical right was less a product of an overreaching German nationalism, Walser insisted, than the pitiful result of social anomie. In fact, its resort to national rhetoric was possible only because it has been neglected by "the opinion makers, the politicians, the intellectuals."

---

[56] Ibid., 913–15. For commentary, see Stephen Brockmann, *Literature and German Reunification* (Cambridge, 1999).

[57] Martin Walser, "November 1989," *Werke*, 11:916, 927.

[58] Martin Walser, "Deutsche Sorgen I" (December 1989), *Werke*, 11:928.

[59] Martin Walser, "Die Geburt der Tragödie aus dem Geist des Gehorsams" (1996), *Werke*, 11:1081. Close to Walser in this regard is Konrad Löw, *"Das Volk ist ein Trost": Deutsche und Juden 1933–1945 im Urteil der jüdischen Zeitzeugen* (Munich, 2006).

These elites were to blame for the right-wing radicalism by not making Germans feel at home in Germany, he implied.[60]

He continued his attack in a speech in 1994 significantly entitled "On Free and Unfree Speech," in which he complained that public speech codes inhibited his free expression of conscience. The public moralization about the two German dictatorships was particularly dangerous. "There is at the moment a terror of virtue of political correctness that makes free speech a mortal [*halsbrecherischen*] risk." Intellectuals engaged in the "public testing" of others' consciences, a practice manifesting the "banality of good."[61] Prescription regarding how to think and feel about dictatorial pasts in the manner of a catechism, even being hounded to make public statements of contrition as was Christa Wolf, undermined the delicate process of reflection about guilt that takes place in the individual conscience. The Non-German German "cultivation of taboos in the name of enlightenment" was demoralizing the unified Germany.[62]

These were the themes that Walser expressed in distilled form in his controversial 1998 Paulskirche speech upon winning the Peace Prize of the German Book Trade. The sense of stigmatization was especially prevalent in his disgust that only Germans were considered a people of whom it could be said that they still harbor genocidal fantasies. The intellectuals were the agents of this defamation. They "want to hurt us, because they think we deserve it." They also continually instrumentalized Auschwitz, first by having used it to justify the division of Germany, and now to bully writers into thematizing Holocaust issues in their work. And they who feel responsible for the consciences of others – he appeared to be referring to Habermas and Grass – were the ones who want to erect a "monumentalization of our disgrace" in the form of the Berlin Holocaust memorial.[63]

Revealing of Walser's political emotions as his speech was, the subsequent face-to-face discussion with the German Jewish leaders, Ignatz Bubis and Salomon Korn, organized and published by the *Frankfurter Allgemeine Zeitung*, was revelatory. Here the emotional interjection of rapid exchanges – which he later regretted – uncovered Walser's own unconscious fantasies more clearly than the guarded phrases he had used in his carefully prepared speeches.[64] He began by reporting that he had received more than one thousand letters supporting his speech, which he interpreted as a "singular consciousness raising"

---

[60] Martin Walser, "Deutsche Sorgen II" (1993), *Werke*, 11:999–1000. In this essay, Walser reprises his discomfort with the media, intellectuals' justification of German division, and their hostility to national feeling.

[61] Martin Walser, "Über Freie und unfreie Rede" (1994), *Werke*, 11:1051–53.

[62] Ibid., 1059.

[63] Martin Walser, *Erfahungen beim Verfassen einer Sonntagsrede: Friedenspreis der Deutschen Buchhandels 1998* (Frankfurt, 1998), 17–20.

[64] Nine years after the affair, Walser regretted his hostility to Bubis, though he did not retract his views. "Martin Walser bereut Verhaltung gegenüber Ignatz Bubis," *Spiegel Online* (March 16, 2007), http://www.spiegel.de/kultur/literatur/0,1518,472183,00.html, viewed April 20, 2007.

and "liberation of the conscience." The people's voice had been heard finally, and they complained about stigma: that "one feels as a German in a state of being accused [*Beschuldigtenzustand*]"; and that they feel "treated like a criminal on probation who has to constantly demonstrate his resocialization because one does not otherwise believe him." In fact, he continued, "Germans have to prove that they are human, because otherwise they are not."[65] Walser, too, complained about stigma, rejecting the entreaty of moderation by the Israeli ambassador to Germany, Avi Primor, because of "the stain on the dress," by which he meant Germany's criminal past. Where is that stain on me, asked Walser? Why do others say contemporary Germans are tainted?[66]

The media (i.e., Non-German Germans) were his principal object of scorn. The incessant public representation of the Holocaust was effectively a declaration that Germans were accused (*Beschuldigung*). Its aim was not education but "the domestication of conscience and manipulation of conscience." But Jews were to blame, too, for the persistence of German stigma. Thus, Walser took Bubis to task for appearing at the site of the arson attack against German Turks in Rostock in August 1993 because his presence linked current issues to the Nazi past. Pretending to speak on behalf of the people, Walser informed his interlocutors that they "can't bear that [link] any longer, and they don't want to hear it any longer, and they have a right to that, because they have nothing more to do with that nightmarish spook [*Spuk*: the Nazis]." Plainly, any public expression of opinion on current affairs by a Jewish leader in Germany would have highlighted the stigmatized past. For that reason, he told Bubis and Korn that, because Jews had not been subject to the same temptations as Germans under Hitler, they were in no position to judge Germans. Jews ought to be silent and respect the sensitivities of the perpetrator collective.[67] Klaus von Dohnanyi, who had similarly questioned Bubis's right to criticize Walser because Jews may not have behaved differently from other Germans toward non-Jewish victims of Nazis had they not been persecuted, asked for Jewish restraint, because "we [Germans] are all vulnerable."[68] The German German's solidarity was with other German Germans, not with the victims of his or her ancestors.

This solidarity with one's own was evident in Walser's defense of the letters he received. Their writers were not anti-Semites, he insisted against the suspicion of Bubis and Korn, who were alarmed by the rhetoric of "liberation" from political correctness, which they took to mean the collapse of the taboo on public anti-Semitism. In fact, there was no real anti-Semitism in the country, Walser retorted. The right-wing political parties were carried by protest

[65] "Wovon zeugt die Schande wenn nicht von Verbrechen," *Frankfurter Allgemeine Zeitung* (November 28, 1998). Reprinted in Frank Schirrmacher, ed., *The Walser-Bubis Debatte: Eine Dokumentation* (Frankfurt, 1999), 446, 451, 462.

[66] Avi Primo, "Der Fleck auf dem Rock. Keine Frage der Schuld, sondern der Verantwortung – Meine Antwort an Walser," *Frankfurter Allgemeiner Zeitung* (December 9, 1998).

[67] "Wovon zeugt die Schande wenn nicht von Verbrechen," 454, 452.

[68] Klaus von Dohnanyi, "Wie sind alle Verletzbar," *Frankfurter Allgemeine Zeitung* (November 17, 1998).

voters, and, besides, right-wing parties existed in other countries as well. What about objections to the proposed Berlin memorial that it would be defaced? Bubis responded. Was there not in fact a dangerous minority? Walser's reply was a stunning revelation of his views about the innocence of the people and corruption of elites: "If a memorial is constructed that provokes the people to defile it . . . "[69] Non-German Germans and Jews, he was saying, were to blame for any stigmatized behavior by Germans.[70] His unconscious historical large-group fantasy was that Jews and Non-German Germans would cease trying to stigmatize the German people. Or that they disappear altogether.

---

[69] "Wovon zeugt die Schande wenn nicht von Verbrechen," 463.

[70] Social scientists call this reaction "secondary anti-Semitism," but Walser is so anxious about the threat that the stigmatized past presents to the survival of the German nation that he is blind to his own resentments: Werner Bergmann and Rainer Erb, *Anti-Semitism in Germany: The Post-Nazi Epoch since 1945*, trans. Belinda Cooper and Allison Brown (New Brunswick, 1997).

12

Political Theology and the Dissolution
of the Underlying Structure

The culture wars in the Federal Republic have been based on the struggle between Non-German Germans who advocated transforming the national culture
and German Germans who resisted such a transformation. These rival projects
were as much theological as political. Non-German Germans advocated an
anamnestic memory culture committed to retrospective solidarity with the victims of the Holocaust, whereas German Germans urged an *amnesiac* memory
that expressed the identity needs of the "perpetrator collective." These polarized positions reflected the underlying structure of postwar German memory but
began to dissolve with the generational change early in the twenty-first century.
With the evolution of basic trust in the republic's institutions, the consensus
about how its political culture began was fashioned.

Contesting Sacrifice

Martin Walser was not alone in criticizing the Non-German German memory culture. Hermann Lübbe sympathized with Walser's situation when he was
attacked in 1999. "It is bizarre," Lübbe wrote, "to regard one's own crimes as
memorializable." As with Walser, the problem lay with Non-German Germans'
disordered relationship to nation and memory. "We are embarrassed and feel
pushed around by the arrogance with which the converted puffs himself up
into the ideal of moral certainty." In their hands, the Berlin memorial became
a weapon with which they could manipulate their fellow citizens. "The memorial serves as the opportunity to accuse others about their moral shortcomings
in their relationship to the past. One's own idea of the memorial represents
the better conscience for which the others ought to strive." And like Walser,
Lübbe reiterated that a memorial to the victims was not for the perpetrators
to erect, and that it represented a "pride in sin" (*Sündenstolz*), an inverted
hypernationalism.[1]

---

[1] Hermann Lübbe, *Aufklärung anlaßhalber: Philosophische Essays zu Politik, Religion und Moral*
(Gräfelfing, 2001), 241–44.

A number of German Jewish commentators expressed similar ambivalence about the redemptive dimension of the Non-German German cryptotheology. Iconoclastic German Jewish commentator Henryk M. Broder observed of the Berlin memorial that it was a gesture of (Non-German) Germans who wanted to clear their consciences. He doubted whether the memorial had anything really to do with Jews: "And the murdered Jews for whom the memorial is erected can rest content that they have made a substantial contribution to the new German conscience culture."[2] Had Germans been truly contrite, they would have built one decades earlier when former Nazis were still prominent in society.[3] Now it was easy to memorialize dead Jews. In fact, remembrance was profitable: "The Germanization of the Holocaust has been a successful experiment in transforming historical liability into moral capital – the interest on the investment alone far exceeds what has been paid out to victims in 'compensation.'" All the while, he lamented that no one seemed interested in compensating the other surviving victims: homosexuals, Roma, so-called euthanasia victims, and those soldiers sentenced as deserters.[4] Not surprisingly, he had little time for the likes of Anna Rosmus, who had written that "[a]s a second-generation German I felt not only terribly ashamed, but also guilty.... I considered it my responsibility to stand up and speak out against it."[5] She also profited from her good conscience.[6]

Members of that leftist sect, the "Anti-Germans,"[7] like Eike Geisel, were predictably ambivalent about the motives of Non-German Germans in advocating the memorial. He also saw ambivalent motives at work: "Auschwitz had a good ending, after all." And a new German collective could celebrate its good rebirth: "The Ashes [of the dead] are the stuff for a Good Conscience," was the title of one of his typically polemical articles.[8] The German arrogation of

[2] Henryk M. Broder, "Deutschmeister des Trauerns," in Ute Heimrod, Günter Schlüsche, and Horst Seferens, eds., *Der Denkmalstreit – das Denkmal: Die Debatte um das "Denkmal für die ermordeten Juden Europas." Eine Dokumentation* (Berlin, 1999), 433. Originally published in *Der Spiegel* (April 17, 1995), 222–24.

[3] Henryk M. Broder, "Abgestürzte Flugzeuge," *Der Tagesspiegel* (January 17, 1995). Reprinted in Heimrod, Schlüsche, and Seferens, *Der Denkmalstreit,* 238.

[4] Henryk M. Broder, "Problem, Shock, and Trauma," in Broder, *A Jew in the New Germany,* ed. Sander L. Gilman and Lilliam M. Friedberg (Urbana and Chicago, 2004), 112. Originally published in Henryk M. Broder, *Volk und Wahn* (Berlin, 1996), 214–28.

[5] Anna E. Rosmus, "A Troublemaker in a Skirt," in Alan L. Berger and Naomi Berger, eds., *Second Generation Voices: Reflections by Children of Holocaust Survivors and Perpetrators* (Syracuse, 2001), 283. See also Anna Rosmus-Weniger, *Widerstand und Verfolgung am Beispiel Passaus, 1933–1939* (Passau, 1983).

[6] Henryk M. Broder, "To Each Her Market Value," in Broder, *A Jew in the New Germany,* 133–38. Originally published in Henryk M. Broder, *Jedem das Seine* (Berlin, 1999), 21–29.

[7] See the new journal, *Promodo: Zeitschrift in eigener Sache,* 1 (October 2005), 46, www.promodo-online.org, which carried an announcement for an "antideutsche Konferenz": "Kritik und Parteilichkeit Aufruf zur antideutschen Konferenz am 18. und 19. November 2005 in Berlin." See also www.redaktion-bahamas.org and www.jungleworld.org. A critique by a former anti-German is Robert Kurz, *Die Antideutsche Ideologie: Vom Antifaschismus zum Krisenimperialismus* (Münster, 2003).

[8] Eike Geisel, "Die Asche ist der Stoff für das gute Gewissen," *Der Tagesspiegel* (January 6, 1995).

murdered Jews went so far as a "spiritual cannibalism not unlike the behavior of members of a wild tribe that consumes the brain or other body parts of a killed enemy in order to assume its perceived quality."[9] Geisel saw the exemplar of this disturbing trend in Leah Rosh, the media personality who has been agitating for the memorial since the 1980s. For she had changed her name from the "Aryan" Edith to Leah in order to transform herself into a "pseudo-Jewess" (*Neigungsjüdin*) and reserved the right to speak on behalf of dead Jews while marginalizing the participation of living ones.[10]

If Geisel's rhetoric seemed excessive, Rosh had made herself an easy target. "In the name of the dead and the survivors, I now call for the creation of these memorials," she declared in 1988.[11] Seven years later, she told the leader of German Jewry Heinz Galinski to "keep out of this, the descendants of the perpetrators are building the memorial, not the Jews."[12] If she thereby counted herself as a member of the perpetrator collective, she did so in the capacity as Germany's foremost stigma manager: "We Germans have to make a clearly visible sign [*ein weithin sichtbares Zeichen*] in order to document publicly that we accept the burden of our history, that we are pondering a new chapter in our history."[13] Her extraordinary gesture in 2005 of placing the tooth of a Holocaust victim on a stele at the Berlin Memorial was regarded by the German Jewish commentator Rafael Seligman as symptomatic of a broader problem: "I am concerned not about the spiritual condition of a Ms. Rosh but rather about a society that blindly follows this woman and her actionism."[14] He was uncomfortable with the embracing of the Jews by the likes of Rosh and her collaborator, the historian Eberhard Jäckel, who treated Jews only as victims. This attention was suffocating and denuded Jews of vitality while allowing German politicians to decline to erect local, event-specific memorials because they could point to the big, abstract one in Berlin. Seligman urged Germans and Jews to reject a sacrificial interpretation of the Holocaust in the Berlin

---

[9] Eike Geisel, "Die Fähigkeit zu mauern," in his *Triumph des Guten Willens: Gute Nazis und selbsternannte Opfer. Die Nationalisierung der Erinnerung*, ed. Klaus Bittermann (Berlin, 1998), 62–63. Originally in *Konkret* (May 1, 1995).

[10] Geisel, "Die Fähigkeit zu mauern," 63. See also his "Lebenshilfe von toten Juden," *Junge Welt* (May 15, 1994).

[11] Leah Rosh, "Kriegsdenkmäler – Ja, Holocaust-Denkmal – Nein?" *Vorwärts* (November 5, 1988). Reprinted in Heimrod, Schlüsche, and Seferens, *Der Denkmalstreit*, 52.

[12] Interview, "'Keine Denkpause': Über die Kritik am Holocaust-Denkmal," *Der Spiegel* (July 10, 1995), 55. Reprinted in Heimrod, Schlüsche, and Seferens, *Der Denkmalstreit*, 464. The Berlin Jewish community was unimpressed by its marginalization in the decision-making process. See Jeffrey M. Peck, *Being Jewish in the New Germany* (New Brunswick, 2006), 38.

[13] Leah Rosh, "Ein Denkmal für die ermordeten Juden Europas," in Förderkreis zur Errichtung eines Denkmals für die ermordeten Juden Europas, ed., *Ein Denkmal für die ermordeten Juden Europas* (Berlin, 1990). Reprinted in Heimrod, Schlüsche, and Seferens, *Der Denkmalstreit*, 775.

[14] Seligmann quoted in Marlies Emmerich, "Stilfragen," *Berliner Zeitung* (May 13, 2005). See the analysis of Broder, Brumlik, and Seligman in Peck, *Being Jewish in the New Germany*, 72–77.

memorial. "The Jews must not allow themselves to be stamped as sacrificial lambs again!"[15]

Like Broder, Seligman thought the memorial was a means of avoiding stigma. "The bad conscience of the perpetrator people determines that the Germans attempt to buy themselves free with money and the capacity for a certain Chutzpah."[16] Broder was astonished at how the stigma of the memorial could be rendered as stigmata. "Once, years ago on a journey abroad, I spoke with a German consul. This man said to me that we need this memorial. I asked him, Who was this 'we'? And he said the Foreign Ministry. For our work abroad. Great, I said, a pity my mother does not live any longer. She would have been delighted that she was not in the camp for nothing."[17] The consul bore out the observation of the political scientist Peter Reichel that "coming to terms with the past" had become a German "export business," indeed, that some Germans thought of themselves as the "world champions" in this event, despite Habermas's warning that "Maybe this is something that *someone else* can say."[18] Not surprisingly, even conservative politicians sometimes hailed the stigmata as the basis of a renewed national identity and shared the view of left-wing historian Lutz Niethammer that Germany's compensation payments to the Jews meant "we could be thoroughly proud in a national sense."[19] Journalist Arno Widdmann could note that Germans no longer bowed their heads before the memorial: "It is our pride."[20]

Pride and Stigma

But who or what is the entity that experiences "pride in sin" (*Sündenstolz*)? Surely not the entire citizenry of the Federal Republic, which includes, in the

[15] Rafael Seligman, "Genug bemitleidet: Gegen ein deutsches Holocaust-Memorial," *Der Spiegel* (January 16, 1995), 162–63.

[16] Ibid.

[17] "'Das ist die Fortsetzung des Dritten Reichs': Was soll, was kann, was hilft das Berliner Holocaust-Mahnmal? Ein Streitgespräch mit Henryk M. Broder und Wolfgang Menge" *Der Tagesspiegel* (June 6, 2005).

[18] "Verlogenes Steinfeld," interview with Peter Reichel by Gunnar Krüger, *ZDF Heute.de Magazin* (May 9, 2005), http://www.heute.de/ZDFheute/drucken/1,3733,2296105,00.html. For commentary, see Norbert Frei, "Gefühlte Geschichte," *Die Zeit* (October 21, 2004); Jürgen Habermas, *The Past as Future*, trans. Max Pensky (Lincoln and London, 1994), 28. Following Habermas here is Lars Rensmann, "Baustein der Erinnerungspolitik. Die Politische Textur der Bundestagsdebatte über ein zentrale 'Holocaust-Mahnmal,'" in Micha Brumlik, Hajo Funke, and Lars Rensmann, *Umkämpftes Vergessen: Walser-Debatte, Holocaust-Mahnmal und neuere deutsche Geschichtspolitik* (Berlin, 2000), 165. It should be noted, however, that in other contexts Habermas regards the remembrance of past suffering as contributing to the "dissolution of guilt on the part of the present with respect to the past." Drawing on the political theology of Helmut Peukert, he wrote of "anamnestic redemption of an injustice, which cannot of course be undone but can at least be virtually reconciled through remembering": Jürgen Habermas, *The Philosophical Discourse of Modernity*, trans. Frederick G. Lawrence (Cambridge, Mass., 1987), 15.

[19] Karl Wilds, "Identity Creation and the Culture of Contrition: Recasting Normality in the Berlin Republic," *German Politics*, 9:1 (2000), 94–95.

[20] Arno Widdmann, "Berliner Mahnmal-Reflexe," *Berliner Zeitung* (August 3, 1999).

words of Habermas, "German/German and German/Jewish citizens."[21] One could add Turkish/German citizens. So while wanting Germans to extend citizenship rights to every resident irrespective of ethnicity, he insisted that the sin pertains only to ethnic Germans because they stood "in a link of tradition that they share with the perpetrator generation," namely, "one's own parents and grandparents who made [Jews] strangers, excluded them as enemies, humiliated them as subhumans, and excoriated and exterminated them as people who were not people."[22] For this reason, he thought that the Germans "can't sneak out of the perpetrator role."[23] In arguing in these terms, he and others like the German Jewish professor of pedagogy Micha Brumlik opened themselves to the criticisms of nationalists such as Augstein and Walser that an inherited-sin accusation was implicit in the Berlin memorial, indeed that it was a *Schandmal* (memorial of disgrace) that had been imposed on the country by the burden of shame, that is, by foreign expectations. In order to escape this particularist rendering of the Holocaust – *the* Germans as an object of scorn – Habermas argued that Germans ought not to worry about what others think of them. Instead, they should erect the memorial as a radical gesture of German self-determination, an "act of taking responsibility for one's own life history," a notion he borrowed from Kierkegaard.

Did this recourse to existentialist philosophy allow Habermas to answer the skeptics and avoid the problem of thinking in terms of collectives? In fact, he himself doubted Kierkegaard's decisionistic belief that one could "dispose over his identity as property," because identity was always intersubjectively constructed. Identity entails the gaze of the other.[24] So there was no avoiding what non-Germans think of Germans and their memory politics after all. In other words, the viability of any German identity was in part dependent on its affirmation by foreigners. The memorial must be recognized by them, too, for it to perform a commemorative and sacrificial function. Indeed, it was erected with the approval of world opinion in mind. The philosopher Agnes Heller was more consistent on this point than Habermas. She understood that "the pangs of conscience" felt by violating self-legislated norms were "not signals of any debt we owe to others but of one we owe to ourselves." That experience was interior and therefore not publicly externalizable. The experience of shame – and stigma – had different consequences. "We can only ritually mitigate the pangs of conscience *if we transform them into shame via confession* when the

---

[21] Jürgen Habermas, "Brief an Peter Eisenman," in Heimrod, Schlüsche, and Seferens, *Der Denkmalstreit*, 1185.

[22] Jürgen Habermas, "Der Zeigefinger: Die Deutschen und ihr Denkmal," *Die Zeit* (March 31, 1999).

[23] Nicola Frowein, "Wenig Platz für Trauer," *ZDF Heute.de Magazin* (May 10, 2005), http://www.heute.de/ZDFheute/inhalt/7/0,3672,2290343,00.html; Adam Krzeminski, interview with Jürgen Habermas, "Europa ist heute in einem miserablen Zustand," *Die Welt* (May 4, 2005). Habermas also wrote of "Sündenbewusststein," in Habermas, *Die nachholende Revolution* (Frankfurt, 1990), 156.

[24] Jürgen Habermas, *Postmetaphysical Thinking: Philosophical Essays*, trans. William Mark Hohengarten (Cambridge, Mass., 1992), 162, 170.

Others will tell us how the debt can and must be repaid."[25] By erecting a memorial, Non-German Germans were signaling to the world that Germany is cleansing itself of sin, and that a new country had been born.

Karl Jaspers encountered these dilemmas in his *The Question of German Guilt.* Forty years before Habermas, he told Germans to interpret their predicament less as the punishment of the victors than as an opportunity for German self-purification and regeneration. He wanted, in the words of Paul Ricoeur, to convert "vengeful expiation to educative expiation – in short, to amendment."[26] And yet, as much as Jaspers tried to avoid collective categories – "A people as a whole can be neither guilty nor innocent, neither in the criminal nor in the political... nor in the moral sense" – he too found the question of collective reputation intruding. "There remains shame for something that is always present, that may be discussed in general terms, if at all, but can never by concretely revealed."[27] He rejected the collective guilt accusations, but ultimately held, as Habermas was to argue decades later, that "[t]here is a sort of collective moral guilt in a people's way of life which I share as an individual, and from which grow political realities."[28]

Unlike Habermas, however, Jaspers made an elementary distinction, also drawn by contemporaries such as the leftist Roman Catholic publicist Eugen Kogon, between political guilt for permitting the Nazis to come to power, and moral and metaphysical guilt for their crimes.[29] *Collective* guilt inhered only in the former. The conflation of the two types of guilt by Habermas and others has converted the accusation of collective political guilt into one of biblical proportions in view of the Holocaust's status as the ultimate symbol of secular evil. It leads predictably to the defensive posture typified by Germans in the late 1940s and Kathi-Gesa in 1998, who do not want to feel vicariously liable for the Holocaust. The purpose of Jaspers's book was to show Germans how to "talk with each other" by distinguishing between different types of guilt; because Germans had been implicated in the regime in different ways, types of guilt and responsibility needed to be identified and distinguished. The subsequent, acrimonious, public discussion of the Nazi past characterized by accusation and innuendo, moral righteousness and finger pointing, indicates that the advice of Jaspers and Kogon has not been heeded.

Moreover, they were addressing Germans who had experienced the Nazi regime, not their grandchildren and great grandchildren. Were they to bear the "mark of Cain," as some nationalists fear? Referring to other cases in world

[25] Agnes Heller, *The Power of Shame: A Rational Perspective* (London, 1985), 27–28 (emphasis in the original).

[26] Paul Ricouer, *The Symbolism of Evil*, trans. Emerson Buchanan (Boston, 1967), 102.

[27] Karl Jaspers, *The Question of German Guilt*, trans. E. B. Ashton (New York, 1961), 41, 33.

[28] Ibid., 76; Mark W. Clark, "A Prophet without Honour: Karl Jaspers in Germany, 1945–48," *Journal of Contemporary History*, 37:2 (2002), 208; Andrew Schaap, "Guilty Subjects and Political Responsibility: Arendt, Jaspers and the Resonance of the 'German Question' in the Politics of Reconciliation," *Political Studies*, 49 (2001), 749–66.

[29] Eugen Kogon, "Gericht und Gewissen," *Frankfurter Hefte*, 1:1 (April 1946), 25–37.

history, Hermann Lübbe argued that the accusation of collective guilt of a people did not persist indefinitely through the generations.[30] Nonetheless, some German Jewish commentators seemed to lean in that direction. Micha Brumlik rejected collective guilt for a collective shame to which he saw no end, whereas Seligman happily referred to Germans in the 1990s as a perpetrator people.[31] At the same time, Ignatz Bubis regarded the relationship between Germans and Jews as that between debtor and creditor. "A creditor approaches a debtor and gives him a repayment notice. The debtor does not react. The creditor gives him notice again. The debtor does not react again. After the third time, the debtor becomes exasperated. He says, as long as you demand payment, I won't pay. But when he was given notice, he did not pay either."[32] Plainly, this analogy is inappropriate. Bubis would not have regarded the debt as dischargable in any straightforward manner, as if a line could be drawn in a historical ledger. He too was caught in the dilemma of demanding that Germans experience their nationality only in negative terms while other ethnicities could enjoy citizenship but retain hyphenated identities.

For three generations, Germans have had to wrestle with the dilemmas of regenerating their collective life after the Holocaust. How were they supposed to relate to Jews, for instance? On the one hand, survivors like Eva Hoffman insisted that no reconciliation or accommodation was possible between them.[33] Foreign observers have followed this intuition in seeing the persistence of Nazi ideology even in the Non-German German identification with Jews; the "[Jewish] survivors are expropriated once more, only now not their property or citizenship but the struggles and memories of their survivorship."[34] On this reading, Germans and Jews ought to respect the rupture wrought by the Holocaust, even though the ontological distinction between Germans and Jews had been intrinsic to the radical nationalist project of German anti-Semites.

On the other hand, Germans were equally criticized for not accepting the victim's perspective as their own. Foreigner and Non-German Germans consistently expressed dismay that German Germans did not sufficiently come to terms with their past by incorporating Jews into the collective "we" and thereby continued to regard them as a non-German other.[35] It was in this vein

[30] Lübbe, *Aufklärung anlaßhalber*, 241–44.

[31] Micha Brumlik, "Gewissen, Gedenken und anamnetische Solidariät," *Universitas*, 53 (1998), 1148; Seligman, "Genug bemitleidet."

[32] "'Moral verjährt nicht': Ignatz Bubis über der Auschwitz-Debatte und seine Auseinandersetzung mit Martin Walser und Klaus von Dohnanyi," *Der Spiegel* (November 30, 1998), 51.

[33] Eva Hoffman, *After Such Knowledge: Memory, History and the Legacy of the Holocaust* (New York, 2004), 111: "The gulf – moral, political, affective – between the victim and the perpetrator is almost absolute."

[34] Eric L. Santner, *Stranded Objects: Mourning, Memory, and Film in Postwar Germany* (Ithaca, 1990), 41; cf. Gabriele Rosenthal, "National Socialism and Antisemitism in Intergenerational Dialogue," in Gabriele Rosenthal, ed., *The Holocaust in Three Generations: Families of Victims and Perpetrators of the Nazi Regime* (London, 1998), 244–45.

[35] Jan-Holger Kirsch, *Nationaler Mythos oder historische Trauer? Der Streit um ein zentrales "Holocaust-Mahnmal" für die Berliner Republik* (Cologne, 2003); Sigrid Weigel, *Bilder*

that the sixty-eighter generation, which eventually fastened on the Jewish fate – "I identified with Jews, because I felt myself to be persecuted by my family" – was criticized because it was at times markedly anti-Zionist.[36] An associated dilemma was the question of whose sensitivities – Jews' or Germans' – ought to be respected in public discourse. Augstein and others proclaimed how vulnerable German Germans were to stigmatization, while Bubis and Habermas pleaded with all Germans to show proper regard for the feelings of the victims' descendants.

Anamnestic and Amnesiac Memory

The Non-German German position was not just an ideology. It was a political theology based on the thought of the Roman Catholic priest Johann Baptist Metz, who was in turn influenced by Walter Benjamin, Theodor W. Adorno, Ernst Bloch, and Jürgen Habermas, his contemporary and friend. Writing in 1972, for instance, Metz urged Christians to adopt a theology of solidarity with the poor and oppressed based on what he called the "dangerous memory of freedom" of Christ's sacrifice. The memory of undeserved suffering, he argued, subverted a purely affirmative attitude to the past and, therefore, to the present. As for Habermas, the Holocaust was not then the focus of such an antihistoricism. The perceived problem was an industrial society run by technocrats not subject to effective democratic control. The enemy was the past conceived in terms of historicism, empty time gradually filled with progress, a theodicy that justified the suffering of past victims in the name of the greater good of contemporary society. History written from the victors' standpoint, then, is amnesiac. It attributed normative status to the present: what was past was past – above all, the suffering of the innocent – so let not memory of them disturb the present. The only motivation to cast off slavery in such a system, Metz thought, was the "*memorial passionis*" of the sacrificed Lord.

The imagination of future freedom is nourished from the memory of suffering, and freedom degenerates wherever those who suffer are treated more or less as a cliché and degraded to a faceless mass. Hence the Christian *memoria* becomes "subversive remembrance," which shocks us out of ever becoming prematurely reconciled to the "facts" and "trends" of our technological society.[37]

des kulturellen Gedächtnisses: Beiträge zur Gegenwartsliteratur (Dülmen-Hiddingsel, 1994), 199.

[36] Barbara Köster, "Rüsselheim July 1985," in Daniel Cohn-Bendit, ed., *Wir haben sie so geliebt, die Revolution* (Frankfurt, 1987), 244, quoted Dagmar Herzog, "Post-Holocaust Memory and the Sexual Revolution," *Critical Inquiry*, 24:2 (1998), 442; Jack Zipes, "Return of the Repressed," *New German Critique*, 31 (1984), 207.

[37] Johann Baptist Metz, "The Future in the Memory of Suffering," *Concilium*, 6:8 (1972), 19; Metz, *Faith in History and Society: Toward a Practical Fundamental Theology* (London, 1980), 88–89. The link between Metz and Benjamin is lucidly discussed in Steven T. Ostovich, "Epilogue: Dangerous Memories," in Alon Confino and Peter A. Fritzsche, eds., *The Work of Memory: New Directions in the Study of German Society and Culture* (Urbana, 2002), 239–56. See also his "Dangerous Memories and Reason in History," *KronoScope*, 5:1 (2005), 41–57.

By contrast, history written from the standpoint of the victims, or that expresses solidarity with them, is anamnestic.[38] Such a perspectival memory was not simply a memorial of resignation or apolitical remembrance. Standing with the victims of "progress" affected how we comported ourselves to the present and future political community. A redeemed community was one so conscious of the crimes committed in its history that henceforth it was committed to ensuring that the price of its progress was not the further suffering of the innocent: "Resurrection mediated by way of the memory of suffering means: The dead, those already vanquished and forgotten, have a meaning which is as yet unrealized. The potential meaning of our history does not depend only on the survivors, the successful and those who make it."[39]

By the 1990s, the Holocaust had become the foundational event of suffering for Metz: "For me Auschwitz signaled a horror that transcends all familiar theologies, a horror that makes every noncontextual talk about God appear empty and blind." The question of theodicy was now framed in terms of the genocide of the Jews: "For an anamnestic reason, being attentive to God means hearing the silence of those who have disappeared."[40] The Holocaust had profound implications for Christianity. It was "the catastrophe of our history, out of which we can find a way only through a radical change of direction achieved via new standards of action." The question of Auschwitz entailed reevaluating its roots and emphasizing Christianity's Hebraic rather than Greek origins. And this rethinking meant that the "apocalyptic-messianic wisdom of Judaism" ought to be appropriated by Christianity, because this wisdom "continually suspends all reconciliations from entering our history," that is, it resisted premature accommodation with extant reality in the name of an unfulfilled future, a conservative temptation he believed was all too apparent in Christianity.[41] A religiopolitical sensibility based on an eschatology in which God would raise the dead and dispense justice reflected a messianic theory of experience: anamnestic memory anticipated redemption at the end of time.[42]

It was one thing for Metz to advocate a new start for Christians based on the rupture he thinks the Holocaust entails for the church; it was quite another for

---

[38] Ostovich, "Epilogue: Dangerous Memories," 241–42. For background of anamnestic culture in Greek philosophy, especially with Aristotle, see Paul Ricoeur, *Memory, History, Forgetting*, trans. Kathleen Blamey and David Pellauer (Chicago and London, 2004).

[39] Metz, "The Future in the Memory of Suffering," 20.

[40] Johann Baptist Metz, "Suffering unto God," *Critical Inquiry*, 20 (Summer 1994), 611, 615.

[41] Johann Baptist Metz, "Christians and Jews after Auschwitz," in Ilya Levkov, ed., *Bitburg and Beyond: Encounters in American, German and Jewish History* (New York, 1987), 510; Metz, *Faith in History and Society* (New York, 1979). Cf. Bruce T. Morrill, *Anamnesis as Dangerous Memory: Political and Liturgical Theology in Dialogue* (Collegeville, Minn., 2000); Ekkehard Schuster and Reinhold Bochert-Kimmis, *Hope against Hope: Johann Baptist Metz and Elie Wiesel Speak Out on the Holocaust* (Mahwah, N.J., 1999).

[42] Jürgen Habermas, "Consciousness-Raising of Redemptive Criticism – The Contemporaneity of Walter Benjamin," *New German Critique*, 17 (Spring 1979), 51; Christian Lenhardt, "Anamnestic Solidarity: The Proletariat and Its *Manes*," *Telos*, 25 (1975), 131–54; Helmut Peukert, *Science, Action, and Fundamental Theology: Toward a Theology of Communicative Action*, trans. James Bohman (Cambridge, Mass., 1984), 206–44.

these ideas to be secularized and addressed to Germans as a whole. Yet that is precisely what Non-German Germans entreated. The theological dimension of Habermas's political project was effectively admitted when he explicitly invoked anamnestic memory as the only defensible orientation for postwar Germans.

There is the obligation incumbent upon us in Germany...to keep alive, without distortion and not only in an intellectual form, the memory of the suffering of those who were murdered by German hands. It is especially those dead who have a claim to the weak anamnestic power of a solidarity that later generations can continue to practice only in the medium of a remembrance that is repeatedly renewed, often desperate, and continually on one's mind. If we were to brush aside this Benjaminian legacy, our fellow Jewish citizens and the sons, daughters, and grandchildren of all those who were murdered would feel themselves unable to breathe in our country.[43]

As might be expected, Metz expressed sympathy with Habermas in the Historians' Dispute of the mid-1980s. He wondered whether

our coming to terms with the catastrophe of Auschwitz is so uncertain and discordant because we lack the spirit that was to have been irrevocably extinguished in Auschwitz; because we lack the anamnestically constituted Spirit necessary to perceive adequately what happened to us in this catastrophe – and to what we call "Spirit" and "Reason"; in a word: because we lack a culture of anamnestic Spirit. In place of remembrance, there is an evolutionarily colored history that presupposes that what is past is past and that no longer considers it a challenge to reason that every time a part of our past is successfully historicized, it is also forgotten in a sense.[44]

Habermas also perceived parallels between Metz's theologically grounded eschatology and the "countertradition" in German thought on which he set so much store: what "stretches from Jakob Böhme and Franz Baader, via Schelling and Hegel, to Bloch and Adorno, [and] transforms the experience of the negativity of the present into the driving force of dialectical reflection. Such reflection is intended to break the power of the past over what is to come."[45] Micha

[43] Jürgen Habermas, "Historical Consciousness and Post-Traditional Identity: The Federal Republic's Orientation to the West," in his The New Conservatism: Cultural Criticism and the Historian's Debate, trans. Shierry Weber Nicholsen (Cambridge, Mass., 1994), 233. Metz himself observes that anamnestic reason was foundational of Habermas's notion of communicative reason, namely, the preparedness to listen to the other and not to use language as an instrument of domination. Metz, "Suffering unto God"; Habermas expounds on the centrality of anamnestic consciousness to his social theory in his The Philosophical Discourse of Modernity, trans. Frederick G. Lawrence (Cambridge, Mass., 1991), 14–16.

[44] Johann Baptist Metz, "Anamnestic Reason: A Theologian's Remarks on the Crisis of the Geisteswissenschften," in Alex Honneth et al., eds., Cultural-Political Interventions in the Unfinished Project of Enlightenment, trans. Barbara Fultner (Cambridge, Mass., 1992), 191.

[45] Jürgen Habermas, "Israel or Athens: Where Does Anamnestic Reason Belong? Johann Baptist on Unity amidst Multicultural Plurality," in his The Liberating Power of Symbols: Philosophical Essays (Cambridge, 2001), 78–89; Habermas, The Philosophical Discourse of Modernity, trans. Frederick G. Lawrence (Cambridge, Mass., 1987), 14. Expressing skepticism about Habermas's invocation of this concept is Max Pensky, "On the Use and Abuse of Memory: Habermas, 'Anamnestic Solidarity,' and the Historikerstreit," Philosophy and Social Criticism, 15:4 (1989), 351–81.

Brumlik, who invoked Metz's notion of an "anamnestic culture,"[46] likewise situated his advocacy of the Berlin memorial in terms of Jewish religious themes. He was wont to quote Adorno: "The only philosophy which can be responsibly practiced in the face of despair is the attempt to contemplate all things as they would present themselves from the standpoint of redemption."[47] Behind this notion lay the Hassidic and Kabbalistic theology of redemption, Brumlik told German newspaper readers, which taught that God's and one's own exile would be ended, and the world healed, when the reasons for the exile were remembered. Referring to Benjamin, he wrote that a "weak messianic power" could be granted to previous generations by remembering their suffering. Because such formulations were too metaphysical for political operationalization, he entreated a profane version in which the dead were accepted into one's moral community by paying public respect to one's victims.[48]

In its secular, Western version, anamnestic memory made the Holocaust the normative standard that guided policy, an effective implementation of Adorno's injunction that the new categorical imperative ought to be preventing a future Auschwitz.[49] "Never again" was the expression of this temporal-moral sensibility, and it affected grand strategy, as Joschka Fischer's justification of German military participation in the NATO Kosovo campaign demonstrated.[50] By 2000 the minister for culture, Michael Naumann, could proclaim that the anamnestic spirit was now government policy. The planned memorial to the Berlin Murdered Jews of Europe would incarnate it.

Although the memorial could bestow "honor" on Germany, it should not lead to collective German happiness.[51] Indeed, Brumlik went to great lengths to stress than an anamnestic culture entailed deferring a comfortable accommodation with reality. "Perspectives must be fashioned that displace and estrange the world, reveal it to be, with its rifts and crevices, as indigent and distorted as it will appear one day in messianic light." Such a culture reflected a "sad but unreconciled perspective on history and its victims" in contrast to an amnesiac

---

[46] Micha Brumlik, "Jedes Mahnmal muß an der Nichtdarstellbarkeit des Holocaust scheitern," *Die Tageszeitung* (April 1, 1995), in Heimrod, Schlusche, and Seferens, *Der Denkmalstreit*, 510–11.

[47] Micha Brumlik, "Messianischer Blick oder Wille zum Glück: Kryptotheologie der Walser-Bubis-Debatte," in Brumlik, Funke, and Rensmann, *Umkämpftes Vergessen*, 130. The Adorno quotation is taken from *Minima Moralia: Reflections from a Damaged Life*, trans. E. F. N. Jephcott (London, 1974), 247.

[48] Micha Brumlik, "Das Geheimnis der Erlösung: Der Erinnerungs-Funktion des Berliner Mahnmals," *Frankfurter Rundschau* (December 19, 1998), in Heimrod, Schlusche, and Seferens, *Der Denkmalstreit*, 1193–94.

[49] Theodor W. Adorno, *Negative Dialectics*, trans. E. B. Ashton (London, 1973), 365; Jeffrey C. Alexander, "On the Social Construction of Moral Universals: The 'Holocaust' from War Crime to Trauma Drama," *European Journal of Social Theory*, 5:1 (2002), 5–85.

[50] Jeffrey Lantis, "The Moral Imperative of Force: The Evolution of German Strategic Culture in Kosovo," *Comparative Strategy*, 21:1 (2001–2), 21–46.

[51] Brumlik, "Das Geheimnis der Erlösung," in Heimrod, Schlusche, and Seferens, *Der Denkmalstreit*, 1194.

one based on reconciliation, forgiveness, and a belief in the beauty of the world as it was.[52] The identity advocated by the left was thus a "torn and unhappy consciousness," which it felt was the only honest and authentic comportment to the German past.[53]

It is remarkable that Non-German Germans thought that such a melancholy nonidentity should find many takers in the German population. Germans were not offered much in return other than vague, theological sounding promises about the benefits of "coming clean with oneself" (*mit sich selbst ins Reine kommen*). Not for nothing did Non-German Germans often sound like Christian preachers, calling down damnation on those who did not follow their high road. "The Germans cannot walk away from this past...without abandoning themselves or drifting off into some dreamland. The denial of historical thinking does not do away with the past – but it is injurious to the present."[54] Brumlik's belief that nonethnic German citizens would take on this "hypothesis of the German past" seemed like a vain hope.[55] Why would anyone want to accept this history as their own?[56]

The contrast with Walser's evocation of a viable Germanness could not be more stark. That his apotheosis of the nation was as much a political theology as that of his critics was evident in a little-noted passage he wrote in 1979 in which he expressed his yearning for the "bliss of trust" (*Vertrauensseligkeit*) and "connectedness" (*Verbindlichkeit*) that he felt was impossible in Germany because of its division, because of Auschwitz, and because of the banning of innocence. To cure the spiritual sickness caused by its excessive egoism, Germany required cooperation, social engagement, and solidarity, which he saw in entities that transcended the self, like "the people," "the nation," and "God." He had no problem with poetry after Auschwitz.[57] But whereas Americans and Russians, for instance, could enjoy their nationality, foreigners and domestic intellectuals forbade Germans this pleasure. Indeed, German intellectuals prevented Germans from rediscovering a viable history by blaming the century's

[52] Brumlik, "Messianischer Blick oder Wille zum Glück," in Brumlik, Funke, and Rensmann, *Umkämpftes Vergessen*, 133.

[53] Hajo Funke and Dietrich Neuhaus, "Einleitung," in Funke and Neuhaus, eds., *Auf dem Weg zur Nation? Über deutsche Identität nach Auschwitz* (Frankfurt, 1989), 7.

[54] Michael Geyer, "The Place of the Second World War in German Memory and History," *New German Critique*, 71 (Spring–Summer, 1997), 12. For a good example of the Non-German German path to redemption, see Michael Geyer and Miriam Hansen, "German-Jewish Memory and National Consciousness," in Geoffrey H. Hartman, ed., *Holocaust Memory: The Shapes of Memory* (Cambridge, Mass., 1994), 175–90.

[55] Brumlik, "Gewissen, Gedenken und anamnetische Solidariät," 1143–53.

[56] Friederike Eigler, "Memory, Moralism and Coming to Terms with the Present: Martin Walser and Zafer Senocak," in Silke Arnold-de-Simone, ed., *Memory Traces: 1989 and the Question of German Cultural Identity* (Oxford and New York, 2005), 55–78; Leslie Adelson, "The Turkish Turn in Contemporary German Literature and Memory Work," *Germanic Review*, 77:4 (2002), 326–38.

[57] For a lucid discussion of this famous phrase of Adorno, see Michael Rothberg, "After Adorno: Culture in the Wake of Catastrophe," *New German Critique*, 72 (Fall 1997), 45–81.

catastrophes on the *Volk* and especially its lower-middle class (*Kleinbürgertum*). In fact, the German people had been "humiliated and plundered" in the First World War, for which it was no more guilty than other nations. Feudal-capitalist elites continued this pattern between the wars, and exploited the suffering of the people in order to enlist them in a terrible conflict, yet afterward the intellectuals perversely held the *Kleinbürger* responsible for the war and Holocaust.[58]

The theme of popular innocence was also a feature of Walser's speech on Victor Klemperer's famous wartime diaries. What Walser liked about them was their clean distinction between the people and the regime, the latter of which was responsible for the campaign of racial hatred.[59] Klemperer was also a model German for another reason: he would not let the Nazis dictate to him about whether he should feel German. "From Victor Klemperer one can learn how to treat one's own conscience rather than watching over that of others."[60] The parallel Walser wished Germans to entertain was between the imposition of alien norms on the people by the Nazis and that on the people in the Federal Republic by its intellectuals. In both cases, ordinary people had to learn a sort of foreign language to master the public sphere.[61]

Brumlik for one did not miss the apologetic intent in Walser's arguments, but they were not only nationalist in orientation; for Brumlik, they were a secularized form of Protestant existentialism with anti-Semitic overtones. For not only did Walser rely on Hegel and Heidegger for his contention that the conscience was a radically solitary inwardness, but he also invoked the contemporary German theologian Eberhard Jüngel (b. 1934), whose Lutheranism posited a sinister binary opposition between the God of law of the Old Testament and the spiritual freedom of the New Testament.[62] Brumlik presented no evidence that Walser was utilizing Lutheran anti-Judaic categories. More plausible is that Walser shared Luther's concern about the emptiness of outward religious observance, a concern based less on his well-known antipathy to Judaism than on his critique of Aristotle and the scholastic theology of the Roman Catholic Church, which was, of course, what led him to stand before its authorities to defend his conscience by (allegedly) saying, "here I stand," in the manner of Walser himself. Walser had grown up as a Roman Catholic and felt oppressed by the duty of confession.[63]

---

[58] Martin Walser, "Händedruck mit Gespenstern," in Jürgen Habermas, ed., *Stichworte zur "Geistigen Situation der Zeit,"* 2 vols. (Frankfurt, 1979), 1:47–49.

[59] Martin Walser, "Das Prinzip Genauigkeit: Über Victor Klemperer," *Werke*, vol. 12 (Frankfurt, 1997), 804.

[60] Ibid., 803.

[61] Stuart Taberner, "A Manifesto for Germany's 'New Right'?: Martin Walser, the Past, Transcendence, Aesthetics, and *Ein Springender Brunnen,*" *German Life and Letters*, 53:1 (2000), 140.

[62] Brumlik, "Messianischer Blick oder Wille zum Glück," in Brumlik, Funke, and Rensmann, *Umkämpftes Vergessen*, 128–29.

[63] Martin Walser, "Über Freie und unfreie Rede" (1994), *Werke*, vol. 11 (Frankfurt, 1997), 1047.

Jüngel's theology was also an important inspiration in a less obvious but significant way. It was not his political theology, which rejected Metz's call for corporate Christian activism.[64] It was his theology of justification. Because personhood was based on intersubjectivity, a community could call on individuals to justify themselves before some duly constituted authority. Individuals could show themselves to be innocent and thereby justified, but what about the sinner? Only God, through the sacrifice of his son who gave the gift of life by taking upon himself the sin of the world, could justify the sinner. And in Jüngel's orthodox Lutheranism, the sinner played no part in her redemption. She was saved by faith alone (*sola fide*). There could be no mediator, whether human or semidivine, like Mary. God's love could not be earned. "It occurs unconditionally – or it is not love. When it has mercy on sinners, God's love does not turn to those worthy or deserving of love, but to those who have deformed themselves, those unworthy of love, those first made worthy of love through God's love."[65]

Now Walser rejected the proposition that he – or any German – needed to justify himself before anyone, especially the public through the media. Nor did the Germans require a mediator, like the media, for their salvation because their secular god – the nation – took the communal sin upon itself and gave life at the same time in the manner of the "happy exchange" between sinner and God described by Luther. Individuals could not bear the guilt of Auschwitz because the crime was communal; the nation therefore assumed responsibility: "What we did in Auschwitz we did as a nation, and for this reason this nation must persist as a nation."[66] Walser thereby came to the opposite conclusion to Habermas and Non-German Germans based on the same understanding of German guilt!

The vehemence with which Walser insisted on the right of individual conscience was remarkable and warrants investigation. His invocation of the Danish Christian existentialist theologian Søren Kierkegaard made his preoccupation clear. Walser was drawn to Kierkegaard because the Dane helped him regard the attempt to institutionalize stigma as a campaign to persecute, even liquidate, German nationality. "My holy Kierkegaard said it is unethical to judge the inner life of another by their behavior. A grain of respect for the conscience of others would do us all good at this time. Can one not imagine, please, what Heidegger thought and felt when he discovered the enormity of the Nazi regime in its entirety?"[67] In asking for sympathy for the likes of Heidegger, Walser was rehearsing the Kierkegaardian themes about the authentic source

---

[64] Eberhard Jüngel, "Toward the Heart of the Matter," *Christian Century*, 108:7 (1991), 229–30.

[65] Eberhard Jüngel, "On the Doctrine of Justification," *International Journal of Systematic Theology*, 1:1 (1999), 41.

[66] "Wovon zeugt die Schande wenn nicht von Verbrechen," *Frankfurter Allgemeine Zeitung* (November 28, 1998), reprinted in Frank Schirrmacher, ed., *The Walser-Bubis Debatte: Eine Dokumentation* (Frankfurt, 1999), 443; Walser, "Auschwitz und kein Ende," 632–33.

[67] Walser, "Über freie und unfreie Rede," 1054–55.

of conversion. Becoming a Christian issued from inner struggle rather than participation in so-called Christian society. It entailed making the individual dependent on the self rather than others, a turning inward that led to feelings of anxiety about disordered relationships and a consciousness of finitude, then dependence on God, and finally a leap of faith. Truth inhered in this inward process rather than in subscription to objectively and publicly articulated dogmas.[68]

Kierkegaard was led to this existentialist approach by his disgust with contemporary Danish society. The smugness of the established Lutheran Church in Denmark, whose prominent theologians had adopted Hegel's philosophy of religion and state, conspired against authentic Christian interiority. The newspaper culture of the 1840s in Denmark appalled him, too, because it likewise promoted an abstraction – public opinion – over the integrity of concrete, individual, lived experience, which he thought was the only avenue to truth. Finally, the Christian establishment had made its peace with the liberal egoism of early capitalism and thereby violated the radical Christian message of renouncing wealth and status.[69]

The lessons that Walser drew from Kierkegaard were clear. Freedom was not an expression of what we chose – the acceptable view of the Holocaust – but how we made our decisions. Just as official Christianity distracted from the existential decision for Christ, the inner stages of awakening through dread that are necessary for a true, personal faith, so did ritualized Holocaust memory inhibit coming to terms with its meaning. An established civil religion – Holocaust memory – impeded the readiness and ability of Germans to grapple inwardly with Auschwitz.[70] Because accepting the consequences of guilt and disgrace was so difficult, Germans required full autonomy. They must be entrusted to wrestle with their consciences on their own, without moralizing. In fact, Walser insisted, the conscience could not process guilt if it is coerced into conforming to official views. Terms like "singularity" and "relativization" – which signified stigma – made Walser "shy away" (*schrecke ich zurück*).[71] He thus bitterly opposed the "instrumentalization of this past for acceptance rituals and political correctness tests, for improvisations of the... moral organ of the feuilletons. I, at any rate, prefer to be ashamed without encouragement than with it. I don't blush on command. Moreover, I believe that we are a kind of people whom something bad like this would leave no peace. One can leave

---

[68] Louis P. Pojman, "Kierkegaard on Faith and Freedom," *Philosophy of Religion*, 27 (1990), 41–61.

[69] George Pattison, *Kierkegaard: Religion and the Nineteenth-Century Crisis of Culture* (Cambridge, 2002), 33–34; Karl Löwith, *From Hegel to Nietzsche: The Revolution in Nineteenth-Century Thought*, trans. David E. Green, foreword by Hans-Georg Gadamer (New York, 1964), 349, 359, 364.

[70] As he pointed out to his critics, his target was not education in schools and the like, but the media's incessant depiction of Holocaust images. Martin Walser, "Wovon zeugt die Schande, wenn nicht von Verbrechen," *Frankfurter Allgemeine Zeitung* (November 28, 1998).

[71] Walser, "Über freie und unfreie Rede," 1056.

us to ourselves."[72] Just as Kierkegaard had attacked the official, Hegelianized Christianity of his day, so Walser attacked the "Hegel of the Federal Republic," Habermas, for publicly questioning the conscience of others.[73] And just as, in the end, the individual could choose not to accept divine grace, so Non-German Germans and others must be prepared to accept that Germans might not come to the same conclusions as the Non-German Germans.

Walser's Kierkegaardian insights into how conscience functioned have not been sufficiently appreciated in the debate about his Paulskirche speech. When it is read with his previous, more elaborated statements on the topic, we witness a tortured attempt to confront an unbearable past. So appalled was he by the images of the Holocaust that he admitted to being physically unable to look at them. He could not leave the perpetrator collective to enjoy emotional relief by standing with the victims. He conceded the guilt of his nation, and the complicity of all Germans in the genocide. He thought that they should ponder the Holocaust in their consciences, even as he insisted that Germans were likely to close off their minds if they felt lectured to about the appropriate feeling to experience.[74]

And yet, as much as he was prepared to lend Auschwitz a traumatic meaning – one whose excess of meaning exploded attempts to grasp or master it in concepts or narratives – Walser ultimately denuded it of collective implications. In fact, he used the Holocaust to reinforce what he regarded as an attenuating German national consciousness. By insisting that the Holocaust was purely a matter for the individual conscience, no one could gain an epistemological vantage point from which to determine its meaning. "There is no position that I could reach from which I could have a firm view about what was done; or at least one that the victim could acknowledge and the perpetrator bear. Every image of Auschwitz smashes every possible coming to terms [abkommen] with this past, which cannot become one."[75] Consequently, no grounds existed for a public memorialization of the Holocaust; that would entail the imposition of a unitary meaning.

Walser's Kierkegaardian insistence on the inviolability of individual conscience and its direct relationship with God thus performed an important function. It vitiated the efficacy of rituals and symbols manifesting institutionalized, communal worship, as noted by Brumlik, who himself advocated the

---

[72] Ibid., 1060.

[73] Ibid., 1052. It is unknown whether Walser is aware of Habermas's own extensive use of Kierkegaard. Habermas, *Postmetaphysical Thinking*, 162; Habermas, "Moral Consciousness and Communicative Action," in Habermas, *The New Conservatism*, 260–63. Cf. Martin J. Matustik, "Kierkegaard's Radical Existential Praxis; or, Why the Individual Defies Liberal, Communitarian, and Postmodern Categories," in Martin J. Matustik and Merold Westphal, eds., *Kierkegaard in Post/Modernity* (Bloomington and Indianapolis, 1995), 245; Matustik, "Existence and the Communicatively Competent Self," *Philosophy and Social Criticism*, 24:3 (1999), 93–120; Matustik, *Postnational Identity: Critical Theory and Existential Philosophy in Habermas, Kierkegaard, and Havel* (New York and London, 1993).

[74] See especially Walser, "Auschwitz und kein Ende," 632–33.

[75] Ibid., 633; Walser, "Über freie und unfreie Rede," 1056: "There is no normative relationship to this guilt, no standardization of confirmation [Bekennens]."

Berlin memorial as a form of "liturgical memory."[76] It was all very well for Walser to disparage the official, public commemoration of the Holocaust, but how else was memory of it supposed to be transmitted? The same criticism was made of Kierkegaard's antiecclesiology.[77] Communicative memory, lasting three generations, needs to become cultural memory by its concretion in rites, rituals, and institutions for the community to reproduce its identity.[78]

Walser effectively wanted the Holocaust memory to disappear from German consciousness by preventing its institutionalization as cultural memory. Even though "we" Germans were irredeemably linked to the perpetrators, such a memory was designed as the nation's glue rather than its solvent. It was a perversion of memory, therefore, for the Holocaust to be used to undermine national solidarity. What was primary for Walser, then, was not consciousness of the Holocaust but national consciousness. The nation bore the burden of Auschwitz, but that burden had no negative implications for the nation, whose existence he took as a self-evident good.

Walser's elevation of the nation to divine status was by no means orthodox Protestantism. His "relationlessness," his existing purely for oneself, oblivious to the needs of recognition of others – such as the descendants of the Holocaust's victims – exemplified a sinful alienation from God and his creation.[79] Moreover, his hypostatization of the solitary conscience ignored the tradition in Lutheran theology that taught that the individual required communal guidance because the unsaved conscience was corrupted by sin. The distinction between an informed and a captive conscience was the difference between its objective and subjective dimensions. To avoid the solipsism of the latter, the individual was bound to account to the deliberative community of his or her co-believers.[80] In this respect, Walser's use of Kierkegaard could be contrasted with that of Habermas. Whereas Walser wanted to protect the individual from official Holocaust commemoration, Habermas sought to inure Germans to the seductions of nationalist modes of identification that he saw emanating from elites like Walser.[81]

Walser was hardly alone in feeling lectured to about the Holocaust. Even the German Jewish journalist Henryk Broder complained about the memorial in Walserian terms, writing that he "hated architecture that tells him how he

[76] Brumlik, "Gewissen, Gedenken und anamnetische Solidariät," 1143–53. Traces of German Pietism were also discernible in Walser's idealization of free communication between authentic individuals, whose community prefigured a redeemed state of wholeness and therefore represented a "secularized eschatology": Georg Pfleiderer, "Gewissen und Öffentlichkeit: Ein Deutungsvorschlag zur Walser/Bubis-Kontroverse," Zeitschrift für Evangelische Ethik, 4 (1999), 254.

[77] Pojman, "Kierkegaard on Faith and Freedom."

[78] Jan Assmann, "Collective Memory and Cultural Identity," New German Critique, 65 (1995), 128.

[79] Jüngel, "On the Doctrine of Justification."

[80] Martha Ellen Stortz, "Solus Christus or Sola Viscera? Scrutinizing Lutheran Appeals to Conscience," Dialog: A Journal of Theology, 44:2 (2005), 146–51.

[81] Habermas, Postmetaphysical Thinking, 162; Habermas, "Moral Consciousness and Communicative Action," in Habermas, The New Conservatism, 260–63.

should feel."[82] It seemed virtually forgotten that Karl Jaspers's *Die Schuld-frage* (The Question of German Guilt), described by Anson Rabinbach as "the founding text of the new narrative of the 'European German,' of a neutral, anti-militarist, and above all ethical Germany," was also dripping in Kierkegaar-dian themes of individual as well as collective sin and redemption.[83] "Either acceptance of the guilt not meant by the rest of the world but constantly repeated by our conscience comes to be a fundamental trait of our German self-consciousness – in which case our soul goes the way of transformation – or we subside into the average triviality of indifferent, mere living."[84] Con-trary to the assertions of his critics, Jaspers insisted on political communication between Germans in addition to private introspection.[85] For such communica-tion to occur, however, Germans needed to respect each others' consciences by moving beyond the clichéd accusations and denials that began to mark public and private discussions of the Nazi regime immediately after the war.

The debate about Walser's infamous Paulskirche speech showed that Jaspers's concern was well placed. He was either roundly condemned by Non-German Germans as someone who wanted to forget Auschwitz and draw a line under the past, or defended by German Germans as a persecuted patriot who allowed them to feel good about being German. Walser's complaint that "the warners never speak of their own wrestling with guilt" was borne out by the denunciatory tone of his critics who blithely presumed they were on the side of the angels.[86]

Trusting Germans?

These dilemmas about the integrity of German conscience reflected the underly-ing structure of national memory. Should it be "instructed" by the community of worshipers, as Lutheran theology put it, by "nonconformist" intellectuals? Or did this very instruction represent an intolerable moralization of politics that led to the unjust hounding of public figures who breached the language games of Non-German Germans? The answer boiled down to a question of basic trust. Could Germans be trusted to wrestle with their consciences? Walser thought

---

[82] "'Das ist die Fortsetzung des Dritten Reiches': Was soll, was kann, was hilft das Berliner Holocaust-Mahnmal? Ein Streitgespräch mit Henryk M. Broder und Wolfgang Menge," *Der Tagesspiegel* (June 9, 2005).

[83] Anson Rabinbach, *In the Shadow of Catastrophe: German Intellectuals between Apocalypse and Enlightenment* (Berkeley, 1997), 132; cf. Dan Diner, *Beyond the Conceivable: Studies on Germany, Nazism, and the Holocaust* (Berkeley, 2000), 219. Already in the 1960s, Jaspers was prophesying that Germany's "future lay not in the recovery of the nation sate but in its overcoming": Karl Jaspers, *Freiheit und Wiedervereinigung: Über Ausgaben der deutschen Politik* (Munich, 1960), 53.

[84] Jaspers, *The Question of German Guilt*, 117.

[85] Typical of this criticism is Dagmar Barnouw, *Visible Spaces: Hannah Arendt and the German-Jewish Experience* (Bloomington, 1990), 161–64.

[86] Walser, "Über freie und unfreie Rede," 1056.

they could; it was the public sphere that was corrupted, not the population.[87] In a neat symmetry, Habermas thought they could not. Jaspers might have agreed with him. His optimism about the German conscience in the 1940s lessened with time as he witnessed the apathy of Germans about the "question of German guilt." Writing twenty years after his *Die Schuldfrage*, and having migrated to Switzerland, he complained that: "The reality was completely different from what I had hoped for in 1945. Very soon there was no more talk of an intellectual reconstruction. . . . Politically, the will for a democratic reconstruction resulting from an inner conversion was lost. From 1948 a new state began with new assumptions. The years 1945–1948 were finished."[88] Certainly, Jaspers did not possess basic trust in German political culture in the 1960s, worrying about its militarism and authoritarian potential.[89]

But what about sixty years after the war? By the first decade of the twenty-first century, the fourth generation since 1945 had grown up in families without a living member who experienced the Nazi regime. The oral transmission of cultural memory of the Nazi period then ceased. The intensity of feelings of pollution subsided just as the traditions of Federal Republican life offered more sources of identification. The sense of indignation and disgust occasioned by stories of former SS officers receiving pensions while their surviving victims received nothing abated. The signs are that this fourth generation of Germans after the Holocaust began to place trust in the country's institutions. This newly won basic trust was the basis of a new republican consensus on the country's political culture.

Much of the public culture had been remade by Non-German Germans. Even the national soccer team of the 2006 World Cup comprised in part Polish-born stars and was coached by a young American-based former player married to a Chinese American. Non-German Germans cheered for them as much as anyone else.[90] Because such a new patriotism was based not on continuities with the generations that experienced the Second World War but on the achievements and culture of the Federal Republic, it was possible for them to feel good about their nationality – their "we-ness" – as well as acknowledge the memory of the Holocaust. The tension between German identity and Holocaust memory was resolved because responsibility for the evil past was laid at the door of a former Germany, a Germany of existential significance to members of the "forty-fiver" generation like Walser and Habermas.[91] For many older Germans, the new Berlin memorial continued to represent a stigma. Martin Hohmann expressed the anxiety in biblical terms when he said that there have been "nearly three

[87] Jan-Werner Müller, *Another Country: German Intellectuals, Unification and National Identity* (New Haven and London, 2000), 175.

[88] Karl Jaspers, "Warum ich Deutschland verlassen habe," in his *Schicksal und Wille* (Berlin 1967), 52, quoted in Clark, "A Prophet without Honour," 215.

[89] Karl Japsers, *Wohin treibt die Bundesrepublik?* (Munich, 1966).

[90] Christoph Amend, "Innere Entspannung. Weshalb junge Deutsche ein gelassenes Verhältnis zu ihrem Land haben," *Die Zeit* (June 22, 2006).

[91] Cf. Brumlik, "Gewissen, Gedenken und anamnetische Solidariät," 1145.

generations of penance time [*Bußzeit*] until now. It should not become six or seven. To that extent, the monument would be a monumental expression of our inability to forgive ourselves."[92] As might be expected, German Germans advocated the parable of the Prodigal Son who was accepted back into the family and whose errors were never mentioned again, while Non-German Germans continued to cast the national story in terms of Cain and Abel.[93] These were the irreconcilable positions of German memory. These memories are of increasingly less existential significance for the youth of the twenty-first century. With the development of basic trust in the Berlin Republic, the underlying structure that had marked German memory for sixty years gradually came to an end.

Biblical themes provide guidance. The Cain and Abel tale was misunderstood by German Germans. God placed Cain under his protection whereupon he thrived and founded cities. God also limited inherited sin to the third or fourth generation. This decision reflects the development of social remembrance. Three to four generations are needed for communicative memory to become cultural memory: when the oral transmission of experience is superseded by institutionalized memory.[94] This transition occurred with the generation of young Germans in 2006.

With this generational change, the Berlin Memorial to the Murdered Jews of Europe became less a stigma or stigmata than a lucrative tourist attraction, an object of indifference, or de facto playground for schoolchildren.[95] The fact that the foreign journalists and academics were no longer alarmed by flag waiving German soccer supporters during the World Cup indicated that they no longer participated in the construction of the German stigma.[96] That in August 2006 Israel was prepared for German troops to patrol the border with Lebanon also indicated the country's international rehabilitation.[97] "The old clichés have been replaced by a new, positive and more fair image of Germany," said British Prime Minister Tony Blair during the 2006 World Cup.[98] To be sure, foreigners and many Germans continued to scrutinize the country's memory politics. After the terrorist attacks on September 11, 2001, some in the West

---

[92] "Wer ist Martin Hohmann?" *Süddeutsche Zeitung* (October 31, 2003).

[93] Lübbe, *Aufklärung anlaßhalber*, 241.

[94] Assmann, "Collective Memory and Cultural Identity," 126; Assmann, *Das kulturelle Gedächtnis: Schrift, Erinnerung und politische Identität in frühen Hochkulturen* (Munich, 1992).

[95] Arno Widmann, "The Berlin Republic: An Attempt by a Member of the Old German Federal Republic to Come to Terms with the Country He Lives In," *Berliner Zeitung* (May 28, 2005).

[96] This fact relieved German observers. Gunter Gebauer, "A Time to Make Friends in Germany – Looking Back a the World Cup in Germany," *Goethe Institute Online*, http://www.goethe.de/ges/pok/thm/ppd/en1628368.htm; Matthias Matussek, "Ein neues deutsches Gefühl," *Spiegel Online International* (June 1, 2006), http://www.spiegel.de/kultur/gesellschaft/o,1518,419214,00.html.

[97] Roger Boyes and Richard Beeston, "German Troops May Face Jews – As Part of Mission for Peace," *Times* (London) (August 16, 2006).

[98] Tony Blair quoted in David Crossland, "From Humorless to Carefree in 30 Days: Germany's World Cup Reinvention," *Spiegel Online International* (July 10, 2006), http://www.spiegel.de/international/o,1518,426063,00.html.

began to worry about the German reluctance to sign up to the global "war on terror." Paradoxically, now German pacifism was thought to signify an unmastered past.[99] Younger Germans are no longer vulnerable to such attempts to revive German stigma in the service of partisan geopolitics. People living in Germany continue to negotiate their identity dilemmas around the axes of ethnicity and immigration – just like any other country.

---

[99] Jeffrey Herf, "Politics and Memory in West and East Germany since 1961 and in Unified Germany since 1990," *Journal of Israeli History*, 23:1 (2004), 40–64.

Index

Lightning Source UK Ltd.
Milton Keynes UK
UKOW040736290312

189799UK00001B/6/P